THOM.

CW00926262

THE

HISTORY

OF THE

ROYAL SOCIETY

OF

LONDON

FOR THE IMPROVING OF

NATURAL KNOWLEDGE

Elibron Classics
www.elibron.com

Elibron Classics series.

© 2005 Adamant Media Corporation.

ISBN 1-4021-6397-5 (paperback)
ISBN 1-4021-5407-0 (hardcover)

This Elibron Classics Replica Edition is an unabridged facsimile
of the edition published in 1722, London.

Let this Book, Intituled, *The Hiſtory of the* ROYAL SOCI-
ETY *of* LONDON, *for the improving of* Natural Knowledge,
be Printed.

WILLIAM MORRICE.

NULLIUS VERBA.

IN

THE
HISTORY
OF THE
ROYAL SOCIETY
OF
L O N D O N,
For the Improving of
NATURAL KNOWLEDGE.

By *THO. SPRAT*, D. D. late Lord
Bifhop of *ROCHESTER*.

The THIRD EDITION Corrected.

L O N D O N:

Printed for J. KNAPTON, J. WALTHOE,
B. and S. TOOKE, D. MIDWINTER, B.
COWSE, J. TONSON, R. ROBINSON,
J. WILFORD, and S. CHAPMAN. 1722.

( )

TO THE

KING.

Sir,

*F all the Kings of Eu-
rope, Your Majesty was
the first, who confirm'd
this noble Design of Ex-
periments, by Your own Example,
and by a publick Establishment. An
Enter-*

The Epistle Dedicatory.

Enterprise *equal to the most renown'd Actions of the best* Princes. *For, to increase the Powers of all Mankind, and to free them from the Bondage of Errors, is greater Glory than to enlarge* Empire, *or to put Chains on the Necks of conquer'd* Nations.

What Reverence all Antiquity *had for the* Authors *of* natural Discoveries, *is evident by the diviner Sort of Honour they confer'd on them. Their Founders of* philosophical Opinions *were only admir'd by their own* Sects: *Their* valiant Men *and* Generals *did seldom rise higher than to* Demy-Gods *and* Heroes: *But the* Gods *they worshiped with* Temples *and* Altars, *were those who instructed the* World *to* plow, *to* sow, to plant, *to* spin, *to* build Houses, *and to find out* new Countries. *This Zeal indeed, by*
which

The Epiſtle Dedicatory.

which they expreſs'd their Gratitude to ſuch Benefactors, degenerated into Superſtition; yet has it taught us, *that a higher Degree of Reputation is due to* Diſcoverers, *than to the* Teachers *of* ſpeculative Doctrines, *nay even to* Conquerors *themſelves.*

Nor has the true God *himſelf omitted to ſhew his Value of* vulgar Arts. *In the whole* Hiſtory *of the firſt* Monarchs *of the World, from* Adam *to* Noah, *there is no mention of their* Wars, *or their* Victories : *All that is recorded is this*, *they liv'd ſo many Years, and taught their* Poſterity *to keep* Sheep, *to till the* Ground, *to plant* Vineyards, *to dwell in* Tents, *to build* Cities, *to play on the* Harp *and* Organs, *and to work in* Braſs *and* Iron. *And if they deſerv'd a* ſacred Remembrance, *for one* natural *or* mechanical

The Epiſtle Dedicatory.

cal Invention, *Your* Majeſty *will certainly obtain* immortal Fame, *for having eſtabliſh'd a perpetual Succeſ-ſion of* Inventors.

I am,

May it pleaſe Your Majeſty,

Your Majeſty's moſt humble,

and moſt obedient

Subject and Servant,

THO SPRAT.

TO THE
ROYAL SOCIETY.

I.

PHILOPHY, *the great and only Heir*
Of all that human Knowledge which has bin
Unforfeited by Man's rebellious Sin,
Though full of Years He do appear,
(Philosophy, I say, and call it, He,
For whatsoe'er the Painter's Fancy be,
It a male Virtue seems to me)
Has still been kept in Non-age till of late,
Nor manag'd or enjoy'd his vast Estate:
Three or four thousand Years one would have thought,
To Ripeness and Perfection might have brought
A Science so well bred and nurst,
And of such hopeful Parts too at the first.
But, oh! the Guardians and the Tutors then,
(Some negligent, and some ambitious Men)
Would ne'er consent to set him free,
Or his own natural Powers to let him see,
Lest that should put an end to their Authoritie.

II.

That his own Business he might quite forget,
They' amus'd him with the Sports of wanton Wit,
With the Deserts of Poetry they fed him,
Instead of solid Meats t'encrease his Force;
Instead of vigorous Exercise, they led him
Into the pleasant Labyrinths of ever-fresh Discourse:
Instead of carrying him to see
The Riches which do hoarded for him lye

B

In

In Nature's endless Treasury,
They chose his Eye to entertain
(His curious, but not covetous Eye)
With painted Scenes, and Pageants of the Brain.
Some few exalted Spirits this latter Age has shown,
That labour'd to assert the Liberty
(From Guardians, who were now Usurpers grown)
Of this old Minor *still, captiv'd Philosophy ;*
  But 'twas Rebellion call'd to fight
  For such a long oppressed Right.
Bacon *at last, a mighty Man, arose,*
  Whom a wise King and Nature chose
  Lord Chancellor of both their Laws,
And boldly undertook the injur'd Pupils Cause.

III.

Authority, which did a Body boast,
Though 'twas but Air condens'd, and stalk'd about,
Like some old Giant's more gigantic Ghost,
  To terrify the learned Rout
With the plain Magic of true Reason's Light,
  He chac'd out of our Sight,
Nor suffer'd living Men to be misled
  By the vain Shadows of the Dead : *(tome fled ;*
To Graves, from whence it rose, the conquer'd Phan-
  He broke that monstrous God which stood
In midst of th' Orchard, and the whole did claim,
  Which with a useless Scythe of Wood,
  And something else not worth a Name,
  (Both vast for Shew, yet neither fit
  Or to defend, or to beget ;
  Ridiculous and senseless Terrors !) made
Children and superstitious Men afraid.
  The Orchard's open now, and free ;
Bacon *has broke that Scare-crow Deity ;*

Come

I

Come, enter, all that will,
Behold the ripened Fruit, come gather now your Fill.
  Yet still, methinks, we fain would be
  Catching at the forbidden Tree,
  We would be like the Deity,
When Truth and Falshood, Good and Evil, we
Without the Senses Aid within our selves would see;
  For 'tis God only who can find
  All Nature in his Mind.

IV.

From Words, which are but Pictures of the Thought,
(Though we our Thoughts from them perversly drew)
To Things, the Mind's right Object, he it brought:
Like foolish Birds to painted Grapes we flew;
He sought and gather'd for our Use the true;
And when on Heaps the chosen Bunches lay,
He pres's'd them wisely the mechanic Way,
Till all their Juice did in one Vessel join,
Ferment into a Nourishment Divine,
  The thirsty Soul's refreshing Wine.
Who to the Life an exact Piece would make,
Must not from others Work a Copy take;
  No, not from Rubens or Vandike;
  Much less content himself to make it like
Th' Ideas and the Images which lye
In his own Fancy, or his Memory,
  No, he before his Sight must place,
  The natural and living Face;
  The real Object must command,
Each Judgment of his Eye, and Motion of his Hand.

V.

From these and all long Errors of the Way,
In which our wandring Predecessors went,
And like th' old Hebrews many Years did stray,

In *Deſarts but of ſmall Extent*,
Bacon, *like* Moſes, *led us forth at laſt*,
  The barren Wilderneſs he paſt,
  Did on the very Border ſtand
  Of the bleſt promis'd Land,
And from the Mountain's Top of his exalted Wit,
  Saw it himſelf, and ſhew'd us it.
But Life did never to one Man allow
Time to diſcover Words, and conquer too ;
Nor can ſo ſhort a Line ſufficient be
To fathom the vaſt Depths of Nature's Sea :
  The Work he did we ought t' admire,
And were unjuſt if we ſhould more require
From his few Years, divided 'twixt th' Exceſs
Of low Afflittion, and high Happineſs :
For who on Things remote can fix his Sight,
That's always in a Triumph, or a Fight ?

VI.

From you, great Champions, we expect to get
Theſe ſpacious Countries but diſcover'd yet ;
Countries where yet inſtead of Nature, we
Her Images and Idols worſhip'd ſee :
Theſe large and wealthy Regions to ſubdue,
Though Learning has whole Armies at Command,
  Quarter'd about in every Land,
A better Troop ſhe ne'er together drew.
  Methinks, like Gideon's *little Band*,
  God with Deſign has pickt out you,
To do theſe noble Wonders by a few :
When the whole Hoſt he ſaw, they are (ſaid he)
  Too many to o'ercome for me ;
  And now he chuſes out his Men,
  Much in the way that he did then :
  Not thoſe many whom he found
  Idly extended on the Ground,

To

To drink with their dejected Head
The Stream, just so as by their Mouths it fled:
  No, but those few who took the Waters up,
And made of their laborious Hands the Cup.

VII.

Thus you prepar'd, and in the glorious Fight
  Their wondrous Pattern too you take :
Their old and empty Pitchers first they brake,
And with their Hands then lifted up the Light.
  Iö! Sound too the Trumpets here!
Already your victorious Lights appear ;
New Scenes of Heaven already we espy,
  And Crowds of golden Worlds on high ;
Which from the spacious Plains of Earth and Sea,
  Could never yet discover'd be
By Sailors or Chaldæans watchful Eye.
Nature's great Works no Distance can obscure,
No Smalness her near Objects can secure.
  You've taught the curious Sight to press
  Into the privatest Recess
Of her imperceptible Littleness.
She with much stranger Art than his who put
  All th' Iliads in a Nut,
The numerous Work of Life does into Atoms shut.
  You've learn'd to read her smallest Hand,
And well begun her deepest Sense to understand.

VIII.

Mischief and true Dishonour fall on those
Who would to Laughter or to Scorn expose
So virtuous and so noble a Design,
So human for its Use, for Knowledge so Divine.
The Things which these proud Men despise, and call
  Impertinent, and vain, and small,

Those

Those smallest Things of Nature let me know,
Rather than all their greatest Actions do.
Whoever would deposed Truth advance
    Into the Throne usurp'd from it,
Must feel at first the Blows of Ignorance,
    And the sharp Points of envious Wit.
So when by various Turns of the celestial Dance,
    In many thousand Years
    A Star, so long unknown, appears,
Though Heaven it self more beauteous by it grow,
It troubles and alarms the World below,
Does to the Wise a Star, to Fools a Meteor show.

IX.

With Courage and Success you the bold Work begin;
    Your Cradle has not idle been:
None e'er but Hercules and you could be
At five Years Age worthy a History.
    And ne'er did Fortune better yet
    Th' Historian to the Story fit:
    As you from all old Errors free
And purge the Body of Philosophy;
    So from all modern Follies He
Has vindicated Eloquence and Wit.
His candid Stile like a clean Stream does slide,
    And his bright Fancy all the way
    Does like the Sun-shine in it play;
It does like Thames, the best of Rivers, glide,
Where the God does not rudely overturn,
    But gently pour the crystal Urn,
And with judicious Hand does the whole Current guide.
H' as all the Beauties Nature can impart,
And all the comely Dress without the Paint of Art.

A. COWLEY.

AN

ADVERTISEMENT

TO THE

READER.

THE *Reader is entreated to take No-*
tice, that much of this Difcourfe
was written and printed above
two Years before the reft: For this
Caufe, in the firft and fecond Books, he may
chance to find fome Expreffions, that by reafon
of the difference of Time may feem not well to
agree with the laft: But thofe having pafs'd
the Prefs fo long ago, were out of my Power
of changing them; and therefore I will refer
it to his Kindnefs to do it for me.

I muft alfo acquaint him, that in the Title
of my Book I have taken a Liberty, which
may be liable to Exception: I have call'd it a
Hiftory of the Royal Society ; *whereas the*
firft Part wholly treats of the State of the
Ancient

Ancient Philofophy; *and the third chiefly contains a Defence and Recommendation of* experimental Knowledge *in general: So that it is only the fecond Book that peculiarly defcribes their Undertaking. But for my Excufe I may alledge the Example of many of the* Ancients, *who have often from the principal Part of their Works given Title to all the reft: In their Imitation, though this Book does treat of many Subjects that are not Hiftorical, yet I have prefum'd to name the whole a* Hiftory, *becaufe that was the main End of my Defign.*

The Style perhaps in which it is written, is larger and more contentious than becomes that Purity and Shortnefs which are the chief Beauties of hiftorical Writings: But the Blame of this ought not fo much to be laid upon me, as upon the Detractors of fo noble an Inftitution: For their Objections and Cavils againft it, did make it neceffary for me to write of it, not altogether in the way of a plain Hiftory, *but fometimes of an* Apology.

THE

(1)

THE

HISTORY

OF THE

Inſtitution, Deſign, and *Progreſs,*

OF THE

ROYAL SOCIETY

OF

L O N D O N,

For the Advancement of experimental Philoſophy.

The FIRST PART.

 Shall here preſent to the World, an
Account of the *firſt Inſtitution* of
the *Royal Society*; and of the *Pro-*
greſs, which they have already made:
In hope, that this learned and inquiſitive Age, will either think their
Indeavours worthy of its *Aſſiſtance*; or elſe will
be thereby provok'd, to attempt ſome *greater En-*
terprize (if any ſuch can be found out) for the

Sect. I.
The Preface,
and Deſign
of this Diſ-
courſe.

A   Bene-

Benefit of human Life, by the Advancement of
Real Knowledge.

Perhaps this Task, which I have propos'd to my
felf, will incur the Cenfure of many judicious Men,
who may think it an over-hafty, and prefumptuous
Attempt; and may object to me, that the *Hiftory*
of an Affembly which begins with fo great Expectations, ought not to have been made publick
fo foon; till we could have produced very many
confiderable *Experiments*, which they had try'd,
and fo have given undeniable *Proofs* of the Ufefulnefs of their Undertaking.

In anfwer to this, I can plead for my felf, that
what I am here to fay, will be far from preventing
the Labours of others in adorning fo worthy a Subject; and is *premis'd* upon no other account, than
as the nobleft Buildings are firft wont to be reprefented in a few *Shadows*, or fmall *Models*; which
are not intended to be equal to the chief Structure it felf, but only to fhew in little, by what
Materials, with what *Charge*, and by how *many
Hands*, that is afterwards to be rais'd. Although,
therefore, I come to the Performance of this Work,
with much lefs *Deliberation*, and *Ability*, than the
Weightinefs of it requires; yet, I truft, that the
Greatnefs of the *Defign* it felf, on which I am to fpeak,
and the *Zeal* which I have for the *Honour* of our
Nation, which have been the chief Reafons that
have mov'd me to this Confidence of Writing, will
ferve to make fomething for my *Excufe*. For what
greater matter can any Man defire, about which to
employ his Thoughts, than the Beginnings of an *Illuftrious Company*, which has already laid fuch excellent Foundations of fo much Good to *Mankind?*
Or,

Or, what can be more delightful for an *English* Man
to confider, than that notwithftanding all the late
Miferies of his Country, it has been able in a fhort
Time fo well to recover it felf, as not only to at-
tain to the Perfection of its *former* Civility, and
Learning, but alfo to fet on foot a *new* Way of
Improvement of Arts, as *great* and as *beneficial* (to
fay no more) as any the wittieft or the happieft
Age has ever invented?

But befides this, I can alfo add, in my Defence,
that though the *Society*, of which I am to write, is
not yet four Years old, and has been of neceffity
hitherto chiefly taken up, about *preparatory Affairs*;
yet even in this Time, they have not wholly neglected their *principal End*, but have had Succefs,
in the Trial of many remarkable Things; of which
I doubt not, but I fhall be able, as I pafs along, to
give Inftances enough to fatisfy the Curiofity of all
fober Inquirers into Truth. And in fhort, if for no
other End, yet certainly for this, a Relation of
their firft Original ought to be expos'd to the View
of Men: That by laying down, on what courfe of
Difcovery they intend to proceed, the *Gentlemen
of the Society* may be more folemnly engag'd, to
profecute the fame. For now they will not be able,
handfomely to draw back, and to forfake fuch honourable Intentions; when the World fhall have
taken notice, that fo many prudent Men have gone
fo far, in a Bufinefs of this univerfal Importance,
and have given fuch undoubted *Pledges* of many
admirable Inventions to follow.

I fhall therefore divide my Difcourfe into thefe
three general Heads.

Sect. II.
*The Division
of the Dif-
courfe.*

A 2   The

The *first* shall give a short View of the *Ancient* and *Modern* Philosophy; and of the most famous Attempts, that have been made for its *Advancement:* That by observing wherein others have *excell'd*, and wherein they have been thought to *fail*, we may the better shew, what is to be expected from these new Undertakers; and what mov'd them, to enter upon a Way of Inquiry, different from that, on which the former have proceeded.

The *second* shall consist of the *Narrative* it self: And out of their *Registers*, and *Journals*, which I have been permitted to peruse, shall relate the first Occasions of their Meetings, the Incouragement, and Patronage, which they have receiv'd; their *Patent*, their *Statutes*, the whole Order and Scheme of their *Design*, and the *Manner* of their Proceedings.

The *third* shall try, to assert the *Advantage* and *Innocence* of this Work, in Respect of all *Professions*, and especially of *Religion*; and how proper, above others, it is, for the present Temper of the *Age* wherein we live.

On the *first* and *last* of these Particulars, it is not needful that I should long insist: Because several *great Men* have already so much prevented me about them; that there is hardly any thing can be spoken, in which I shall not almost tread in their very *Footsteps*. But yet it is requisite, that something be here said to that purpose, though it be only in *Repetition:* Because I perceive, that there is still much prejudice remaining on many Men's Minds, towards any *new* Discoveries in *natural* Things. This I shall try to remove, not that I imagine, that those Reasons can have any great effect

fect in my *weak Hands,* which were not able fully to
prevail, when they were inforc'd by the Eloquence
of thofe *excellent Men,* who have gone before me
in this Argument: But I rather truft to the inclination of the *Age* it felf, wherein I write; which (if
I miftake not) is far more prepar'd to be perfuaded
to promote fuch Studies, than any other Time that
has gone before us.

And firft, let us obferve the Practice of the beft, Sect. III.
and the civileft Nations, amongft the *Ancients*; and *The Philofo-*
a little trace out the Courfe which they follow'd, to *phy of the*
enrich their Countries, by the introducing of *For-* *Eaft.*
eign Arts, or a fearching into *New.*

It is evident, from the univerfal Teftimony of
Hiftory, that all Learning and Civility were deriv'd
down to us from the *Eaftern* Parts of the World.
There it was, that Mankind arofe: And there they
firft difcover'd the Ways of Living, with Safety,
Convenience and Delight. It is but juft, that we
fhould attribute the original of *Aftronomy, Geometry,*
Government, and many Sorts of Manufactures, which
we now enjoy, to the *Affyrians,* the *Chaldeans,* and
Egyptians. And as to them we owe the *Invention*;
fo from them proceeded the firft *Corruption* of Knowledge. It was the cuftom of their wife Men, to
wrap up their Obfervations on Nature, and the
Manners of Men, in the dark Shadows of *Hierogly-*
phicks; and to conceal them, as facred *Myfteries,* from
the Apprehenfions of the Vulgar. This was a fure
Way to beget a Reverence in the People's Hearts towards *themfelves*: But not to advance the true Philofophy of *Nature.* That ftands not in need of fuch
Artifices to uphold its credit: But is then moft likely

to thrive, when the Minds, and Labours of Men of all Conditions, are join'd to promote it, and when it becomes the Care of united Nations.

Into the *Eaft*, the firft inquifitive Men amongft the *Grecians* travelled : By what they obferved there, they ripened their own imperfect Conceptions, and fo return'd to teach them at Home. And that they might the better infinuate their Opinions into their Hearers Minds, they fet them off with the Mixture of *Fables* and the Ornaments of *Fancy*. Hence it came to pafs, that the firft Mafters of Knowledge amongft them, were as well *Poets*, as *Philofophers* ; for *Orpheus, Linus, Mufæus,* and *Homer,* firft foftned Men's natural Rudenefs; and by the Charms of their Numbers, allur'd them to be inftructed by the feverer Doctrines of *Solon, Thales,* and *Pythagoras.* This was a Courfe, that was ufeful at firft, when Men were to be delightfully deceiv'd to their own Good : But perhaps it left fome ill Influence on the whole Philofophy of their Succeffors ; and gave the *Grecians* occafion ever after of exercifing their Wit, and their Imagination, about the Works of Nature, more than was confiftent with a fincere Inquiry into them.

Sect. IV. *The Philofophy of Greece.* When the fabulous Age was paft, *Philofophy* took a little more Courage; and ventured more to rely upon its own Strength, without the Affiftance of *Poetry.* Now they began to gather into Affemblies, and to increafe their Intereft : And according to the different Temper of the *Grecians,* from the *Eaftern* Nations, fo were their Arts propagated in a different Way from theirs. The *Greeks,* being of a vigorous, and active Humour, eftablifh'd their Philo-

*

fophy

fophy in the *Walks,* and *Porches,* and *Gardens,* and
fuch publick places about their Cities; whereas the
graver and more referv'd *Ægyptians,* had confin'd
it to their *Temples.*

In *Greece,* the moft confiderable (and indeed
almoft the only fuccefsful) Tryals, that were made
in this way, were at *Athens* ; the Wit of whofe Inhabitants, was, 'tis true, admirably fit for the reducing of Philofophy into *Method,* and for the adorning of it with the nobleft Words, when once it had
been before completed in its Subftance : But yet
their Genius was not fo well made, for the under-
going of the firft *Drudgery* and *Burden* of *Obfervation*
which is needful for the *Beginning* of fo difficult a
Work. This will appear, if we remember, that they
were the Mafters of the Arts of Speaking to all their
Neighbours; and fo might well be inclin'd, rather
to choofe fuch Opinions of Nature, which they might
moft elegantly exprefs, than fuch, which were more
ufeful, but could not fo well be illuftrated by the
Ornaments of Speech. Befides this, their *City* was
the general *School,* and Seat of *Education;* and
therefore the Epitomes of Knowledge beft ferved
their turn, to make their Scholars, in a fhort time,
finifh the courfe of their Studies, and go home fatisfied with a Belief of their own Proficience, and
their Teacher's Wifdom. They were alfo commonly (as moft of the other *Grecians*) Men of hot, earneft, and hafty Minds ; and fo lov'd rather to make
fudden Conclufions, and to convince their Hearers
by Argument, than to *delay* long, before they fixt
their Judgments; or to attend with fufficient Patience the Labour of Experiments. But to fay no more,
they had but a *narrow Territory* ; and the conditi-

on of thofe times, would not allow a very large
Commerce with foreign Nations: they were much
exercis'd in the civil Affairs of their Country: they
had almoft a perpetual War at home, or abroad:
which Kinds of bufie and active Life breed men up
indeed for great Employments: but not fo well for
the diligent, private, and fevere Examination of
thofe little and almoft infinite Curiofities, on which
the true Philofophy muft be founded.

Sect. V.   In that City therefore, the Knowledge of *Nature*
The Original had its Original, before either that of *Difcourfe;* or
of the Phi- of *human Actions*; but it was quickly forc'd to
lofophical give way to them both: For it was not yet come
Sects. to a fufficient Ripenefs, in the time of *Socrates*; and
he, by the Authority of his admirable Wit, made all
parts of Philofophy to be taken off from a Condition of encreafing much farther, that they might be
immediately ferviceable to the Affairs of Men, and
the ufes of Life.   He was one of the firft Men, that
began to draw into fome Order, the confus'd and
obfcure Imaginations of thofe that went before him:
and to make way for the compofing of Arts, out of
their fcattered Obfervations.   All thefe various Subjects, the Vaftnefs of his Soul comprehended in his
cafual Difputations: but after his Death they were
divided amongft his Followers, according to their
feveral Inclinations. From him moft of the fuc-
ceeding *Sects* defcended: and though every one
of them had its different Principles and Rendezvoufes; yet they all laid claim to this one common
Title of being *his Difciples*.   By this means, there
was a moft fpecious Appearance of the Increafe of
Learning: all places were fill'd with Philofophical
                                                    Dif-

Difputes: Controverfies were rais'd : Factions were made: Many Subtilities of confuting, and defending, were invented: But fo inftead of joining all their Strength to overcome the Secrets of Nature (all which would have been little enough, though ever fo wifely manag'd) they only did that, which has undone many fuch great Attempts ; before they had yet fully conquer'd her, they fell into an open Diffenfion, to which of them her Spoils did belong.

'Tis true, at the fame time, fome few Men did continue an earneft, and laborious Purfuit, after *natural Caufes, and Effects* ; and took that Courfe, which, if it had met with as much Encouragement, as the others had, would without queftion have produc'd extraordinary Things. But thefe Philofophers, digging deep, out of the fight of Men ; and ftudying more, how to *conceive* Things aright, than how to *fet off*, and perfuade their Conceptions, to others ; were quickly almoft quite overwhelm'd, by the more plaufible and talkative Sects.

This was the fuccefs of that famous Age of the *Grecian* Learning, in refpect of natural Knowledge. They ftay'd not for an Information fufficient for fuch a noble Enterprize: They would not fuffer their Pofterity, to have any Share with them, in the Honour of performing it : But too fuddenly, for prefent Ufe, they clap'd up an entire Building of Sciences : And therefore it is not to be wonder'd, if the *hafty Fabrick,* which they rais'd, did not confift of the beft Materials.

But at laft with their Empire, their Arts alfo were tranfported to *Rome :* The great Spirit of their Lawgivers,

Sect. VI.
The Philofo-phy amongft the Romans.

B

givers, and Philofophers, in Courfe of Time, degenerating into Rhetoricians, and wandring Teachers
of the Opinions of their private Sects.   Amongft
the *Romans,* the ftudies of Nature met with little,
or no Entertainment.   They fcarce ever dream'd of
any other Way of Philofophy, than only juft reducing into new Method, and eloquently tranflating
into their own Language, the Doctrines, which they
had receiv'd from the *Greeks*.   And it was a long
time too, before even that could obtain any Countenance amongft them.   For, in the firft warlike and
bufie Ages of that State, they only apply'd themfelves to a Severity of moral Virtue ; indeavour'd after no other Skill, than that of the Cuftoms, and
Laws of their Country, the Ceremonies of their Religion, and the Arts of Government : Efteeming e-
very Thing that came out of *Greece,* as an out-landifh
Fafhion, which would corrupt the Manners of their
Youth ; and allure them, from that Strictnefs of Difcipline, and Integrity of Life, by which they had inlarg'd the Bounds of their Common-wealth : Till
at length their Power being increas'd, and their Minds
a little foftned by the Greatnefs of their Commands,
and having tafted of the Pleafures of the Eaft ; they
were content too, by degrees, to admit their Philofophy.   And yet all the Ufe, that they made of it at
laft, was only, either that they might thereby make
their Speech more plentiful ; or elfe , that when
they were at leifure from civil Affairs, they might
have that as a Companion, and Comfort of their Retirements.

Sect. VII.
The Philofo-   This was the Condition of Philofophy, when the
phy of the Chriftian Religion came into the World. That main-
Primitive
Church.   tain'd

tain'd it felf in its firft Age, by the Innocence, and
Miracles, and Sufferings of its Founder, and his Apoftles.   But after their Deaths, when Chriftianity began to fpread into the fartheft Nations, and when
the Power of Working Wonders had ceas'd : It was
thought neceffary for its Increafe, that its Profeffors
fhould be able to defend it, againft the Subtilities of
the Heathens; by thofe fame ways of Arguing, which
were then in ufe, among the Heathen Philofophers.
It was therefore on this Account, that the Fathers,
and chief Doctors of our Church , apply'd themfelves to the Peripatetick, and Platonick Sects ; but
chiefly to the Platonick : Becaufe that feem'd to
fpeak plainer about the Divine Nature ; and alfo,
becaufe the Sweetnefs, and Powerfulnefs of *Plato's*
Writings, did ferve as well to make them popular
Speakers, as Difputers. Having thus provided themfelves againft their Adverfaries, they eafily got the
Victory over them : And though the idolatrous Gen-
tiles had kept the Inftruments of difputing, in their
own Hands, fo many hundred Years ; yet they foon
convinced them, of the Ridiculoufnefs of their Worfhip, and the Purity, and the Reafonablenefs of ours.
   But now the Chriftians having had fo good Succefs, againft the Religions of the Heathens, by their
own Weapons; inftead of laying them down when
they had done, unfortunately fell to manage them
one againft another. So many fubtile Brains having
been fet on work, and warm'd againft a Foreign
Enemy : When that was over, and they had nothing
elfe to do (like an Army that returns victorious, and
is not prefently disbanded) they began to fpoil, and
quarrel amongft themfelves. Hence that Religion,
which at firft appear'd fo innocent, and peaceable,

and fitted for the benefit of human Society; which
confifted in the plain, and direct Rules, of good Life,
and Charity, and the Belief in a Redemption by one
Savior, was miferably divided into a thoufand intricate Queftions, which neither advance true Piety, nor
good Manners.   Hence arofe all the Herefies of thofe
times.   Againft thefe, befides the force of Difputation, the Church obtain'd the Arm of the Civil Magiftrate : and fo at laft by the help of many General
Councils, got them extinguifh'd ; if I may fay they
were extinguifh'd, feeing in this Age wherein we live,
we have feen moft of them unhappily revived.   But
ftill by this means, there was no Knowledge in Requeft,
but the Difputative Philofophy.   For while things were
in this pofture, and fo many great Wits ingag'd in the
heats of Controverfie : it was not to be expected, that
they fhould look out for farther affiftance, than the
Arts, which were already prepar'd ; or that they fhould
make any confiderable Indeavours, about new Inventions, and the tedious Tryal of Experiments.   Nor can
we much blame them for it : feeing in a time of War,
every Man will rather fnatch up that Armor which he
finds ready made, than ftay till Men go to the Mine,
and digg out new Ore, and refine, and harden it a
better way; in hope to have his Weapons of a
ftronger, and nobler Metal at laft.   .

Nor was that Age unfit for fuch an Enterprife, only on the Account of thefe Wars of the Tongue :
But alfo by Reafon of the miferable Diftempers of the
civil Affairs of the World, about that time : which
were chiefly occafion'd by the *Roman* Army's ufur-
ping the Right of choofing Emperors, and by the
invafions of Barbarous Nations, which overwhelm'd
the greateft Part of *Europe*. Amidft thefe Diftractions,

it

it was impoſſible for any thing of this Nature to have
proſper'd : And in ſo vaſt an Inundation of Ignorance, which carry'd away with it the very grown
and aged Trees themſelves (thoſe Parts of Learning
which had taken Root, ſo many Generations paſt) it
would have been in vain, to have committed any
new Plants to the Ground. Such Studies as theſe, as
they muſt receive Encouragement from the Sovereign Authority, ſo they muſt come up in a peaceful
Time, when Men's Minds are at Eaſe, and their Imaginations not diſturb'd, with the Cares of preſerving their Lives, and Fortunes.

To go on therefore with the Matter of Fact : Ha- Sect. VIII.
ving left that diſmal bloody Age, we come into a *The Philoſo-*
Courſe of Time, which was indeed far quieter : *phy under the*
But it was like the Quiet of the Night, which is dark *Church of*
withal. The Biſhops of *Rome* taking the Opportu- *Rome.*
nity of the Decay of the *Roman* Empire, had wreſt-
eſt from it ſo many Privileges, as did at laſt wholly
deſtroy it : And while it was gaſping for Life, forc'd
it to make what Will and Teſtament they pleas'd.
Being thus eſtabliſh'd, and making *Rome*, whoſe Name
was ſtill venerable, the Seat of their Dominion,
they ſoon obtain'd a Supremacy over the Weſtern
World. Under them for a long Space together Men
lay in a profound Sleep. Of the univerſal Ignorance of thoſe Times; let it ſuffice to take the Teſtimony of *William* of *Malmsbury*, one of our ancient
Engliſh Hiſtorians, who ſays, that even amongſt the
Prieſts themſelves, he was a Miracle that could underſtand *Latin*. Thus they continued ; till at laſt,
that Church adopted, and cheriſh'd, ſome of the Peripatetic Opinions, which the moſt ingenious of the
Monks,

Monks, in their solitary and idle Course of Life,
had lighted upon. This Sect was excellently well
made for their Turn. For by hovering so much, in
general Terms, and Notions, it amus'd Men's Minds,
in Things that had not much Difficulty: And so the
Laity being kept blind, were forc'd in all Things to
depend on the Lips of the *Roman Clergy.* From that
time even down to the *Reformation,* the *Gentlemen*
of all these Countries, imploying themselves, chiefly
in Arms, and Adventures abroad : And the Books of
the *Ancients,* being either destroy'd by the *Goths,*
and *Vandals* ; or those which escap'd their Fury, lying cover'd with Dust in the Libraries of *Monasteries* ; few or none regarded any of the Arts of Wit,
and Reason, besides the *Church-men.*

This, I will take the Boldness to say, must needs
be very injurious to the Increase of *general Learning.*
For though I shall justly affirm to the Honour of
that *sacred Profession,* that all Knowledge has been
more search'd into, and promoted by *them,* than by
any other *Order* of Men, even from the *Egyptians*
Times, (whose *Priests* in good part invented, or at
least preserv'd, the Learning of the *East*) down to our
present Age : Yet I must also add, that whenever all
the studious Spirits of a Nation, have been reduc'd
within the Temple's Walls, that Time is naturally liable to this Danger, of having its Genius more intent, on the different Opinions in *Religion,* and the
Rites of Worship, than on the Increase of any other
Science. Of this I shall give two Instances : one,
from the *Ancients,* the other, from *our selves.*

It is manifest, that amongst the *Jews,* all the Men
of Letters still apply'd themselves to the understanding of their *Law:* That being the publick Way

*   of

of Preferment , to the highest Places of Judicature
and Authority in the State. For that many Fraterni-
ties were erected, and (as I may call them) *Judaical
Monasteries* constituted.   Hence came all the Interpretations on the Writings of their *great Law-giver :*
Which at last grew so numerous, and various amongst
themselves, that *Chrift,* when he came, could hardly find any thing of *Moses his Mind,* in all they had
writ : But perform'd more himself towards the Ex-
planation of the *Law,* in *two Chapters,* than they
had done in all their infinite Volumes.   But while
they were so excessively busie, about such Sorts of Contemplations, the other Parts of Learning were neglected : Little or no Footsteps of Philosophy remaining amongst them, except only the Memory of that
History of Plants, which was not written by any of
Aaron's Family, but by their *wisest King.*

But my other Instance comes nearer home, and it
is of the *School-men.* Whose Works when I consider,
it puts into my Thoughts , how far more impor-
tantly a good Method of Thinking, and a right
Course of apprehending Things, does contribute towards the attaining of Perfection in true Knowledge,
than the strongest, and most vigorous Wit in the
World, can do without them.   It cannot without
Injustice be deny'd, that they were Men of extraordinary Strength of Mind : They had a great Quick-
ness of Imagination, and Subtility of distinguishing :
They very well understood the Consequence of Propositions : Their natural Endowments were excellent :
Their Industry commendable : But they lighted on a
wrong Path at first, and wanted Matter to contrive :
And so, like the *Indians,* only express'd a wonderful
Artifice,

Sect. IX.
*The Philoso-
phy of the
School-men.*

Artifice, in the ordering of the fame Feathers into a thoufand Varieties of Figures. I will not infift long on the Barbaroufnefs of their Stile ; though that too muft juftly be cenfur'd : For all the *ancient Philo-fophers*, though they labour'd not to be full and a-dorn'd in their Speech, yet they always ftrove to be eafie, natural, and unaffected. *Plato* was allow'd by all to be the chief Mafter of *Speaking*, as well as of *Thinking*. And even *Ariftotle* himfelf, whom alone thefe Men ador'd, however he has been fince us'd by his *Commentators*, was fo careful about his Words, that he was efteem'd one of the pureft, and moft polite Writers of his Time. But the want of good Language, not being the *School-men*'s worft defect, I fhall pafs it over, and rather ftop a little, to examine the *Matter* it felf, and *Order* in which they proceeded.

The *Subjects* about which they were moft con-verfant, were either fome of thofe *Arts*, which *Ariftotle* had drawn into Method, or the more fpecula-tive Parts of our *Divinity*. Thefe they commonly handled after this Fafhion. They began with fome general Definitions of the Things themfelves, ac-cording to their univerfal Natures , then divided them into their Parts, and drew them out into feve-ral Propofitions, which they laid down as Problems : Thefe they controverted on both fides; and by many Niceties of Arguments, and Citations of Authori-ties, confuted their Adverfaries, and ftrengthned their own Dictates. But though this notional War had been carry'd on with far more Care, and Calmnefs amongft them, than it was : Yet it was never able to do any great Good towards the Enlargement of Knowledge; becaufe it rely'd on *general Terms*,

*   which

which had not much Foundation in *Nature*, and alfo becaufe they took no other Courfe, but that of *Difputing.*

That this infifting altogether on eftablifh'd *Axioms,* is not the moft ufeful Way, is not only clear in fuch airy Conceptions, which they manag'd; but alfo in thofe Things, which lye before every Man's obfervation, which belong to the Life and Paffions, and Manners of Men; which, one would think, might be fooner reduc'd into ftanding Rules. As for example; to make a prudent Man in the Affairs of State, it is not enough, to be well vers'd in all the Conclufions, which all the *Politicians* in the World have devis'd, or to be expert in the Nature of Government and Laws, Obedience and Rebellion, Peace and War: Nay rather a Man that relyes altogether on fuch univerfal Precepts, is almoft certain to mifcarry. But there muft be a Sagacity of Judgment in particular Things; a Dexterity in difcerning the Advantages of Occafions; a Study of the Humour, and Intereft of the People he is to govern: The fame is to be found in *Philofophy*; a thoufand fine Argumentations, and Fabricks in the Mind, concerning the Nature of *Body, Quantity, Motion,* and the like, if they only hover a-loof, and are not fquar'd to particular Matters, they may give an empty Satisfaction, but no benefit, and rather ferve to *fwell,* then *fill* the Soul.

But befides this, the very way of *Difputing* itfelf, and inferring one Thing from another alone, is not at all proper for the fpreading of Knowledge. It ferves admirably well indeed, in thofe Arts, where the Connection between the Propofitions is neceffary, as in the *Mathematicks,* in which a long Train of *Demonftrations,* may be truly collected, from the certainty of

C   the

the firſt Foundation : But in things of probability only, it ſeldom or never happens, that after ſome little Progreſs, the main Subjeċt is not left, and the Contenders fall not into other Matters, that are nothing to the Purpoſe : For if but one Link in the whole Chain be looſe, they wander far away, and ſeldom, or never recover their firſt Ground again. In brief, *Diſputing* is a very good Inſtrument, to ſharpen Men's Wits, and to make them verſatile, and wary Defenders of the Principles, which they already know : but it can never much augment the *ſolid Subſtance* of *Science* itſelf : And methinks compar'd to *Experimenting*, it is like *Exerciſe* to the Body in Compariſon of *Meat* : For Running, Walking, Wreſtling, Shooting, and other ſuch aċtive Sports, will keep Men in Health, and Breath, and a vigorous Temper : but it muſt be a ſupply of new Food that muſt make them grow : ſo it is in this Caſe ; much Contention, and Strife of Argument, will ſerve well to explain obſcure things, and ſtrengthen the weak, and give a good, ſound, maſculine, Colour, to the whole Maſs of Knowledge : But it muſt be a continued addition of Obſervations, which muſt nouriſh, and increaſe and give new Blood, and Fleſh, to the *Arts* themſelves.

But this has been only hitherto ſpoken, againſt the *Method* of the *School-men* in general ; on ſuppoſition, that they took the beſt Courſe, that could be in that Kind. I ſhall now come to weigh that too. For it may eaſily be prov'd, that thoſe very Theorics, on which they built all their ſubtile Webs, were not at all colleċted, by a ſufficient Information from the things themſelves ; which if it can be made out, I hope, it will be granted, that the Force and Vigour of their Wit did more hurt, than good : and

only

only ferv'd to carry them the fafter out of the right
Way, when they were once going. The *Peripateticks* themfelves do all grant, that the firft Rife of
Knowledge muft be from the *Senfes*, and from an In-
duction of their Reports: Well then; how could
the *School-men* be proper for fuch a Bufinefs, who
were ty'd by their Cloyftral Life to fuch a Strictnefs of Hours, and had feldom any larger Profpects
of *Nature*, than the Gardens of their *Monafteries*?
It is a common Obfervation, that Men's Studies are
various according to the different Courfes of Life,
to which they apply themfelves; or the Tempers of
the Places, wherein they live. They who are bred
up in *Commonwealths*, where the greateft Affairs are
manag'd by the Violence of popular Affemblies, and
thofe govern'd by the moft plaufible Speakers, bufie themfelves chiefly about *Eloquence*; they who
follow a *Court*, efpecially intend the Ornament of
Language, and *Poetry*, and fuch more delicate Arts,
which are ufually there in moft Requeft: they who
retire from human things, and fhut themfelves up
in a narrow Compafs, keeping Company with a very
few, and that too in a folemn way, addict themfelves, for the moft part, to fome melancholy Contemplations, or to *Devotion*, and the Thoughts of
another World. That therefore which was fitteft for
the *School-men's* way of life, we will allow them:
But what forry Kinds of Philofophy muft they needs
produce, when it was a part of their *Religion*, to
feparate themfelves, as much as they could, from the
Converfe of Mankind? when they were fo far from
being able to difcover the Secrets of *Nature*, that
they had fcarce Opportunity, to behold enough of
its common Works. If any fhall be inclinable to follow

low the Directions of such Men in natural Things,
rather than of those, who make it their Employment ; I shall believe, they will be irrational enough,
to think, that a Man may draw an exacter Descrip-
tion of *England*, who has never been here, than the
most industrious Mr. *Cambden*, who had travel'd
over every Part of this Country, for that very Purpose.

Whoever shall soberly profess, to be willing to
put their Shoulders under the Burthen of so great
an Enterprize, as to represent to Mankind the whole
Fabrick, the Parts, the Causes, the Effects of Nature ; ought to have their Eyes in all Parts, and to
receive Information from every Quarter of the Earth ;
they ought to have a constant universal Intelligence ;
all Discoveries should be brought to them ; the Trea-
suries of all former Times should be laid open before
them ; the Assistance of the present should be allow'd
them : So far are the narrow Conceptions of a few
private Writers, in a dark Age, from being equal
to so vast a Design.   There are indeed some Operations of the Mind, which may be best perform'd by
the simple Strength of Men's own particular Thoughts;
such are Invention, and Judgment, and Disposition :
For in them a Security from Noise, leaves the Soul
at more Liberty, to bring forth Order, and fashion
the Heap of Matter, which had been before supply'd
to its Use.   But there are other Works also, which
require as much Aid, and as many Hands, as can be
found: And such is this of Observation ; which
is the great Foundation of Knowledge ; some
must gather, some must bring, some separate, some
examine; and to use a similitude, (which the present Time of the Year, and the ripe Fields, that lye
                                                    before

before my Eyes, fuggeft to me) it is in *Philofophy*, as
in *Husbandry*; wherein we fee, that a few Hands
will ferve to meafure out, and fill into Sacks, that
Corn, which requires very many more Labourers, to
fow, and reap, and bind, and bring it into the Barn.

But now it is time for me to difmifs this fubtle Generation of Writers; whom I would not have profecuted fo far, but that they are ftill efteem'd by fome
Men, the only Mafters of Reafon. If they would
be content with any thing lefs than an Empire in
Learning, we would grant them very much. We
would permit them to be great and profound Wits,
as *Angelical*, and *Seraphical*, as they pleas'd; we
would commend them, as we are wont to do *Chaucer*; we would confefs, that they are admirable in
Comparifon of the Ignorance of their own Age: And,
as Sir *Philip Sidney* faid of him, we would fay of them;
that it is to be wonder'd, how they could fee fo clearly then, and we can fee no clearer now: But that
they fhould ftill be fet before us, as the great Oracles of all Wit, we can never allow. Suppofe, that
I fhould grant, that they are moft ufeful in the Controverfies of our *Church*, to defend us againft the Herefies, and Schifms of our Times; what will thence
follow, but that they ought to be confin'd within
their own Bounds, and not be fuffer'd to hinder the
Enlargement of the Territories of other *Sciences*? Let
them ftill prevail in the *Schools*, and let them govern
in Difputations: But let them not over-fpread all
Sorts of Knowledge. That would be as ridiculous,
as if, becaufe we fee, that Thorns, and Briers, by
Reafon of their Sharpnefs, are fit to ftop a Gap, and
keep out wild Beafts; we fhould therefore think,
they deferv'd to be planted all over every Field.

And

And yet I fhould not doubt, (if it were not fome-what improper to the prefent Difcourfe) to prove, that even in *Divinity* it felf, they are not fo neceffa-ry, as they are reputed to be: and that all, or moft of our Religious Controverfies, may be as well deci-ded, by plain Reafon, and by Confiderations, which may be fetch'd from the *Religion* of *Mankind*, the Nature of *Government*, and *human Society*, and *Scripture* it felf, as by the Multitudes of Authorities, and Subtleties of Difputes, which have been hereto-fore in Ufe.

Sect. X.
The Reftora-tion of Learning.
And now I am come to the Time within our View, and to the *third great Age* of the *flourifhing* of *Learn-ing*.   Whether this Recovery of Knowledge did hap-pen by the benefit of *Printing*, invented about that Time, which fhew'd a very eafie Way of communica-ting Men's Thoughts one to another; or whether it came from the Hatred, which was then generally conceiv'd againft the Blindnefs, and Stupidity, of the *Roman Fryars*; or from the *Reformation*, which put Men upon a ftricter Inquiry into the Truth of things; whatever the *Caufe* was, I will not take much Pains to determine: But I will rather obferve, what Kinds of Knowledge have moft flourifh'd upon it.   If we compare this *Age* of *Learning*, with the *two for-mer*; we fhall find, that this does far exceed both the other in its Extent: there being a much larger Plat of Ground, fown with Arts and Civility at this time, than either when the *Grecian* or *Roman* Em-pires prevail'd.   For then (efpecially under the *Ro-mans*) fo many Nations being united under one *Do-minion*, and reduc'd into the Form of *Provinces*: that Knowledge which they had was chiefly confin'd

I   to

to the Walls of the *Imperial Cities* themſelves. But
now (not to inſiſt on the Learning of far remote
Countries, of which we have only imperfeɛt Relations; but to contraɛt our Obſervation to *Chriſtendom* alone) there being ſo many different *States*, and
Governments in *Europe*, every Country ſets up for itſelf: almoſt in every place, the liberal Arts (as they
are call'd) are cheriſh'd, and publick Allowance is
made for their Support. And in this Compaſs, the infinite Numbers of Wits, which have appear'd ſo thick
for theſe many Years, have been chiefly taken up a-
bout ſome of theſe three Studies; either the *Writings*
of the *Antients*, or *Controverſies* of *Religion*, or *Affairs* of *State*.

The Firſt thing that was undertaken, was to re-
ſcue the excellent Works of former *Writers* from Obſcurity. To the better performing of this, many
things contributed about that time. Amongſt which,
as to us in *England*, I may reckon (and that too, it
may be, not the leaſt, whatever the Aɛtion was in itſelf,) the Diſſolution of *Abbyes :* whereby their Libraries came forth into the Light, and fell into induſtrious Men's Hands, who underſtood how to make
more Uſe of them, than their ſlothful Poſſeſſors had
done. So that now the *Greek* and *Latin* Tongues
began to be in Requeſt ; and all the ancient Authors,
the *Heathen Philoſophers, Mathematicians, Orators,
Hiſtorians, Poets*, the various Copies, and Tranſlati-
ons of the *Bible*, and the *Primitive Fathers* were
produc'd. All theſe, by the ſeveral Tranſcriptions,
and the Ignorance of the Tranſcribers, had very many
different Readings, and many Parts wholly loſt; and
by the Diſtance of Times, and Change of Cuſtoms,
were

*Seɛt. XI.
The Reco-
very of the
Antients.*

were grown obscure. About the interpreting, explaining, supplying, commenting on these, almost all the first Wits were employed. A Work of great Use, and for which we ought to esteem our selves much beholden to them. For indeed, if they had not completed that Business, to our Hands, we of this Age, had not been so much at Leisure, as now I hope we are, to prosecute new Inventions. If they had not done it, we should; of which we ought not to doubt, seeing we behold, that even now, when the Soil of Criticism is almost quite barren, and hardly another Crop will come, yet many learned Men cannot forbear spending their whole Labour in toyling about it; what then should we have done, if all those Books had come down untouch'd to our Hands?

We cannot then, with any Sobriety, detract from the *Criticks*, and *Philologists*, whose Labours we enjoy. But we ought rather to give them this Testimony, that they were Men of admirable Diligence: and that the Collections, which they have made, out of the Monuments of the *Ancients*, will be wonderfully advantageous to us, if the right Use be made of them; if they be not set before us, only that we may spend our whole Lives in their Consideration, and to make the Course of Learning more difficult: But if they be imploy'd, to direct us in the Ways that we ought to proceed in Knowledge for the future; if by shewing us what has been already finish'd, they point out to us, the most probable Means, to accomplish what is behind. For methinks, that Wisdom, which they fetch'd from the Ashes of the Dead, is something of the same Nature with Ashes themselves; which, if they are kept up in Heaps together, will be ufelefs: But if they are fcattered upon living Ground, they will make it more fertile, in the bring-ing forth of various Sorts of Fruits. To thefe Men then we are beholden, that we have a fairer Pro-fpect about us: to them we owe, that we are not ig-norant of the Times that are gone before us; which to be, is (as *Tully* fays) *to be always Children.* All this, and much more, is to be acknowledg'd : But then we fhall alfo defire of them, that they would content themfelves with what is their Due: that by what they have difcover'd, amongft the Rubbifh of the *Antients*, they would not contemn the Treafures, either lately found out, or ftill unknown ; and that they would not prefer the *Gold* of *Ophir*, of which now there is no mention but in Books, before the prefent Mountains of the *Weft Indies.*

Thus I pafs over this Sort of *reviv'd Learning.* And now there comes into our View another remarkable Occafion of the Hindrance of the Growth of *expe-rimental Philofophy,* within the Compafs of this bright Age; and that is the great a-do which has been made, in raifing, and confirming, and refuting fo many different Sects, and Opinions of the *Chriftian Faith.* For whatever other Hurt or Good comes by fuch holy fpeculative Wars (of which whether the Benefit or Mifchief over-weighs, I will not now exa-mine) yet certainly by this means, the Knowledge of Nature has been very much retarded. And (to ufe that Metaphor, which an excellent *Poet* of our Nation turns to another purpofe) that Shower has done very much Injury by falling on the Sea, for which the Shepherd and the Plough-man call'd in vain ; The Wit of Men has been profufely pour'd out

Sect. XII.
Religious Controverfies and Arts of

D

on

on *Religion,* which needed not its help, and which
was only thereby made more tempeftuous; while it
might have been more fruitfully fpent, on fome Parts
of Philofophy, which have been hitherto barren, and
might foon have been made fertile.

But befides this, there have been alfo feveral o-
ther *Profeffions,* which have drawn away the Inclinations of Men, from profecuting the naked and unin-
tereffed Truth.   And of thefe I fhall chiefly name
the *Affairs* of *State,* the Adminiftration of civil Government, and the Execution of Laws.   Thefe by
their fair Dowry of Gain and Honour, have always
allur'd the greateft Part of the Men of Art, and Reafon, to addict themfelves to them : while the Search
into feverer Knowledge has been look'd on, as a Study
out of the Way, fitter for a melancholy Humorift, or
a retir'd weak Spirit, than to make Men equal to Bufinefs, or ferviceable to their Country.   And in this,
methinks, the *experimental Philofophy* has met with
very hard Ufage : For it has commonly, in Men's Cen-
fures, undergone the Imputation of thofe very Faults,
which it endeavours to correct in the *verbal.*   That
indeed may be juftly condemn'd for filling Men's
Thoughts with imaginary Ideas of Conceptions, that
are no way anfwerable to the practical Ends of Life :
But this, on the other fide, (as I fhall fhortly make out)
is the fureft Guide, againft fuch notional Wandrings ;
opens our Eyes to perceive all the Realities of Things ;
and clears the Brain, not only from Darknefs, but
falfe or ufelefs Light.   This is certainly fo in the
Thing it felf : But the greateft Part of Men have
ftill apprehended the contrary.   If they can bring
fuch Inquirers under the fcornful Titles of *Philofo-*
phers, or *Scholars,* or *Virtuofi,* it is enough : They pre-

fently conclude them to be Men of another World, only fit Companions for the Shadow, and their own melancholy Whimfies : looking on thofe who dig in the Mine of Nature, to be in as bad a Condition, as the *King* of *Spain's* Slaves in *Peru*, condemn'd for ever to that Drudgery, and never to be redeem'd to any other Imployment. And is not this a very une-qual Proceeding? While fome over-zealous *Divines* do reprobate natural Philofophy as a carnal Know-ledge, and a too much minding worldly Things ; the Men of the World, and Bufinefs, on the other fide, efteem it merely as an idle Matter of Fancy, and as that which difables us from taking right Meafures in human Affairs. Thus, by the one Party, it is cen-fur'd for ftooping too low; by the other, for foar-ing too high : fo that, methinks, it is a good Ground to conclude, that it is guilty of neither of thefe Faults, feeing it is alike condemn'd by both the Ex-tremes. But I fhall have a fitter Occafion to examine this hereafter. However it be, it is not to be won-der'd, if Men have not been very zealous about thofe Studies, which have been fo far remov'd from prefent Benefit, and from the Applaufe of Men. For what fhould incite them to beftow their Time, and Art, in revealing to Mankind thofe Myfteries, for which, it may be, they would be only defpis'd at laft? How few muft there needs be, who will be willing to be impoverifh'd for the common Good? while they fhall fee all the Rewards, which might give Life to their Induftry, paffing by them, and be-ftow'd on the Deferts of eafier Studies? and while they, for all their Pains, and publick Spirit, fhall on-ly perhaps be ferved, as the poor Man was in the *Fable*; who, while he went down into the Well, in Affurance,

that

that he fhould find a mighty Treafure there, was in the mean Time robb'd by his Companions, that ftay'd above, of his Cloak, and all the Booty that he had before gotten?

The Philofo-phy of the Moderns.
And yet, notwithftanding all thefe unfortunate Hindrances, there have been many commendable Attempts in this Way, in the Compafs of our Memories, and the Age before us. And though they have been for the moft part carry'd on, by the private Diligence of fome few Men, in the midft of a thoufand Difficulties, yet it will not be unprofitable to recount fome of them; if it were only to give a fair Ground of Hope, how much Progrefs may be made by a form'd and regular *Affembly*, feeing fome fingle Hands, with fo fmall Encouragement, could difpatch fo much of the Work.

There are five *new Ways* of *Philofophy*, that come into my Obfervation.

Sect. XIII. Modern Dogmatifts.
The firft is, of thofe, who, out of a juft Difdain, that the *Antients* fhould ftill poffefs a Tyranny over our Judgments, began firft to put off the Reverence that Men had born to their Memories; and handling them more familiarly, made an exact Survey of their Imperfections: But then, having rejected them, they purfue their Succefs too far, and ftrait fell to form and impofe new Theories on Men's Reafon, with an Ufurpation as great as that of the others: An Action, which we that live in this Age, may refemble to fome Things that we have feen acted on the Stage of the World: For we alfo have beheld the Pretenders to publick Liberty, turn the greateft *Tyrants* themfelves. The firft part of thefe Men's Performance is very much to be prais'd: They have made the

Ground open and clear for us; they have remov'd
the Rubbifh; which, when one great Fabrick is to
be pull'd down, and another to be erected in its
ftead, is always efteem'd well nigh half the whole
Work: Their Adventure was bold, and hazardous:
They touch'd Men's Minds in their tendereft Part,
when they ftrove to pluck off thofe Opinions,
which had, by long Cuftom, been fo clofely twin'd
about them: They freed our Underftandings from
the Charms of vain Apparitions, and a Slavery to
dead Men's Names. And we may well guefs, that the
abfolute Perfection of the *true Philofophy* is not now
far off, feeing this firft great and neceffary Preparation for its coming, is already taken off our Hands.
For methinks there is an Agreement, between the
Growth of *Learning*, and of *Civil Government*. The
Method of the Rife and Increafe of that, was this:
At firft in every Country there prevail'd nothing
but Barbarifm and Rudenefs: All Places were terrible with *Giants*, and Enchantments, and infolent
Ufurpers: Againft thefe there firft arofe fome mighty
Heroes, as *Hercules*, *Thefeus*, and *Jafon*: Thefe fcowr'd
the World, redrefs'd Injuries, deftroy'd Monfters;
and for this they were made *Demi-gods*. But then
they gave over, and it was left to the great Men,
who fucceeded them, as *Solon*, and *Lycurgus*, to accomplifh the Work, to found Common wealths, to
give Laws, to put Juftice in its Courfe: And why
may I not now prefume, (as many others have done
before me) to reduce thefe Stories to a philofophical Senfe? Firft then, the Phantafms, and Fairies, and
venerable Images of Antiquity, did long haunt the
World; againft thefe we have had our Champions;
and without all queftion, they had the better of the
Caufe

Caufe ; and now we have good Ground to truft, that thefe Illufions being well over, the laft finifhing of this great Work is nigh at Hand, and is referv'd for this Undertaking.

So then, thus far they did well. But in the fecond Part of their Enterprize, they themfelves feem to me to have run into the fame Miftake, for which we chiefly complain'd againft thofe *Ancients*, whofe Authority they deftroy'd. The greateft occafion of our diffenting from the *Greek Philofophers*, and efpecially from *Ariftotle*, was, that they made too much Hafte to feize on the Prize, before they were at the End of the Race ; that they fix'd and determin'd their Judgments, on general Conclufions too foon, and fo could not afterwards alter them, by any new Appearances, which might reprefent themfelves. And may we not fuppofe, that Pofterity will have the fame Quarrel at thefe Men's Labours ? We do not fall foul upon Antiquity, out of any Singularity of Opinion, or a prefumptuous Confidence of the Strength of our Wits above theirs ; we admire the Men, but only diflike the Method of their Proceedings. And can we forbear murmuring, if we fee our *Cotemporaries* difdain them, and yet imitate their Failings ? If we muft conftitute a Sovereignty over our Reafons ; I know not why we fhould not allow this Dominion to the *Ancients*, rather than to any one of the Moderns. They are all dead long fince ; and though we fhould be over-reach'd by them in fome few Falfehoods, yet there is no Danger, left they fhould increafe them upon us ; whereas, if we once hang on the Lips of the wifeft Men now living ; we are ftill in their Power, and under their Difcipline, and fubject to be led by all their Dictates for the future. It is true indeed, a diligent *Inquirer* of thefe Times may gather as much Experience, and in probability, conclude as rightly, as a whole *Academy*, or Sect of theirs could ; yet I fhall ftill deny, that any one Man, though he has the nimbleft, and moft univerfal Obfervation, can ever, in the Compafs of his Life, lay up enough Knowledge, to fuffice all that fhall come after him to reft upon, without the Help of any new Inquiries.

And if we fuppofe the beft, that fome one Man, by wonderful Sagacity, or extraordinary Chance, fhall light upon the true Principles of natural Philofophy ; yet what will be the Profit of fuch univerfal Demonftrations, if they are only fitted for Talk, and the folving of Appearances? Will there be any great Matter, whether they are certain, or doubtful ; old, or new ; if they muft be only bounded to a Syftem, and confin'd to Difcourfe ? The true Philofophy muft be firft of all begun, on a fcrupulous, and fevere Examination of Particulars : from them there may be fome general Rules with great Caution drawn : But it muft not reft there, nor is that the moft difficult Part of its Courfe. It muft advance thofe Principles, to the finding out of new Effects, through all the Varieties of Matter ; and fo both the Courfes muft proceed orderly together ; from experimenting to demonftrating, and from demonftrating to experimenting again. I hope I fhall content my Reader, if I only give one Inftance in this Cafe. It is probable, that he who firft difcover'd, that all Things were order'd in *Nature* by *Motion*; went upon a better Ground, than any before him. But now if he will only manage this, by nicely difputing about the Nature, and Caufes of

Motion

Motion in general, and not profecute it through all particular Bodies; to what will he at laft arrive, but only to a better Sort of *Metaphyficks?* And it may be, his Followers, fome Ages hence, will divide his Doctrine into as many Diftinctions, as the *School-men* did that of *Matter* and *Form*; and fo the whole Life of it will alfo vanifh away into Air and Words, as that of theirs has already done.

Sect. XIV. But it is time for me to give over this Argument;
The ill effects in which, I fear, that what I have already faid, will
of dogmatical alarm fome excellent Men, whofe Abilities I admire;
Philofophy. who may perhaps fufpect, that it has been with a particular Reflection. I might fay for my felf, that firft they muft pafs Sentence on themfelves, before they can think fo, feeing I have nam'd no Man. But I will rather fincerely profefs, that I had no fatyrical Senfe, but only declar'd againft *Dogmatifts* in general. And I cannot repent my having done it, while I perceive there are two very dangerous Mifchiefs, which are caus'd by that way of Philofophy. The one is, that it makes Men give over, and believe that they are fatisfy'd, too foon. This is of very ill Confequence; for thereby Men's Induftry will be flackned, and all the Motives to any farther Purfuit taken away. And indeed this is an Error, which is very natural to Men's Minds; they love not a long and a tedious Doubting, though it brings them at laft to a real Certainty; but they choofe rather to conclude prefently, than to be long in Sufpence, though to better purpofe. And it is with moft Men's Underftandings, as with their Eyes; to which thofe feem more delightful Profpects, where Varieties of Hills and Woods do foon bound their Wandrings, than where there is one
large

large fmooth *Champagn*, over which they may fee much farther, but where there is nothing to delay, and ftop, and divert the Sight.

But the other ill Effect, of which I fhall take notice, is, that it commonly inclines fuch Men, who think themfelves already refolv'd, and immoveable in their Opinions, to be more imperious, and impatient of Contradiction, than becomes the Calmnefs, and unpaffionate Evennefs of the true philofophical Spirit. It makes them prone to undervalue other Men's Labours, and to neglect the real Advantage, that may be gotten by their Affiftance; left they fhould feem to darken their own Glory. This is a Temper of Mind of all others the moft pernicious; to which I may chiefly attribute the Slownefs of the Increafe of Knowledge amongft Men. For what great Things can be expected, if Men's Underftandings fhall be as it were always in the warlike State of Nature, one againft another? If every one be jealous of another's Inventions, and ftill ready to put a Stop to his Conquefts? Will there not be the fame wild Condition in Learning, which had been amongft Men, if they had always been difpers'd, ftill preying upon and fpoiling their Neighbours? If that had ftill continued, no Cities had been built, no Trades found out, no Civility taught: For all thefe noble Productions came from Men's joining in Compacts, and entring into *Society*. It is an ufual faying, that *where the natural Philofopher ends, the Phyfician muft begin:* And I will alfo add, that *the natural Philofopher is to begin, where the moral ends.* It is requifite, that he who goes about fuch an Undertaking, fhould firft know himfelf, fhould be well practis'd in all the modeft, humble, friendly Virtues; fhould be willing

E   to

The HISTORY *of*

to be taught, and to give way to the Judgment of
others. And I dare boldly fay, that a plain induftrious Man, fo prepar'd, is more likely to make a
good Philofopher, than all the high, earneft, inful-
ting Wits,who can bear neither Partnerfhip, nor Oppofition. The *Chymifts* lay it down, as a neceffary
Qualification of their happy Man, to whom God
will reveal their ador'd *Elixir*, that he muft be rather
innocent, and virtuous, than knowing. And if I
were to form the Character of a true Philofopher,
I would be fure to make that the Foundation: Not
that I believe, God will beftow any extraordinary
Light in Nature, on fuch Men more than others ;
but upon a bare rational Account: For certainly,
fuch Men, whofe Minds are fo foft, fo yielding, fo
complying, fo large, are in a far better Way, than
the bold and haughty Afferters; they will pafs by
nothing, by which they may learn; they will be always ready to receive, and communicate Obfervations ; they will not contemn the Fruits of others
Diligence ; they will rejoice to fee Mankind bene-
fited, whether it be by themfelves or others.

Sect. XV.
TheRevivers
of the Anci-
ent Sects.

The fecond Endeavours have been of thofe, who
renounc'd the Authority of *Ariftotle* ; but then reftor'd fome one or other of the *Ancient Sects* in his
ftead. If fuch Men's Intentions were only, that we
might have before us the Conceptions of feveral
Men of different Ages, upon the Works of Nature,
without obliging us to an implicit Confent to all that
they affirm ; then their Labours ought to be receiv'd
with great Acknowledgements: For fuch a general
Profpect will very much inlarge, and guide our Inquiry ; and perhaps alfo will help to hinder the Age
from

from ever falling back again into a Subjection to one usurping Philosopher. But if their Purpose was, to erect those Schools which they reviv'd, into as absolute a Power, as the *Peripateticks* had heretofore; if they strive to make a Competition between *Aristotle* and *Epicurus*, or *Democritus*, or *Philolaus*; they do not contribute very much, towards the main Design : For towards that, it is not enough, that the *Tyrant* be chang'd; but the *Tyranny* it self must be wholly taken away.

The *third* Sort of *new Philosophers* have been Sect. XVI. those, who have not only disagreed from the An-*Modern Ex-* *cients*, but have also propos'd to themselves the right *perimenters.* Course of slow and sure *Experimenting*; and have prosecuted it as far, as the Shortness of their own Lives, or the Multiplicity of their other Affairs, or the Narrowness of their Fortunes, have given them leave. Such as these we are to expect to be but few; for they must divest themselves of many vain Conceptions, and overcome a thousand false Images, which lye like Monsters in their Way, before they can get as far as this. And of these, I shall only mention one great Man, who had the true Imagination of the whole Extent of this Enterprise, as it is now set on foot; and that is, the Lord *Bacon*; in whose Books there are every where scattered the best Arguments, that can be produc'd for the Defence of experimental Philosophy, and the best Directions, that are needful to promote it : All which he has already adorn'd with so much Art; that if my Desires could have prevail'd with some excellent Friends of mine, who engag'd me to this Work, there should have been no other Preface to the *History* of the *Royal So-*

ciety.

ciety, but fome of his Writings. But methinks, in this one Man, I do at once find enough Occcafion, to admire the Strength of human Wit, and to bewail the Weaknefs of a mortal Condition. For is it not wonderful, that he, who had run through all the Degrees of that *Profeffion*, which ufually takes up Men's whole Time; who had ftudied, and practis'd, and govern'd the *common Law*; who had always liv'd in the Crowd, and born the greateft Burden of civil Bufinefs; fhould yet find Leifure enough for thefe retir'd Studies, to excel all thofe Men, who feparate themfelves for this very purpofe? He was a Man of ftrong, clear, and powerful Imaginations; his Genius was fearching and inimitable; and of this I need give no other Proof, than his Style it felf; which as, for the moft part, it defcribes Men's Minds, as well as Pictures do their Bodies, fo it did his above all Men living. The Courfe of it vigorous, and majeftical; the Wit bold, and familiar; the Comparifons fetch'd out of the Way, and yet the more eafie: In all expreffing a Soul, equally skill'd in Men, and Nature. All this and much more is true of him ; but yet his *Philofophical Works* do fhew, that a fingle and bufie Hand can never grafp all this whole Defign, of which we treat. His Rules were admirable ; yet his *Hiftory* not fo faithful, as might have been wifh'd, in many Places; he feems rather to take all that comes, than to choofe, and to heap, rather than to regifter. But I hope this Accufation of mine can be no great Injury to his Memory; feeing, at the fame time, that I fay he had not the Strength of a thoufand Men, I do alfo allow him to have had as much as twenty.

The

The next Philofophers, whom I fhall touch upon,
are the *Chymifts*, who have been more numerous, in
this latter Age, than ever before.　And without queftion, they have lighted upon the right Inftrument of
great Productions and Alterations; which muft for
the moft part be perform'd by Fire.　They may be
divided into three Ranks: Such, as look after the
Knowledge of Nature in general : fuch, as feek out,
and prepare Medicines; and fuch, as fearch after Riches, by Trafmutations, and the great *Elixir*.　The
two firft have been very fuccefsful, in feparating,
compounding, and changing the Parts of Things; and
in fhewing the admirable Powers of Nature, in the
raifing of new Confiftencies, Figures, Colours, and
Virtues of Bodies: And from their Labours, the true
Philofophy is like to receive the nobleft Improvements.　But the Pretenfions of the third Kind are,
not only to indow us with all the Benefits of this
Life, but with Immortality it felf :　And their Succefs has been as fmall, as their Defign was extravagant.　Their Writers involve them in fuch Darknefs;
that I fcarce know, which was the greateft Task, to
underftand their Meaning, or to effect it.　And in the
Chafe of the *Philofopher's Stone*, they are fo earneft,
that they are fcarce capable of any other Thoughts;
fo that if an Experiment lye ever fo little out of
their Road, it is free from their Difcovery; as I have
heard of fome Creatures in *Africk*, which ftill going
a violent Pace ftrait on, and not being able to
turn themfelves, can never get any Prey, but what
they meet juft in their Way.　This Secret they profecute fo impetuoufly, that they believe they fee fome
Footfteps of it, in every Line of *Mofes, Solomon*, or
Virgil.　The Truth is, they are downright *Enthufiafts*
　　　　　　　　　　　　　　　　　　about

about it. And feeing we caft *Enthufiafm* out of *Divinity* it felf, we fhall hardly fure be perfuaded, to admit it into Philofophy. It were perhaps a vain Attempt, to try to cure fuch Men of their groundlefs Hopes. It may be they are happier now, as they are: And they would only cry out with the Man in *Horace*, that their Friends, who had reftor'd them to a perfect Senfe, had murder'd them. But certainly, if they could be brought to content themfelves with moderate Things, to grow rich by Degrees, and not to imagine, they fhall gain the *Indies* out of every *Crucible*; there might be wonderful Things expected from them. And of this we have good Affurance, by what is come abroad from diverfe eminent Perfons; amongft whom fome are Members of the *Royal Society*. And, if it were not already excellently perform'd by others, I might here fpeak largely, of the Advantages that accrue to Phyfick, by the induftrious Labours of fuch *Chymifts*, as have only the difcreet, and fober Flame, and not the wild Lightning of the others Brains.

Sect. XVIiI *Thofe that have handled particular Subjects.* But the laft Kind, that I fhall name, has been of thofe, who confcious of human Frailty, and of the Vaftnefs of the Defign of an *univerfal Philofophy*, have feparated, and chofen out for themfelves, fome particular Subjects, about which to beftow their Diligence. In thefe, there was lefs Hazard of Failing; thefe by one Man's Induftry, and conftant Indeavours, might probably at laft be overcome: And indeed they have generally reap'd the Fruits of their Modefty. I have but one Thing to except againft fome few of them; that they have been fometimes a little too forward to conclude upon *Axioms*, from what they

they have found out, in some particular Body. But that is a Fault, which ought to be overwhelm'd by their other Praises: And I shall boldly affirm, that if all other Philosophical Matters had been as well and as throughly sifted, as some admirable Men of this Age have manag'd some parts of *Astronomy, Geometry, Anatomy*, &c. there would scarce any Burden have remain'd on the Shoulders of our Posterity ; but they might have sat quietly down, and injoy'd the Pleasure of the true *Speculative* Philosophy, and the Profit of the *Practical*.

To all these Proceedings, that I have mention'd, there is as much Honor to be paid, as can be due to any one single human Wit: But they must pardon us, if we still prefer the joint Force of many Men.

And now it is much to be wondred, that there was never yet such an *Assembly* erected, which might proceed on some standing Constitutions of Experimenting. There have, 'tis true, of late, in many Parts of *Europe*, some Gentlemen met together, submitted to common Laws, and form'd themselves into *Academies* : But it has been, for the most part, to a far different Purpose ; and most of them only aim'd at the smoothing of their Stile, and the Language of their Country. Of these, the first arose in *Italy* : where they have since so much abounded, that there was scarce any one great City without one of these *Combinations*. But that, which excel'd all the other, and kept it self longer untainted from the Corruptions of Speech, was the *French Academy* at *Paris*. This was compos'd of the noblest Authors of that Nation ; and had for its *Founder*, the *Great Cardinal de Richelieu* : who, amongst all his Cares, whereby he esta-

Sect. XIX. *Modern Academies for Language.*

✳   blish'd,

blifh'd and enlarg'd that *Monarchy* fo much, did often refrefh himfelf by directing, and taking an Account of their Progrefs.   And indeed in his own Life
he found fo great Succefs of this Inftitution, that he
faw the *French Tongue* abundantly purified, and beginning to take place in the Weftern World, almoft
as much as the *Greek* did of old, when it was the
Language of Merchants, Soldiers, Courtiers, and
Travellers.   But I fhall fay no more of this *Academy*,
that I may not deprive my Reader of the Delight of
perufing their own *Hiftory*, written by *Monfieur de
Peliffon*; which is fo mafculinely, fo chaftly, and fo
unaffectedly done, that I can hardly forbear envy-
ing the *French Nation* this Honour; that while the
Englifh Royal Society has fo much out-gone their *Illuftrious* Academy, in the Greatnefs of its Undertaking,
it fhould be fo far fhort of them in the Abilities of its
Hiftorian.   I have only this to allege in my Excufe;
that as they undertook the Advancement of the Elegance of Speech, fo it became their *Hiftory* to have
fome Refemblance to their Enterprize: Whereas the
Intention of ours being not the Artifice of Words,
but a bare Knowledge of Things; my Fault may be
efteem'd the lefs, that I have written of *Philofophers*
without any Ornament of *Eloquence.*

Sect. XX.   I hope now, it will not be thought a vain Digref-
A Propofal fion, if I ftep a little afide, to recommend the forming
for erecting of fuch an *Affembly* to the Gentlemen of our Nation.
an Englifh   I know indeed, that the *Englifh Genius* is not fo airy
Academy.   and difcurfive, as that of fome of our Neighbors,
but that we generally love to have Reafon fet out in
plain undeceiving Expreffions; as much as they to
have it deliver'd with Colour and Beauty.   And be-
              *   fides

fides this, I underftand well enough, that they have
one great Affiftance to the Growth of Oratory,
which to us is wanting; that is, that their Nobility
live commonly clofe together in their Cities, and
ours for the moft part fcattered in their Country
Houfes. For the fame reafon, why our Streets are
not fo well built as theirs, will hold alfo, for their
exceeding us in the Arts of Speech : They prefer the
Pleafures of the Town, we thofe of the Field;
whereas it is from the frequent Converfations in Cities, that the Humour, and Wit, and Variety, and
Elegance of Language, are chiefly to be fetch'd.
But yet, notwithftanding thefe Difcouragements, I
fhall not ftick to fay, that fuch a Project is now feafonable to be fet on foot, and may make a great Reformation in the manner of our Speaking and Writing.
Firft, the Thing it felf is no way contemptible : For
the Purity of Speech, and Greatnefs of Empire have,
in all Countries, ftill met together. The *Greeks*
fpake beft, when they were in their Glory of Conqueft. The *Romans* made thofe Times the Stan-
ftard of their Wit, when they fubdued, and gave
Laws to the World: And from thence, by degrees, they declin'd to Corruption, as their Valour,
their Prudence, and the Honor of their Arms did decay; and at laft, did even meet the *Northern Nations*
half way in *Barbarifm*, a little before they were over-
run by their *Armies*.

But befides, if we obferve well the *Englifh Language*, we fhall find, that it feems at this time, more
than others, to require fome fuch Aid, to bring it to
its laft Perfection. The Truth is, it has been hitherto a little too carelefly handled; and, I think, has
had lefs Labour fpent about its polifhing than it deferves.

F

ferves. Till the time of *King Henry* the *Eighth*, there was fcarce any Man regarded it, but *Chaucer*; and nothing was written in it, which one would be willing to read twice, but fome of his *Poetry*. But then it began to raife itfelf a little, and to found tolerably well. From that Age, down to the beginning of our late *Civil Wars*, it was ftill fafhioning, and beautifying it felf. In the Wars themfelves, which is a time wherein all Languages ufe, if ever, to increafe by extraordinary degrees; (for in fuch bufie and active times, there arife more new Thoughts of Men, which muft be fignified, and varied by new Expreffions) then, I fay, it receiv'd many fantaftical Terms, which were introduc'd by our *Religious Sects*; and many outlandifh Phrafes, which feveral *Writers*, and *Tranflators*, in that great Hurry, brought in; and made free as they pleas'd; and withal it was inlarg'd by many found and neceffary Forms and Idioms; which it before wanted. And now, when Men's Minds are fomewhat fettled, their Paffions allay'd, and the Peace of our Country gives us the Opportunity of fuch Diverfions; if fome fober and judicious Men would take the whole Mafs of our Language into their Hands, as they find it, and would fet a Mark on the ill Words, correct thofe which are to be retain'd; admit and eftablifh the good, and make fome Emendations in the Accent and Grammar; I dare pronouce, that our *Speech* would quickly arrive at as much Plenty, as it is capable to receive; and at the greateft Smoothnefs, which its Derivation from the rough *German* will allow it.

Nor would I have this new *Englifh Academy* confin'd only to the weighing Words and Letters; but there may be alfo greater Works found out for it. By

many

many Signs we may guefs, that the Wits of our Nation are not inferior to any other; and that they have an excellent Mixture of the Spirit of the *French* and the *Spaniard*: and I am confident, that we only want a few more ftanding Examples, and a little more Familiarity with the Antients, to excel all the Moderns. Now the beft Means that can be devis'd to bring that about, is to fettle a fixt and *impartial Court* of *Eloquence*; according to whofe Cenfure, all Books, or Authors, fhould either ftand or fall. And above all, there might be recommended to them one principal Work, in which we are yet defective; and that is, the compiling of a *Hiftory* of our late *Civil Wars*. Of all the Labors of Men's Wit and Induftry, I fcarce know any that can be more ufeful to the World than *Civil Hiftory*; if it were written, with that Sincerity and Majefty, as it ought to be, as a faithful Idea of human Actions. And it is obfervable, that almoft in all civilis'd Countries, it has been the laft thing, that has come to Perfection. I may now fay, that the *Englifh* can already fhew many induftrious and worthy Pieces in this kind: But yet, I have fome prophetical Imagination in my Thoughts, that there is ftill behind fomething greater than any we have yet feen, referv'd for the Glory of this Age. One Reafon of this my ftrong Perfuafion is a Comparifon, that I make, between the Condition of our *State*, and that of the *Romans*. They at firft wrote, in this way, not much better than our *Monks*: only regiftring, in an undigefted manner, fome few naked Breviaries of their Wars, and Leagues, and Acts of their City Magiftrates. And indeed they advanc'd forward by very flow Degrees: For I remember, that *Tully* fomewhere complains, in thefe

Words:

Words : *Historia nondum Latinis Literis illustrata.*
But it was in the peaceful Reign of *Augustus,* after the
Conclusion of their long Civil Wars, that most of
their perfect *Historians* appear'd. And it seems to
me, that we may expect the same Progress amongst us.
There lye now ready in Bank the most memorable
Actions of twenty Years; a Subject of as great Dignity and Variety, as ever pass'd under any Man's
Hands; the Peace which we Enjoy, gives Leisure
and Encouragement enough; the Effects of such a
Work would be wonderfully advantageous to the
Safety of our Country, and to *His Majesty's* Interest:
for there can be no better Means to preserve his Subjects in Obedience for the future, than to give them
a full View of the Miseries that attend Rebellion.
There are only therefore wanting, for the finishing
of so brave an Undertaking, the united Endeavors of
some publick Minds, who are conversant both in
Letters and Business: and if it were appointed to be
the Labor of one or two Men to compose it, and of
such an *Assembly* to revise and correct it, it might
certainly challenge all the Writings of past or present Times.

But, I see, I have already transgress'd : for I know
it will be thought unadvisedly done, while I was in-
forcing a weightier Design, to start, and to follow
another of less Moment. I shall therefore let it pass
as an extravagant Conceit : only I shall affirm, that the
Royal Society is so far from being like to put a Stop to
such a Business, that I know many of its Members,
who are as able as any others, to assist in the bringing it into Practice.

Thus I have dispatch'd my first general Head ; in
which, it may be, it was not needful to have staid so

long :

long; feeing, I am confident, I have faid nothing, but what was before very well known, and what paffes about in common Difcourfe.

I did on purpofe omit the *learned Age* of the *Arabians*, in its proper Place; becaufe I was refolv'd, as I came down, to keep my felf as near as I could, within the Bounds of *Chriftendom*. But I fhall now add, concerning them, that their Studies alfo were principally bent, upon expounding *Ariftotle*, and the *Greek Phyficians*. They were, without Queftion, Men of a deep and fubtile Wit; which is a Character, that (it may be) in all Ages has belong'd more juftly to the Tempers of the Southern, than of the Northern Countries. Of this they have left many noble Teftimonies behind them; fo many, that (if we believe fome worthy and induftrious Men of our own Nation, who have fearch'd into their Monuments) they might even almoft be compar'd to *Rome* and *Athens* themfelves. But they injoy'd not the Light long enough: It brake forth upon the Point of their greateft Conquefts; it mainly confifted, in underftanding the Ancients; and what they would have done, when they had been weary of them, we cannot tell: For that Work was not fully over, before they were darkened by that, which made even *Greece* it felf barbarous, the *Turkifh Monarchy*. However, that Knowledge, which they had, is the more remarkable, becaufe it fprang up, in that Part of the World, which has been almoft always perverfly unlearned. For methinks, that fmall Spot of civil Arts, compar'd to their long Courfe of Ignorance, before and after, bears fome Refemblance with that Country it felf; where there are fome few little Vallies, and

Sect. XXI. The Philofophy of the Arabians.

+ Wells,

Wells, and pleafant Shades of *Palm-Trees*; but thofe lying in the midft of Deferts, and unpaffable Tracts of Sands.

But now it being a fit Time to ftop, and breath a while, and take a Review of the Ground, that we have pafs'd. It would be here needful for me, to make an Apology for my felf, in a Matter, which, if it be not before-hand remov'd, may chance to be very prejudicial to Men's good Opinion of the *Royal Society* it felf, as well as of its *Hiftorian*. I fear, that this *Affembly* will receive Difadvantage enough, from my weak Management of their Caufe, in many other Particulars; fo that I muft not leave them, and my felf unjuftified, in this, wherein we have fo much Right on our Sides. I doubt not then, but it will come into the Thoughts of many *Criticks* (of whom the World is now full) to urge againft us, that I have fpoken a little too fparingly of the Merits of former Ages; and that this Defign feems to be promoted, with a malicious Intention of difgracing the Merits of the *Ancients*.

But firft, I fhall befeech them, calmly to confider; whether they themfelves do not more injure thofe great Men, whom they would make the Mafters of our Judgments, by attributing all Things to them fo abfolutely; than we, who do them all the Juftice we can, without adoring them? It is always efteem'd the greateft Mifchief a Man can do thofe whom he loves, to raife Men's Expectations of them too high, by undue and impertinent Commendations. For thereby not only their Enemies, but indifferent Men, will be fecretly inclin'd to be more watchful over their Failings, and to confpire in beating down their Fame.

Fame. What then can be more dangerous to the
Honour of Antiquity ; than to set its Value at such
a Rate, and to extol it so extravagantly, that it can
never be able to bear the Trial, not only of envi-
ous, but even of impartial Judges? It is natural to
Men's Minds, when they perceive others to arrogate
more to themselves, than is their Share ; to deny
them even that, which else they would confess to be
their Right. And of the Truth of this, we have an
Instance of far greater Concernment, than that which
is before us: And that is, in *Religion* it self. For
while the *Bishops* of *Rome* did assume an Infallibility, and a sovereign Dominion over our Faith ; the *reformed Churches* did not only justly refuse to grant
them that, but some of them thought themselves oblig'd to forbear all Communion with them, and would
not give them that Respect, which possibly might belong to so ancient and so famous a *Church* ; and
which might still have been allowed it, without any
Danger of Superstition.

But to carry this Dispute a little farther ; what is
this, of which they accuse us? They charge us with
Immodesty in neglecting the Guidance of wiser and
more discerning Men, than our selves. But is not this
rather the greatest Sign of Modesty, to confess, that
we our selves may err, and all Mankind besides? To
acknowledge the Difficulties of Science ; and to submit our Minds, to all the least Works of Nature?
What Kind of Behavior do they exact from us in this
Case? That we should reverence the Footsteps of
Antiquity? We do it most unanimously. That we
should subscribe to their Sense, before our own? We
are willing, in Probabilities ; but we cannot, in Matters of Fact ; for in them we follow the most ancient
Author

Author of all others, even *Nature* it felf. Would
they have us make our Eyes behold Things, at no
farther Diſtance, than they ſaw? That is impoſſible;
feeing we have the Advantage of ſtanding upon their
Shoulders. They ſay, it is Inſolence, to prefer our
own Inventions before thoſe of our *Anceſtors*. But
do not even they the very ſame Thing themſelves, in
all the pretty Matters of Life? In the Arts of War,
and Government; in the making, and aboliſhing of
Laws; nay even in the Faſhion of their Cloaths, they
differ from them, as their Humour or Fancy leads
them. We approach the Ancients, as we behold their
Tombs with Veneration; but we would not therefore be confin'd to live in them altogether; nor
would (I believe) any of thoſe, who profeſs to be
more addicted to their Memories. They tell us, that
in this Corruption of Manners, and Sloth of Men's
Minds, we cannot go beyond thoſe, who ſearch'd
ſo diligently, and concluded ſo warily before us. But
in this they are confuted by every Day's Experience.
They object to us *Tradition*, and the Conſent of all
Ages. But do we not yet know the Deceitfulneſs of
ſuch Words? Is any Man, that is acquainted with the
Craft of founding *Sects*, or of managing Votes in *popular Aſſemblies*, ignorant, how eaſie it is to carry
Things in a violent Stream? And when an Opinion has
once maſter'd its firſt Oppoſers, and ſettled it ſelf in
Men's Paſſions or Intereſts; how few there be, that
coldly conſider, what they admit for a long Time after? So that when they ſay, that *all Antiquity* is a-
gainſt us; 'tis true, in Shew, they object to us the
Wiſdom of many Ages; but in Reality, they only
confront us, with the Authority of a few leading
Men. Nay, what if I ſhould ſay, that this Honour for
the

the dead, which fuch Men pretend to, is rather a worſhiping of themſelves, than of the *Antients*? It may be well prov'd, that they are more in Love with their own *Commentaries*, than with the *Texts* of thoſe, whom they ſeem to make their Oracles; and that they chiefly doat on thoſe Theories, which they themſelves have drawn from them; which, it is likely, are almoſt as far diſtant from the original Meaning of their *Authors*, as the Poſitions of the *new Philoſophers* themſelves.

But to conclude this Argument (for I am weary of walking in a Road ſo trodden) I think I am able to confute ſuch Men by the Practice of thoſe very *Antients*, to whom they ſtoop ſo low. Did not they truſt themſelves, and their own Reaſons? Did not they buſie themſelves in Inquiry, make new Arts, eſtabliſh new Tenents, overthrow the old, and order all Things as they pleas'd, without any ſervile Regard to their Predeceſſors? The *Grecians* all, or the greateſt Part of them, fetch'd their Learning from *Egypt*; and did they blindly aſſent to all that was taught them by the *Prieſts* of *Iſis* and *Oſiris*? If ſo; then why did they not, together with their Arts, receive all the infinite Idolatries, which their Maſters embrac'd? Seeing it is not to be queſtion'd, but the *Egyptians* deliver'd the Rites of their Religion to Strangers, with as much Solemnity at leaſt, as they did the Myſteries of their *Hieroglyphicks*, or *Philoſophy*. Now then, let *Pythagoras*, *Plato*, and *Ariſtotle*, and the reſt of their wiſe Men, be our Examples, and we are ſafe. When they travell'd into the *Eaſt*, they collected what was fit for their Purpoſe, and ſuitable to the Genius of their Country, and left the Superfluities behind them: They brought home ſome

G   of

of their ufeful Secrets; but ftill counted their wor-
fhiping a Dog, or an Onion, a Cat, or a Crocodile,
ridiculous. And why fhall not we be allow'd the
fame Liberty, to diftinguifh, and choofe what we
will follow ? Efpecially, feeing in this, they had a
more certain Way of being inftructed by their Teachers, than we have by them : They were prefent on
the Place : They learn'd from the Men themfelves,
by word of Mouth, and fo were in a likely Courfe
to apprehend all their Precepts aright; whereas we
are to take their Doctrines, fo many hundred Years
after their Death, from their Books only, where they
are for the moft part fo obfcurely exprefs'd, that they
are fcarce fufficiently underftood by the *Grammarians*,
and *Linguifts* themfelves, much lefs by the *Philofophers*.

In few Words therefore, let fuch Men believe,
that we have no Thought of detracting from what was
good in former Times : But, on the contrary, we have
a mind to beftow on them a folid Praife, inftead of a
great, and an empty. While we are raifing new Obfervations upon Nature, we mean not to abolifh the
old, which were well and judicioufly eftablifh'd by
them : No more, than a *King*, when he makes a new
Coin of his own, does prefently call in that, which
bears the Image of his Father ; he only intends thereby to increafe the current Money of his Kingdom,
and ftill permits the one to pafs, as well as the other.
It is probable enough, that upon a frefh Survey, we
may find many Things true, which they have before
afferted ; and then will not they receive a greater
Confirmation, from this our new and fevere Approbation, than from thofe Men, who refign up their Opinions to their Words only ? It is the beft Way of ho-

z   nouring

nouring them, to feparate the certain Things in them, from the doubtful: For that fhews, we are not fo much carried towards them, by rafh Affection, as by an unbyafs'd Judgment. If we would do them the moft Right, it is not neceffary we fhould be perfectly like them in all Things. There are two principal Ways of preferving the Names of thofe that are paft; the one, by *Pictures*; the other, by *Children*: The *Pictures* may be fo made, that they may far nearer refemble the Original, than *Children* do their Parents; and yet all Mankind choofe rather to keep themfelves alive by Children, than by the other. It is beft for the *Philofophers* of this Age to imitate the *Antients* as their *Children*; to have their Blood deriv'd down to them; but to add a new Complexion, and Life of their own: While thofe, that indeavour to come near them in every Line, and Feature, may rather be call'd their dead *Pictures* or *Statues*, than their *genuine Off-fpring*.

The End of the FIRST PART.

THE
HISTORY
OF THE
ROYAL SOCIETY.

The SECOND PART.

Section I.
*The Division
of the Narration.*

Hus I am, at length, arriv'd at the second Part of my Method, the *Narration* it self. This I shall divide into three Periods of Time, according to the several Degrees of the *Preparation, Growth*, and *complete Constitution* of the *Royal Society.*

The first shall consist of the *first Occasions* of this Model, and the Men, who first devis'd to put it in Execution; and shall end where they began to make it a form'd and *regular Assembly.*

The second shall trace out their *first Attempts*, till they receiv'd the public Assistance of *Royal Authority.*

The third shall deliver what they *have done* since they were made a *Royal Corporation.*

It may seem perhaps, that in passing through the first of these, I go too far back, and treat of Things, that may appear to be of too private and domestick Concernment, to be spoken in this publick Way. But if this *Enterprize*, which is now so well establish'd, shall be hereafter advantageous to Mankind (as I make no scruple to foretel that it will)

it

it is but juft, that future Times fhould hear the *Names* of its firft *Promoters:* That they may be able to render particular Thanks to them, who firft conceiv'd it in their Minds, and practis'd fome little Draught of it long ago. And befides, I never yet faw an Hiftorian that was clear from all Affections; that, it may be, were not fo much to be call'd *Integrity,* as a ftoical *Infenfibility :* Nor can I, more than others, refift my Inclinations, which ftrongly force me to mention that, which will be for the Honour of that Place, where I receiv'd a great Part of my Education. It was therefore fome Space after the End of the Civil Wars at *Oxford,* in Doctor *Wilkins* his Lodgings, in *Wadham College,* which was then the Place of Refort for virtuous and learned Men, that the firft Meetings were made, which laid the Foundation of all this that follow'd. The *Univerfity* had at that time many Members of its own, who had begun a *free way* of Reafoning; and was alfo frequented by fome *Gentlemen* of Philofophical Minds, whom the Misfortunes of the Kingdom, and the Security and Eafe of a Retirement amongft Gown-men, had drawn thither.

Their firft Purpofe was no more than only the Satisfaction of breathing a freer Air, and of converfing in Quiet one with another, without being ingag'd in the Paffions and Madnefs of that difmal Age. And from the Inftitution of that *Affembly,* it had been enough if no other Advantage had come but this : That by this means there was a Race of young Men provided againft the next Age, whofe Minds receiving from them their firft Impreffions of *fober* and *generous Knowledge,* were invincibly arm'd againft all the Inchantments of *Enthufiafm.* But what is more, I may

Sect. II. *The Meetings at Oxford.*

venture

2

venture to affirm, that it was in good Meafure by the Influence which thefe Gentlemen had over the reft, that the *Univerfity* it felf, or at leaft, any Part of its Difcipline and Order, was fav'd from Ruin. And from hence we may conclude, that the fame Men have now no Intention of fweeping away all the Honour of Antiquity in this their new Defign ; feeing they imploy'd fo much of their Labour and Prudence in preferving that *moft venerable Seat* of ancient Learning, when their fhrinking from its Defence would have been the fpeedieft Way to have deftroy'd it. For the Truth of this, I dare appeal to all unintereftted Men, who knew the Temper of that Place; and efpecially to thofe who were my own Cotemporaries there; of whom I can name very many, whom the happy Reftoration of the Kingdom's Peace found as well inclin'd to ferve their *Prince* and the *Church,* as if they had been bred up in the moft profperous Condition of their Country. This was undoubtedly fo: Nor indeed could it be otherwife; for fuch *fpiritual Frenfies,* which did then bear Rule, can never ftand long, before a clear and a *deep Skill* in *Nature.* It is almoft impoffible, that they, who converfe much with the Subtilty of *Things,* fhould be deluded by fuch *thick Deceits.* There is but one better Charm in the World, than *real Philofophy,* to allay the Impulfes of the *falfe Spirit*; and that is, the bleffed Prefence and Affiftance of the *true.*

Nor were the good Effects of this Converfation only confin'd to *Oxford:* But they have made themfelves known in their printed Works, both in our own, and in the learned Language; which have much conduc'd to the Fame of our Nation *abroad,* and to the fpreading of profitable Light *at home.* This, I truft,

truft, will be univerfally acknowledg'd, when I fhall have nam'd the Men. The principal and moft conftant of them were Doctor *Seth Ward*, then Lord Bifhop of *Exeter*, Mr. *Boyle*, Dr. *Wilkins*, Sir *William Petty*, Mr. *Matthew Wren*, Dr. *Wallis*, Dr. *Goddard*, Dr. *Willis*, Dr. *Bathurft*, Dr. *Chriftopher Wren*, Mr. *Rook*, befides feveral others, who join'd themfelves to them, upon Occafions. Now I have produc'd their Names I am a little at a ftand how to deal with them. For, if I fhould fay what they deferve ; I fear it would be interpreted Flattery, inftead of Juftice : And yet I have now lying in my Sight, the Example of an *Elegant Book*, which I have profefs'd to admire, whofe Author fticks not to make large Panegyricks on the Members of that *Affembly*, whofe *Relation* he writes. But this Precedent is not to be follow'd by a *young Man*, who ought to be more jealous of publick Cenfure, and is not enough confirm'd in the good Liking of the World, to think, that he has fuch a weighty and difficult Work, as the making of Characters, committed to him. I will therefore pafs by their Praifes in Silence ; though I believe, that what I might fay of them, would be generally confefs'd ; and that if any ingenuous Man, who knows them, or their Writings, fhould contradict me, he would alfo go near to gainfay himfelf, and to retract the Applaufes, which he had fome Time or other beftow'd upon them.

For fuch a candid and unpaffionate Company, as that was, and for fuch a gloomy Seafon, what could have been a fitter Subject to pitch upon than *Natural Philofophy ?* To have been always toffing about fome *Theological Queftion*, would have been, to have made that their private Diverfion, the Excefs of which

which they themfelves diflik'd in the publick : To
have been eternally mufing on *Civil Bufinefs*, and the
Diftreffes of their Country, was too melancholy a
Reflexion : It was *Nature* alone, which could plea-
fantly entertain them in that Eftate. The Contemplation of that, draws our Minds off from paft, or
prefent Misfortunes, and makes them Conquerors
over Things, in the greateft publick Unhappinefs :
while the Confideration of *Men*, and *human Affairs*,
may affect us with a thoufand various Difquiets ; *that*
never feparates us into moral Factions ; that gives us
room to differ, without Animofity ; and permits us
to raife contrary Imaginations upon it, without any
Danger of a *Civil War*.

Their *Meetings* were as frequent, as their Affairs
permitted : their Proceedings rather by Action, than
Difcourfe ; chiefly attending fome particular Trials,
in *Chymiftry* or *Mechanicks :* they had no Rules nor
Method fix'd : their Intention was more to communicate to each other their Difcoveries, which they
could make in fo narrow a Compafs, than an united, conftant, or regular Inquifition.   And methinks,
their Conftitution did bear fome Refemblance to the
Academy lately begun at *Paris :* where they have at
laft turn'd their Thoughts from *Words* to experimental *Philofophy*, and perhaps in Imitation of the
Royal Society.   Their Manner likewife, is to affemble
in a private Houfe, to reafon freely upon the Works
of Nature ; to pafs Conjectures, and propofe Problems, on any Mathematical, or Philofophical Matter, which comes in their Way.   And this is an Omen,
on which I will build fome Hope, that as they agree
with us in what was done at *Oxford*, fo they will go
on farther, and come by the fame Degrees, to erect
                                                another

another *Royal Society* in *France*. I promife for thefe
Gentlemen here (fo well I know the Generofity of
their Defign) they will be moft ready to accept
their Affiftance. To them, and to all the Learned
World befides, they call for Aid. No difference of
Country, *Intereft*, or Profeffion of *Religion*, will
make them backward from taking or affording
Help in this Enterprize. And indeed all *Europe*, at
this time, have two general Wars, which they ought
in Honour to make; the one a *holy*, the other a *philofophical*: The one againft the common Enemy of
Chriftendom, the other alfo againft powerful and
barbarous Foes, that have not been fully fubdued almoft thefe fix thoufand Years, *Ignorance*, and *falfe
Opinions*. Againft thefe, it becomes us, to go forth
in one common Expedition: All civil Nations joyn-
ing their *Armies* againft the one, and their *Reafon* a-
gainft the other; without any petty Contentions a-
bout Privileges, or Prudence.

   Thus they continued without any great Intermif- Sect. III.
fions, till about the Year 1638. But then being call'd *Their firft*
away to feveral Parts of the Nation, and the great- *Meetings at*
eft Number of them coming to *London*, they ufual- London.
ly met at *Grefham* College, at the *Wednefday's*, and
Thurfday's Lectures of Dr. *Wren*, and Mr. *Rook* ; where
there join'd with them feveral eminent Perfons of their
common Acquaintance : The Lord *Vifcount Brouncker*, the now Lord *Brereton*, Sir *Paul Neil*, Mr. *John
Evelyn*, Mr. *Henfhaw*, Mr. *Slingsby*, Dr. *Timothy
Clarke*, Dr. *Ent*, Mr. *Ball*, Mr. *Hill*, Dr. *Crone*, and
diverfe other Gentlemen, whofe Inclinations lay the
fame way. This Cuftom was obferv'd once, if not
twice a week, in Term-time, till they were fcat-
                    H   ter'd

ter'd by the miferable Diftractions of that fatal Year ;
till the Continuance of their Meetings there might
have made them run the Hazard of the Fate of *Archi-*
medes: For then the place of their Meeting was
made a *Quarter* for *Soldiers.* But, to make hafte
through thofe dreadful Revolutions, which cannot be
beheld upon Paper without Horror, unlefs we remember, that they had this one happy Effect, to o-
pen Men's Eyes to look out for the true Remedy ; upon this follow'd the *King's* Return ; and that wrought
by fuch an admirable Chain of Events, that if we either regard the *Eafinefs,* or *Speed,* or *bleffed Iffue* of the
Work, it feems of it felf to contain Variety and Pleafure enough, to make Recompence for the whole
twenty Years Melancholy that had gone before.
This I leave to another kind of Hiftory to be defcrib'd. It fhall fuffice my purpofe, that Philofophy
had its Share in the Benefits of that glorious Action :
For the *Royal Society* had its beginning in the wonderful pacifick Year, 1660. So that if any Conjectures
of good Fortune, from extraordinaty *Nativities,* hold
true, we may prefage all Happinefs to this Undertaking. And I fhall here join my folemn Wifhes, that
as it began in that Time, when our Country was
freed from Confufion and Slavery ; fo it may, in its
Progrefs, redeem the Minds of Men from Obfcurity,
Uncertainty, and Bondage.

Sect. IV.
The Begin-
ning of the
Royal Soci-
ety.

These Gentlemen therefore finding the Hearts of
their Countrymen inlarg'd by their Joys, and fitted
for any noble Propofition ; and meeting with the
Concurrence of many worthy Men, who, to their immortal Honor, had follow'd the King in his Banifhment, Mr. *Erskin,* Sir *Robert Moray,* Sir *Gilbert Tal-*
bot,

bot, &c. began now to imagine fome greater Thing, and to bring out experimental Knowledge from the *Retreats,* in which it had long hid it felf, to take its Part in the *Triumphs* of that univerfal Jubilee. And indeed Philofophy did very well deferve that Reward, having been always Loyal in the worft of Times: For though the King's Enemies had gain'd all other Advantages; though they had all the Garrifons, and Fleets, and Ammunitions, and Treafures, and Armies on their fide; yet they could never, by all their Victories, bring over the Reafon of Men to their Party.

While they were thus ordering their Platform, there came forth a Treatife, which very much haften'd its Contrivance: and that was a Propofal by Mafter *Cowley,* of erecting a Philofophical College. The Intent of it was, that in fome places near *London,* there fhould liberal Salaries be beftow'd on a competent Number of Learned Men, to whom fhould be committed the Operations of Natural Experiments. This Model was every way practicable; unlefs perhaps, in two Things, he did more confult the Generofity of his own Mind, than of other Men's: the one was the *Largenefs of the Revenue,* with which he would have his College at firft indow'd; the other, that he impos'd on his Operators a fecond Task of great Pains, the *Education of Youth.*

The laft of thefe is indeed a matter of great Weight; the Reformation of which ought to be ferioufly examin'd by prudent Men. For it is an undeniable Truth, which is commonly faid, that there would be Need of fewer Laws, and lefs Force to govern Men, if their Minds were rightly inform'd, and fet ftrait, while they were young, and pliable. But perhaps this Labor is not fo proper for Experimenters to undergo; for it would not only devour too much of their Time, but it would go near to make them a little more *magifterial* in Philofophy, than became them; by being long accuftom'd to command the Opinions, and direct the Manners, of their Scholars. And as to the other Particular, the large Eftate which he requir'd to the Maintenance of his College; it is evident, that it is fo difficult a Thing to draw Men in to be willing to divert an antient Revenue, which has long run in another Stream, or to contribute out of their own Purfes, to the fupporting of any new Defign, while it fhews nothing but Promifes, and Hopes; that, in fuch cafes, it were (it may be) more advifeable to begin upon a fmall Stock, and fo to rife by degrees, than to profefs great Things at firft, and to exact too much Benevolence all in one Lump together. However, it was not the excellent Author's Fault, that he thought better of the Age than it did deferve. His Purpofe in it was like himfelf, full of Honor and Goodnefs: Moft of the other Particulars of his Draught the *Royal Society* is now putting in Practice.

I come now to the fecond Period of my Narration; wherein I promis'd to give an Account of what they did, till they were publickly own'd, incourag'd, and confirm'd by Royal Favor. And I truft, that I fhall here produce many Things, which will prove their Attempts to be worthy of all Men's Incouragement: though what was perform'd in this Interval may be rather ftyl'd the *Temporary Scaffold* about the Building, than the *Frame it felf.* But in my Entrance upon this Part, being come to the Top of the Hill, I begin to tremble, and to apprehend the Greatnefs of
                                                                        my

my Subject. For I perceive, that I have led my Readers Minds on, by fo long and fo confident a Speech, to expect fome wonderful Model, which fhall far exceed all the former, that I have acknowledg'd to have been imperfect. Now, though this were really fo, as I believe it is; yet I queftion, how it will look, after it has been disfigur'd by my unskilful Hands. But the Danger of this ought to have deter'd me in the Beginning: It is now too late to look back; and I can only apply my felf to that *good Nature*, which a *great Man* has obferv'd to be fo peculiar to our *Nation*, that there is fcarce an Expreffion to fignify it, in any other Language. To this I muft fly for Succour, and moft affectionately intreat my Country-men, that they would interpret my Failings to be only Errors of Obedience to fome, whofe Commands, or Defires, I could not refift; and that they would take the Meafure of the *Royal Society*, not fo much from my lame Defcription of it, as from the Honour and Reputation of many of thofe Men, of whom it is compos'd.

I will here, in the firft place, contract into few Words, the whole *Sum* of their *Refolutions*; which I fhall often have occafion to touch upon in *Parcels*. Their Purpofe is, in fhort, to make faithful *Records* of all the Works of *Nature*, or *Art*, which can come within their Reach; that fo the prefent Age, and Pofterity, may be able to put a Mark on the Errors, which have been ftrengthned by long Prefcription; to reftore the Truths, that have lain neglected; to pufh on thofe, which are already known, to more various Ufes; and to make the way more paffable, to what remains unreveal'd. This is the Compafs of their Defign.

Sect. V.
A Model of their whole Defign.

Defign. And to accomplifh this, they have endeavour'd, to feparate the Knowledge of *Nature*, from
the Colours of *Rhetorick*, the Devices of *Fancy*, or the
delightful Deceit of *Fables*. They have labor'd to inlarge it, from being confin'd to the Cuftody of a
few, or from Servitude to private Interefts. They
have ftriven to preferve it from being over-prefs'd by
a confus'd Heap of vain and ufelefs Particulars; or
from being ftreitghned and bound too much up by
general Doctrines. They have tried to put it into a
Condition of perpetual Increafing; by fettling an in-
violable Correfpondence between the Hand and the
Brain. They have ftudied, to make it not only an
Enterprife of one Seafon, or of fome lucky Opportunity; but a Bufinefs of Time; a fteady, a lafting,
a popular, an uninterrupted Work. They have attempted, to free it from the Artifice, and Humors,
and Paffions of Sects; to render it an Inftrument,
whereby Mankind may obtain a Dominion over
Things, and not only over one another's *Judgments*:
And laftly, they have begun to eftablifh thefe Re-
formations in Philofophy, not fo much, by any folem-
nity of Laws, or Oftentation of Ceremonies, as by
folid Practice and Examples; not by a glorious
Pomp of Words; but by the filent, effectual, and un-
anfwerable Arguments of real Productions.

   This will more fully appear, by what I am to fay
on thefe four Particulars, which fhall make up this
Part of my Relation, the *Qualifications* of their *Members*; the *Manner* of their *Inquiry*; their *Weekly Affemblies*; and their *Way* of *Regiftring*.

Sect. VI.
*The Qualifi-
cations of the
Members of
the Royal So-
ciety.*
   As for what belongs to the *Members* themfelves
that are to conftitute the *Society*: It is to be noted,
                                *
                                                that

that they have freely admitted Men of different Religions, Countries, and Professions of Life. This they were oblig'd to do, or else they would come far short of the Largeness of their own Declarations. For they openly profess, not to lay the Foundation of an *English, Scotch, Irish, Popish*, or *Protestant* Philosophy; but a Philosophy of *Mankind*.

That the *Church of England* ought not to be apprehensive of this free Converse of various Judgments, I shall afterwards manifest at large. For the present, I shall frankly assert, that our *Doctrine*, and *Discipline*, will be so far from receiving Damage by it; that it were the best Way to make them universally embrac'd, if they were oftner brought to be canvass'd amidst all Sorts of Dissenters. It is dishonorable, to pass a hard Censure on the Religions of all other Countries: It concerns them, to look to the Reasonableness of their Faith; and it is sufficient for us, to be establish'd in the Truth of our own. But yet this Comparison I may modestly make; that there is no one Profession, amidst the Several Denominations of Christians, that can be expos'd to the Search and Scrutiny of its Adversaries, with so much safety as ours. So equal it is, above all others, to the general Reason of Mankind; such honorable Security it provides, both for the Liberty of Men's Minds, and for the Peace of Government; that if some Men's Conceptions were put in Practice, that all wise Men should have two Religions; the one, a *publick*, for their Conformity with the People, the other, a *private*, to be kept to their own Breasts; I am confident, that most considering Men, whatever their first were, would make ours their second, if they were well acquainted with it. Seeing therefore our Church would be in

They admit Men of all Religions.

so

fo fair a Probability of gaining very much, by a frequent Contention and Encounter with other Sects:
It cannot be indanger'd by this Affembly; which
proceeds no farther, than to an unprejudic'd Mixture with them.

Of all Coun-   By their *naturalizing* Men of all Countries, they
tries.   have laid the Beginnings of many great Advantages
for the future.   For by this Means, they will be able,
to fettle a *conftant Intelligence*, throughout all civil
Nations,   and make the *Royal Society* the general
Bank and Free-port of the World : A Policy,
which whether it would hold good in the *Trade* of
England, I know not ; but fure it will in the *Philofophy*.   We are to overcome the Myfteries of all
the Works of Nature; and not only to profecute fuch
as are confin'd to one Kingdom, or beat upon one
Shore : We fhould not then refufe to lift all the Aids,
that will come in, how remote foever.   If I could
fetch my Materials whence I pleas'd, to fafhion the
Idea of a perfect Philofopher; he fhould not be all
of one *Clime*, but have the different Excellencies of
feveral Countries. Firft, he fhould have the *Induftry,
Activity*, and *inquifitive Humor* of the *Dutch, French,
Scotch*, and *Englifh*, in laying the ground Work, the
Heap of Experiments: And then he fhould have added the cold, and *circumfpect*, and *wary* Difpofition
of the *Italians* and *Spaniards*, in meditating upon
them, before he fully brings them into Speculation. All
this is fcarce ever to be found in one fingle Man ; feldom in the fame Country-men : It muft then be fup-
plied, as well as it may, by a *publick Council*, wherein the various Difpofitions of all thefe Nations may
be blended together. To this purpofe, the *Royal Society* has made no Scruple to receive all inquifitive
                          *
                                        Strangers

Strangers of all Countries into its Number. And this they have conftantly done, with fuch peculiar Refpect, that they have not oblig'd them to the Charge of Contributions; they have always taken Care, that fome of their Members fhould affift them in interpreting all that pafs'd, in their publick Affemblies; and they have freely open'd their Regifters to them, thereby inviting them to communicate foreign Rarities, by imparting their own Difcoveries. This has been often acknowledg'd by many learned Men, who have travel'd hither; who have been introduc'd to their Meetings, and have admir'd the Decency, the Gravity, the Plainnefs, and the Calmnefs of their Debates. This they have publifh'd to the World; and this has rous'd all our Neighbours to fix their Eyes upon *England.* From hence they expect the great Improvements of Knowledge will flow; and though, perhaps, they fend their *Youth* into other Parts to learn *Fafhion,* and *Breeding*; yet their *Men* come hither for nobler Ends, to be inftructed in the *Mafculine,* and the *folid Arts of Life*; which is a Matter of as much greater Reputation, as it is more honourable to teach Philofophers, than Children.

By their Admiffion of Men of all *Profeffions,* thefe *Of all Pro-*
two Benefits arife: The *one,* that every *Art,* and eve-*feffions.*
ry Way of Life already eftablifh'd, may be fecure of receiving no Damage by their Counfels. A Thing which all new Inventions ought carefully to confult. It is in vain to declare againft the Profit of the moft, in any Change that we would make. We muft not always deal with the violent Current of popular Paffions, as they do with the furious *Eager* in the *Severn*; where the fafeft Way is to fet the Head of the Boat directly againft its Force. But here Men muft

follow the Shore; wind about leifurably; and infinuate their ufeful Alterations by foft and unperceivable
Degrees. From the Negle&t of this Prudence, we
often fee Men of great Wit, to have been overborn
by the Multitude of their Oppofers; and to have
found all their fubtile Proje&ts too weak for Cuftom
and Intereft: While being a little too much heated
with a Love of their own Fancies, they have rais'd to
themfelves more Enemies than they needed to have
done, by defying at once too many Things in Ufe.
But here this Danger is very well prevented. For
what Sufpicion can *Divinity*, *Law*, or *Phyfick*, or
any other Courfe of Life have, that they fhall be impair'd by thefe Men's Labors; when they themfelves
are as capable of fitting amongft them as any others?
Have they not the fame Security that the whole Nation has for its Lives and Fortunes? Of which this is
efteem'd the Eftablifhment, that Men of all Sorts
and Qualities, give their Voice in every Law that is
made in *Parliament*. But the other Benefit is, that
by this equal Balance of all Profeffions, there will no
one Particular of them overweigh the other, or make
the *Oracle* only fpeak their *private* Senfe; which
elfe it were impoffible to avoid. It is natural to
all Ranks of Men, to have fome one Darling, upon which their Care is chiefly fix'd. If *Mechanicks*
alone were to make a Philofophy, they would bring
it all into their Shops, and force it wholly to confift
of Springs, and Wheels, and Weights; if *Phyficians*,
they would not depart far from their Art; fcarce any
Thing would be confider'd, befides the *Body* of *Man*,
the *Caufes*, *Signs*, and *Cures* of Difeafes. So much
is to be found in Men of all Conditions, of that
which is call'd *Pedantry* in Scholars; which is nothing

thing elſe but an obſtinate Addiction to the Forms
of ſome private Life, and not regarding general Things
enough. This Freedom therefore, which they uſe,
in embracing all Aſſiſtance, is moſt advantageous to
them ; which is the more remarkable, in that they
diligently ſearch out, and join to them, all extraordinary Men, though but of ordinary Trades. And
that they are likely to continue this comprehenſive
Temper hereafter, I will ſhew by one Inſtance ; and
it is the Recommendation which the *King* himſelf
was pleaſed to make, of the judicious Author of *the*
Obſervations on the Bills of Mortality : In whoſe
Election, it was ſo far from being a Prejudice, that
he was a Shop-keeper of *London* ; that his Majeſty
gave this particular Charge to his Society, that if they
found any more ſuch Tradeſmen, they ſhould be ſure
to admit them all, without any more ado. From
hence it may be concluded, what is their Inclination towards the manual Arts ; by the careful Regard
which their *Founder* and *Patron*, has engag'd them
to have for all Sorts of *Mechanick Artiſts.*

But, though the *Society* entertains very many Men Sect. VII.
of *particular Profeſſions*, yet the far greater Num- *It conſiſts*
ber are *Gentlemen*, free and unconfin'd. By the Help *chiefly of*
of this there was hopeful Proviſion made againſt *two* *Gentlemen.*
Corruptions of Learning, which have been long complain'd of, but never remov'd : The *one*, that *Knowledge*
ſtill degenerates to conſult *preſent Profit* too ſoon ; the
other, that *Philoſophers* have been always *Maſters* and
Scholars ; ſome impoſing, and all the other ſubmitting ;
and not as equal Obſervers without Dependence.

The firſt of theſe may be call'd, the *marrying* of *Arts* *The Advan-*
too ſoon ; and putting them to Generation before *tages of this*
they come to be of Age ; and has been the Cauſe of
I 2 much

much Inconvenience. It weakens their Strength; it makes an unhappy Difproportion in their Increafe; while not the *beft*, but the *moft gainful* of them flourifh: But above all, it diminifhes that very Profit for which Men ftrive. It bufies them about poffeffing fome petty Prize; while Nature it felf, with all its mighty Treafures, flips from them; and fo they are ferv'd like fome foolifh Guards; who, while they were earneft in picking up fome fmall Money, that the Prifoner drop'd out of his Pocket, let the Prifoner himfelf efcape, from whom they might have got a great Ranfom. This is eafily declaim'd againft, but moft difficult to be hindred. If any Caution will ferve, it muft be this; to commit the Work to the Care of fuch Men, who, by the Freedom of their Education, the Plenty of their Eftates, and the ufual Generofity of noble Blood, may be well fuppos'd to be moft averfe from fuch fordid Confiderations.

The fecond Error, which is hereby endeavour'd to be remedied, is, that the Seats of Knowledge have been for the moft part heretofore, not *Laboratories*, as they ought to be; but only *Schools*, where fome have *taught*, and all the reft *fubfcrib'd*. The Confequences of this are very mifchievous. For firft, as many *Learners* as there are, fo many Hands and Brains may ftill be reckon'd upon as ufelefs. It being only the *Mafter's* part to examine, and obferve; and the Difciples, to fubmit with Silence to what they conclude. But befides this, the very Inequality of the Titles of *Teachers* and *Scholars*, does very much fupprefs and tame Men's Spirits; which though it fhould be proper for Difcipline and Education; yet is by no means confiftent with a free philofophical Confultation. It is undoubtedly true; that fcarce any Man's
Mind,

Mind is so capable of *thinking strongly*, in the Presence
of one whom he *fears* and *reverences*, as he is when
that Restraint is taken off. And this is to be found,
not only in these weightier Matters; but also to give
a lighter instance in the Arts of *Discourse* and *Raillery*
themselves. For we have often seen Men of bold
Tempers, that have over-aw'd and govern'd the Wit
of most Companies; to have been disturb'd, and dumb,
and bashful as Children, when some other Man has
been near, who us'd to out-talk them. Such a kind of
natural Sovereignty there is in some Men's Minds over
others; which must needs be far greater, when it is advanc'd by long Use, and the *venerable Name* of a *Master*. I shall only mention one *Prejudice* more, and
that is this; that from this only Teaching, and Learning, there does not only follow a Continuance, but an
Increase of the Yoak upon our Reasons: For those
who take their Opinions from others Rules, are commonly stricter Imposers upon their Scholars, than their
own Authors were on them, or than the first Inventors
of Things themselves are upon others. Whatever
the Cause of this be; whether the first Men are made
meek and gentle by their long Search, and by better
understanding all the Difficulties of Knowledge; while
those that learn afterwards, only hastily catching
Things in small *Systems*, are soon satisfy'd, before they
have broken their Pride, and so become more imperious; or whether it arises from hence, that the same
Meanness of Soul, which made them bound their
Thoughts by other Precepts, makes them also *insolent*
to their Inferiors; as we always find *Cowards* the
most *cruel*; or whatever other Cause may be alledg'd,
the Observation is certain, that the *Successors* are usu-
ally more positive and tyrannical, than the *Beginners* of Sects.   If

If then there can be any Cure devis'd for this, it muft be no other than to form an *Affembly* at one Time, whofe Privileges fhall be the fame ; whofe Gain fhall be in common; whofe *Members* were not brought up at the Feet of each other. But after all, even this cannot be free from Prevarication in all future Ages. So apt are fome to diftruft, and others to confide too much in themfelves; fo much Sweetnefs there is, in leading Parties ; fo much Pride in following a Faction ; fuch various Artifices there are to enfnare Men's *Paffions*, and foon after their *Underftandings*. All thefe Hazards, and many more, are to be fuppos'd ; which it is impoffible for mortal Wit wholly to forefee, much lefs to avoid. But yet we have lefs Ground of Jealoufie from this Inftitution than any other, not only becaufe they only deal in Matters of *Fact*, which are not fo eafily perverted ; but alfo upon Security of the Inclinations of the greateft Part of the *Members* of the *Society* it felf. This, I hope, moft Men will acknowledge ; and I will take the Permiffion to fay in general of them, that in all *paft* and *prefent* Times, I am confident there can never be fhewn fo great a Number of *Cotemporaries* in fo narrow a Space of the World, that lov'd Truth fo zealoufly fought it fo conftantly ; and upon whofe Labors Mankind might fo freely rely. This I fpeak, not out of Bravery to *Foreigners* (before whofe Eyes, I believe, this negligent Difcourfe will never appear) but to the learned Men of this *Nation*, who are better Judges of what I fay. And this too, I dare affirm, in an *Age*, wherein I expect to be condemn'd of Falfhood or Partiality for this Character, which I have given. For fo it happens, that we are now arriv'd at that exceffive cenfuring Humor, that he who takes upon him to command any

thing,

tning, though ever fo worthy, will raife to himfelf
far more Enemies than Friends. And indeed this
Sowrnefs of *Criticifm*, which now bears down all
before it, is very injurious to the Honor of our Country. For by defpifing Men for not being abfolutely
excellent, we keep them from being fo; while *Admonitions* join'd with *Praifes*, and *Reproofs* with
Directions, would quickly bring all Things to a higher Perfection. But the Rudenefs of fuch *Criticks* I
do not fo much regard, as the Objections of foberer
Men, who have a real good Will to the Promotion of
this Defign, and yet may be a little diffatisfied in this
Place. For here efpecially they may doubt of two
Things ; the firft, whether the *Royal Society* being fo
numerous as it is, will not in fhort Time be diverted
from its primitive Purpofe ; feeing there will be fcarce
enough Men of philofophical Temper always found to
fill it up ; and then others will crowd in, who have not
the fame Bent of Mind ; and fo the whole Bufinefs will
infenfibly be made rather a Matter of Noife and Pomp,
than of real Benefit ! The fecond, Whether their Number being fo large, will not affright private Men from
imparting many profitable Secrets to them ; left they
fhould thereby become common, and fo they be depriv'd of the Gain, which elfe they might be fure of,
if they kept them to themfelves.

To the firft I fhall reply, That this Scruple is of no
Force, in Refpect of *the Age wherein we live.* For
now the Genius of *Experimenting* is fo much difpers'd,
that even in this *Nation*, if there were one or two
more fuch *Affemblies* fettled, there could not be wanting able Men enough to carry them on. All Places and
Corners are now bufie and warm about this Work :

Sect. VIII.
A Defence of
the Large-
nefs of their
Number.

                                                  and

and we find many noble Rarities to be every Day given in not only by the Hands of learned and profess'd Philosophers; but from the Shops of *Mechanicks*; from the Voyages of *Merchants*; from the Ploughs of *Husbandmen*; from the Sports, the Fish-ponds, the Parks, the Gardens of *Gentlemen*; the Doubt therefore will only touch *future Ages*. And even for them too, we may securely promise, that they will not, for a long Time, be barren of a Race of inquisitive Minds, when the Way is now so plainly trac'd out before them; when they should have tasted of these first Fruits, and have been excited by this Example. There was scarce ever yet, any the meanest Sect, or the most contemptible Opinion, that was utterly extinguish'd in its Cradle. Whether they deserv'd to live, or not, they all had their Course; some longer, some shorter; according as they could combine with the Interests or Affections of the Countries where they began. What Reason then have we to bode ill alone to this *Institution*, which is now so earnestly embrac'd; and which, the older it grows, cannot but still appear more inoffensive? If we only requir'd *perfect Philosophers*, to manage this Employment, it were another Case. For then I grant it were improbable, that threescore, or an hundred such should meet in one Time. But here it is far otherwise: If we cannot have a sufficient Choice of those that are skill'd in all *Divine* and *Humam* Things (which was the ancient Definition of a Philosopher) it suffices, if many of them be plain, diligent, and laborious Observers: such, who though they bring not much Knowledge, yet bring their Hand, and their Eyes uncorrupted: such as have not their Brains infected by false Images, and can honestly assist in the *examining* and *registring*

I

what

what the others reprefent to their View. It feems
ftrange to me, that Men fhould confpire to believe
all things more perplex'd, and difficult, than indeed
they are. This may be fhewn in moft other Matters;
but in this particular in hand, it is moft evident. Men
did generally think, that no Man was fit to meddle in
Matters of this Confequence, but he that had bred himfelf up in a long Courfe of Difcipline for that Purpofe;
that had the Habit, the Gefture, the Look of a Philofopher : Whereas Experience, on the contrary, tells us,
that greater Things are produc'd by the *free* way, than
the *formal*. This Miftake may well be compar'd to the
Conceit we had of *Soldiers*, in the beginning of the
civil Wars. None was thought worthy of that Name,
but he that could fhew his Wounds, and talk aloud of
his Exploits in the *Low Countries:* Whereas the
whole Bufinefs of fighting, was afterwards chiefly perform'd by *untravel'd Gentlemen, raw Citizens*, and
Generals that had fcarce ever before feen a Battle. But
to fay no more, it is fo far from being a Blemifh, that
it is rather the Excellency of this Inftitution, that *Men
of various Studies* are introduc'd. For fo there will
be always many fincere Witneffes ftanding by, whom
Self-love will not perfuade to report falfly, nor Heat
of Invention carry to fwallow a Deceit too foon; as
having themfelves no Hand in the making of the Experiment, but only in the *Infpection*. So cautious
ought Men to be, in pronouncing even upon Matters
of Fact. The whole Care is not to be trufted to *fingle*
Men; not to a *Company* all of *one Mind*; not to *Philofophers*; not to *devout* and religious Men *alone* : By
all thefe we have been already deluded; even by thofe
whom I laft nam'd, who ought moft of all to abhor Falfhood; of whom yet many have mul-

K

tiplied

tiplied upon us infinite Stories and falfe Miracles, without any regard to Confcience or Truth.

To the fecond Objection I fhall briefly anfwer; that if all the Authors, or Poffeffors of extraordinary Inventions, fhould confpire to conceal all that was in their Power from them ; yet the *Method* which they take will quickly make abundant Reparation for that Defect. If they cannot come at Nature in its particular *Streams*, they will have it in the *Fountain.* If they could be fhut out from the Clofets of *Phyficians*, or the Work-houfes of *Mechanicks*; yet with the fame, or with better Sorts of Inftruments, on more Materials, by more Hands, with a more rational Light, they would not only reftore again the old Arts, but find out perhaps many more of far greater Importance. But I need not lay much Strefs upon that Hope ; when there is no Queftion at all, but all, or the greateft part of fuch *domeftick Receipts* and Curiofities, will foon flow into this *publick Treafurie.* How few Secrets have there been, though ever fo gainful, that have been long conceal'd from the whole World by their *Authors ?* Were not all the leaft Arts of Life at firft private? Were not *Watches*, or *Locks*, or *Guns*, or *Printing*, or lately the *Bow-dye*, devis'd by *particular Men*, but foon made *common ?* If neither *Chance*, nor *Friendfhip*, nor *Treachery* of Servants, have brought fuch Things out ; yet we fee *Oftentation* alone to be every Day powerful enough to do it. This Defire of Glory, and to be counted *Authors*, prevails on all, even on many of the dark and referv'd *Chymifts* themfelves ; who are ever printing their greateft Myfteries, though indeed they feem to do it with fo much Reluctancy, and with a Willingnefs to hide ftill ; which makes their *Style* to refemble the *Smoke*, in which they deal.

deal. Well then, if this Difpofition be fo *univerfal*, why fhould we think, that the Inventors will be only tender and backward to the *Royal Society*; from which they will not only reap the moft *folid Honor*, but will alfo receive the ftrongeft Affurances of ftill retaining the *greateft part of the Profit* ? But if all this fhould fail, there ftill remains a Refuge, which will put this whole Matter out of Difpute : and that is, that the *Royal Society* will be able by Degrees to purchafe fuch extraordinary Inventions, which are now clofe lock'd up in *Cabinets* ; and then to bring them into one common Stock, which fhall be upon all Occafions expos'd to all Men's Ufe. This is a moft *heroick Intention* : For by fuch Concealments, there may come very much Hurt to Mankind. If any certain Remedy fhould be found out againft an *Epidemical* Difcafe ; if it were fuffer'd to be ingrofs'd by one Man, there would be great Swarms fwept away, which otherwife might be eafily fav'd. I fhall inftance in the *Sweating-Sicknefs*. The *Medicine* for it was almoft infallible : But, before that could be generally publifh'd, it had almoft difpeopled whole Towns. If the fame Difeafe fhould have return'd, it might have been again as deftructive, had not the Lord *Bacon* taken Care, to fet down the particular Courfe of *Phyfick* for it, in his Hiftory of *Henry the feventh*, and fo put it beyond the Poffibility of any private Man's invading it. This ought to be imitated in all other *fovereign Cures* of the like Nature, to avoid fuch dreadful Cafualties. The *Artificers* fhould reap the common Crop of their *Arts* : but the *Publick* fhould ftill have *Title* to the miraculous Productions. It fhould be fo appointed, as it is in the Profits of Men's Lands ; where the Corn, and Grafs, and Timber, and fome coarfer Metals belong to the

Owner: But the *Royal Mines,* in whofe Ground
foever they are difcover'd, are no Man's Propriety,
but ftill fall to the *Crown.*

Thefe therefore are the *Qualities* which they have
principally requir'd in thofe whom they admitted;
ftill referving to themfelves a Power of *increafing,*
or keeping to their Number, as they faw Occafion.
By this Means, they have given Affurance of an eternal Quietnefs and Moderation, in their experimental
Progrefs; becaufe they allow themfelves to differ in
the weightieft Matter, even in the *Way of Salvation*
it felf. By this they have taken Care, that nothing
fhall be fo remote as to efcape their Reach; becaufe
fome of their *Members* are ftill fcattered abroad, in
moft of the habitable Parts of the Earth. By this
they have provided, that no profitable Thing fhall
feem too mean for their Confideration, feeing they
have fome amongft them, whofe Life is employ'd
about *little* Things, as well as *great.* By this they
have broken down the Partition-wall, and made a
fair Entrance, for *all Conditions of Men* to engage in
thefe Studies; which were heretofore affrighted from
them, by a groundlefs Apprehenfion of their Charge-
ablenefs and Difficulty. Thus they have form'd that
Society, which intends a *Philofophy,* for the Ufe of
Cities, and not for the Retirements of *Schools,* to refemble the *Cities* themfelves; which are compounded of all Sorts of Men, of the *Gown,* of the *Sword,*
of the *Shop,* of the *Field,* of the *Court,* of the *Sea;*
all mutually affifting each other.

Sect. IX.   Let us next confider what *Courfe of Inquiry* they
Their Courfe take, to make all their Labours unite for the Service
of Inquiry. of Mankind: And here I fhall infift on their *Expence,*
their *Inftruments,* their *Matter,* and their *Method.*

Of

Of the Stock, upon which their *Expence* has been hitherto defray'd, I can say nothing that is very *magnificent*; seeing they have relied upon no more than some small *Admiſſion-money*, and *weekly Contributions* amongſt themſelves. Such a *Revenue* as this can make no great Sound, nor amount to any *vaſt Sum*. But yet I ſhall ſay this for it, that it was the only way which could have been begun, with a Security of Succeſs, in that Condition of Things. The *publick Faith* of *experimental Philoſophy*, was not then ſtrong enough, to move Men and Women of all Conditions, to bring in their Bracelets and Jewels, towards the carrying of it on. Such Affections as thoſe may be rais'd by a miſ-guided Zeal; but ſeldom, or never, by calm and unpaſſionate Reaſon. It was therefore well ordain'd, that the firſt Benevolence ſhould come from the *Experimenters themſelves*. If they had ſpeedily at firſt call'd for *mighty Treaſures*; and ſaid aloud, that their Enterprize requir'd the *Exchequer of a Kingdom*; they would only have been contemn'd as vain *Projectors*. So ready is Mankind to ſuſpect all new Undertakings to be Cheats, and *Chimæras*; eſpecially, when they ſeem *chargeable*; that it may be, many excellent Things have been loſt by that Jealouſie. Of this we have a fatal Inſtance amongſt our ſelves. For it was this fear of being circumvented, that made one of our wiſeſt *Kings* delay *Columbus* too long, when he came with the Promiſe of a *new World*; whereas a little more Confidence in his *Art*, and a ſmall Charge in furniſhing out ſome few Ships, would have yearly brought all the Silver of the *Weſt-Indies* to *London*, which now arrives at *Sevil*.

This Suſpicion, which is ſo natural to Men's Breaſts,

could not any way harm the *Royal Society's* Eftablifh-ment; feeing its firft Claims, and Pretenfions were fo modeft. And yet I fhall prefume to affure the World; that what they fhall raife on thefe mean Foundations, will be more anfwerable to the *Largenefs* of their Intentions, than to the *Narrownefs* of their Beginnings. This I fpeak fo boldly, not only becaufe it is almoft generally found true; that thofe Things, which have been *fmall* at firft, have oftner grown *greater*, than thofe which have begun upon a wider Bottom, which have commonly *ftood at a Stay* : But alfo in Refpect of the prefent prevailing *Genius* of the *Englifh* Nation. It is moft ufually found, that every People has fome one Study or other in their View, about which their Minds are moft intent, and their Purfes readier to open. This is fometimes a Profufion in *Habit* and *Diet*; fometimes *religious Buildings*; and fometimes the *civil Ornaments* of their Cities and Country. The firft of thefe will fhortly vanifh from amongft us, by the irrefiftible Correction of the King's own Example; the *next* is of late Years very fenfibly abated : and it is the *laft* of the three towards which Men's Defires are moft propenfe. To evidence this; I think it may be calculated, that fince the *King's* Return, there have been more *Acts* of *Parliament*, for the *clearing* and *beautifying* of Streets, for the *repairing* of *Highways*, for the *cutting* of *Rivers*, for the *Increafe* of *Manufactures*, for the fetting on foot the Trade of Fifhing, and many other fuch publick Works, to adorn the State, than in diverfe Ages before. This *general Temper* being well weigh'd; it cannot be imagin'd, that the *Nation* will withdraw its Affiftance from the *Royal Society* alone; which does not intend to ftop at fome *particular Benefit,* but goes to the Root of *all noble Inventions*, and propofes an infallible Courfe to make *England* the Glory of the Weftern World.

This my Love and my Hopes prompt me to fay. But befides this, there is one Thing more, that perfuades me, that the *Royal Society* will be *immortal*, and that is, that if their Stock fhould ftill continue narrow, yet even upon that, they will be able to free themfelves from all Difficulties, and to make a conftant Increafe of it, by their managing. There is fcarce any Thing has more hindred *the truePhilofophy*, than a vain Opinion, that Men have taken up, that Nothing could be done in it, to any purpofe, but upon a *vaft Charge*, and by a *mighty Revenue*. Men commonly think, that the *Pit*, in which (according to *Democritus*) Truth lyes hid, is bottomlefs; and that it will devour, whatever is thrown into it, without being the fuller. This falfe Conception had got fo much Ground, that affoon as a Man began to put his Hands to *Experiments*, he was prefently given over, as impoverifh'd and undone. And indeed the Enemies of real Knowledge, had fome Appearance of Reafon to conclude this heretofore; becaufe they had feen the great Eftates of fome *Chymifts* melted away, without any Thing left behind, to make Recompence. But this Imagination can now no longer prevail: Men now underftand, that Philofophy needs not fo great a Prodigality to maintain it; that the moft *profitable* Trials are not always the moft *coftly*; that the beft Inventions have not been found out by the *richeft*, but by the moft *prudent* and *induftrious* Obfervers; that the right *Art* of *Experimenting*, when it is once fet forward, will go near to fuftain it felf. This I fpeak, not to ftop Men's future Bounty, by a philofophical Boaft,

that

that the *Royal Society* has enough already: But rather
to encourage them to caſt in more Help; by ſhewing them, what Return may be made from a little, by a
wiſe Adminiſtration.

Of the Variety and Excellence of the *Inſtruments*,
which it lyes in their Power to uſe, I will give no o-
ther Proof, than the wonderful Perfection to which
all manual Arts have of late Years arriv'd. Men now
generally underſtand, to employ thoſe very Tools
which the *Antients* lent us, to infinite more Works
than formerly; they have alſo *of late* devis'd a great
Multitude of all Sorts, which were before *unknown*;
and beſides we may very well expect, that Time will
every Day bring forth *more*. For according as the
Matter to work upon does abound, the greater Plenty
of *Inſtruments* muſt by Conſequence follow; ſuch a
Connexion there is between *Inventions*, and the *Means*
of inventing, that they mutually increaſe each other.

I might be as large, as I pleaſed, in this Particular;
in running through ſome Part of all the innumerable
Arts of the *weſtern World*; and it were not difficult
to ſhew, that the ordinary Shops of *Mechanicks* are
now as full of *Rarities*, as the *Cabinets* of the former
nobleſt Mathematicians. But I will leave that Subject,
which is ſo familiar to all; and chooſe rather, to fetch
a Confirmation of this, even from thoſe Countries,
which (after the Manner of the *Antients*) we call
barbarous. And in going thither for an Example, I
have a farther End. In my foregoing Diſcourſe, I
tried to make out the Advantages of the *modern* Times
above the *antient*; by following the Progreſs of
Learning, down through their Tracts, to which *Scho-*
                                                    lars
                        2

lars ufually confine it; I will now alfo ftrengthen that Argument, by briefly comparing the Skill, and the Works of the *unlearned* Parts of the *prefent* World with thofe that are *paft*. The antient *Barbarians* then, thofe *Nations* I mean, who lay without the Circle of thofe Arts which we admire; the *Gauls*, the *Britains*, the *Germans*, the *Scythians*, have fcarce left any Footfteps behind them, to fhew that they were rational Men. Moft of them were favage in their *Practices*; grofs in their *Contrivances*; ignorant of all, that might make Life either fafe, or pleafant. Thus it was with them, and this all Hiftory fpeaks with one Voice; whereas the *Barbarians* of our Times (if I may take the Liberty ftill to ufe that Word, which the Pride of *Greece* firft brought into Fafhion) the *Turks*, the *Moors*, the *Eaft-Indians*, and even the *Americans*, though they too are utterly unacquainted with all our Sciences; yet by the Help of an *univerfal Light*, which feems to over-fpread this *Age*, are in feveral *Handicrafts* moft ready, and dextrous; infomuch that in fome, they can fcarce be imitated by the *Europeans* themfelves. I fhall leave it to any Man to conjecture from hence, which of thefe two Times has the prerogative; and how much better Helps are Probably to be found at this Day, in the moft *civil Countries*; when we now find fo much Artifice, amongft thofe our *Cotemporaries*, who only follow *rude*, and *untaught* Nature.

Of the *Extent* of the *Matter*, about which they have been already converfant, and intend to be hereafter; there can be no better Meafure taken, than by giving a *general Profpect* of all the Objects of Men's Thoughts; which can be nothing elfe, but either *God*, or *Men*, or *Nature*.

Sect. XI. Their Matter.

L. As

As for the firſt, they meddle no otherwiſe with *divine Things*, than only as the *Power*, and *Wiſdom*, and *Goodneſs* of the *Creator* is diſplay'd in the admirable Order and Workmanſhip of the Creatures. It cannot be deny'd, but it lies in the *natural Philoſopher*'s Hands, beſt to advance that Part of *Divinity*; which, though it fills not the Mind with ſuch *tender* and *powerful Contemplations,* as that which ſhews us Man's *Redemption* by a *Mediator*; yet it is by no means to be paſs'd by unregarded, but is an excellent Ground to eſtabliſh the other. This is a *Religion,* which is confirm'd by the unanimous Agreement of all Sorts of Worſhips, and may ſerve in reſpect to *Chriſtianity,* as *Solomon*'s Porch to the *Temple*; into the one the *Heathens* themſelves did alſo enter, but into the other, only God's *peculiar People.*

In Men, may be conſider'd the *Faculties* and Operations of their *Souls,* the *Conſtitution of their Bodies,* and the *Works of their Hands.* Of theſe, the *firſt* they omit; both becauſe the Knowledge and Direction of them have been before undertaken, by ſome *Arts,* on which they have no mind to intrench, as the *Politicks, Morality,* and *Oratory*; and alſo becauſe the *Reaſon,* the *Underſtanding,* the *Tempers,* the *Will,* the *Paſſions* of Men, are ſo hard to be reduc'd to any certain Obſervation of the *Senſes,* and afford ſo much Room to the *Obſervers* to falſify or counterfeit; that if ſuch Diſcourſes ſhould be once entertain'd, they would be in Danger of falling into *talking,* inſtead of *working,* which they carefully avoid. Such Subjects therefore as theſe they have hitherto kept out. But yet, when they ſhall have made more Progreſs in *material* Things, they will be in a Condition of pronouncing more boldly on them too. For though Man's *Soul*
and

and *Body* are not only one *natural Engine* (as fome have thought) of whofe Motions of all Sorts, there may be as certain an Account given, as of thofe of a Watch or Clock ; yet by long ftudying of the *Spirits*, of the *Blood*, of the *Nourifhment*, of the Parts, of the *Difeafes*, of the *Advantages*, of the Accidents which belong to *human Bodies* (all which will come within their Province) there may, without Queftion, be very near Guefles made, even at the more *exalted* and *immediate* Actions of the *Soul* ; and that too, without deftroying its *fpiritual* and *immortal* Being.

Thefe two Subjects, *God,* and the *Soul,* being only forborn, in all the reft they wander at their Plea-fure : In the Frame of *Men's Bodies,* the Ways for ftrong, heathful, and long Life ; in the *Arts of Men's Hands,* thofe that either *Neceffity, Convenience,* or *Delight* have produc'd *;* in the *Works* of *Nature,* their Helps, their Varieties, Redundancies, and Defects; and in bringing all thefe to the *Ufes* of *human Society.*

In their *Method* of *inquiring,* I will obferve how they have behav'd themfelves in Things that might be brought within their *own Touch* and *Sight* ; and how in thofe, which are fo remote, and hard to be come by, that about them they were forc'd to truft *the Reports of others.* Sect. XII. *Their Method of Inquiry.*

In the firft Kind, I fhall lay it down as their *fun-damental Law,* that whenever they could poffibly get to *handle* the Subject, the *Experiment* was ftill per-form'd by fome of the *Members* themfelves. The want of this *Exactnefs* has very much diminifh'd the Credit of former *Naturalifts;* it might elfe have feem'd ftrange, that fo many Men of Wit, fetting fo many Hands on work, being fo watchful to catch up all Re-

lations,

lations, from Woods, Fields, Mountains, Rivers, Seas, and Lands; and scattering their Pensions so liberally; should yet be able to collect so few Observations, that have been judicious or useful. But the Reason is plain; for while they thought it enough, to be only *Receivers* of others Intelligence; they have either employ'd *ignorant* Searchers, who knew not how to digest or distinguish what they found; or *frivolous*, who always lov'd to come home laden, though it were but with Trifles; or (which is worst of all) *crafty*, who having perceiv'd the Humors of those that paid them so well, would always take care to bring in such Collections as might seem to agree with the Opinions and Principles of their *Masters*, however they did with *Nature* it self.

This Inconvenience the *Royal Society* has escap'd, by making the whole Process pass under its own Eyes. And the Task was divided amongst them, by one of these two Ways. First, it was sometimes refer'd to some *particular Men*, to make Choice of what *Subject* they pleased, and to follow their own Humor in the *Trial*; the *Expence* being still allow'd from the general Stock. By which Liberty, that they afforded, they had a very necessary Regard to the Power of *particular Inclinations*; which in all Sorts of *Knowledge* is so strong; that there may be numberless Instances given of Men, who in some Things have been altogether *useless*, and yet in others have had such a vigorous and *successful* Faculty, as if they had been born and form'd for them alone.

Or else secondly, the *Society* it self made the Distribution, and deputed whom it thought fit for the Prosecution of such or such Experiments. And this they did, either by allotting the *same Work* to *several*

Men,

Men, feparated one from another; or elfe by *joining* them into *Committees*, (if we may ufe that Word in a philofophical Senfe, and fo in fome Meafure purge it from the ill Sound which it formerly had.) By this *Union* of *Eyes* and *Hands* there do thefe *Advantages* arife. Thereby there will be a full *Comprehenfion* of the Object in *all* its Appearances; and fo there will be a mutual Communication of the Light of one *Science* to another; whereas *fingle Labors* can be but as a Profpect taken upon one fide. And alfo by this fixing of feveral Men's Thoughts upon one Thing, there will be an excellent Cure for that *Defect*, which is almoft unavoidable in great *Inventors*. It is the Cuftom of fuch earneft and powerful Minds, to do wonderful Things in the *Beginning*; but fhortly after, to be over-born by the Multitude and Weight of their own Thoughts; then to yield, and cool by little and little; and at laft grow weary, and even to loath that, upon which they were at firft the moft eager. This is the wonted Conftitution of *great Wits*; fuch tender Things are thofe exalted Actions of the Mind; and fo hard it is, for thofe Imaginations, that can run fwift and mighty Races, to be able to travel a long and a conftant Journey. The Effects of this Infirmity have been fo remarkable, that we have certainly loft very many *Inventions*, after they have been in part fafhion'd, by the meer *languifhing* and *negligence* of their *Authors*. For this, the beft Provifion muft be, to join many Men together; for it cannot be imagin'd, that they fhould be all fo violent and fiery; and fo by this mingling of Tempers, the *impetuous* Men not having the whole Burthen on them, may have Leifure for Intervals to recruit their firft Heat : and the more *judicious*, who are not fo foon poffefs'd with fuch Raptures, may carry

on

on the others ſtrong Conceptions, by ſoberer Degrees, to a full Accompliſhment.

Sect. XIII.
Their way of
Inquiry into
remote Mat-
ters.
This they have practis'd in ſuch Things whereof the Matter is common, and wherein they may repeat their Labours as they pleaſe. But in *foreign* and *remote* Affairs, their *Intentions* and their *Advantages* do far exceed all others. For theſe, they have begun to ſettle a *Correſpondence* through all Countries; and have taken ſuch Order, that in ſhort Time there will ſcarce a Ship come up the *Thames*, that does not make ſome return of *Experiments*, as well as of *Merchandize*.

This their Care of an *univerſal Intelligence* is befriended by *Nature* it ſelf, in the Situation of *England*: For, lying ſo as it does, in the Paſſage between the *Northern* Parts of the World and the *Southern*; its *Ports* being open to all Coaſts, and its *Ships* ſpreading their *Sails* in all *Seas*; it is thereby *neceſſarily* made, not only *Miſtreſs* of the *Ocean*, but the moſt proper *Seat* for the Advancement of *Knowledge*. From the *Poſitions* of Countries ariſe not only their ſeveral Shapes, Manners, Cuſtoms, Colours, but alſo their *different Arts* and *Studies*. The *Inland* and *Continent* we ſee do give Laws to Diſcourſe, to Habits, to Behaviour; but thoſe that border upon the *Seas*, are moſt properly ſeated to bring home Matter for *new Sciences*, and to make the ſame Proportion of Diſcoveries above others in the *intellectual* Globe, as they have done in the *Material*.

Upon this Advantage of our Iſland, there is ſo much Streſs to be laid towards the Proſperity of this Deſign, that if we ſhould ſearch through all the World for a perpetual Habitation, wherein the univerſal Philoſophy might ſettle it ſelf, there can none be found,
I   which

which is comparable to *London*, of all the former, or
prefent Seats of Empire. *Babylon*, that was the *Capi-*
tal City of the firft *Monarchy*, was fituated in a Cham-
pion Country, had a clear and uncloudy Air; and
was therefore fit enough to promote one part of *Natu-*
ral Knowledge, the *Obfervations* of the *Heavens :* But
it was a Mid-land Town, and regarded not the Traffick of Foreigners, abounding with its own Luxury
and Riches. *Memphis* was improper, upon the fame
account; for *Egypt* was a *Land content with its own*
Plenty, admitting Strangers, rather to inftruct them,
than to learn any thing from them. *Carthage* ftood not
fo well for a Refort for *Philofophers*, as for *Pirates*; as
all the *African* Shore continues at this Day. As for
Rome, its Fortune was read by *Virgil*; when he faid,
that *it only ought to excel in the Arts of Ruling*. *Con-*
ftantinople, though its prefent *Mafters* were not *barba-*
rous, yet is too much fhut up by the Straits of *Helle-*
fpont. *Vienna* is a Frontier Town, and has no Communication with the *Ocean*, but by a long Compafs a-
bout. *Amfterdam* is a place of Trade, without the Mixture of Men of freer Thoughts. And, even *Paris* it
felf, though it is far to be preferr'd before all the others
for the Refort of learned and inquifitive Men to it, yet is
lefs capable, for the fame Reafons for which *Athens*
was, by being the Seat of *Gallantry*, the *Arts of Speech*,
and *Education*. But it is *London* alone, that enjoys moft
of the other's Advantages without their Inconveniences. It is the Head of a *mighty Empire*, the greateft
that ever commanded the *Ocean :* It is compos'd of
Gentlemen, as well as *Traders :* It has a large Intercourfe with all the *Earth :* It is, as the *Poets* defcribe
their *Houfe* of *Fame*, a City, where all the Noifes and
Bufinefs in the World do meet: and therefore this
Honour

Honour is juftly due to it, to be the *conftant* place of *Refidence* for that *Knowledge*, which is to be made up of the Reports and Intelligence of all Countries.

To this I will add; That we have another Help in our Hands, which almoft forces this Crown on the Head of the *Englifh* Nation: and that is, the *noble* and *inquifitive Genius* of our *Merchants*. This cannot be better fhewn, than by comparing them with thofe of that one Country, which only ftands in Competition with us for Trade. The *Merchants* of *England* live honourably in foreign Parts; thofe of *Holland* meanly, minding their Gain alone: ours converfe freely, and learn from all ; having in their Behaviour very much of the *Gentility* of the Families, from which fo many of them are defcended : The others when they are abroad, fhew, that they are only a Race of plain *Citizens,* keeping themfelves moft within their own Cells, and Ware-houfes; fcarce regarding the Acquaintance of any, but thofe with whom they traffick. This *Largenefs* of ours, and *Narrownefs* of their living, does, no doubt, conduce very much to enrich them ; and is, perhaps, one of the Reafons that they can fo eafily under-fell us: But withal it makes ours the moft *capable,* as theirs *unfit,* to promote fuch an *Enterprife,* as this of which I am now fpeaking. For indeed, the Effects of their feveral Ways of Life are as different : Of the *Hollanders,* I need fay no more, but of the *Englifh Merchants* I will affirm, that in all forts of Politenefs, and Skill in the *World* and *human Affairs,* they do not only excell them, but are equal to any other fort of Men amongft us.

This I have fpoken, not to leffen the Reputation of that *induftrious People* : But, that I might (if it were poffible) inflame their Minds to an Emulation of this

+   Defign:

Defign. They have all things imaginable to ftir them up; they have the Examples of the greateft *Wits* of other Countries, who have left their own Homes, to retire thither, for the Freedom of their Philofophical Studies : They have one Place (I mean the *Hague*) which may be foon made the very Copy of a Town in the *New Atlantis*; which for its Pleafantnefs, and for the Concourfe of Men of all Conditions to it, may be counted, above all others, (except *London*) the moft advantageoufly feated for this Service.

These have been the Privileges and Practices of the *Royal Society*, in Things foreign and native. It would now be needlefs to fet down all the Steps of their Progrefs about them; how they obferv'd all the Varieties of *Generations* and *Corruptions*, natural and artificial; all the Increafings and Leffenings, Agreements and Oppofitions of Things; how, having found out a *Caufe*, they have applied it to many other *Effects*, and the *Effects* to different *Caufes*; how they are wont to change the Inftruments, and Places, and Quantities of Matter, according to Occafions; and all the other Subtilties and Windings of Trial, which are almoft infinite to exprefs. I fhall only, in paffing, touch on thefe two Things, which they have moft carefully confulted.

The one is, not to prefcribe to themfelves any certain *Art* of *Experimenting*, within which to circumfcribe their Thoughts; but rather to keep themfelves free, and change their Courfe, according to the different Circumftances that occur to them in their Operations, and the feveral Alterations of the Bodies on which they work. The true *Experimenting* has this one thing infeparable from it, never to be a *fix'd* and *fettled Art*, and never to be *limited* by conftant Rules. This, perhaps, may be fhewn too in other *Arts*; as in

M

that of *Invention*, of which, though in *Logick* and *Rhetorick* so many Bounds and Helps are given; yet I believe very few have argued or discoursed by those *Topicks*. But whether that be unconfin'd, or no, it is certain that *Experimenting* is; like that which is call'd *Decence* in human Life: which, though it be that, by which all our Actions are to be fashion'd, and though many things may be plausibly said upon it; yet it is never wholly to be reduc'd to *standing Precepts*; and may almost as easily be *obtain'd*, as defin'd.

Their other Care has been, to regard the *least* and the *plainest* Things, and those that may appear at *first* the most *inconsiderable*, as well as the *greatest Curiosities*. This was visibly neglected by the *Antients*. The *Histories* of *Pliny, Aristotle, Solinus, Ælian*, abounding more with pretty Tales, and fine monstrous Stories, than sober, and fruitful Relations. If they could gather together some extraordinary Qualities of *Stones* or *Minerals*, some Rarities of the *Age*, the *Food*, the *Colour*, the *Shapes* of *Beasts*, or some *Virtues* of *Fountains*, or *Rivers*, they thought they had perform'd the chiefest Part of *Natural Historians*. But this Course is subject to much Corruption: It is not the true following of *Nature*; for that still goes on in a steady Road, nor is it so extravagant, and so artificial in its Contrivances, as our Admiration, proceeding from our Ignorance, makes it. It is also a Way that, of all others, is most subject to be deceiv'd; for it will make Men inclinable to bend the Truth much awry, to raise a specious Observation out of it. It stops the severe Progress of *Inquiry*, infecting the Mind, and making it averse from the true *Natural Philosophy*: It is like *Romances*, in respect of *True History*; which,

by

by multiplying Varieties of extraordinary Events and
furprifing Circumftances, makes that feem dull and
taftelefs. And, to fay no more, the very Delight which
it raifes, is nothing fo folid; but, as the Satisfaction
of *Fancy*, it affects us a little in the beginning, but
foon wearies and furfeits: whereas a juft *Hiftory* of
Nature, like the Pleafure of *Reafon*, would not be,
perhaps, fo quick and violent, but of far longer Continuance in its Contentment.

Their *Matter* being thus collected, has been
brought before their *weekly Meetings*, to undergo a
juft and a full Examination. In them their principal Endeavours have been, that they might enjoy the Benefits of a *mix'd Affembly*, which are Largenefs of Obfervation, and Diverfity of Judgments, without the
Mifchiefs that ufually accompany it; fuch as Confufion, Unfteadinefs, and the little Animofities of divided
Parties. That they have avoided thefe Dangers for
the time paft, there can be no better Proof than their
conftant Practice; wherein they have perpetually
preferv'd a fingular Sobriety of debating, Slownefs
of confenting, and Moderation of diffenting. Nor
have they been only free from *Faction*, but from the
very *Caufes* and *Beginnings* of it. It was in vain for
any Man amongft them, to ftrive to prefer himfelf before another; or to feek for any great Glory from
the Subtilty of his Wit; feeing it was the inartificial
Procefs of the *Experiment*, and not the *Acutenefs* of
any Commentary upon it, which they have had in Veneration. There was no Room left, for any to *attempt*
to heat their own, or other's Minds, beyond a due
Temper; where they were not allow'd to expatiate,
or amplifie, or connect fpecious Arguments together.

Sect. XIV.
*Their week-
ly Affemblie.*

M 2
They

They could not be much exafperated one againft another in their Difagreements, becaufe they acknowledge, that there may be feveral Methods of Nature, in producing the fame Thing, and all equally
good; whereas they that contend for Truth by talking, do commonly fuppofe that there is but one Way
of finding it out. The Differences which fhould chance
to happen, might foon be compos'd; becaufe they
could not be grounded on Matters of Speculation, or
Opinion, but only of Senfe; which are never wont
to adminifter fo powerful Occafions of Difturbance
and Contention, as the other. In brief, they have
efcap'd the Prejudices that ufe to arife from Authority, from Inequality of Perfons, from Infinuations, from
Friendfhips; but above all, they have guarded themfelves againft themfelves, left the Strength of their
own Thoughts fhould lead them into Error; left their
good Fortune in one Difcovery fhould prefently confine them only to one way of Trial; left their Failings fhould difcourage, or their Succefs abate their Diligence. All thefe *excellent philofophical Qualities*
they have by long Cuftom made to become the peculiar Genius of this *Society*; and to defcend down to
their Succeffors, not only as *circumftantial Laws*,
which may be neglected, or alter'd, in the Courfe of
Time, but as the very *Life* of their Conftitution; to
remain on their Minds, as the *Laws* of *Nature* do in
the Hearts of Men; which are fo near to us, that we
can hardly diftinguifh, whether they were taught us by
Degrees, or rooted in the very Foundation of our Being.

Sect. XV. It will not be here feafonable, to fpeak much of
The Ceremo- the *Ceremonies* which they have hitherto obferv'd in
nies of their
Meetings. thefe *Meetings*; becaufe they are almoft the fame,
I   which

which have been fince eftablifh'd by their *Council,* which we fhall have a more proper Occafion to pro- duce hereafter. Let this only be faid in brief, to fa- tisfy the curious.

The *Place* where they hitherto affembled, is *Gre-* *fham-College*; where, by the Munificence of a Citi- zen, there have been Lectures for feveral *Arts* in- dow'd fo liberally, that if it were beyond Sea, it might well pafs for an *Univerfity.* And indeed, by a rare Happinefs in the Conftitution (of which I know not where to find the like Example) the Profeffors have been from the Beginning, and chiefly of late Years, of the moft learned Men of the Nation; though the Choice has been wholly in the Difpofal of Citizens. Here the *Royal Society* has one *publick Room* to meet in, another for a *Repofitory* to keep their Inftruments, Books, Rarities, Papers, and whatever elfe belongs to them; making ufe befides, by Permiffion, of feve- ral of the other Lodgings, as their Occafions do re- quire. And, when I confider the Place it felf; methinks it bears fome Likenefs to their Defign. It is now a *Col-* *lege,* but was once the Manfion-houfe of one of the *greateft Merchants* that ever was in *England :* And fuch a *Philofophy* they would build; which fhould firft wholly confift of *Action* and *Intelligence,* before it be brought into *Teaching* and *Contemplation.*

Their Time is every *Wednefday,* after the Lecture of the *Aftronomy* Profeffor; perhaps, in Memory of the firft Occafions of their Rendezvoufes.

Their *Elections,* perform'd by *Balloting*; every Member having a Vote; the Candidates being nam'd at one Meeting, and put to the *Scrutiny* at another.

Their *chief Officer* is the *Prefident ;* to whom it belongs to call, and diffolve their *Meetings* ; to *propofe* the

the Subject; to *regulate* the Proceedings; to *change* the Inquiry from one thing to another; to *admit* the Members who are elected.

Besides him, they had at first a *Regifter*, who was to take Notes of all that pafs'd; which were afterwards to be reduc'd into their *Journals* and *Regifter Books*. This Task was first *perform'd* by Dr. *Croone*. But they since thought it more neceffary, to appoint two *Secretaries*, who are to reply to all Addreffes from Abroad, and at Home; and to publish whatever shall be agreed upon by the *Society*. Thefe are at prefent, Dr. *Wilkins*, and Mr. *Oldenburgh*, from whom I have not ufurp'd this first Imployment of that Kind; for it is only my Hand that goes, the Subftance and Direction came from one of them.

This is all that I have to fay concerning their *ceremonial Part*. In moft other Things, they bounded themfelves to no ftanding Orders, there being nothing more intended in fuch *Circumftances*, than Convenience and Order. If any shall imagine, they have not limited themfelves to *Forms* enough, to keep up the Gravity, and Solemnity of fuch an Enterprize, they are to confider, that fo much Exactnefs and Curiofity of Obfervances, does not fo well befit *Inquirers*, as *Sects* of Philofophy, or Places appointed for Education, or thofe who fubmit themfelves to the Severity of fome religious Order. The Work which the *Society* propofes to it felf, being not fo fine, and eafie, as that of Teaching is; but rather a painful digging, and tolling in *Nature*; it would be a great Incumbrance to them, to be ftreightned to many ftrict *Punctilios*; as much as it would be to an *Artificer*, to be loaded with many Cloaths, while he is labouring in his Shop.

But

But having made so much Haste through *the formal
Part of these their Meetings*, I shall not so soon dispatch *the substantial*; which consists in *directing, judging, conjecturing, improving, discoursing*, upon *Experiments*.

Towards the first of these Ends, it has been their usual Course, when they themselves appointed the Trial, to propose one Week some particular *Experiments*, to be prosecuted the next ; and to debate before Hand, concerning all Things that might conduce to the better carrying them on.   In this *preliminary Collection*, it has been the Custom, for any of the *Society*, to urge what came into their Thoughts, or Memories concerning them ; either from the Observations of others, or from *Books*, or from their own *Experience*, or even from common *Fame* it self. And in performing this, they did not exercise any great Rigour of choosing and distinguishing between *Truths* and *Falshoods*; but amass altogether as they came the certain Works, the Opinions, the Guesses, the Inventions, with their different Degrees and Accidents, the Probabilities, the Problems, the general Conceptions, the miraculous Stories, the ordinary Productions, the Changes incident to the same Matter in several Places, the Hindrances, the Benefits, of *Airs*, or *Seasons*, or *Instruments ;* and whatever they found to have been begun, to have fail'd, to have succeeded, in the Matter which was then under their Disquisition.

Sect. XVI.
Their directing Experiments.

This is a most necessary Preparation, to any that resolve to make a perfect Search.   For they cannot but go blindly, and lamely, and confusedly about the Business, unless they have first laid before them a full *Account* of it.   I confess the excellent *Monsieur des*

I
Cartes

Cartes recommends to us another Way in his *philoſo-phical Method*; where he gives this Relation of his own Progreſs; that after he had run through the uſual Studies of Youth, and ſpent his firſt Years in an active Life; when he retir'd to ſearch into *Truth,* he at once rejected all the *Impreſſions,* which he had before re-ceiv'd, from what he had heard and read, and wholly gave himſelf over to a Reflection on the naked *Ideas* of his own Mind. This he profeſs'd to do, that he might lay aſide all his *old Imaginations,* and begin anew to write on a white and unblotted *Soul.* This, perhaps, is more allowable in Matters of *Contemplation,* and in a *Gentleman,* whoſe chief Aim was his own Delight; and ſo it was in his own Choice, whether or no he would go farther to ſeek it, than his own Mind: But it can by no means ſtand with a practical and univerſal *Inquiry.* It is impoſſible, but they, who will only tranſcribe their own Thoughts, and diſdain to mea-ſure or ſtrengthen them by the Aſſiſtance of others, ſhould be in moſt of their Apprehenſions too narrow, and obſcure; by ſetting down Things for general, which are only peculiar to themſelves. It cannot be avoided, but they will commit many groſs Miſtakes; and beſtow much uſeleſs Pains by making themſelves wilfully *ignorant* of what is already known, and what conceal'd. It was tried among the *Antients,* to find out the pure and primitive Language of the World, by breeding up a Child ſo, that he might never hear any Man ſpeak. But what was the Event of that Trial? Inſtead of obtaining that End, the Child was made abſolutely dumb thereby. And the like Succeſs will that *Philoſopher* find, who ſhall expect, that, by the keeping his Mind free from the *Tincture* of all o-thers *Opinions,* it will give him the otiginal and un-
infected

infected *Truths* of Things. All *Knowledge* is to be got the fame way that a Language is, by *Induſtry, Uſe,* and *Obſervation.* It muſt be receiv'd, before it can be drawn forth. 'Tis true, the Mind of Man is a Glaſs, which is able to repreſent to it ſelf, all the Works of *Nature* : But it can only ſhew thoſe Figures, which have been brought before it : It is no *magical Glaſs,* like that with which *Aſtrologers* uſe to deceive the ignorant; by making them believe, that therein they may behold the Image of any *Place,* or *Perſon* in the World, though ever ſo far remov'd from it. I know it may be here ſuggeſted; that they, who buſie themſelves much abroad about learning the Judgments of others, cannot be unprejudic'd in what they think. But it is not the *knowing,* but the peremptory *Addic-tion* to others *Tenets,* that ſowers and perverts the *Underſtanding.* Nay, to go farther; that Man, who is throughly acquainted with all Sorts of *Opinions,* is very much more unlikely, to adhere obſtinately to any one particular, than he whoſe Head is only fill'd with Thoughts, that are all of one Colour.

It being now ſo requiſite, to premiſe this general Collection, it could not be better made, than by the *joint Labours* of the whole *Society.* It were an into-lerable Burthen, if it were wholly caſt on the *Experi-menters* themſelves. For, it is not only true, that thoſe who have the beſt Faculty of *experimenting,* are commonly moſt averſe from reading Books ; and ſo it is fit, that this *Defect* ſhould be ſupplied by others Pains: But alſo it would too much tire, and waſte or at leaſt divert their Spirits, before they came to the main Work: Whereas the *Task* being ſhar'd amongſt ſo great a Number, will become not much more than a Buſineſs of *Delight.* Well then, by

N   this

this firſt *Comment* and *Diſcourſe* upon the *Experiment*; he that is to try it, being preſent, and having ſo good an Opportunity, of comparing ſo many other Men's Conceptions with his own, and with the *Thing* it ſelf, muſt needs have his Thoughts more enlarg'd, his Judgment confirm'd, his Eyes open'd to diſcern, what moſt compendious Helps may be provided; what part of it is more or leſs uſeful, and upon what ſide it may be beſt attempted: The *Truths*, which he learns this way, will be his Pattern; the *Errors* will be his Sea-marks, to teach to avoid the ſame Dangers; the very Falſhoods themſelves will ſerve to enlarge, though they do not inform his *Underſtanding*. And, indeed, a thouſand more Advantages will hereby come into the Minds of the moſt ſagacious and acute *Inquirers*, which they would never have compaſs'd, if they had been only left to themſelves. I remember my Lord *Bacon* ſomewhere ſays; *That it is one of the greateſt Secrets of Nature, that Men's Paſſions are more capable of being rais'd to higher Degrees in Company, than in Solitude*; *and that we ſooner grieve, fear, rejoice, love, admire, when we behold many others ſo mov'd, than when we are alone.* This is true; and the ſame may be as well affirm'd of moſt other Actions of the Mind. In *Aſſemblies*, the *Wits* of moſt Men are ſharper, their *Apprehenſions readier*, their *Thoughts fuller*, than in their *Cloſets*. Of this there is an undoubted Proof in the *Art of ſpeaking*. For, let the wittieſt and moſt eloquent Men think as largely as they can, on any Subject in private; yet, when they come into the publick, and eſpecially, when they have heard others ſpeak before them, their *Argument* appears quite another thing to them; their former Expreſſions ſeem too flat and cold for their preſent

Thoughts;

Thoughts; their Minds fwell, and are enlightned,
as if at that time they were poffefs'd with the *Souls* of
the whole Multitude, before whom they ftand.

Thofe, to whom the Conduct of the *Experiment* Sect. VII.
is committed, being difmifs'd with thefe Advantages, *Their judg-*
do, as it were, carry the Eyes and the Imaginati-*ing of the*
ons of the whole Company into the *Laboratory* with *Matter of*
them. And after they have perform'd the *Trial*, they *Fact.*
bring all the *Hiftory* of its *Procefs* back again to the
Teft. Then comes in the fecond great Work of the
Affembly; which is to *judge* and *refolve* upon the Matter of *Fact.* In this Part of their Imployment, they
us'd to take an exact View of the Repetition of the
whole Courfe of the *Experiment*; here they obferv'd
all the *Chances*, and the *Regularities* of the Proceeding; what *Nature* does willingly, what con-
ftrain'd; what with its own Power, what by the Suc-
cours of Art; what in a conftant Road, and what
with fome kind of Sport and Extravagance; induftrioufly marking all the various Shapes into which it
turns it felf, when it is perfued, and by how many fecret Paffages it at laft obtains its End; never giving it
over till the whole *Company* has been fully fatisfied of
the Certainty and Conftancy; or, on the other fide,
of the abfolute Impoffibility of the Effect. This *cri-*
tical and *reiterated Scrutiny* of thofe Things, which
are the plain Objects of their Eyes, muft needs put
out of all reafonable Difpute the Reality of thofe
Operations, which the *Society* fhall pofitively determine to have fucceeded. If any fhall ftill think it a
juft *philofophical Liberty*, to be jealous of refting on
their Credit, they are in the right; and their *Diffent-*
ings will be moft thankfully receiv'd, if they be eftablifh'd on folid Works, and not only on *Prejudices*, or

Suspicions. To the *Royal Society* it will be at any time
almost as acceptable, to be *confuted*, as to *discover* ;
seeing, by this means, they will accomplish their
main *Design :* others will be inflam'd ; many more
will labour ; and so the *Truth* will be obtain'd between them ; which may be as much promoted by
the *Contentions* of Hands, and Eyes; as it is commonly injur'd by those of Tongues.   However, that
Men may not hence undervalue their *Authority*, because they themselves are not willing to impose, and
to usurp a *Dominion* over their *Reason*; I will tell
them, that there is not any one Thing, which is now approv'd and practis'd in the World, that is confirm'd
by stronger Evidence, than this which the *Society*
requires ; except only the *Holy Mysteries of our
Religion*. In almost all other Matters of *Belief*, of
Opinion, or of *Science ;* the Assurance, whereby Men
are guided, is nothing near so firm, as this.   And I
dare appeal to all *sober Men ;* whether, seeing in all
Countries, that are govern'd by Laws, they expect
no more, than the Consent of two or three Wit-
nesses in Matters of Life and Estate ; they will not
think, they are fairly dealt withal in what concerns
their *Knowledge,* if they have the concurring Testimonies of *Threescore or an Hundred.*

Sect.XVIII.   The *History* of the *Trial* perform'd being thus se-
Their conjec- cur'd, I will next declare, what Room they allow'd for
turing on the conjecturing upon the *Causes*; about which they also
Causes. took some Pains, though in a far different Way from
the antient *Philosophers* ; amongst whom, scarce any
thing else was regarded, but such *general Contemplations.* This indeed is the *fatal Point,* about which so
many of the greatest *Wits* of all Ages have miscar-
I   ried ;

ried ; and commonly, the greater the Wit, the more
has been the Danger : So many wary Steps ought to
be troden in this uncertain Path ; such a Multitude of
pleasing *Errors*, false *Lights*, disguised *Lies*, deceit-
ful *Fancies* must be escap'd ; so much Care must be
taken to get into the right Way at first ; so much, to
continue in it ; and at last, the greatest Caution still
remaining to be us'd ; lest when the Treasure is in our
View, we undo all, by catching at it too soon, with
too greedy and rash a Hand. These and many more
are the Difficulties to be pass'd ; which I have here
with less Apprehension reckon'd up, because the Remedy is so nigh. To this *Work* therefore the *Society* ap-
proaches, with as much Circumspection and Modesty, as human Connsels are capable of : They have
been cautious, to shun the overweening *Dogmatizing*
on Causes on the one Hand ; and not to fall into a
speculative Scepticism on the other ; and whatever Causes they have with just Deliberation found to hold good
they still make them increase their Benefits, by farther experimenting upon them ; and will not permit
them to rust or corrupt, for want of Use. If after all
this, they shall not seem wholly to have remov'd the
Mischiefs, that attend this *hazardous Matter* ; they
ought rather to be judg'd, by what they have done towards it above others, than by what they have not provided against ; seeing the Thing it self is of that Nature, that it is impossible to place the Minds of Men
beyond all Condition of erring about it.

The first *Danger* that I shall observe in this kind, is
an *over-hasty*, and *precipitant* concluding upon the
Causes before the *Effects* have been enough search'd
into ; a finishing the *Roof* before the *Foundation* has
been well laid.   For this, I shall first allege this Cure ;
that,

that though the *Experiment* was but the private Task
of one or two, or fome fuch fmall Number; yet the
conjecturing, and *debating* on its *Confequences*, was
ftill the Imployment of their full and folemn *Affemblies*. I have already, upon feveral Occafions, prefer'd
Companies before *fingle Endeavours* in *philofophical*
Matters; and yet I am not afham'd here to repeat it
again; efpecially, feeing in this place it is moft apparent, to which of them the Prerogative of Freedom,
and Clearnefs of Judging belongs. To this Purpofe
I fhall affirm, that there can never be found, in the
Breaft of any particular *Philofopher*, as much Wari-
nefs, and Coldnefs of Thinking, and rigorous Examination, as is needful, to a folid *Affent*, and to a
lafting *Conclufion*, on the whole Frame of *Nature*. How
can it be imagin'd, that any fingle Mind can comprehend and fuftain long enough the Weight of fo many
different *Opinions*, and infinite *Obfervations*; when
even the beft *Mathematicians* are foon tir'd with a
long Train of the moft delightful *Propofitions*, which
were before made to their Hands? Or, if there could
be a Man of that Vaftnefs of *Soul*; yet, how can we be
affur'd, that he would hold the *Scale* even? Where have
we ever had an Example of fo much Streightnefs and
Impartiality of Judgment, to perfuade us, that the
calmeft Philofopher will not be infenfibly inclin'd to
prefer his own *Doctrines*, before thofe of a Stranger?
We fee all the World flatter themfelves in their
Strength, Beauty, nay, even (as fome have noted) in
their very *Statures*; the loweft Men fcarce believing,
but that they are tall enough. Why then fhould they be
fingly trufted in their Votes about their own Thoughts;
where the Comparifon of Wit makes them more ea-
gerly concern'd? If we follow the *Philofopher* home
into

into his Study, we fhall quickly difcover, by how many *plaufible Degrees*, the wifeft Men are apt to deceive themfelves into a *fudden Confidence* of the Certainty of their Knowledge. We will fuppofe him to begin his *Inquiry* with all the Sincerity imaginable: refolving to pafs by no fmall Miftake, and to forgive to himfelf no flight Error in the *Account*; with thefe *fair Purpofes*, he pitches on fome *particular Subject*; this he turns and tortures every way, till, after much Labour, he can make fome Gueffes at its *Caufes*: upon this his Induftry increafes; he applies the fame Matter to feveral other Operations; he ftill finds the Effects anfwer his Expectations: Now he begins to mould fome *general Propofition* upon it; he meets with more and more Proofs to confirm his *Judgment*: thus he grows, by little and little, warmer in his *Imaginations*; the Delight of his Succefs fwells him; he triumphs and applauds himfelf for having found out fome *important Truth*: But now his Tryal begins to flacken; now *Impatience* and *Security* creep upon him; now he carelefly admits whole Crowds of Teftimonies, that feem any way to confirm that *Opinion*, which he had before eftablifh'd; now he ftops his Survey, which ought to have gone forward to many more *Particulars*; and fo at laft this *fincere*, this *invincible Obferver*, out of Wearinefs, or Prefumption, becomes the moft negligent in the latter part of his Work, in which he ought to have been the moft exact. Such is the univerfal Inclination of Mankind, to be mifled by themfelves; which I have mention'd, not to beat down the Credit of any particular *Philofophers*, whofe *Superftructures* have not been anfwerable to the Strength of their firft *Affertions*; but I have only complain'd of it in general, as we ufe to do of Man's Mortality, and being

ing

ing fubject to difeafes; the aggravating of which common Infirmities can never be efteem'd by any private Man, as an effect of *Malice* or *ill Nature*.

But now, on the other fide, this *Doubtfulnefs* of Thoughts, this *Fluctuation*, this *Slownefs* of concluding, which is fo ufeful in this Cafe, is fo natural to a Multitude of Counfellors, that it is frequently urg'd againft them, as their *infeparable Imperfection*. Every Man has this Argument in his Mouth, wherewith to condemn a great and mixt Number of Advifers; that their *Deliberations* are fo tedious, that commonly the *Seafons of Action* are loft, before they can come to any Refult. 'Tis true, this Unweildinefs, and want of Difpatch, is moft deftructive in *Matters of State* and *Government*; as Chriftendom lately felt : But it has a quite contrary influence on *Philofophy*. It is not here the moft fpeedy, or the fwifteft Determination of Thoughts, that will do the Bufinefs: here many Delays are requir'd: here he that can make a *folid Objection*, or ask a *feafonable Queftion*, will do more Good, than he who fhall boldly fix on a hundred *illgrounded Refolutions*. Every Rub is here to be fmooth'd; every Scruple to be plan'd; every thing to be forefeen; the Satisfaction of the Reafon of all paft, prefent, and future Times to be defign'd : fo that here, that which is fo much cried down in *Policy*, a ftriving ftill to do better, can never be too much regarded.

Nor is the *Society* only fore-arm'd againft this great *Inconvenience*, this Rafhnefs of fettling upon Caufes, by the Multitude of Judges that are to be fatisfied; but alfo by their indifferent hearing of all *Conjectures*, that may be made from the Tenets of any *Sect of Philofophy*; and by touching every Effect that comes before them, upon all the *Varieties of Opinions*, that

that have been either of late found out, or reviv'd.
By this Equality of Respect to all Parties, it has allow'd a sufficient Time to ripen whatever it debated :
By this too it has made it self the common *Cherish-*
er, and *Umpire* of them all ; and has taken the right
Way of finding out, what is good in any one of them.
A Course, which if the Antients had more follow'd,
their Sects would not so soon have destroy'd each o-
ther.   It was a most perverse Custom amongst their
Disciples, not to make any *strict Choice*, to leave some,
and embrace others of their Masters Doctrines, but
to swallow all at once.   He that became a *Stoick*, an
Epicurean, a *Peripatetick*, in *Logick*, or *Moral Phi-*
losophy, or *Physicks*, never stuck presently to assent
to whatever his Founder had said in all the other
Sciences ; though there was no Kind of Connexion between his Doctrines in the one, and the other.
Thus was the whole Image of *Philosophy* form'd in
their Minds all together : and what they receiv'd so
carelesly, they defended the same way ; not in Parcels, but in Gross.   Of this the Errors are apparent ;
for by so *partially* believing all forts of Tenets, they
had no Time to be fully convinc'd ; and so became rather *formal* Afferters of them, than *judicious*.   And by
thus adhering to all, without making any Distinction
between the Truths and Falshoods, Weaknesses and
Strengths of *their Sects* ; they denied to themselves a
far more *calm* and *safe Knowledge*; which might have
been compounded out of them all, by fetching something from one, and something from another.

This the *Royal Society* did well foresee ; and therefore did not regard the Credit of *Names*, but *Things* :
rejecting or approving nothing, because of the Title
which it bears ; preferving to it self the Liberty of re-
O   fusing

fuſing or liking, as it found ; and ſo advancing its Stock, by a *ſure* and a *double Increaſe*; by adding *new Diſcoveries*, and retaining *antient Truths*. A Large-neſs and Generoſity, which certainly is an excellent *Omen* of its Eſtabliſhment. In this, methinks, it excels any *other Sect*; as the *Roman Commonwealth* did that of *Venice*. The latter began upon a ſmall Stock, and has been careful to preſerve it ſelf unmingled, beſtowing the Freedom of its City very ſparingly : And we ſee, it has been ſtill on the defenſive, making no great Pro-greſs in the World ; whereas the *Romans*, by a far more frank and honourable Counſel, admitted all, that deſir'd to be their Confederates ; gave the Liber-ty of *Roman Citizens* to whole Towns and Coun-tries; excluded none, but thoſe that would *obſtinately* ſtand out ; and ſo deſervedly extended their Empire, as far as the Bounds of the *civil World* did reach.

The ſecond Miſchief in this great matter of Cauſes is an *eternal Inſtability* and *Averſion* from aſſigning of any.   This ariſes from a violent and imprudent Haſte to avoid the firſt. So eaſy is the Paſſage from one Extreme to another ; and ſo *hard* it is to ſtop in that little Point, wherein the Right does conſiſt.   The Truth is, they are both almoſt equally pernicious ; nothing *found* is to be expected from thoſe, who will fix blindly on whatever they can lay hold on ; and no-thing *great* from them, who will always wander ; who will never leave diſputing, whether they dream, or wake, whether there is any Motion, whether they have any Being, or no ; the *one* can produce nothing but *unwholſome* and *rotten* Fruits ; and the *other*, for Fear of that, will endeavour to have no *Harveſt*, nor *Autumn* at all.

To this Fault of *Sceptical Doubting*, the *Royal So-ciety*

ciety may perhaps be fuspected to be a little too much inclin'd; becaufe they always profeffed to be fo backward from *fettling* of *Principles*, or *fixing* upon *Doctrines*. But if we fairly confider their Intentions, we fhall foon acquit them. Though they are not yet very daring, in eftablifhing Conclufions; yet they lay no Injunctions upon their Succeffors not to do the fame, when they fhall have got a fufficient Store for fuch a Work. It is their Study, that the way to attain a *folid Speculation* fhould every Day be more and more perfued; which is to be done by a long forbearing of *Speculation* at firft, till the Matters be ripe for it; and not by madly rufhing upon it in the very beginning. Though they do not contemplate much on the *general* Agreements of Things, yet they do on the *particular*; from whence the others alfo will in time be deduc'd. They are therefore as far from being *Scepticks*, as the greateft *Dogmatifts* themfelves. The *Scepticks* deny all, both *Doctrines* and *Works*. The *Dogmatifts* determine on *Doctrines*, without a fufficient refpect to *Works*: and this Affembly, though we fhould grant, that they have wholly omitted *Doctrines*, yet they have been very pofitive and affirmative in their *Works*. But more than this, it muft alfo be confefs'd, that fomtimes after a full Infpection, they have ventur'd to give the Advantage of Probability to one Opinion, or Caufe, above another: Nor have they run any manner of Hazard by thus concluding, For firft, it is likely, they did hit the *right*, after fo long, fo punctual, and fo gradual an Examination: or if we fuppofe the worft, that they fhould fometimes judge *amifs* (as we cannot but allow them ay, feeing it will not be juft to beftow Infallibility on them alone, while we deny it to all others)

yet

yet they have taken Care, that their *weaker Reasonings*, and even their *Errors*, cannot be very prejudicial to Posterity. The Causes, upon which they have agreed, they did not presently extend beyond their due Strength to all other Things, that seem to bear some Resemblance to what they tried. Whatever they have resolv'd upon, they have not reported, as *unalterable Demonstrations*, but as *present Appearances* : delivering down to future Ages, with the good Success of the Experiment, the *Manner* of their Progress, the *Instruments*, and the several Differences of the *Matter*, which they have applied : so that, with their Mistake, they give them also the Means of finding it out. To this I shall add, that they have never affirm'd any thing concerning the Cause, till the Trial was past : whereas, to do it before, is a most venomous thing in the making of *Sciences*; for whoever has fix'd on his *Cause* before he has experimented, can hardly avoid fitting his *Experiment*, and his Observations, to his own *Cause*, which he had before imagin'd, rather than the *Cause* to the Truth of the *Experiment* it self. But, in a word, they have hitherto made little other Benefit of the *Causes*, to which they have consented, than that thereby they might have a firm footing, whereon *new Operations* may proceed. And for this Work, I mean a Continuation and Variation of the *Inquiry*, the tracing of a *false* Cause doth very often so much conduce, that, in the Progress, the *right* has been discover'd by it. It is not to be question'd, but many Inventions of great Moment have been brought forth by Authors, who began upon Suppositions, which afterwards they found to be untrue. And it frequently happens to *Philosophers*, as it did to *Columbus*; who first believ'd the *Clouds*, that hover'd about the Continent, to be

the

the firm *Land:* But this Miſtake was happy; for, by
failing towards them, he was led to what he ſought;
ſo by proſecuting of *miſtaken Cauſes*, with a Reſolu-
tion of not giving over the Perſuit, they have been
guided to the *Truth* it ſelf.

The laſt Defect is the rendring of Cauſes barren;
that when they have been found out, they have been
ſuffer'd to lye idle; and have been only us'd, to increaſe Thoughts, and not Works. This Negligence is
of all others the moſt dangerous; it is a *Shipwrack* in
the end of the *Voyage*, and thence the more to be piti-
ed: It is a Corruption, that both hinders Additions,
and eats out the Knowledge that has been already obtain'd: It is the Fault of *Philoſophers*, and not of meer
Inquirers; of thoſe that have been *ſucceſsful*, and not
of the *Unfortunate* in their Search; and therefore it is
as the Miſcarriages of thoſe, that are proſperous in human Actions; which are always obſerv'd to be more
deſtructive, and harder to be cur'd, than the Failings
of the afflicted, or thoſe that are ſtill in Perſuit.

To this the *Royal Society* has applied a double Pre- Sect. XIX.
vention; both by endeavouring to ſtrike out *new* *Their way of*
Arts, as they go along; and alſo, by ſtill improving *Improving.*
all to *new Experiments*.

Of the Poſſibility of their performing the firſt, and
the Method, which is to be taken about it, I ſhall
ſhortly ſpeak in another Place: It is enough here, to
ſay; that by this, they have taken Care, to ſatisfy the
Hopes of the *preſent Times*; which elſe might juſtly
languiſh, and grow cold about this Enterpriſe; if they
once ſaw, that nothing would be ripe in their Days;
but that all was to come up *hereafter*, for the Advantage of thoſe that are yet unborn. They conſulted
the

the Good of *future* Times, but have not neglected their *own*; they have practis'd both the Parts of *good Husbandry*, planting Trees, and sowing Corn. This latter, for their own speedy Benefit and Support; and the other for the Profit, and Ornament of after-Ages.

Nor have they suffer'd their Diligence to be swallow'd up, by the Pleasures and Enjoyments of *present* Discoveries; but have still submitted their noblest Inventions, to be made Instruments and Means for the finding out of *others*. This certainly is the most comprehensive and unerring Method; at once to make use of that Assistance they give, and to force them to be farther helpful to greater Ends. There is nothing of all the Works of Nature so inconsiderable, so remote, or so fully known; but, by being made to reflect on other Things, it will at once enlighten them, and shew it self the clearer. Such is the Dependence amongst all the Orders of Creatures; the inanimate, the sensitive, the rational, the natural, the artificial; that the Apprehension of one of them is a good Step towards the understanding of the rest: And this is the highest Pitch of *human Reason*; to follow all the Links of this Chain, till all their Secrets are open to our Minds; and their Works advanc'd, or imitated by our Hands. This is truly to command the World; to rank all the *Varieties*, and *Degrees* of Things, so orderly one upon another, that standing on the Top of them, we may perfectly behold all that are below, and make them all serviceable to the Quiet, and Peace, and Plenty of Man's Life. And to this Happiness, there can be nothing else added; but that we make a second Advantage of this *rising Ground*, thereby to look the nearer into Heaven:

An Ambition, which though it was punifh'd in the *old World* by an *univerfal Confufion*, when it was manag'd with *Impiety* and *Infolence*; yet, when it is carried on by that *Humility* and *Innocence*, which can never be feparated from true Knowledge; when it is defign'd, not to *brave* the Creator of all Things, but to *admire* him the more; it muft needs be the utmoft Perfection of *human Nature*.

Thus they have directed, judg'd, conjectur'd upon, and improved *Experiments*. But laftly, in thefe, and all other Bufineffes, that have come under their Care; there is one thing more, about which the *Society* has been moft folicitous; and that is, the Manner of their *Difcourfe*; which, unlefs they had been very watchful to keep in due Temper, the whole Spirit and Vigour of their *Defign* had been foon eaten out, by the Luxury and Redundance of *Speech*. The ill Effects of this Superfluity of Talking, have already overwhelm'd moft other *Arts* and *Profeffions*; infomuch, that when I confider the Means of *happy Living*, and the Caufes of their Corruption, I can hardly forbear recanting what I faid before; and concluding, that *Eloquence* ought to be banifh'd out of all *civil Societies*, as a thing fatal to Peace and good Manners. To this Opinion I fhould wholly incline, if I did not find, that it is a Weapon, which may be as eafily procur'd by *bad* Men, as *good*; and that, if thefe fhould only caft it away, and thofe retain it; the *naked Innocence* of Virtue would be, upon all Occafions, expos'd to the *armed Malice* of the Wicked. This is the chief Reafon, that fhould now keep up the Ornaments of Speaking in any Requeft, fince they are fo much degenerated from their original Ufefulnefs. They were at firft,

Sect. XX. Their manner of Difcourfe.

no

no doubt, an admirable Inftrument in the Hands of
wife Men; when they were only employ'd to defcribe
Goodnefs, Honefty, Obedience, in larger, fairer, and
more moving Images; to reprefent *Truth,* cloath'd with
Bodies; and to bring *Knowledge* back again to our very
Senfes, from whence it was at firft deriv'd to our Under-
ftandings. But now they are generally chang'd to worfe
Ufes; they make the *Fancy* difguft the beft Things, if
they come found and unadorn'd ; they are in open De-
fiance againft *Reafon*; profeffing not to hold much
Correfpondence with that; but with its Slaves, *the*
Paffions; they give the Mind a Motion too changeable and bewitching, to confift with *right Practice*.
Who can behold, without Indignation, how many
Mifts and Uncertainties, thefe fpecious *Tropes* and *Fi-*
gures have brought on our Knowledge ? How many
Rewards, which are due to more profitable and difficult *Arts*, have been ftill fnatch'd away by the eafie
Vanity of *fine Speaking* ! For now I am warm'd with
this juft Anger, I cannot withold my felf, from betray-
ing the Shallownefs of all thefe feeming Myfteries ;
upon which, we *Writers*, and *Speakers*, look fo big.
And in few Words, I dare fay, that of all the Studies of Men, nothing may be fooner obtain'd, than
this vicious Abundance of *Phrafe,* this Trick of *Meta-*
phors, this Volubility of *Tongue*, which makes fo great
a Noife in the World. But I fpend Words in Vain ;
for the Evil is now fo inveterate, that it is hard to know
whom to *blame,* or where to begin to *reform*. We
all value one another fo much, upon this beautiful Deceit ; and labour fo long after it, in the Years of
our Education; that we cannot but ever after think
kinder of it, than it deferves. And indeed, in moft
other Parts of Learning, I look on it to be a Thing al-
                              *   moft

moft utterly defperate in its Cure ; and I think it may be plac'd amongft thofe *general Mifchiefs* ; fuch as the *Diffention* of Chriftian Princes, the *Want of Practice* in Religion, and the like ; which have been fo long fpoken againft, that Men are become infenfible about them ; every one fhifting off the Fault from himfelf to others; and fo they are only made bare Common Places of Complaint. It will fuffice my prefent Purpofe, to point out, what has been done by the *Royal Society*, towards the correcting of its Exceffes in *natural Philofophy* ; to which it is, of all others, a moft profeft Enemy.

They have therefore been more rigorous in putting in Execution the only Remedy, that can be found for this *Extravagance*; and that has been a conftant Refolution, to reject all the Amplifications, Digreffions, and Swellings of Style; to return back to the primitive Purity and Shortnefs, when Men deliver'd fo many *Things*, almoft in an equal Number of *Words*. They have exacted from all their Members, a clofe, naked, natural way of Speaking ; pofitive Expreffions, clear Senfes ; a native Eafinefs ; bringing all Things as near the mathematical Plainnefs as they can; and preferring the Language of Artizans, Countrymen, and Merchants, before that of Wits, or Scholars.

And here, there is one Thing not to be pafs'd by ; which will render this eftablifh'd Cuftom of the *Society* well nigh everlafting ; and that is the general Conftitution of the Minds of the *Englifh*. I have already often infifted on fome of the Prerogatives of *England* ; whereby it may juftly lay Claim, to be the Head of a *philofophical League*, above all other Countries in *Europe :* I have urg'd its Situation, its prefent Genius, and the Difpofition of its Merchants ; and

P many

many more fuch *Arguments* to encourage us, ftillre-
main to be us'd : But of all others, this which I
am now alleging, is of the moft weighty and important Confideration.   If there can be a true Character given of the *univerfal Temper* of any Nation
under Heaven ; then certainly this muft be afcrib'd
to our Country-men; that they have commonly an
unaffected Sincerity ; that they love to deliver their
Minds with a found Simplicity ; that they have the
middle Qualities, between the referv'd fubtile Southern, and the rough unhewn Northern People ; that
they are not extremely prone to fpeak ; that they are
more concern'd what others will think of the Strength,
than of the Finenefs of what they fay; and that an
univerfal Modefty poffeffes them.   Thefe Qualities
are fo confpicuous, and proper to our Soil ; that we
often hear them objected to us, by fome of our Neighbour Satyrifts, in more difgraceful Expreffions.   For
they are wont to revile the *Englifh*, with a want of
Familiarity ; with a melancholy Dumpifhnefs ; with
Slownefs, Silence, and with the unrefin'd Sullennefs
of their Behaviour.   But thefe are only the Reproa-
ches of Partiality, or Ignorance ; for they ought rather to be commended for an honorable Integrity ;
for a Neglect of Circumftances and Flourifhes; for
regarding Things of *greater* Moment, more than *lefs* ;
for a Scorn to deceive as well as to be deceiv'd ; which
are all the beft Indowments, that can enter into
a *philofophical Mind.* So that even the Pofition of
our Climate,the Air,the Influence of the Heaven, the
Compofition of the *Englifh* Blood; as well as the Em-
braces of the Ocean, feem to join with the Labours of
the *Royal Society*,to render our Country a Land of *experimental Knowledge.* And it is a good Sign, that

2   Nature

Nature will reveal more of its Secrets to the *English*, than to others; because it has already furnish'd them with a Genius so well proportion'd, for the receiving and retaining its Mysteries.

And now, to come to a Close of the second Part of the *Narration :* The *Society* has reduc'd its principal Observations, into one *common Stock*; and laid them up in publick *Registers*, to be nakedly transmitted to the next Generation of Men; and so from them, to their Successors. And as their Purpose was, to heap up a mixt Mass of *Experiments*, without digesting them into any perfect Model; so to this End, they confin'd themselves to no order of Subjects; and whatever they have recorded, they have done it, not as complete Schemes of Opinions, but as bare unfinish'd Histories.

Sect. II.
Their Way
of Registring.

In the Order of their *Inquisitions*, they have been so free; that they have sometimes committed themselves to be guided, according to the Seasons of the Year; sometimes, according to what any Foreigner, or *English* Artificer, being present, has suggested; sometimes, according to any extraordinary Accident in the Nation, or any other Casualty, which has hapned in their Way. By which roving and unsettled Course, there being seldom any Reference of one Matter to the next; they have prevented others, nay even their own Hands, from corrupting or contracting the Work; they have made the raising of *Rules* and *Propositions*, to be a far more difficult *Task*, than it would have been, if their *Registers* had been more *Methodical*. Nor ought this Neglect of Consequence and Order, to be only thought to proceed from their *Carelesness*; but from a mature and well grounded

Preme-

Premeditation. For it is certain, that a too fudden Striving to reduce the _Sciences_, in their Beginnings, into Method, and Shape, and Beauty, has very much retarded their Increafe. And it happens to the Invention of Arts, as to Children in their younger Years; in whofe Bodies, the fame _Applications_, that ferve to make them ftrait, flender, and comely, are often found very mifchievous, to their Eafe, their Strength, and their Growth.

By their fair, and equal, and fubmiffive way of _Regiftring_ nothing but _Hiftories_, and _Relations_; they have left Room for others, that fhall fucceed, to _change_, to _augment_, to _approve_, to _contradict_ them at their Difcretion. By this, they have given _Pofterity_ a far greater Power of judging them, than ever they took over thofe that went before them. By this, they have made a firm _Confederacy_, between their own _prefent Labours_, and the Induftry of _future Ages_; which how beneficial it will prove hereafter, we cannot better guefs, than by recollecting, what Wonders it would in all Likelihood have produc'd e'er this, if it had been begun in the Times of the _Greeks_, or _Romans_, or _Schoolmen_; nay even in the laft Refurrection of Learning. What Depth of _Nature_ could by this Time have been hid from our View? What Faculty of the Soul would have been in the dark? What Part of human Infirmities not provided againft? If our Predeceffors, a thoufand, nay even a hundred Years ago, had begun to add by little and little to the Store, if they would have endeavour'd to be _Benefactors_, and not _Tyrants_ over our Reafons; if they would have communicated to us, more of their _Works_, and lefs of their _Wit_.

This Complaint, which I here take up, will appear
the

the jufter, if we confider, that the firft *learned Times*
of the Antients, and all thofe, that follow'd after them,
down to this Day, would have receiv'd no Prejudice
at all; if their *Philofophers* had chiefly beftow'd their
Pains, in making *Hiftories of Nature*, and not in *forming* of *Sciences.* Perhaps indeed the Names of fome
particular Men, who had the Luck to compile thofe
Syftems and *Epitomes* which they gave us, would
have been lefs glorious than they are: Though that
too may be doubted; and, (if we may conclude any
Thing furely, upon a Matter fo changeable as *Fame* is)
we have reafon enough to believe, that thefe latter
Ages would have honour'd *Plato, Ariftotle, Zeno,*
and *Epicurus,*as much,if not more, than now they do;
if they had only fet Things in a way of propagating
Experiences down to us, and not impos'd their *Imaginations* on us, as the only *Truths.* This may be
well enough fuppos'd, feeing it is common to all Mankind, ftill to efteem dearer the Memories of their
Friends, than of thofe that pretend to be their
Mafters.

But this Matter of *Reputation,* was only the *private*
Concernment of five, or fix. As for the Intereft of
thofe Times in general, I will venture to make good,
that in all Effects of *true Knowledge,* they might have
been as happy, without thofe *Bodies of Arts,* as they
were with them; *Logick,* and the *Mathematicks* only excepted. To inftance in their *Phyficks*; they were
utterly ufelefs,in refpect of the good of Mankind; they
themfelves did almoft confefs fo much, by referving
their *natural Philofophy,* for the Retirements of their
wife Men. What Help did it ever bring to the Vulgar?
What vifible Benefit to any City or Country in the
World? Their *Mechanicks,* and *Artificers* (for whom

the

the true *natural Philofophy* fhould be principally intended, were fo far from being affifted by thofe *abf-
trufe Doctrines*; that perhaps fcarce any one of thofe
Profeffions, and Trades, has well underftood *Ariftotle's Principles of Bodies*, from *his own* Time down
to *ours*. Hence then we may conclude, that thofe
firft Times, wherein thefe *Arts* were made, had been
nothing damag'd; if, inftead of raifing fo many *fpeculative Opinions*, they had only minded the laying of
a *folid Ground-work*, for a vaft Pile of *Experiments*,
to be continually augmenting through all Ages.

　　And I will alfo add; that, if fuch a Courfe had been
at firft fet on Foot, *Philofophy* would by this means
have been kept clofer to *material Things*; and fo, in
Probability, would not have undergone fo many *Eclipfes*, as it has done ever fince. If we reckon from its firft
fetting forth in the *Eaft*; we fhall find, that in fo long
a Tract of Time, there have not been above four or
five hundred Years, at feveral Intervals, wherein it
has been in any Requeft in the World. And if we
look back on all the Alterations and Subverfions of
States, that have hapned in civil Nations, thefe three
thoufand Years; we may ftill behold, that the *Sciences of Men's Brains*, have been always fubject to be
far more injur'd by fuch Viciffitudes, than the *Arts
of their Hands*. What Caufe can be affign'd for this?
Why was Learning the firft Thing, that was conftantly
fwept away, in all Deftructions of Empire, and foreign Inundations? Why could not that have weather'd
out the Storm, as well as moft Sorts of Manufactures;
which, though they began as foon, or before the other,
yet they have remain'd, through all fuch Changes, unalter'd; except for the better? The Reafon of this
is evident. It is, becaufe *Philofophy* had been fpun
out,

out to fo fine a Thread, that it could be known but
only to thofe who would throw away all their whole
Lives upon it. It was made too fubtile for the *common* and *grofs* Conceptions of Men of Bufinefs. It had
before in a Meafure been banifh'd by the Philofophers
themfelves, out of the World, and fhut up in the
Shades of their Walks. And by this means, it was firft
look'd upon as moft *ufelefs*, and fo fit fooneft to be
neglected. Whereas if at firft, it had been made to
converfe more with the Senfes, and to affift familiarly
in all Occafions of *human Life*; it would, no doubt,
have been thought needful to be preferv'd, in the
moft *active* and *ignorant* Time. It would have e-
fcap'd the Fury of the barbarous People, as well as
the Arts of *Ploughing*, *Gardening*, *Cookery*, *Making
Iron and Steel*, *Fifhing*, *Sailing*, and many more
fuch neceffary Handicrafts have done.

And it is too late to lament this Error of the Antients, feeing it is not now to be repair'd. It is enough,
that we gather from hence, that by bringing *Philofophy* down again to Men's Sight and Practice, from
whence it was flown away fo high, the *Royal Society*
has put it into a Condition of ftanding out againft the
Invafions of *Time*, or even *Barbarifm* it felf; that by
eftablifhing it on a firmer Foundation than the *airy
Notions* of Men alone, upon all the *Works of Nature*;
by turning it into one of the *Arts* of *Life*, of which
Men may fee there is daily need; they have provided,
that it cannot hereafter be extinguifh'd, at the Lofs of
a Library, at the Overthrowing of a Language, or at
the Death of fome few *Philofophers*; but that Men
muft lofe their *Eyes* and *Hands*, and muft leave off
defiring to make their *Lives* convenient or pleafant,
before they can be willing to *deftroy* it.

Thus

Sect. XXI.   Thus far I was come in my intended *Work*, when
The Occasion my *Hand* was stop'd, and my *Mind* disturb'd from
of the Hin-
drance of the writing, by the two greatest Disasters that ever befel
publishing our *Nation*, the *fatal Infection*, which overspread
this History. the City of *London* in sixty five, and the *dreadful fir-*
ing of the City it self in the Year insuing.   These two
Calamities may well be sufficient to excuse the *Delay*
of publishing this *Book*; when the one of them devour'd as many *Men*, and the other as many *Books*,
as the cruellest Incursion of the *Goths* and *Vandals*
had ever done.

The *Plague* was indeed an irreparable Damage to
the whole Kingdom; but that which chiefly added
to the Misery, was the *Time* wherein it happen'd.   For
what could be a more deplorable Accident, than that
so many *brave Men* should be cut off by the *Arrow*
that flies in the dark, when our Country was ingag'd
in a *foreign War*, and when their Lives might have
been honourably ventur'd on a glorious Theatre in
its Defence? And we had scarce recover'd this *first*
Misfortune. when we receiv'd a *second* and a deeper
Wound; which cannot be equal'd in all *History*, if
either we consider the Obscurity of its *Beginning*, *the*
irresistible Violence of its Progress, the Horror of its
Appearance, or the Wideness of the Ruin it made,
in one of the most renown'd *Cities* of the World.

Yet when, on the one side, I remember what *De-*
solation these Scourges of Mankind have left behind
them ; and on the other, when I reflect on the *Mag-*
nanimity wherewith the English Nation did support the Mischiefs; I find, that I have not more
Reason to *bewail* the one, than to *admire* the
other.

                                                      Upon

Upon our Return after the abating of the *Plague*, what elſe could we expect, but to ſee the *Streets* unfrequented, the *River* forſaken, the *Fields* deform'd with the *Graves* of the *dead,* and the *Terrors* of *Death* ſtill abiding on the Faces of the living? But inſtead of ſuch diſmal Sights, there appear'd almoſt the ſame Throngs in all publick Places, the ſame Noiſe of *Buſineſs,* the ſame Freedom of Converſe, and, with the Return of the *King,* the ſame Chearfulneſs returning on the Minds of the *People* as before.

Nor was their *Courage* leſs, in ſuſtaining the *ſecond Calamity,* which deſtroy'd their *Houſes* and *Eſtates.* This the greateſt Loſers indur'd with ſuch undaunted Firmneſs of Mind, that their Example may incline us to believe, that not only the beſt *natural,* but the beſt *moral* Philoſophy too, may be learn'd from the Shops of *Mechanicks.* It was indeed an admirable Thing to behold, with what *Conſtancy* the meaneſt Artificers ſaw all the *Labours* of their *Lives,* and the *Support* of their *Families* devour'd in an inſtant. The Affliction, 'tis true, was widely ſpread over the whole Nation ; every Place was fill'd with Signs of *Pity* and *Commiſeration* ; but thoſe who had ſuffer'd moſt, ſeem'd the leaſt affected with the Loſs : No *unmanly Bewailings* were heard in the few *Streets* that were preſerv'd ; they beheld the Aſhes of their *Houſes,* and *Gates,* and *Temples,* without the leaſt Expreſſion of Puſillanimity. If *Philoſophers* had done this, it had well become their Profeſſion of Wiſdom ; if *Gentlemen,* the Nobleneſs of their *Breeding* and *Blood* would have requir'd it : But that ſuch Greatneſs of Heart ſhould be found amongſt the poor *Artizans,* and the obſcure *Multitude,* is no doubt one of the moſt honourable Events that ever happen'd. Yet ſtill there is one *Circumſtance* behind,

hind, which may raise our Wonder higher ; and that is, that amidst such horrible *Ruins*, they still prosecuted the *War* with the same *Vigour* and *Courage*, against three of the most powerful States of all *Europe*. What Records of Time, or Memory of past Ages, can shew us a greater Testimony of an invincible and heroick *Genius* than this, of which I now speak? that the Sound of the *Heralds* proclaiming new *Wars* should be pleasant to the People, when the sad Voice of the *Bell-man* was scarce yet gone out of their Ears? That the Increase of their Adversaries *Confederates*, and of their own *Calamities*, should be so far from affrighting them ; that they rather seem'd to receive from thence a *new Vigour* and *Resolution*? and that they should still be eager upon *Victories* and *Triumphs*, when they were thought almost quite exhausted, by so great Destructions?

Sect. XXII.
The third Part of the Narration. From this *Observation* my Mind begins to take Comfort, and to presage, that as this *terrible Disease* and *Conflagration*, were not able to darken the Honour of our *Prince's Arms*; so they will not hinder the many noble *Arts*, which the *English* have begun under his *Reign*, on the Strength of these Hopes and Incouragements. I will now return to my former thoughts, and to the finishing of my interrupted *Design*. And I come with the more Earnestness to perfect it, because it seems to me, that from the sad Effects of these Disasters, there may a new and a powerful *Argument* be rais'd, to move us to double our Labours about the *Secrets of Nature*.

A *new* City is to be built, on the most advantageous Seat of all *Europe* for Trade and Command. This therefore is the fittest Season for Men to apply their
Thoughts

Thoughts to the improving of the *Materials* of Building, and to the inventing of better *Models* for *Houfes*, *Roofs*, *Chimnies*, *Conduits*, *Wharfs*, and *Streets*: all which have been already under the Confideration of the *Royal Society*; and that too, before they had fuch a fad Occafion of bringing their *Obfervations* into Practice. The Mortality of this *Peftilence* exceeded all others of later Ages; but the Remembrance of it fhould rather enliven than damp our *Induftry*. When Mankind is overrun with fuch horrible Invafions of *Death*, they fhould from thence be univerfally alarm'd, to ufe more Diligence about preventing them for the future.

It is true, that terrible *Evil* has hitherto, in all Countries, been generally too ftrong for the former Remedies of *Art*. But why fhould we think, that it will continue fo for ever? Why may we not believe, that in all the vaft Compafs of natural Virtues of Things yet conceal'd, there is ftill referv'd an *Antidote*, that fhall be equal to this *poyfon*? If in fuch Cafes we only accufe the *Anger* of *Providence*, or the *Cruelty* of *Nature*, we lay the Blame where it is not juftly to be laid. It ought rather to be attributed to the *Negligence* of Men themfelves, that fuch *difficult Cures* are without the Bounds of their *Reafon's Power*.

If all Men had defponded at firft, and funk under the Burden of their own *Infirmities*, almoft every little Wound, or Pain of the leaft *Member*, had been as deadly, as the *Plague* at this time. It was by much Inquiry, and Ufe, that moft of the mildeft Difeafes became *curable*. And every firft Succefs of this kind, fhould always ftrengthen our Affurance of farther Conquefts, even over this greateft *Terror* of Mankind. Diftruft, and Defpair of our own Endeavours, is as

great

great a Hindrance in the Progrefs of the *true Philofo-phy*, as it is wont to be in the Rife of Men's private Fortunes. Whoever aims not at the *greateft* Things, will feldom proceed much farther than the *leaft*. Whoever will make a right and a fortunate Court-fhip to *Nature*, he cannot enterprife or attempt too much: for *She* (as it is faid of other *Miftreffes*) is alfo a Miftrefs, that fooneft yields to the *forward* and the *bold*.

I have hitherto defcrib'd the firft *Elements*, on which the *Royal Society* arofe, and fupported its Be-ginnings: I have trac'd its Progrefs from the firft private Indeavours of fome of its *Members*, till it be-came united into a *regular Conftitution*; and from thence I have related their firft *Conceptions* and *Practi-ces*, towards the Settling of an univerfal, conftant, and impartial Survey of the whole *Creation*. There now remains to be added in this third Part of my *Narra-tion*, an Account of the *Incouragements* they have re-ceiv'd from abroad, and at home; and a particular Enumeration of the *principal Subjects*, about which they have been employ'd, fince they obtain'd the *Royal Confirmation*.

Sect.XXIII.   I will firft begin with the *Efteem*, which all the ci-
The Reputa- vil World abroad has conceiv'd of their *Enterprife*:
tion and Cor- And I mention this with the more Willingnefs, becaufe
refpondence I believe that our *Nation* ought juftly to be reprov'd,
of the R. S. for their Excefs of natural *Bafhfulnefs*, and for their
abroad. Want of Care, to have their moft excellent Things re-prefented to Strangers with the beft Advantage. This filent and referv'd Humour has no doubt been very prejudicial to us, in the Judgment that our Neigh-bours have often made, not only concerning the Con-

*
dition

dition of our *Learning*, but alfo of our *political Af-*
fairs. I will therefore trefpafs a little on this *Difpo-*
fition of my *Countrymen,* and affirm, that as the *Eng-*
lifh Name does manifeftly get Ground, by the Bravery
of their *Arms,* the Glory of their *Naval Strength,*
and the Spreading of their *Commerce*; fo there has been
a remarkable Addition to its Renown, by the Succefs, which all our *Neighbours* expect from this *Af-*
fembly.

It is evident, that this *fearching Spirit,* and this Affection to *fenfible Knowledge,* does prevail in moft
Countries round about us.   'Tis true, the Conveniences for fuch Labours are not equal in all Places. Some
want the Affiftance of others *Hands*; fome the Contribution of others *Purfes;* fome the Benefit of excellent *Inftruments,* fome the *Patronage* of the
Civil *Magiftrates :* But yet according to their feveral *Powers,* they are every where intent on fuch
practical Studies. And the moft confiderable Effects
of fuch Attempts throughout *Europe* have been ftill
recommended to this *Society,* by their *Authors,* to be
examin'd, approv'd, or corrected.

The Country, that lyes next to *England* in its Si-   *In* France.
tuation is *France*; and that is alfo the neareft to it, in
its Zeal for the Promotion of *Experiments.* In that
Kingdom, the *Royal Society* has maintain'd a perpetual Intercourfe, with the moft eminent Men of *Art*
of all Conditions ; and has obtain'd from them, all
the Help which might juftly be hop'd for, from the *Vi-*
gour, and *Activity,* and *Readinefs* of Mind, which is
natural to that People. From their *Phyficians, Chirur-*
geons, and *Anatomifts,* it has receiv'd many faithful *Re-*
lations of extraordinary *Cures*; from their moft judicious
Travellers the Fruits of their *Voyages*; from their moft
famous

famous *Mathematicians*, diverfe *Problems*, which have
been folv'd many different Ways; from their *Chymifts* the effects of their *Fires*; and from others of
their beft *Obfervers*, many Rarities, and Difcourfes
of their *Fruits, Silk, Wine, Bread, Plants, Salt*, and
fuch natural Productions of their Soil. And to inftance once for all, it has been affectionately invited
to a mutual *Correfpondence* by the *French Academy*
of *Paris*: In which Invitation, there is one Expreffion, that ought not to be pafs'd over in Silence; that
they acknowledge the *Englifh Nation*, to have many
Advantages for the propagating of *real Philofophy*,
which are wanting to all others. This Confeffion is
true: Yet thefe Advantages, unlefs they had been improv'd by this *Inftitution*, had been only as thofe,
that we have for Fifhing, Objections and Arguments
of our Sloth.

In Italy.   In *Italy* the *Royal Society* has an excellent Privilege of receiving and imparting *Experiments*, by
the Help of one of their own *Fellows*, who has the
Opportunity of being *Refident* there for them, as well
as for the *King*. From thence they have been earneft-
ly invited to a mutual Intelligence, by many of their
moft *noble Wits*, but chiefly by the *Prince Leopoldo*,
Brother to the great Duke of *Tufcany*; who is the
Patron of all the *inquifitive Philofophers* of *Florence*;
from whom there is coming out under his Name an
Account of their Proceedings call'd *Ducal Experiments*. This Application to the *Royal Society* I have
mention'd, becaufe it comes from that Country, which
is feldom wont to have any great Regard to the *Arts* of
thefe *Nations*, that lye on this fide of their Mountains.

In Germany.   In *Germany*, and its neighbouring Kingdoms, the
                                                    Royal

Royal Society has met with great Veneration; as appears by several Testimonies in their late *printed Books*, which have been submitted to its Censure; by many *Curiosities* of *Mechanick Instruments*, that have been transmitted to it; and by the *Addresses* which have been sent from their *Philosophical Inquirers*. For which Kinds of Enterprizes the Temper of the *German* Nation is admirably fit, both in respect of their peculiar Dexterity in all Sorts of manual *Arts*, and also in Regard of the plain and unaffected Sincerity of their *Manners*; wherein they so much resemble the *English*, that we seem to have deriv'd from them the Composition of our *Minds*, as well as to have descended from their *Race*.

In the *Low-Countries*, their Interest, and Reputation has been establish'd, by the Friendship of some of their chief learned Men, and principally of *Hugenius*. This Gentleman has bestow'd his Pains, on many Parts of the *Speculative*, and *practical Mathematicks*, with wonderful Successes. And particularly his applying the Motion of *Pendulums* to Clocks, and Watches, was an excellent *Invention*. For thereby there may be a Means found out of bringing the *Measures* of *Time*, to an exact *Regulation*; of which the Benefits are infinite. In the Prosecution of such *Discoveries*, he has often requir'd the Aid of this *Society*; he has receiv'd the Light of their *Trials*, and a Confirmation of his own, and has freely admitted their *Alterations* or *Amendments*. And this learned Correspondence with him, and many others, is still continued, even at this present Time, in the Breach between our *Countries*: Their great Founder, and Patron still permitting them to maintain the Traffick of *Sciences*, when all
other

In the low Countries.

other *Commerce* is intercepted. Whence we may guefs, what may be expected from the peaceful Part of our *King's Reign;* when his very Wars are manag'd without Injury to the *Arts* of *Civil Knowledge.*

Vifits of Foreigners. But not to wander any farther in *Particulars*, it may perhaps in *general* be fafely computed, that there has been as large a Communication of Foreign *Arts*, and *Inventions* to the *Royal Society*, within this fmall Compafs of Time, as ever before did pafs over the *Englifh* Chanel, fince the very firft Tranfportation of *Arts* into our *Ifland.* And that this Benefit will ftill increafe by the Length of Time is indubitable, from the *Reception*, which has been given to the *Scholars*, *Nobility*, *Embaffadors*, and Foreign *Princes*, who of late Years have travell'd hither, to behold a *Country*, which had been the Stage of fo famous a War, and fo miraculous a Peace. All thefe have ftill vifited the *Royal Society*, as one of the firft and *nobleft Fruits* of our *Reftoration.* From hence they have return'd Home, with a free Engagement of their Affiftance; the *Men of Learning* affuring it of a Contribution of their *Labours*, and the *Statefmen* and *Princes* of their *Authority* and Indeavours, in fatisfying all *philofophical Qaeries*, with which they have been plentifully furnifh'd.

It would be a ufelefs Pomp to reckon up a *Catalogue* of their *Names*; efpecially feeing they are already recorded with Gratitude, in a more lafting *Monument*, the *Regifter* of the *Society.* Only it will not, I think, be amifs, if I mention the Vifit of one *Prince*, becaufe it may afford us a profitable Obfervation. When the Duke of *Brunfwick* and *Lunenburgh* was introduc'd into their weekly *Affembly*, and had fubfcrib'd his Name to their *Statutes*; there was accor-

ding

ding to the Cuftom, one of the *Fellows* appointed, to
interpret to him, what Experiments were produc'd,
and examin'd at that Meeting. But his *Highnefs* told
them, that it was not neceffary they fhould put themfelves to that Trouble; for he well underftood our
Language, having been drawn to the Study of it, out
of a Defire of reading our *Philofophical Books.*
From whence there may this Conclufion be made,
that if ever our *Native Tongue* fhall get any Ground
in *Europe,* it muft be by augmenting its *experimental
Treafure.* Nor is it impoffible, but as the *Feminine*
Arts of *Pleafure* and *Gallantry* have fpread fome of
our neighbouring Languages to fuch a vaft Extent; fo
the *Englifh Tongue* may alfo in time be more enlarg'd,
by being the Inftrument of conveying to the World
the *Mafculine* Arts of *Knowledge.*

I now come to relate, what *Incouragements* this
Defign has receiv'd at home in its native *Soil.* And I
will affure my *Reader,* that the *Original* of the *Royal
Society* has found a general *Approbation* within ourfelves, and that the moft prudent Men of all Profeffions and Interefts, have fhewn by their Refpects to
thefe hopeful Beginnings, that there is a *Reverence*
due to the firft Trials and Intentions, as well as to the
laft Accomplifhment of generous Attempts.

Sect.XXIV.
*The Incour-
agements the
R. S. has re-
ceiv'd at
home.*

Of our chief and moft wealthy *Merchants* and *Citizens,* very many have affifted it with their Prefence;
and thereby have added the induftrious, punctual, and
active *Genius* of Men of *Traffick,* to the quiet,
fedentary, and referv'd Temper of Men of *Learning.*
They have contributed their *Labours*; they have
help'd their *Correfpondence*; they have employ'd

*From our Ci-
tizens.*

R   their

their *Factors* Abroad to anfwer their *Inquiries*; they have laid out in all Countries for *Obfervations*; they have beftow'd many confiderable Gifts on their *Treafury* and Repofitory. And chiefly there is one *Bounty* to be here inferted, which for the fingular Benefit that may be expected from it, deferves the *Applaufe* and *Imitation* of this and future Times. It is the *Eftablifhment* made by Sir *John Cutler*, for the reading on *Mechanicks*, in the Place where the *Royal Society* fhall meet. This is the firft *Lecture* that has been founded of this Kind, amidft all the vaft *Munificence* of fo many *Benefactors to Learning* in this latter Age. And yet this was the moft neceffary of all others. For this has chiefly caus'd the flow Progrefs of *manual Arts*; that the *Trades* themfelves have never ferv'd *Apprentifhips*, as well as the *Tradefmen*; that they have never had any *Mafters* fet over them, to direct and guide their Works, or to vary and enlarge their Operations.

From our Phyficians. Of our *Phyficians*, many of the moft judicious have contributed their *Purfes*, their *Hands*, their *Judgments*, their *Writings*. This they have done, though they have alfo in *London* a College peculiar to their *Profeffion*; which ever fince its firft Foundation, for the Space of a hundred and fifty Years, has given the World a Succeffion of the moft eminent *Phyficians* of *Europe*. In *that* they confine themfelves to the Advancement of *Phyfick*: But in *this*, they have alfo with great Zeal and Ability promoted this *univerfal Infpection*, into all *natural Knowledge*. For without Danger of *Flattery*, I will declare of the *Englifh Phyficians*, that no Part of the World exceeds them, not only in the Skill of their own *Art*, but in *general Learning*; and of very many of that Profeffion I will affirm, that *all Apollo*

Apollo is their own, as it was faid by the beft *Poet* of this Age, of one of the moft excellent of their Number.

Of our *Nobility* and *Gentry,* the moft noble and *illu-* From our *ftrious* have condefcended to labour here with their Nobility. Hands, to impart their *Difcoveries,* to propofe their *Doubts,* to affift and defray the *Charge* of their *Trials.* And this they have done with fuch a univerfal Agreement, that it is almoft the only thing, wherein the *Nobility* of all the three Kingdoms are *united.* In their *Affemblies* for making Laws they are feparated; in their Cuftoms and Manners of Life they differ; and in their Humours too, they are thought not much of kin to each other. But in the *Royal Society* the *Scotch,* the *Irifh,* the *Englifh* Gentry do meet, and communicate, without any Diftinction of *Countries* or Affections. From hence no doubt very much *political,* as well as *philofophical* Benefit will arife. By this means, there is a good Foundation laid for the removing of that Averfion, which the *Englifh* are fometimes obferv'd to exprefs to the *Natives* of thofe Kingdoms; which though perhaps it arifes from the Knowledge of their own *Advantages* above the other, yet it is a great Hindrance to the Growth of the *Britifh Power.* For as a Kingdom divided againft it felf, cannot ftand; fo three Kingdoms divided from each other, in *Tempers, Studies,* and *Inclinations,* can never be great, upon one common Intereft.

Of our *Minifters of State at home,* and our *Embaffa-* From our *dors abroad,* there have been very few employ'd, who Statefmen. are not *Fellows* of the *Royal Society:* and efpecially thefe latter have beftow'd their Pains in *foreign Courts,* to collect *Relations* and Secrets of Nature, as well as of State : For which Service their Way of Life is most convenient, by the Generality of their Converse, the *Privileges* and *Freedom* of their *Dispatches*, and the usual Resort of the most knowing and inquisitive Men to their Company.

From our Soldiers. Our greatest *Captains* and *Commanders* have inroll'd their *Names* in this Number, and have regarded these *Studies :* which are not, as other Parts of *Learning*, to be call'd the *Studies of the Gown ;* for they do as well become the Profession of a *Soldier*, or any other Way of Life. Nor have our most renown'd *Generals* neglected the Opportunities of *philosophical* Inquiries, even in the midst of their greatest *Enterprises*, on which the Fate of *Kingdoms* has depended. They have been furnish'd with Instruments and Directions by the *Royal Society*, and amidst the Tumult of *Wars*, and *Government* of *Fleets*, they have found Leisure to make some *Trials* of *Experiments :* which Works as much excell that of *Declaiming*, which some of the *Roman Generals* us'd in their *Camps*, as it is better to *do*, than to *talk* well.

From our Churchmen. Of our *Churchmen* the greatest and the most *Reverend*, by their Care and Passion, and Endeavours in advancing this *Institution*, have taken off the unjust Scandal from *Natural* Knowledge, that it is an Enemy to *Divinity*. By the perpetual *Patronage* and *Assistance* they have afforded the *Royal Society*, they have confuted the false Opinions of those Men, who believe that *Philosophers* must needs be *irreligious :* they have shewn, that in our *Veneration* of God's *almighty Power*, we ought to imitate the manner of our Respect to *earthly Kings*. For as the greater their *Dominion* is,

I   the

the more Obfervance is wont to be given to their
neareft Servants and Officers: fo the Greatnefs of the
Divine Majefty is beft to be worfhip'd, by the due
honouring and obferving of *Nature,* which is his immediate Servant, and the univerfal *Minifter* of his
Pleafure.

But I make hafte to that, which ought to be efteem'd *Sect.* XXV.
the very *Life* and Soul of this *Undertaking,* the Pro- *From the*
tection and Favour of the *King* and the *Royal Family.* *Royal Fami-*
When the *Society* firft addrefs'd themfelves to his *Ma- ly.*
jefty,* he was pleas'd to exprefs much Satisfaction, that
this Enterprife was begun in *his Reign:* he then re-
prefented to them the Gravity and Difficulty of their
Work, and affur'd them of all the kind Influence of his
Power and *Prerogative.* Since that he has frequently
committed many Things to their *Search:* he has refer'd many foreign *Rarities* to their *Infpection:* he has
recommended many domeftick *Improvements* to their
Care: he has demanded the Refult of their *Trials,* in
many Appearances of *Nature:* he has been prefent,
and affifted with his own Hands, at the performing of
many of their *Experiments,* in his *Gardens,* his *Parks,*
and on the *River.* And befides I will not conceal, that
he has fometimes reprov'd them for the *Slownefs* of
their *Proceedings:* at which Reproofs they have not
fo much Caufe to be afflicted, that they are the Reprehenfions of a *King,* as to be comforted, that they are
the Reprehenfions of his *Love,* and *Affection* to their
Progrefs. For a Teftimony of which *Royal Benignity,*
and to free them from all *Hindrances* and *Occafions* of
Delay, he has given them the Eftablifhment of his
Letters Patents, of which I will here produce an
Epitome.

Charles

CHarles *the Second, by the Grace of God, of* England, Scotland, France, *and* Ireland *King, Defender of the Faith,* &c. *To all unto whom thefe Prefents fhall come, Greeting. Having long refolv'd within our felf to promote the Welfare of Arts and Sciences, as well as that of our Territories and Dominions, out of our princely Affection to all kind of Learning, and more particular Favour to philofophical Studies: Efpecially thofe which indeavour by folid Experiments, either to reform or improve Philofophy. To the intent therefore that thefe Kinds of Study, which are no where yet fufficiently cultivated, may flourifh in our Dominions; and that the learned World may acknowledge us to be, not only the Defender of the Faith, but the Patron and Encourager of all Sorts of ufeful Knowledge.*

Know ye, that we out of our fpecial Grace, certain Knowledge, and meer Motion, have given and granted, and do by thefe Prefents give and grant for us, our Heirs, and Succeffors, That there fhall be for ever a Society, confifting of a Prefident, Council, and Fellows, which fhall be called by the name of the Prefident, Council, and Fellows of the Royal Society of London, *for and improving of natural Knowledge, of which Society we do by thefe Prefents declare our felf to be Founder and Patron. And we do hereby make and conftitute the faid Society by the Name,* &c. *to be a Body corporate, to be continued under the fame Name in a perpetual Succeffion; and that they and their Succeffors, (whofe Studies are to be imployed for the promoting of the Knowledge of natural Things, and ufeful Arts by Experiments. To the Glory of God, and the good of Mankind,) fhall by the aforefaid Name of Prefident, Council,* &c. *be inabled and made capable in Law, to levy, hold, poffefs, and injoy, Lands, Tenements,* &c.

Liberties, Franchiſes, Juriſdictions, for Perpetuity, or Terms of Lives, or Years, or any other Way: as alſo Goods, Chattels, and all other Things of what Nature or Kind ſoever. And alſo by the Name aforeſaid to give, grant, demiſe, or aſſign the ſaid Lands, Goods, &c. and to do all Things neceſſary thereabout. And the ſaid Per-ſons by the Name aforeſaid are inabled to implead, be impleaded, ſue, defend, &c. in any Courts, and before any Judges, Officers, &c. whatſoever of the King, his Heirs, and Succeſſors, in all and ſingular Actions real and perſonal: Pleas, Cauſes, &c. of what kind ſoever, as any of his Subjects within his Kingdom of England, *or Corporations, are by Law capable and inabled to do.*

And the ſaid Preſident, Council, and Fellows are impower'd to have a Common Seal for their Uſe in their Affairs; and from time to time to break, change, and make anew the ſame, as ſhall ſeem expedient unto them.

And his Majeſty, in Teſtimony of his Royal Favour towards the ſaid Preſident, Council, and Fellows, and of his eſpecial Eſteem of them, doth grant a Coat of Arms to them and their Succeſſors, viz. On a Field Ar-gent a Canton of the three Lyons of England: *For a Creſt, an Eagle proper on a Ducal Coronet ſupporting a Shield charged with the Lyons aforeſaid; and for Supporters, two Talbots with Coronets on their Necks. The ſaid Arms to be born, &c. by the ſaid Society upon all Occaſions.*

And that his Majeſty's Royal Intention may take the better Effect for the good Government of the ſaid Society from time to time; It is eſtabliſh'd, that the Council aforeſaid ſhall conſiſt of 21. *Perſons; (whereof the Preſident for the time being always to be one.) And that all Perſons, which within two Months next en-ſuing the Date of the ſaid Charter ſhall be choſen by the*

ſaid

said President *and* Council; *and in all times after the said two Months, by the* President, Council, *and* Fellows [*and noted in a* Register *to be kept for that purpose*] *shall be Fellows of the said Society, and so accounted, and call'd during Life, except by the Statutes of the said Society to be made, any of them shall happen to be amoved. And by how much any* Persons *are more excelling in all kinds of Learning, by how much the more ardently they desire to promote the Honour,* Business, *and Emolument of the said Society, by how much the more eminent they are for Integrity,* Honesty, Piety, Loyalty, *and Good Affection toward his Majesty, his Crown and Dignity; by so much the more fit and worthy such* Persons *are to be judged, for Reception into the Society.*

And for the better Execution of his Royal Grant, his Majesty hath nominated, &c. his trusty and well-beloved William, Viscount Brouncker, *Chancellor to his dearest Consort Queen* Catherine, *to be the first and modern President to continue in the said Office from the Date of the Patent to the Feast of St.* Andrew *next ensuing, and until another Person of the said Council be duly chosen into the said Office. The said Lord* Brouncker *being sworn in all things belonging thereto well and faithfully to execute the said Office, before his right well-beloved and right trusty Cousin and Counsellor,* Edward, *Earl of* Clarendon, *Lord High Chancellor of* England, *in the Words following.*

I *William,* Viscount *Brouncker,* do promise to deal faithfully and honestly in all things belonging to that Trust committed to me, as President of the *Royal Society* of *London,* for improving Natural Knowledge. So help me God. *And*

And his Majesty hath nominated, &c. *the Persons following, His trusty and well-beloved Sir* Robert Moray *Knight, one of his Privy Council in his Kingdom of* Scotland, Robert Boyle *Esquire,* William Brereton *Esquire, eldest Son to the Lord* Brereton, *Sir* Kenelme Digby *Knight, Chancellor to his dearest Mother Queen* Mary, *Sir* Gilbert Talbot *Knight, Master of his Jewel-house, Sir* Paul Neile *Knight, one of the Ushers of his Privy Chamber,* Henry Slingsby *Esquire, one of the Gentlemen of His said Privy Chamber, Sir* William Petty *Knight,* Timothy Clark *Doctor of Physick, and one of his Physicians,* John Wilkins *Doctor of Divinity,* George Ent *Doctor of Physick,* William Erskyne *Esquire, one of his Cupbearers,* Jonathan Goddard *Doctor of Physick,* William Ball *Esquire,* Matthew Wren *Esquire,* John Evelyn *Esq.* Thomas Henshaw *Esquire,* Dudley Palmer *of* Grays Inn *Esquire,* Abraham Hill *of* London *Esquire, and* Henry Oldenburg *Esquire, together with the President aforesaid, to be the first and Modern* 21. *of the Council and Fellows of the Royal Society aforesaid, to be continued in the Offices of the Council aforesaid, from the Date of the Patent to the Feast of St.* Andrew *next following, and from thence till other fit Persons be chosen into the said Offices. The said Persons to be sworn before the President of the Society, for the time being, well and truly to execute the said Offices, according to the Form and Effect of the aforesaid Oath to be administred to the President by the Lord Chancellor as aforesaid. For the administring which Oath to the said Persons, and all others hereafter from time to time to be chosen into the said Council, full Power and Authority is granted to the President for the time being : And the said Persons duly sworn, and all other*

*   S   *from*

from time to time duly chosen into the said Council and sworn, are to aid, advise and assist in all Affairs, Businesses, and Things concerning the better Regulation, Government, and Direction of the Royal Society; and every Member thereof.

Furthermore, Liberty is granted to the said Society, lawfully to make and hold Meetings of themselves, for the searching out and Discovery of natural Things, and Transaction of other Businesses relating to the said Society, when and as often as shall be requisite, in any College, Hall, or other convenient Place in London, *or within* 10 *Miles thereof.*

And Power is granted to the said Society, from time to time to nominate and choose yearly, on St. Andrew's Day, one of the Council aforesaid, for the time being, to be President of the Society, until St. Andrew's Day next ensuing (if he shall so long live, or not be removed for some just and reasonable Cause) and from thence until another be chosen and put into the said Office, the said President so elected, before Admission to that Office, to be sworn before the Council, according to the Form before expressed, who are impower'd to administer the said Oath from time to time, as often as there shall be Cause to chuse a President.

And in Case that the said President, during his Office, shall die, recede, or be removed; then, and so often, it shall be lawful for the Council of the Royal Society, to meet together to chuse one of their Number for President of the said Society, and the Person so chosen and duly sworn, shall have and exercise the Office of President for the remainder of the Year, and until another be duly chosen into the said Office.

And in Case that any one or more of the Council aforesaid shall die, recede, or be remov'd (which Persons or

any

any of them, for *Mifdemeanour, or other reafonable Caufe*, are declar'd to be amoveable by the *Prefident* and the reft of the *Council*) then and fo often it fhall be lawful for the *Prefident*, *Council*, and *Fellows*, to chufe one or more of the *Fellows* of the *Royal Society* in the Room of him or them fo deceafing, receding, or remov'd, to compleat the aforefaid Number of 21 of the *Council*, which *Perfon* or *Perfons* fo chofen, are to continue in Office until St. Andrew's *Day* then next enfuing, and until others be duly chofen the faid *Perfons* being fworn faithfully to execute their *Offices*, according to the true Intention of the *Patent*.

And his *Majefty* doth will and grant unto the faid *Prefident*, *Council*, and *Fellows*, full *Power* and Authority, on St. Andrew's *Day* yearly, to elect, nominate, and change 10 of the *Fellows* of the *Royal Society*, to fupply the *Places* and *Offices* of ten of the aforefaid Number of 21. of the *Council*, declaring it to be his Royal *Will* and *Pleafure*, that ten and no more of the *Council* aforefaid be annually changed and removed by the *Prefident*, *Council* and *Fellows* aforefaid.

And it is granted on the behalf of the faid *Society*, that if it fhall happen, that the *Prefident* be fick, infirm, detain'd in his *Majefty's Service*, or otherwife occupied, fo as he cannot attend the neceffary *Affairs* of the *Society*, then and fo often it fhall be lawful for him to appoint one of the *Council* for his *Deputy*, who fhall fupply his place from time to time, as often as he fhall happen to be abfent, during the whole time of the faid *Prefident's Continuance* in his *Office*, unlefs he fhall in the mean time conftitute fome other of the *Council* for his *Deputy* : And the *Deputy* fo conftituted is impower'd to do all and fingular *Things* which belong to the *Office* of the *Prefident* of the *Royal Society*, and in as amole *Manner* and *Form* as the faid *Prefident may do by virtue of his Majesty's Letters Patents, he the said Deputy being duly sworn before the Council in Form before specified, who are impower'd to administer the Oath as often as the Case shall require.*

It is farther granted to the Society, to have one Treasurer, two Secretaries, two or more Curators of Experiments, one or more Clerk or Clerks, and also two Serjeants at Mace, who may from time to time attend on the President ; all the said Officers to be chosen by the President, Council and Fellows, and to be sworn in Form and Effect before specified, well and faithfully to execute their Offices, which Oath the Council are impower'd to administer : And his Majesty nominates and appoints his well beloved Subjects, the aforesaid William Ball *Esquire, to be the first and modern Treasurer ; and the aforesaid* John Wilkins *and* Henry Oldenburgh, *to be the first and modern Secretaries of the Royal Society, to be continued in the said Offices to the Feast of St.* Andrew *next following the Date of the Patent. And that from time to time and ever hereafter, on the said Feast of St.* Andrew *(if it be not Lord's Day, and if it be Lord's Day, on the next Day after) the President, Council, and Fellows aforesaid, are impower'd to nominate and chuse honest and discreet Men for Treasurer and Secretaries, which are to be of the Number of the Council of the Royal Society, which Persons elected and sworn, in Form before specified, are to exercise and enjoy the said Offices until the Feast of St.* Andrew *next then following.*

And if it shall happen, that the aforesaid Election of the President, Council, Treasurer, and Secretaries, or any of them, cannot be made or perfected on the Feast of St. Andrew *aforesaid ; it is granted to the aforesaid President, Council, and Fellows, that they may lawfully*

no-

nominate and affign another Day, as near to the faid Feaft of St. Andrew *as conveniently may be, for making or perfecting the faid Elections, and fo from Day to Day till the faid Elections be perfected.*

And in Cafe that any of the aforefaid Officers of the Royal Society fhall die, recede, or be remov'd from their refpective Offices, then and fo often it fhall be lawful for the faid Prefident, Council, and Fellows, to choofe one or more into the Office or Offices vacant, to hold the fame during the Refidue of that Year, and until others be duly chofen and fworn in their Places.

Moreover, on the behalf of the Society, it is granted unto the Prefident and Council, that they may affemble and meet together in any College, Hall, or other convenient place in London, *or within ten Miles thereof (due and lawful Summons of all the Members of the Council to extraordinary Meetings being always premifed) and that they being fo met together, have full Power and Authority from time to time, to make, conftitute, and eftablifh fuch Laws, Statutes, Orders, and Conftitutions, which fhall appear to them to be good, ufeful, honeft, and neceffary, according to their Judgments and Difcretions, for the Government, Regulation and Direction of the Royal Society, and every Member thereof: And to do all Things concerning the Government, Éftate, Goods, Lands, Revenues, as alfo the Bufineffes and Affairs of the faid Society: All which Laws, Statutes, Orders, &c. fo made, His Majefty wills and commands, that they be from time to time inviolably obferved, according to the Tenor and Effect of them: Provided that they be reafonable, and not repugnant or contrary to the Laws, Cuftoms, &c. of his Kingdom of* England.

And furthermore, full Power and Authority is given

and

and granted unto the said Society, from time to time to choose one or more Printers and Gravers, and by writing sealed with the common Seal of the Society, and signed by the President for the time being, to grant them Power to print such Things, Matters and Businesses concerning the said Society, as shall be committed to them by the Council from time to time : The said Printers and Gravers, being sworn before the President and Council in Form before specified, which President and Council are impowered to give the said Oath.

And for the greater Advantage and Success of the Society in their Philosophical Studies and Indeavours, full Power and Authority is granted unto them, to require, take, and receive, from time to time, dead Bodies of Persons executed, and the same to anatomise, to all Intents and Purposes, and in as ample Manner and Form as the College of Physicians, and Company of Chirurgeons of London *(by what Names soever the said two Corporations are or may be called) have had and made use of, or may have and use the said Bodies.*

And for the Improvement of such Experiments, Arts, and Sciences, as the Society may be imploy'd in, full Power and Authority is granted unto them from time to time by Letters under the Hand of the President, in the Presence of the Council, to hold Correspondence and Intelligence with any Strangers, whether private Persons, or Collegiate Societies, or Corporations, without any Interruption or Molestation whatsoever : Provided that this Indulgence or Grant be extended to no farther Use than the particular Benefit and Interest of the Society, in Matters Philosophical, Mathematical, and Mechanical.

Full Power and Authority is also granted on the behalf of the Society to the Council, to erect and build one or more Colleges within London, *or ten Miles thereof,*

thereof, of what Form or Quality foever, for Habitati-
on, Affembling, or Meeting of the Prefident, Council
and Fellows, about any Affairs and Bufineffes of the
Society.

And if any Abufes or Differences fhall ever hereaf-
ter arife and happen about the Government or Affairs
of the Society, whence the Conftitution, Progreſs,and
Improvement,or Bufineffes thereof may fuffer or be hin-
dred: In fuch Cafes his Majefty affigns and authori-
fes his right trufty and right well beloved Coufin
and Counfellor, Edward *Earl of* Clarendon *Lord high*
Chancellor of England, *by himfelf during his Life,*
and after his Deceafe the Lord Arch-biſhop of Canterbury, *the Lord Chancellor, or Lord Keeper of the great*
Seal of England, *the Lord high Treaſurer of* England,
the Lord Keeper of the Privy Seal,the Lord Biſhop of
London, *and the two principal Secretaries of State for*
the Time being, or any four or more of them, to compofe
and redreſs any fuch Differences or Abufes.

And laftly, His Majefty ftrictly charges and com-
mands all Juftices, Mayors, Aldermen, Sheriffs, Bai-
liffs, Conftables, and all other Officers, Minifters, and
Subjects whatfoever, from time to time to be aiding
and affifting unto the faid Prefident, Council, and Fel-
lows of the Royal Society, in and about all Things,
according to the true Intention of his Letters Patents.

This is the *Legal Ratification* which {the *Royal*
Society has receiv'd. And in this place I am to render
their publick Thanks to the right honourable the
Earl of Clarendon Lord Chancellor of *England,* to
Sir *Jeffery Palmer* Attorney General, and to Sir *He-*
neage Finch Sollicitor General; who by their chaerful
Concurrence, and free Promotion of this Confirma-
tion, have wip'd away the Afperfion, that has been

I   fcanscandalously caft on the *Profeſſion* of the *Law*, that it is an Enemy to *Learning* and the *civil Arts.* To ſhew the Falſhood of this Reproach, I might inſtance in many *Judges* and *Counſellors* of all Ages, who have been the Ornaments of the *Sciences*, as well as of the *Bar*, and *Courts* of *Juſtice*. But it is enough to declare, that my Lord *Bacon* was a *Lawyer*, and that theſe eminent *Officers* of the *Law*, have completed this Foundation of the *Royal Society* ; which was a Work well becoming the Largeneſs of his Wit to deviſe, and the Greatneſs of their Prudence to eſtabliſh.

Sect.XXIV. *Their Councils and Statutes.* According to the Intention of theſe *Letters Patents*, their *Council* has ever ſince been annually renew'd ; their *Preſident*, their *Treaſurer*, their *Secretaries* choſen : The chief Employments of the *Council* have been to manage their *political Affairs*, to regulate Diſorders, to make Addreſſes, and Applications in their Behalf ; to regard their *Privileges*, to diſperſe *Correſpondents*, but principally to form the Body of their *Statutes*, which I will here inſert.

An Abſtract of the Statutes of the Royal Society.

*VV*Hatever Statute ſhall be made, or repeal'd, the making or repealing of it ſhall be voted twice, and at two ſeveral Meetings of the Council.

This Obligation ſhall be ſubſcrib'd by every Fellow ; or his Election ſhall be void.

WE who have hereto ſubſcrib'd, do promiſe each for himſelf, that we will endeavour to promote the good of the Royal Society of *London*, for the Improvement of natural Knowledge, and to purſue the Ends, for which the ſame was founded ; that we

were

will be prefent at the Meetings of the Society, as often as conveniently we can; efpecially at the anniverfary Elections, and upon extraordinary Occafions; and that we will obferve the Statutes and Orders of the faid Society: Provided, that whenever any of us fhall fignify to the Prefident under his Hand, that he defires to withdraw from the Society, he fhall be free from this Obligation for the future.

Every Fellow fhall pay his Admiffion-Money, and afterwards Contribution towards the defraying of the Charges of Obfervations and Experiments, &c.

The ordinary Meetings of the Royal Society fhall be held once a Week, where none fhall be prefent, befides the Fellows, without the leave of the Society, under the Degree of a Baron in one of his Majefty's three Kingdoms, or of his Majefty's Privy Council; or unlefs he be an eminent Foreigner, and thefe only without the leave of the Prefident.

The Bufinefs of their weekly Meetings fhall be, To order, take account, confider, and difcourfe of, philofophical Experiments and Obfervations; to read, hear, and difcourfe upon, Letters, Reports, and other Papers, containing philofophical Matters; as alfo to view, and difcourfe upon the Productions and Rarities of Nature, and Art; and to confider what to reduce from them, or how they may be improv'd for Ufe or Difcovery.

The Experiments that be made at the Charge of the Society; two Curators at leaft fhall be appointed for the Infpection of thofe which cannot be perform'd before the Society; by them the bare Report of Matter of Fact fhall be ftated and return'd.

The Election of Fellows fhall be made by way of Ballet; and their Admiffion by a folemn Declaration made by the Prefident of their Election.

T

The

The Election of the Council and Officers shall be made once a Year: Eleven of the present Council shall be continued by Lot, for the next Year, and ten new ones chosen in like Manner. Out of this new Council shall be elected a President, Treasurer, and two Secretaries in the same Way.

The President shall preside in all Meetings, regulate all Debates of the Society and Council; State, and put Questions; call for Reports and Accounts from Committees, Curators, and others; summon all extraordinary Meetings upon urgent Occasions, and see to the Execution of the Statutes. The Vice-President shall have the same Power in the Absence of the President.

The Treasurer, or his Deputy, shall receive and keep Accounts of all Money due to the Society, and disburse all Money payable by the Society. He shall pay small Sums by Order of the President under his Hand, but those that exceed five Pounds by Order of the Council. All Bills of Charges for Experiments shall first be sign'd by the Curators. The Accounts of the Treasurer shall be audited four Times a Year, by a Committee of the Council, and once a Year by a Committee of the Society.

The Secretaries are to take Notes of the Orders, and material Passages of the Meetings; to take Care of the Books, Papers, and Writings of the Society; to order, and direct the Clerks in making Entries of all Matters in the Register and Journal-Books of the Society or Council; to draw up such Letters as shall be written in their Name, which shall be approv'd at one of their Meetings; to give notice of the Candidates propounded in order to Election.

The Curators by Office shall have a sufficient Allowance for their Encouragement, which shall increase proportionably with the Revenue of the Society, pro-
vided

vided that it exceed not two hundred Pounds a Year. *They shall be well skilled in philosophical and mathematical Learning, well vers'd in Observations, Inquiries, and Experiments of Nature and Art. They shall take Care of the managing of all Experiments and Observations appointed by the Society or Council, and report the same, and perform such other Tasks, as the Society or Council shall appoint; such as the examining of Sciences, Arts, and Inventions now in use, and the bringing in Histories of natural and artificial Things, &c. They shall be propounded at least a Month before they are chosen. They shall be examin'd by the Council before the Election: To their Election every Member of the Society shall be summon'd: They shall at first be only elected for a Year of Probation, except they be of known Merits; At the end of the Year, they shall be either elected for Perpetuity, or for a longer Time of Probation, or wholly rejected. The Causes of ejecting a Curator shall be the same with ejecting a Fellow, or for fraudulent Dealing and Negligence in the Affairs of the Society, provided that he shall first receive three respective Admonitions. If any Curator shall be disabled by Age, Infirmity, or any Casualty, in the Service of the Society, some Provision shall be made for him during Life, if his Condition requires, according as the Council shall think fit.*

The Clerk shall constantly attend at all Meetings; he shall follow the Directions of the Secretaries, in registring and entring all Matters that shall be appointed: he shall not communicate any thing contain'd in their Books, to any that is not a Fellow. He shall have a certain Rate for what he copies, and a yearly Stipend for his Attendance.

The Printer shall take Care for the printing of such

T 2

Books.

Books as ſhall be committed to him by Order of the Society, or Council; and therein he ſhall obſerve their Directions, as to the Correction of the Edition, the Number of Copies, the Form, or Volume, &c.

The Operators of the Society, when they have any of their Work under their Hands, ſhall not undertake the Work of any other Perſons, which may hinder the Buſineſs of the Society. They ſhall have Salaries for their Attendance.

The common Seal of the Society, ſhall be kept in a Cheſt with three Locks, and three different Keys, by the Preſident, Treaſurer, and one of the Secretaries. The Deeds of the Society ſhall be paſs'd in Council, and ſeal'd by them and the Preſident.

The Books that concern the Affairs of the Society, ſhall be the Charter Book, Statute Book, Journal Books, Letter Books, and Regiſter Books, for the entring of philoſophical Obſervations, Hiſtories, Diſcourſes, Experiments, Inventions.

The Names of Benefactors ſhall be honourably mention'd in a Book provided for that Purpoſe.

In caſe of Death, or Receſs of any Fellow, the Secretaries are to note it in the Margent of the Regiſter, over againſt their Names.

The Cauſes of Ejection ſhall be contemptuous Diſobedience to the Statutes and Orders of the Society; defaming or malicious damnifying the ſame. This ſhall be declar'd by the Preſident at one of the Meetings; and the Ejection recorded.

When theſe Statutes were preſented to his *Majeſty,* he was pleas'd to ſuperſcribe himſelf their *Founder* and *Patron;* his *Royal Highneſs,* and his *Highneſs Prince Rupert,* at the ſame time, declaring themſelves *Fellows.*   ‡   Nor

Nor has the *King* only incourag'd them, by Kindnefs and *Words*, and by *Acts* of *State*; but he has alfo
provok'd them to unwearied Activity in their *Expe-*
riments, by the moft effectual Means of his *Royal Ex-*
ample. There is fcarce any one Sort of *Work*, whofe Advancement they regard; but from his *Majefty's* own
Labours they have receiv'd a *Pattern* for their Indeavours about it. They defign the multiplying and
beautifying of *Mechanick Arts*: And the Noife of
Mechanick Inftruments is heard in *Whitehall* it felf.
They intend the Perfection of *Graving, Statuary,
Limning, Coining*, and all the Works of Smiths, in Iron,
or Steel, or Silver: And the moft excellent *Artifts* of
thefe kinds have Provifion made for their Practice,
even in the Chambers and Galleries of his *Court.*
They purpofe the Trial of all manner of *Operations by
Fire*: And the *King* has under his own Roof found
place for *Chymical Operators.* They refolve to reftore,
to enlarge, to examine *Phyfick*; and the *King* has indow'd the College of *London* with new Privileges,
and has planted a Phyfick Garden under his own Eye.
They have beftow'd much Confideration on the *propagating of Fruits and Trees*: And the *King* has made
Plantations enough, even almoft to repair the Ruins
of a Civil War. They have begun an exact *Survey*
of the *Heavens*; and St. *James's Park* may witnefs,
that *Ptolomy* and *Alphonfo* were not the only *Monarchs*, who obferv'd the Motions and Appearances of
the *Stars.* They have ftudied the promoting of *Architecture* in our Ifland; and the Beauty of our late
Buildings, and the Reformation of his own Houfes, do
fufficiently manifeft his Skill and Inclination to that
Art: of which Magnificence, we had feen more Effects

fects e'er this, if they had not been call'd off by this
War, from Houses of *Convenience*, to those of *Strength*.
They have principally confulted the Advancement of
Navigation; and the *King* has been moft ready to
reward thofe, that fhall difcover the *Meridian*. They
have employ'd much Time in examining *the Fabrick
of Ships*, the Forms of their *Sails*, the Shapes of their
Keels, the Sorts of Timber, the planting of Fir, the
bettering of pitch, and Tar, and Tackling. And in
all *maritime* Affairs of this Nature, his *Majefty* is acknowledg'd to be the beft *Judge* amongft Seamen
and Shipwrights, as well as the moft powerful amongft
Princes.

Sect. XXVIII.   By thefe and many other Inftances it appears, that
*And the pre-*the *King* has not only given Succour to the *Royal So-*
fent Genius *ciety*, in the profecution of their *Labours*; but has alfo
of our Na-
*tion.*led them on their *Way*, and trac'd out to them the
Paths, in which they ought to tread. And with this
propitious Inclination of his *Majefty*, and the higheft
Degrees of Men, the *Genius* of the *Nation* it felf irrefi-
ftibly confpires. If we reflect on all the paft Times
of *Learning* in our *Ifland*; we may ftill obferve fome
remarkable *Accidents*, that retarded thefe *Studies*,
which were ftill ready to break forth, in fpight of all
Oppofition.

Till the Union of the two Houfes of *York* and *Lan-*
cafter, the whole Force of our *Country* was ingag'd in
Domeftick Wars, between the *King* and the *Nobility*,
or in the furious Contentions between the divided
Families: unlefs fometimes fome magnanimous
Prince was able to turn their Strength to foreign
Conquefts. In King *Henry the Seventh* the two *Rofes*
were joyn'd: His Government was like his own
                                                    Temper,

Temper, *clofe, fevere, jealous, avaritious,* and withal
victorious, and *prudent:* but how unprepar'd his Time
was for new Difcoveries, is evident by the flender Account that he made of the Propofition of *Columbus.*
The Reign of King *Henry the Eighth* was *vigorous,
haughty, magnificent, expenfive, learned:* But then
the Alteration of *Religion* began, and that alone was
then fufficient to poffefs the Minds of Men.

The *Government* of King *Edward the Sixth* was
contentious, by reafon of the Factions of thofe who
manag'd his Childhood; and the Shortnefs of his Life
depriv'd us of the Fruits, that might have been expected
from the prodigious Beginnings of the *King* himfelf. That of *Queen Mary* was *weak, melancholy,
bloody* againft the Proteftants, obfcur'd by a foreign
Marriage, and unfortunate by the Lofs of *Calais.* That
of *Queen Elizabeth* was *long, triumphant, peaceable* at
home, and *glorious* abroad. Then it was fhewn, to
what height the *Englifh* may rife, when they are commanded by a *Prince,* who knows how to govern their
Hearts as well as Hands. In her Days the *Reformation*
was fettled, Commerce was eftablifh'd, and *Navigation*
advanc'd. But though Knowledge began abundantly to fpring forth, yet it was not then feafonable for
Experiments to receive a *publick Incouragement:* while
the Writings of Antiquity, and the Controverfies between us and the Church of *Rome,* were not fully
ftudied and difpatch'd.

The *Reign* of King *James* was happy in all the Benefits of *Peace,* and plentifully furnifh'd with Men of
profound *Learning:* But in Imitation of the *King,*
they chiefly regarded the Matters of *Religion* and
Difputation; fo that even my Lord *Bacon,* with all his
Authority in the State, could never raife any *College*
of

of Salomon, but in a *Romance*. That of *King Charles the Firſt* began indeed to be ripe for ſuch undertakings, by reaſon of the Plenty and Felicity of the firſt Years of his *Government*, and the Abilities of the *King* himſelf; who was not only an inimitable *Maſter*, in *Reaſon* and *Eloquence*, but excell'd in very many practical *Arts*, beyond the uſual Cuſtom of *Kings*, nay even beyond the Skill of the beſt *Artiſts* themſelves. But he, alas! was call'd away from the Studies of *Quiet* and *Peace*, to a more dangerous and a more honourable Reputation. The chief Triumphs that Heaven reſerv'd for him, were to be gather'd from his *ſuffering Virtues*: In them he was only exceeded by the Divine Example of our *Saviour*; in Imitation of whoſe Paſſion, thoſe Afflictions, and thoſe Thorns which the rude Soldiers deſign'd for his *Diſgrace* and *Torment*, became his *Glory* and his *Crown*.

The late Times of *Civil War* and *Confuſion*, to make Recompenſe for their infinite Calamities, brought this Advantage with them, that they ſtir'd up Men's Minds from *long Eaſe*, and a *lazy Reſt*, and made them *active*, *induſtrious* and *inquiſitive*: it being the uſual Benefit that follows upon *Tempeſts* and *Thunders* in the *State*, as well as in the *Sky*, that they purifie and clear the *Air*, which they diſturb. But now ſince the *King's* Return, the blindneſs of the former *Ages*, and the Miſeries of this laſt, are vaniſh'd away: now Men are generally weary of the *Relicks* of *Antiquity*, and ſatiated with *Religious Diſputes*: now not only the *Eyes* of Men, but their *Hands* are open and prepar'd to *labour*: Now there is an univerſal *Deſire* and *Appetite* after *Knowledge*, after the peaceable, the fruitful, the nouriſhing *Knowledge*; and not after that of antient Sects, which only yielded hard indigeſtible *Arguments*,

or

or sharp *Contentions* instead of *Food*; which when the Minds of Men requir'd *Bread,* gave them only a *Stone,* and for *Fish* a *Serpent.*

Whatever they have hitherto attempted, on these Principles and Incouragements, it has been carry'd on with a vigorous Spirit, and wonderful good Fortune, from their first Constitution down to this Day. Yet I overhear the Whispers and Doubts of many, who demand, what they have done all this while? And what they have produc'd, that is answerable to these mighty Hopes, which we indeavour to make the World conceive of their Undertaking?

Sect.XXIX.
The Subjects
about which
they have
been employ'd

If those who require this Account, have themselves perform'd any worthy Things, in this Space of Time; it is fit, that we should give them Satisfaction. But they who have done nothing at all, have no reason to up-braid the *Royal Society,* for not having done as much as they fancy it might. To those therefore who ex-cite it to work by their Examples, as well as Words and Reproofs, methinks it were a sufficient Answer, if I should only repeat the Particulars I have already mention'd, wherein the *King* has set on foot a *Refor-mation,* in the Ornaments, and Advantages of our Country. For though the original Praise of all this is to be ascrib'd to the Genius of the *King* himself; yet it is but just, that some Honour should thence des-cend to this Assembly, whose Purposes are conform-able to his Majesty's Performance of that Nature: Seeing all the little Scandals, that captious Humours have taken against the *Royal Society,* have not risen from their general Proceedings, but from a few pretended Offences of some of their private Mem-bers; it is but reason, that we should alledge in their

U   com-

Commendation, all the excellent Defigns, which are
begun by the *King*, who has not only ftil'd himfelf
their *Founder*, but acted as a particular *Member* of
their Company.

· To this I will alfo add, that in this Time, they have
pafs'd through the firft Difficulties of their *Charter*
and Model ; and have overcome all Oppofitions,
which are wont to arife, againft the Beginnings of
great Things. This certainly alone were enough to free
them from all Imputation of Idlenefs, that they have
fram'd fuch an Affembly in fix Years, which was never yet brought about in fix thoufand.   Befides this the
World is to confider, that if any fhall think, the whole
Compafs of their Work might have come to a fudden
Iffue ; they feem neither to underftand the Intentions of the *Royal Society*, nor the Extent of their Task.
It was never their Aim, to make a violent Difpatch.
They know, that Precipitancy in fuch Matters was the
Fault of the Antients : And they have no Mind, to fall
into the fame Error, which they indeavour to correct.
They began at firft on fo large a Bottom, that it is impoffible, the whole Frame fhould be fuddenly compleated.   'Tis true, they that have nothing elfe to do,
but to exprefs, and adorn Conclufions of Knowledge
already made, may bring their Arts to an End, as foon
as they pleafe :   But they who follow the flow and
intricate Method of Nature, cannot have the Seafons
of their Productions, fo much in their own Power.
If we would always exact from them daily or weekly Harvefts ; we fhould wholly cut off the Occafions
of very many excellent Inventions, whofe Subjects
are remote, and come but feldom under their Confideration.   If we would require them, immediately
to reduce all their Labours, to publick and confpicuous

ous Ufe ; by this dangerous Speed, we fhould draw
them off from many of the beft Foundations of Knowledge. Many of their nobleft Difcoveries, and fuch
as will hereafter prove moft ferviceable, cannot inftantly be made to turn to Profit. Many of their
weightieft and moft precious *Obfervations*, are not
always fit to be expos'd to open View: For it is with
the greateft Philofophers, as with the richeft Merchants, whofe Wares of greateft Bulk and Price, lye
commonly out of Sight, in their Warehoufes, and
not in their Shops.

This being premis'd, I will however venture to lay
down a brief Draught of their moft remarkable Particulars; which may be reduc'd to thefe following
Heads: The Queries and Directions they have given
abroad; the Propofals and Recommendations they
have made; the Relations they have receiv'd; the
Experiments they have tried; the Obfervations they
have taken; the Inftruments they have invented; the
Theories that have been propofed; the Difcourfes they have written, or publifhed; the Repofitory and Library; and the Hiftories of Nature,
and Arts, and Works they have collected.

Their Manner of gathering, and difperfing *Que-*
ries, is this. Firft, they require fome of their particular Fellows, to examine all Treatifes and Defcriptions of the Natural and Artificial Productions of
thofe Countries, in which they would be inform'd.
At the fame Time, they employ others to difcourfe
with the Seamen, Travellers, Tradefmen, and Merchants, who are likely to give them the beft Light.
Out of this united Intelligence from Men and Books,
they compofe a Body of Queftions, concerning all

U 2   the

the observable Things of those Places. These Papers being produc'd in their weekly Assemblies, are augmented, or contracted, as they see Occasion. And then the Fellows themselves are wont to undertake their Distribution into all Quarters, according as they have the Convenience of Correspondence : Of this Kind I will here reckon up some of the principal, whose particular Heads are free to all, that shall desire Copies of them for their Direction.

They have compos'd Queries, and Directions, what Things are needful to be observ'd, in order to the making of a natural History in general ; what are to be taken Notice of towards a perfect History of the Air, and Atmosphere, and Weather ; what is is to be observ'd in the Production, Growth, Advancing or Transforming of Vegetables ; what Particulars are requisite, for collecting a compleat History of the Agriculture, which is us'd in several Parts of this Nation.

They have prescrib'd exact Inquiries, and given punctual Advice for the Trial of Experiments of Rarefaction, Refraction, and Condensation ; conncerning the Cause and Manner of the Petrifaction of Wood ; of the Loadstone ; of the Parts of Anatomy, that are yet imperfect ; of Injections into the Blood of Animals ; and transfusing the Blood of one Animal into another ; of Currents ; of the ebbing, and flowing of the Sea ; of the Kinds, and Manner of the feeding of Oysters ; of the Wonders, and Curiosities observable in deep Mines.

They have collected, and sent abroad Inquiries for the *East Indies*, for *China*, for *St. Helena*, for *Teneriff*, or any high Mountain, for *Guinea*, for *Barbary*, and *Morocco*,

Morocco, for *Spain,* and *Portugal,* for *Turky,* for *France,* for *Italy,* for *Germany,* for *Hungary,* for *Transylvania,* for *Poland,* and *Sweden,* for *Iceland,* and *Greenland,* they have given Directions for Seamen in general, and for observing the Eclipses of the Moon; for observing the Eclipses of the Sun by *Mercury,* in several Parts of the World, and for observing the *Satellites* of *Jupiter.*

Of this their Way of Inquiry, and giving Rules for Direction, I will here produce a few Instances; from whose Exactness it may be guess'd, how all the rest are perform'd.

ANS-

ANSWERS

RETURN'D BY

Sir *PHILBERTO VERNATTI*

Refident in *Batavia* in *Java Major*,

To certain Inquiries fent thither by Order of the
Royal Society, and recommended by

Sir *ROBERT MORAY.*

Q. 1. *W*Hether *Diamonds and other precious Stones
grow again, after three or four Years, in the
fame Places where they have been digged out ?*

A. Never, or at leaft as the Memory of Man can
attain to.

Q. 2. *Whether the Quarries of Stone in* India, *near*
Fetipoca, *not far from* Agra, *may be cleft like Logs, and
fawn like Planks, to ceil Chambers, and cover Houfes.*

A. What they are about the Place mentioned, I
have not as yet been well inform'd ; but in *Perfia* not
far from *Cyrus* where the beft Wine groweth, there is
a fort of hard Stone which may be cleft like Fir-
wood, as if it had a Grain in it ; the fame is at the
Coaft *Cormandel* about *Sadrafpatuam* ; where they
make but a Mark in the Stone, fet a Wedge upon it,
with a wooden Hammer, as thick and thin as they
pleafe ; it is ufed commonly for Pavement in Houfes,
one Foot fquare, and fo cheap, that fuch a Stone finely polifh'd cofts not above fix Pence.

Q. 3. *Whe-*

Q. 3. *Whether there be a Hill in* Sumatra *which burneth continually, and a Fountain which runneth pure Balfam.*

A. There is a Hill that burneth in *Sumatra* near *Endrapeor* ; but I cannot hear of any such Fountain ; and I believe that the like Hill is upon *Java Major* opposite to *Batavia* ; for in a clear Morning or Evening, from the Road a Man may perfectly perceive a continual Smoke rise from the top, and vanish by little and little. I have often felt Earthquakes here, but they do not continue long. In the Year 1656, or 57, (I do not remember well the Time) *Batavia* was cover'd in one Afternoon, about two of the Clock, with a black Dust, which being gathered together, was so ponderous, that it exceeded the Weight in Gold. I, at that time, being very ill, did not take much Notice of it, but some have gathered it, and if I light upon it, I shall send you some. It is here thought, it came out of the Hill : I never heard of any that had been upon this Hill's top. *Endrapeor* is counted a mighty unwholesome Place, as likewise all others where Pepper grows ; as *Jamby, Banjar, Balingtoan,* &c. though some impute it to the Hill's burning.

As for the Fountain, it is unknown to us, except *Oleum Terræ* is meant by it, which is to be had in *Sumatra,* but the best comes from *Pegu.*

Q. 4. *What River is that in* Java Major *that turns Wood into Stone ?*

A. There is none such to our Knowledge ; yet I have seen a Piece of Wood with a Stone at the End of it ; which was told me, that was turned into Stone by a River in *Pegu* ; but I took it but for a Foppery ; for diverse *Arbufta* grow in Rocks, which being appro-

I   priated

priated curioufly, may eafily deceive a too hafty Be-
liever.

Q. 5. *Whether it be true, that upon the Coaſt of*
Achin *in* Sumatra, *the Sea, though it be calm, grow-*
eth very high when no Rain falls, but is ſmooth in
Rain, though it blows hard?

A. Sometimes, but not always; the Reaſon is
this, that *Achin* lyeth at the very End and Corner of
Sumatra, as may be feen by the Map, open in the
main Ocean, fo that the Sea comes rowling from the
Cabo de bona Eſperanza, and all that way unto it, and it
is natural to the Sea to have a continual Motion, let it
be never fo calm; which Motion cannot be called a
Wave, neither have I any *Engliſh* for it at prefent,
but in *Dutch* we call it, *Deyninge van Dee Zee,* and
the calmer it is, the higher; the natural Motion of the
Sea elevates very flowly the Water; fo that I have feen
Ships and Junks tofled by thefe *Deynings* in a calm,
(when there is fcarce Wind enough to drive a Bubble)
that a Man can fcarce ftand in them; fome fay this
Motion proceeds from boifterous Winds at Sea far
diftant.   That Rain beats down the fwelling of thefe
Deynings (efpecially if it be vehement) proceeds
naturally from its Weight and Impetuofity.   And it
is obferved, that about *Achin* the Mountains are high
and fteep, from whofe Tops boifterous Winds, called
Travant, come fuddenly (like a Granado-caft) falling
into the Sea, are accompanied commonly with a great
Shower of Rain, and laft not above a Quarter, or at
the moft, half an Hour, which is too fhort a Time to
difturb the Sea, or to caufe a contrary Motion in it,
being fhelter'd by thefe Mountains.

Q. 6. *Whether in the Iſland of* Sambrero, *which*
lyeth Northwards of Sumatra, *about eight Degrees*

I   *Northern*

thern Latitude, there be found such a Vegetable as Mr. James Lancaster *relates to have seen, which grows up to a Tree, shrinks down, when one offers to pluck it up, into the Ground, and would quite shrink, unless held very hard? And whether the same, being forcibly pluck'd up, hath a Worm for its Root, diminishing more and more, according as the Tree groweth in Greatness; and as soon as the Worm is wholly turned into the Tree, rooting in the Ground, and so growing great? And whether the same plucked up young turns, by that time it is dry, into a hard Stone, much like to white Corral?*

A. I cannot meet with any that ever have heard of such a Vegetable.

Q. 7. *Whether those Creatures that are in these Parts plump, and in Season at the full Moon, are lean and out of Season at the new, and the contrary, at the* East-Indies?

A. I find it so here, by Experience at *Batavia,* in Oysters and Crabs.

Q. 8. *What ground there may be for that Relation, concerning Horns taking Root, and growing about* Goa?

A. Inquiring about this, a Friend laught, and told me it was a Jeer put upon the *Portuguese,* because the Women of *Goa* are counted much given to Lechery.

Q. 9. *Whether the* Indians *can so prepare that stupifying Herb* Datura, *that they make it lye several Days, Months, Years, according as they will have it, in a Man's Body, without doing him any hurt, and at the end kill him, without missing half an Hour's time?*

A. The *China* Men in this Place have formerly used *Datura* as a Fermentation, to a Sort of Drink much beloved by the Soldiers and Mariners, called *Suyker-*

X   *bier,*

bier, which makes them raging mad, fo that it is forbidden ftrictly under the Penalty of a great Pain to make ufe of the fame.

Q. 10. *Whether thofe that be ftupified by the Juice of this Herb* Datura, *are recovered by moiftning the Soles of their Feet in fair Water?*

A. No. For I have feen diverfe Soldiers and Mariners fall into the Rivers and Ditches, being ftupified by their Drink aforefaid, who were rather worfe after they were taken out, than better.

Q. 11. *Whether a* Betel *hath fuch Contrariety to the* Durion, *that a few Leaves thereof put to a whole Shopful of* Durions, *will make them all rot fuddenly? And whether thofe who have furfeited on* Durions, *and thereby overheated themfelves, do by laying one Leaf of* Betel *cold upon the Heart, immediately cure the Inflammations and recover the Stomach? This* Betel *being thought to preferve thofe* Indians *from Tooth-ach, loofe Gums, and Scurvy, and from ftinking Breath; fome of it is defired to be fent over with the Fruit* Areica, *and the other Ingredients, and Manner of preparing it.*

A. I have feen that *Betel* Leaves in a fhort time will fpoil a *Durion,* take away its Nature, and turn a fat creamy Subftance into Water. Commonly thofe that eat great Quantities of Durions, eat a *Betel* afterwards as a *Correctorium*; but of laying a Leaf upon the Heart, I have never heard. As for the other Qualities of the *Betel,* I believe they are good, if not abufed; as moft of the *Indians* do, who never are without it in their Mouths, no not fleeping, which corrodes their Teeth, and makes them as black as Jet: It draws from the Head the phegmatick Humours, which are voided by fpitting; fo we ufe it;

*
but

but the *Indians* fwallow down their Spittle, together
with the Juice of the *Betel*, and the *Areica*. The
Manner of preparing it is eafie, being nothing but the
Nut Leaf and *Calx viva*, of which laft each one adds
as much as pleafeth his Palate.   There is a Sort of
of Fruit called *Sivgboa*, which is ufed with the *Areica*, inftead of *Betel*, and can be dried and tranfported
as well as the *Areica*, and hath the fame Force, but a
great deal more pleafant to the Palate.

Q. 12. *Whether the* Papayas, *that beareth Fruit
like a Melon, do not grow, much lefs bear Fruit, unlefs
Male and Female be together?*

A. They grow, as I have feen two in the *Englifh*
Houfe at *Bantam*, and bear little Fruit, which never
comes to Perfection ; but if the Male and Female be
together, the one bears great Fruit, the other nothing
but Flowers.

Q. 13. *Whether the* Arbor Trifte *fheds its Flowers
at the rifing of the Sun, and fhoots them again at the fetting of the Sun? And whether the diftill'd Water
thereof (called* Aqua di Mogli *by the* Portugals) *may
not be tranfported to* England? *And whether at the
rifing of the Sun the Leaves of the* Arbor Trifte *drop
off as well as the Flowers?*

A. There are two Sorts of the *Arbor Trifte* ; one is
called by the *Portugals Trifte de Die*, the other *Trifte
de Noɛ̃te* ; the one fheds its Flowers at the rifing, the
other at the fetting of the Sun ; but neither of them
fhed their Leaves. There is no Body here that underftands the diftilling of Waters ; fome fay this *Aqua
di Mogli* is to be had at *Malaca*, for which I have
writ, and fhall fend it if procurable.

Q. 14. *Whether the* Arbor de Rays, *or Tree of Root,
propagate it felf in a whole Foreft, by fhooting up and*

X 2   *letting*

letting fall Roots from its Branches into the **Ground**, *that spring up again, and so on?*

A. This is true. And we have diverse Trees about *Batavia*, and the like adjacent Iflands, above fifty Foot in the Diameter.

Q. 15. *What kind of Fruit is that in* Jucca, *which grows immediately out of the Tree's Body; and is said to breed the* Plague *if eaten immoderately?*

A. It is a Fruit much like to *Durion*, which groweth in the fame Manner; hath a faint Smell, and fweet waterifh Tafte; for my part I do not affect them : The *Plague* is a Difeafe unknown amongft the *Indians*; but this Fruit, as moft others do, immoderately eaten, caufes a *Dirthea*, which eafily degenerates to a *Tenefmus*, by us called *Peirfing*, a dangerous Sicknefs, and worfe than the *Plague.*

Q. 16. *What Poifon is it the King of* Macaffar *in* Colebees *is said to have particular to himself, which not only kills a Man immediately, that hath received the flighteft Wound by a Dart dipt therein, but also within half an Hour's time, makes the Flefh, touched with it, fo rotten, that it will fall like Snivel from the Bones, and whofe poyfonous Steam will foon fly up to a Wound made with an unpoifoned Dart, if the Blood be only in the flighteft Manner touch'd with a Dart infected with the Poifon? What certainty there is of this Relation?*

A. That there is fuch a Poifon in this King's Poffeffion is moft certain; but what it is, no *Chriftian* hitherto ever knew right. By the Government of *Arnold de Flamminge Van Outfhorn* diverfe have been tortured; yea, killed.

Some fay it is the Gall of a venomous Fifh, others fay it is a Tree which is fo venomous, that thofe who

*   are

are condemned to die, fetch the Poifon, but not one
of an Hundred fcapes Death; the Roots of this Tree
are held an Antidote againft the Poifon; but our
People, when we had War with *Macaffar*, found no
Antidote like to their own or other's Excrements; as
foon as they felt themfelves wounded, they inftantly
took a Dofe of this fame, which prefently provoked to
vomit, and fo, by Repulfion, (as I perceive) and Sweat,
freed the noble Parts from farther Infection. That
a Wound fhould be infected by this Poifon, though not
inflicted by an impoifoned Weapon, is not ftrange to
thofe who ftudy Sympathy; and fet Belief in that
much renowned fympathetical Powder of Sir *Ke-
nelm Digby*. Yet fuch Effects of the *Macaffars* Arts
are unknown to us.

Q. 17. *Whether in* Pegu *and other Places in the*
Eaft Indies, *they ufe a Poifon that kills by fmelling,
and yet the Poifon-Smell is hardly perceived?*

To this no Anfwer was return'd.

Q. 18. *Whether* Camphire *comes from Trees? What
kind of Trees they are in* Borneo, *that are faid to yield
fuch excellent* Camphire, *as that one Pound thereof
is faid to be worth an Hundred of that of* China *and
other Places?*

A. Camphire comes from Trees of an exceffive
Bulk, as you may fee by the Chefts which come
from *Japan* into *Europe*, made of the fame Wood of
Borneo; it comes likewife from Trees, which are faid
to ftand in fandy Ground, and drop like a Gum.

But of late an Experiment is found in *Ceylon*, that
the Root of a Cinamon Tree yields as good *Camphire*, as either *Japan*, or *China*, of which I fhall fend
you a Pattern, being now to be had at prefent here;
as alfo an Oil extracted from the fame Roots, which

reserves

reserves fomething of the Cinamon-fmell; but that may be the Fault of the Diftiller.

Q. 19. *Whether fome of that rare Wood, called* Palo d' Aquila *and* Calamba, *of an extraordinary Value, even in the Country where it groweth, as in* Siam *about* San, *and* Patan, *and in* Cochinchina, *may not be brought over; as alfo fome of thofe ftrange Nefts of* Cochinchina, *made by Birds upon Rocks, of a certain vifcous Froth of the Sea, which Nefts grown dry and hard, are faid to become tranfparent; and when diffolved in Water, ferve excellently to feafon all their Meats?*

A. If the Queftion be made, whether thefe Things may be brought over by Permiffion of the Company? I anfwer; as firft, that their Laws forbid the Tranfportation of all whatfoever, whether neceffary to the Confervation of Health, or Acquifition of Wealth, or Rarities, *&c.* but if the *Query* be concerning the Nature and Subftance of the Wood and Nefts; they are tranfportable, and can fubfift without decaying many Years. *Lignum Aquilæ* is far inferiour to *Calamba*, though not eafie to be difcerned. A Pound of *Calamba* is worth in *Japan* thirty, and fometimes forty Pounds Sterling; the beft comes from *Cambodia*, and feems to be the Pith of the Tree *Aquila* in *Japan*; it is ufed as Incenfe to perfume Cloaths, and Chambers. It is held for a great Cordial, and commonly ufed by that Nation, as alfo the *Chinefe*, *in Defectione fpirituum vitalium*; as in *Paralyfi & Nervorum laxatione & impotentia:* They rub it with *Aqua Cynamomi* upon a Stone, till the Subftance of the Wood is mixt, *ficut pulpa*, with the Water, and fo drink it with Wine, or what they pleafe. The Bird's nefts are a great Reftorative to Nature, and much ufed by the lecherous *Chinefe*.

Q. 20. *Whether the Animal call'd* Abados, *or* Rhinoceros, *hath Teeth, Claws, Flesh, Blood, and Skin, yea his very Dung and Water, as well as his Horns, antidotal? And whether the Horns of those Beasts be better or worse, according to the Food they live upon.*

A. Their Horns, Teeth, Claws, and Blood are esteemed Antidotes, and have the same Use in the *Indian Pharmacopeia* as the *Theriaca* hath in ours; the Flesh I have eaten is very sweet and short. Some Days before the Receipt of your Letter, I had a young one no bigger than a Spaniel Dog, which followed me whereever I went, drinking nothing but *Buffalo* Milk, lived about three Weeks, then his Teeth began to grow, and he got a Looseness and died. 'Tis observed, that Children (especially of *European* Parents) at the breaking out of their Teeth are dangerously sick, and commonly die of the scouring in these Parts. His Skin I have caused to be dried, and so present it unto you, since Fate permits not to send him you living; such a young one was never seen before. The Food I believe is all one to this Animal, being that they are seldom seen but amongst withered Branches, Thistles and Thorns; so that the Horn is of equal Virtue.

Q. 21. *Whether the falsifying of the* China *Musk is not rather done by mixing Oxen and Cow's Livers dried and pulverised with some of the putrified and concrete Flesh and Blood of the* China *Musk-cat, than by beating together the bare Flesh and Blood of this Animal, &c.*

Not answered.

Q. 22. *Whether there be two Sorts of* Gumlac, *one produced from a certain winged* Ant, *the other the* Exudation *of a Tree; the first had in the Islands*

of

of Suachan, *the laſt in the Kingdom of* Marta-
ban ?

A. We know of none but ſuch as drop from Trees,
and come from diverſe Places in *Siam, Cambodia,*
Pegu, &c.

Q. 23. *If the beſt* Ambergreaſe *be found in the*
Iſlands Socotora *and* Aniana, *near* Java? *To endea-*
vour the getting of more certain Knowledge, what it
is ; being reported to be bred in the Bottom of the Sea
like to a thick Mud?

A. The beſt that is in the World comes from the
Iſland *Mauritius;* and is commonly found after a
Storm. The Hogs can ſmell it at a great Diſtance;
who run like mad to it, and devour it commonly before the People come to it. It is held to be a *Zeequal*
Viſcoſity, which being dried by the Sun, turns to ſuch
a Conſiſtence as is daily ſeen. Father *Myavines Iſaac*
Vigny a *French* Man in *Oleron,* hath been a great
Traveller in his Time; and he told me, he ſailed once
in his Youth through ſo many of theſe *Zeequalen,* as
would have loaden ten thouſand Ships; the like having been never ſeen: His Curioſity did drive him to
take up ſome of thoſe, which being dried in the Sun,
were perceived to be the beſt *Ambergreaſe* in the
World; I have ſeen one piece which he kept for a
Memento, and another piece he ſold for 1 3 00 *lib.* ſterl.
This being diſcovered, they ſet ſail to the ſame Place
where theſe *Zeequalen* appeared, and cruiſed there, to
and fro, for the ſpace of ſix Weeks, but could not
perceive any more. Where this Place is ſituated, I
do not know ; but Monſieur *Gentillot,* a *French* Cap-
tain in *Holland,* can tell you.

Q. 24. *To enquire of the* Divers for Pearls *ſtaying*
long under Water; whether they do it by the Aſſiſtance of
any

any thing they carry with them, or by long and often Ufe get a Trick of holding their Breath fo long, at the Ifle of Baharen *near* Ormus ?

A. What they do at *Baharen* is unknown to me, but fince we have had *Tute Corein* in *Ceylon*, where very good Pearls grow, I hear the *Diverfs* Ufe no Artifice. The manner is thus; at a fet time of the Year Merchants come from all Parts, as likewife *Diverfs* with their Boats; each Boat hath a certain Quantity of fquare Stones, upon which Stones the *Divers* go down, and give a Token to their Companions, when they think it time to be hal'd up; each Stone pays Tribute to the Company. The Oifter or Shell-Fifh is not immediately open'd, but laid on Heaps, or in Holes at the Sea-fide. When the diving Time is ended, the Merchants come and buy thefe Heaps, according as they can agree, not knowing whether they fhall get any thing or no. So that this is a meer Lottery. This Pearl-fifhing is dangerous, being the *Diverfs* commonly make their Will, and take Leave of their Friends, before they tread the Stone to go down.

Q. 25. *Whether Cinnamon when firft gathered hath no Tafte at all, but acquires its Tafte and Strength by fifteen Days funning ? And whether the Bark be gathered every two Years in the Ifle of* Ceylon ?

A. The Cinnamon Tree as it groweth is fo fragrant, that it may be fmelt a great Way off before it be feen. And hath even then, a moft excellent Tafte ; fo that by Sunning it lofeth rather than acquires any Tafte or Force; the Tree being pill'd is cut down to the Root; but the young Sprigs after a Year or two give the beft and fineft Cinnamon.

Q. 26. *To learn, if it may be, what Art the Mafter-workmen of* Pegu *have to add to the Colour of their Rubies ?*   Y   *A.* Not

A. Not anfwered.

Q. 27. *To inquire after, and get, if poffible, fome*
of the Bones of the Fifh called Caballa, *which are fo*
powerful in ftopping Blood.

A. 'Tis done, and they fhall follow with the
Dutch Ships.

Q. 28. *Whether at* Hermita, *a Town in* Ethiopia
there are Tortoifes, fo big, that Men may ride upon
them ?

A. It is reported, that there be extraordinary 'great
ones there; I have feen fome Sea Tortoifes here,
of four Foot broad, in oval Form, very low leg'd,
but of that Strength, that a Man may ftand on one :
The manner of catching them, is to turn them with
a Fork upon their Backs.

Q. 29. *Whether there be a Tree in* Mexico, *that*
yields Water, Wine, Vinegar, Oil, Milk, Honey, Wax,
Thread and Needles ?

A. The *Cokos* Trees yields all this and more; the
Nut, while it is green, hath very good Water in it ;
the Flower being cut, drops out great Quantity of Liquor, called *Sury,* or *Taywack,* which drank frefh,
hath the Force, and almoft the Tafte of Wine; grown
fowr, is very good Vinegar; and diftilled, makes very
good Brandy, or *Areck :* The Nut grated, and mingled with Water, tafteth like Milk ; preffed, yields
very good Oil : Bees fwarm in thefe Trees, as well
as in others; Thread and Needles are made of the
Leaves and tough Twigs. Nay, to add fomething
to this Defcription ; in *Amboyna,* they make Bread of
the Body of the Tree, the Leaves ferve to thatch
Houfes, and likewife Sails for their Boats.

Q. 30. *Whether about* Java, *there be Oyfters of that*
vaft Bignefs, as to weigh three hundred Weight ?

*   *A.*

A. I have feen a Shell Fifh, but nothing like an Oyfter, of fuch a Bignefs, the Fifh being falted, and kept in pickle, afterwards boiled, tafteth like Brawn in *England,* and is of an horny Subftance.

Q. 31. *Whether near* Malacca, *there be found in the Gall of certain Swine, a Stone efteemed incomparably above* Bezoar?

A. In that Country, but very feldom, there grows a Stone in the Stomach of a *Porkapine,* called *Pedro Porco;* of whofe Virtue there are large Defcriptions; and the *Hollanders* are now fo fond, that I have feen 400 Dollars of ⅜ given for one no bigger than a Pigeon's Egg. There is Sophiftication as well in that as *Bezoar, Musk, &c.* and every Day new Falfhood, fo that I cannot well fet down here any Rules, but muft be judged by Experience. A falfe one I fend you, which doth imitate very near in Virtue the true one, but is a great deal bigger, and of another Colour.

As for the Obfervations defired of the Iflands St. *Helena,* and *Afcenfion,* they may be better made by the Englifh *Eaft-India* Men, who commonly touch at both Places; but the *Hollander* never, or very feldom.

Q. 32. *Whether it be Winter at the Eaft-fide of the Mountain* Gates, *which come from the North to Cape* Comoryn, *whilft it is Summer on the Weft-fide? and* Vice verfa.

A. Not only there, but likewife on the Ifland of *Zeylon.*

Q. 33. *In what Country* Lignum Aloes *is found, whether it be the Wood of a Tree? or the Root of a Tree? How to know the beft of the Kind?*

A. Lignum Aloes, Lignum *Paradifi,* Culamba, are *Synonyma,* the fame: And the fame Wood comes moft

Y 2 from

from *Cambodia*, and *Siam*; but they say it is brought by the People of *Lawlan*, a Country about *Cambodia*, whence *Musk*, and *Benzoin*, and most *Aromata* come; it is easily distinguished from other Wood by its strong Scent and Richness of Balm in it, which appears in its Blackness; it is of great Value, and hard to be gotten here.

The rest of the *Queries* are not answered, because the Time is short since I received them, and especially, because I cannot meet with any one that can satisfy me, and being unsatisfied my self, I cannot nor will obtrude any Thing upon you, which may hereafter prove fabulous; but shall still serve you with Truth.

A

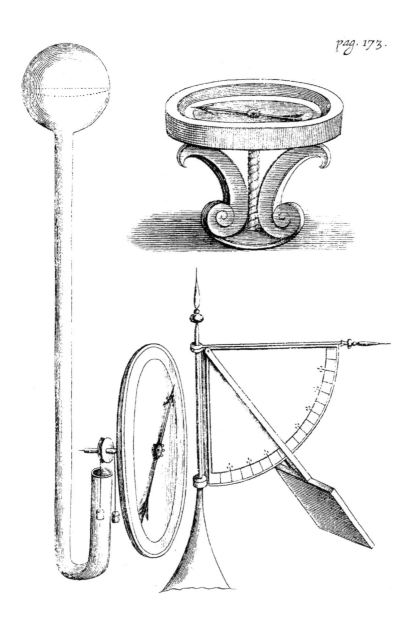

A

M E T H O D

For making a History of the W E A T H E R.

By Mr. *H O O K.*

" FOr the better making a History of the Wea-
" ther, I conceive it requisite to observe,
" 1. The Strength and Quarter of the Winds, and
" to register the Changes as often as they happen;
" both which may be very conveniently shewn, by
" a small Addition to an ordinary Weather-clock.
" 2. The Degrees of Heat and Cold in the Air;
" which will be best observed by a sealed *Thermo-*
" *meter,* graduated according to the Degrees of *Ex-*
" *pansion,* which bear a known Proportion to the
" whole Bulk of Liquor, the Beginning of which
" Gradation, should be that Dimension which the Li-
" quor hath, when encompassed with Water, just
" beginning to freeze, and the Degrees of *Expansion,*
" either greater or less, should be set or marked a-
" bove it, or below it.
" 3. The Degrees of Dryness and Moisture in the
" Air; which may be most conveniently observed by
" a *Hygroscope,* made with the single Beard of a wild
" Oat perfectly ripe, set upright and headed with an
" *Index,* after the Way described by *Emanuel Magnan;*
" the Conversions and Degrees of which may be mea-
" sured by Divisions made on the rim of a Circle, in
" the

" the *Center* of which, the *Index* is turned round :
" The Beginning or Standard of which Degree of
" *Rotation*, should be that, to which the *Index* points,
" when the Beard, being throughly wet, or covered
" with Water, is quite unwreathed, and becomes
" strait. But because of the Smalness of this Part
" of the Oat, the Cod of a wild *Vetch* may be used
" instead of it, which will be a much larger *Index*, and
" will be altogether as sensible of the Changes of the
" Air.

" 4. The Degrees of Pressure in the Air; which
" may be several Ways observed, but best of all with
" an Instrument with Quick-silver, contrived so, as
" either by means of Water, or an *Index*, it may sen-
" sibly exhibit the minute Variations of that Action.

" 5. The Constitution and Face of the Sky or Hea-
" vens; and this is best done by the Eye; here should
" be observed, whether the Sky be clear or clouded;
" and if clouded, after what Manner; whether with
" high Exhalations or great white Clouds, or dark
" thick ones. Whether those Clouds afford Fogs or
" Mists, or Sleet, or Rain, or Snow, &c, Whether
" the under side of those Clouds be flat or waved and
" irregular, as I have often seen before Thunder.
" Which way they drive, whether all one Way, or
" some one way, some another, and whether any of
" these be the same with the Wind that blows below;
" the Colour and Face of the Sky at the rising and
" setting of the Sun and Moon; what Haloes or
" Rings may happen to encompass those Luminaries,
" their Bigness, Form and Number.

" 6. What Effects are produc'd upon other Bo-
" dies: As what Aches and Distempers in the Bodies
" of Men; what Diseases are most rise, as Colds, Fe-
                                              " vors,

" vers, Agues, *&c.* What Putrefactions or other
" Changes are produc'd in other Bodies; as the sweat-
" ing of Marble, the burning blue of a Candle, the
" blasting of Trees and Corn; the unusual Sprouting,
" Growth, or Decay of any Plants or Vegetables; the
" Putrefaction of Bodies not usual; the Plenty or
" Scarcity of Insects; of several Fruits, Grains, Flow-
" ers, Roots, Cattel, Fishes, Birds, any thing notable of
" that Kind. What Conveniences or Inconveniences
" may happen in the Year, in any kind, as by Floods,
" Droughts, violent Showers, *&c.* What Nights pro-
" duce Dews and Hoar-Frosts, and what not?

" 7. What Thunders and Lightnings happen, and
" what Effects they produce; as souring Beer or Ale,
" turning Milk, killing Silk-worms, *&c?*

" Any thing extraordinary in the Tides; as double
" Tides, later or earlier, greater or less Tides than
" ordinary, rising or drying of Springs; Comets or
" unusual Apparitions, new Stars, *Ignes fatui* or
" shining Exhalations, or the like.

" These should all or most of them be diligently
" observed and registred by some one, that is always
" conversant in or near the same Place.

" Now that these, and some others, hereafter to be
" mentioned, may be registred so as to be most con-
" venient for the making of Comparisons, requisite
" for the raising *Axioms*, whereby the Cause or Laws
" of Weather may be found out; it will be desire-
" able to order them so, that the Scheme of a whole
" Month may at one View be presented to the Eye:
" And this may conveniently be done on the Pages of
" a Book in *Folio*, allowing fifteen Days for one side,
" and fifteen for the other. Let each of those Pages
" be divided into Nine Columns, and distinguished by

" per-

" perpendicular Lines; let each of the first six Co-
" lumns be half an Inch wide, and the three last equal-
" ly share the remaining of the Side.

" Let each Column have the Title of what it is to
" contain, in the first at least, written at the Top of it:
" As, let the first Colume towards the left hand, con-
" tain the Days of the Month, or Place of the Sun,
" and the remarkable Hours of each Day. The second,
" the Place, Latitude, Distance, Ages and Faces of
" the Moon. The third, the Quarters and Strength of
" Winds, The fourth, the Heat and Cold of the Sea-
" son. The fifth, the Dryness and Moisture of it. The
" sixth, the Degrees of Pressure. The seventh, the
" Faces and Appearances of the Sky. The eighth, the
" Effects of the Weather upon other Bodies, Thun-
" ders, Lightnings, or any thing extraordinary. The
" ninth, general Deductions, Corollaries or Syllo-
" gisms, arising from the comparing the several *Phæ-*
" *nomina* together.

" That the Columns may be large enough to con-
" tain what they are designed for, it will be necessary,
" that the Particulars be expressed with some Cha-
" racters, as brief and compendious as is possible.
" The two first by the Figures and Characters of the
" Signs commonly us'd in Almanacks. The Winds
" may be exprest by the Letters, by which they are ex-
" prest in small Sea-Cards; and the Degrees of
" Strength by 1, 2, 3, 4, *&c.* according as they are
" marked in the Contrivance in the Weather-cock.
" The Degrees of Heat and Cold may be exprest by
" the Numbers appropriate to the Divisions of the
" *Thermometer.* The Dryness and Moisture, by the
" Divisions in the Rim of the *Hydroscope.* The Pres-
" sure by Figures, denoting the Height of the *Mercu-*
                            *   *rial*

" *rial Cylinder.* But for the Faces of the Sky, they
" are fo many, that many of them want proper Names;
" and therefore it will be convenient to agree upon
" fome determinate ones, by which the moſt uſual
" may be in brief expreſt. As let *Clear* fignify a very
" clear Sky without any Clouds or Exhalations:
" *Checquer'd* a clear Sky, with many great white round
" Clouds, fuch as are very uſual in Summer. *Hazy,*
" a Sky that looks whitiſh, by Reaſon of the Thick-
" neſs of the higher Parts of the Air, by fome Exhala-
" tion not formed into Clouds. *Thick,* a Sky more
" whitened by a greater Company of Vapours: theſe do
" uſually make the *Luminaries* look bearded or hairy,
" and are oftentimes the Cauſe of the Appearance of
" Rings and Haloes about the *Sun* as well as the *Moon.*
" *Overcaſt,* when the Vapours fo whiten and thicken
" the Air, that the *Sun* cannot break through; and of
" this there are very many Degrees, which may be ex-
" preſt by a *little, much, more, very much overcaſt,* &c.
" Let *Hairy* fignify a Sky that hath many fmall, thin,
" and high exhalations, which reſemble Locks of Hair,
" or Flakes of Hemp or Flax: whoſe Varieties may
" be expreſt by *ſtrait* or *curv'd, &c.* according to the
" Reſemblance they bear. Let *Water'd* fignify a Sky
" that has many high thin and fmall Clouds, looking
" almoſt like water'd Tabby, called in fome places a
" Mackeril Sky. Let a Sky be called *Wav'd,* when
" thoſe Clouds appear much bigger and lower, but
" much after the fame manner. *Cloudy,* when the Sky
" has many thick dark Clouds. *Lowring,* when the
" Sky is not very much overcaſt, but hath alfo under-
" neath many thick dark Clouds which threaten
" Rain. The fignification of *gloomy, foggy, miſty, ſleet-*
" *ing, driving, rainy, ſnowy,* Reaches or Racks *va-*
Z   " *riable,*

" *riable, &c.* are well known, they being very com-
" monly ufed.   There may be alfo feveral Faces of
" the Sky compounded of two or more of thefe,
" which may be intelligibly enough expreft by two
" or more of thefe Names. It is likewife defirable, that
" the Particulars of the eighth and ninth Columns
" may be entred in as little Room and as few Words
" as are fufficient to fignify them intelligibly and
" plainly.

" It were to be wifht that there were diverfe in fe-
" veral Parts of the World, but efpecially in diftant
" Parts of this Kingdom, that would undertake this
" Work, and that fuch would agree upon a common
" Way fomewhat after this Manner, that as near as
" could be, the fame Method and Words might be
" made Ufe of.   The Benefit of which Way is eafily
" enough conceivable.

" As for the Method of ufing and digefting thofe
" fo collected Obfervations; That will be more ad-
" vantageoufly confidered when the *Supellex* is pro-
" vided; A Workman being then beft able to fit
" and prepare his Tools for his Work, when he fees
" what Materials he has to work upon.

A

A
S C H E M E,

AT ONE

View representing to the Eye the Observations of the Weather for a Month.

Days of the Month and Place of the Sun.	Remarkable Houses.	Age and Sign of the Moon at Noon.	The Quarters of the Wind and its Strength.	The Degrees of Heat and Cold.	The Degrees of Driness and Moisture.	The Degrees of Pressure.	The Faces or visible Appearances of the Sky.	The notablest Effects.	General Deductions to be made after the Side is fitted with Observations: As,
14 Π 12.46	4 8 12 / 4 8 12	27 ♂9.46. Perigeu.	W. 2 / 3 / 3½ / W.SW.1	9 .³/. / 12½ / 16 / 10⅛ / 7 ½	2 / 2	5 29 1/6 / 8 / 29 1/8 / 9 29 3/8	Clear Blue, but Yellowish in the N. E. clouded toward the S. checker'd Blue.	A great Dew. Thunder, far to the South. A very great Tide.	From the last Q. of the Moon to the Change the Weather was very temperate, but cold for the Season; the Wind pretty constant between N. & W. A little before the last great Wind, and till the Wind rose at its highest, the Quick-silver continu'd descending till it came very low; after which it began to reascend, &c.
15 Π 13.4c	3 4 6 10	28 ♂24.51	N.W. 3 / 4 / N. 2 / 1	9 / 8 ½ / 7	28½ 2 / 2	29 1/4 / 9 / 10 29	A clear Sky all Day, but a little Check-er'd at 4.P.M. at Sunset red and hazy.	Not by much so big a Tide as Yesterday. Thunder in the North.	
16 Π 14.37	10	N. Moon at 7.25. A. M. Π 10.8. &c.	S. 1	10	1 1	10 28 ½	Overcast and very lowr-ing.	No Dew upon the Ground, but very much upon Marble-stones &c.	
		&c.	&c.	&c.	&c.	&c.	&c.	&c.	

DI-

DIRECTIONS

FOR THE

Obfervations of the Eclipfes of the Moon.

By Mr. *ROOKE.*

"EClipfes of the Moon are obferved for two prin-
" cipal Ends ; one *Aftronomical,* that by com-
" paring Obfervations with Calculations, the *Theory*
" of the *Moon's* Motion may be perfected, and the Ta-
" bles thereof reformed : The other *Geographical,*
" that by comparing among themfelves Obfervations
" of the fame *Ecliptical Phafes,* made in diverfe
" Places, the Difference of *Meridians,* or *Longitudes*
" of thofe Places, may be difcovered.

" The Knowledge of the *Eclipfe's* Quantity and
" Duration, the Shadow's, Curvity and Inclination,
" *&c.* conduce only to the former of thefe Ends :
" The exact Time of the Beginning, Middle, and
" End of the *Eclipfes,* as alfo in total ones, the Be-
" ginning and End of total Darknefs, is ufeful for both
" of them.

" But becaufe thefe Times confiderably differ in
" Obfervations made by the bare Eye, from thofe with
" a *Telefcope,* and becaufe the Beginning of *Eclipfes*
" and the End of total Darknefs are fcarce to be ob-
" ferved exactly, even with Glaffes; one not being a-
" ble clearly to diftinguifh between the true Shadow
" and *Penumbra,* unlefs one have feen, for fome Time
" before, the Line, feparating them, pafs along upon
" the

" the Surface of the *Moon* : And laftly, becaufe in
" fmall partial *Eclipfes,* the Beginning and End (and
" in total ones of fhort Continuance in the Shadow,
" the Beginning and End of total Darknefs) are un-
" fit for nice Obfervations, by Reafon of the flow
" Change of Appearances, which the oblique Motion
" of the Shadow then caufeth : For thefe Reafons I
" fhall propound a Method particularly defigned for
" the Accomplifhment of the *geographical* End in
" obferving *Lunar Eclipfes,* free (as far as is poffible)
" from all the mentioned Inconveniences. For,

" Firft, It fhall not be practicable without a *Tele-*
" *fcope.*

" Secondly, The Obferver fhall always have Op-
" portunity, before his principal Obfervation, to note
" the Diftinction between the true Shadow and *Pen-*
" *umbra.*

" Thirdly, It fhall be applicable to thofe Seafons
" of the *Eclipfe,* when there is the fuddeneft Altera-
" tion in the Appearances. To fatisfy all which In-
" tents ;

" Let there be of the eminenteft Spots, difperfed
" over all Quarters of the *Moon's* Surface, a felect
" Number generally agreed on, to be conftantly made
" ufe of to this Purpofe, in all Parts of the World :
" As for Example, thofe which *Hevelius* calleth

" Mons { *Sinai* / *Ætna* / *Porphyrites* / *Serrorum* } *Infula* { *Befvicus* / *Creta* } *Palus* { *Mæoti* / *Maræ-* / *otis.* }

Lacus Niger Major.

2

" Let in each *Eclipse* (not all, but for inftance)
" three of thefe Spots, which then lye neareft to the
" *Ecliptic*, be exactly obferved, when they are firft
" touched by the true Shadow, and again when they
" are juft completely entred into it ; and (if you
" pleafe) alfo in the Decreafe of the *Eclipfe*,when they
" are firft fully clear from the true Shadow : For the
" accurate Determination of which Moments of
" Time (that being in this Bufinefs of main Impor-
" tance) let there be taken *Altitudes* of remarkable
" fixed Stars, on this fide the Line, of fuch as lye
" between the *Æquator* and *Tropic* of *Cancer ;* but
" beyond the Line, of fuch as are fituated towards
" the other *Tropic ;* and in all Places, of fuch, as at
" the time of Obfervation, are about four Hours di-
" ftant from the *Meridian*.

Mr.

Mr. *ROOK'S*
D I S C O U R S E
Concerning the Obſervations of the Eclipſes of the *Satellites* of *Jupiter*.

Longitudinis ſive *Differentiæ* Meridianorum ſcientia eſt vel *Nautica*, vel *Geographica*.
Illa Navis aquæ innatantis ; Hæc Urbium, Inſula-
rum, Promontoriorum, &c. Globo terreſtri adhæren-
tium ſitum inveſtigat.

In Navi, motu vario ſubinde tranſlatâ, Obſervatio
identidem eſt repetenda ; at loci terreni, fixam perpetuò
ſedem obtinentis, poſitionem ſemel determinâſſe ſufficit.

Maria, fluctibus ut plurimum agitata, ſubtilem In-
ſtrumentorum, præſertim Teleſcopii longioris tractati-
onem minime permittunt.

Longitudinis ſcientia Nautica vix unquam de Cœlo
expectanda ; Geographica vero ab Eclipſibus Corpo-
rum cœleſtium præcipuè petenda.

Eclipſes ſunt vel⎰*Veteribus notæ,* ſcil. Solis & Lunæ,
⎱Satellitum Jovis, ante Tubi Optici
　uſum incognitæ.

(Miſſam fecimus Cl. Hugenii Lunulam Saturniam,
Obſervatu difficiliorem.)

Illarum per multa retro ſæcula Obſervationes ; nè
duo quidem loca quantum Meridianorum intercapidinem
habeant, ſatis certò definitum eſſe experimur : harum
verò per pauculos annos adhibendâ diligenti animad-
　2.　　　　　　　　　　　　　　　verſione ;

*verſione; præcipuæ totius terrarum Orbis partes, quo-
modo ad ſe invicem ſitæ ſint, accuratius determina-
tum iri non deſperamus.*

    *Cauſæ, ob quas minùs in hoc negotio præſtitère E-
clipſes Luminarium.*

Sunt $\begin{cases} \text{1. Communis utriſque, ipſarum Raritas} \\ Propria \begin{cases} \text{2. Solari, Parallaxis Lunæ.} \\ \text{3. Lunari, Penumbra Terræ.} \end{cases} \end{cases}$

    *His ergo præferimus Satellitum Jovialium Defectus
frequentiſſimos, ſine ulla Parallaxi, in quibus etiam
Penumbra Jovis prodeſſe magis, quam officere videtur.*

    *Methodus Longitudinis, ex Eclipſibus vel aliis
Phænomenis cæleſtibus, indagandæ duplex eſt : Una,
cum Tempore ad Meridianum Tabularum proprium ſup-
putato, Tempus alibi obſervatum; Altera, Tempora
variis in locis obſervata, inter ſe comparat.*

    *Cum Arti nauticæ prior illa unicè interſerviat, quæ
Motus cæleſtes accuratiùs multò, quam nobis ſperandum
videtur, cognitos ſupponit; ob Aſtronomiæ Imperfectio-
nem, & Obſervationum marinarum Hallucinationem
perpetuo ferè neceſſariam : ſupra pronunciavimus Longitudinis Scientiam nauticam vix unquam de Cœlo
expectandam.*

    *Methodus altera, Geographiæ perficiendæ idonea,
cum non aliam ob cauſam prævium Calculum adhibeat,
niſi ut eo moniti plures, eidem Phænomeno, in diſſitis
locis, obſervando ſimul invigilent; Periodorum atque
Epocharum ἀκρίβειαν minimè deſiderat.*

    *Satellites Jovis numero ſunt quatuor, varia apud
Authores Nomina ſortiti; nos ex diverſis, quæ a Jove
obtinent Intervallis, 1. Intimum, 2. Penintimum,
3. Penextimum, 4. Extimum appellabimus.*

Horum

Horum non niſi uniuſmodi Φαινόμδρον *obſervandum proponimus ; Immerſionem nempè in Umbram Jovis ſive ipſum Eclipſεως initium.*

Solam hanc Φάσιν *ſeligimus, utpote in indiviſibili ferè conſtitutam : Licet enim Luminis Languor atque Diminutio Moram aliquantulam trahere poſſit, omnimoda tamen Extinctio & Evaneſcentia (de qua unicè ſoliciti ſumus) Momento quaſi contingere deprehendetur.*

Ante 8 ⊙ ♃ *Satellites ad Occidentem, Diſci Jovialis Reſpectu, in Deliquia incidunt ; poſt Acronychia, ad Orientem.*

Intimi & (niſi fortè rariſſimè) penintimi Eclipſεων tantum Occidentalium Initia nobis apparere poſſunt : duorum autem remotiorum multa etiam Orientalium Exordia conſpicere licet.

Defectus Medicæorum Obſervatu faciliores reddant. 1. *Major Planetarum Claritas.* 2. *Motus ipſorum tardior.* 3. *Penumbra Jovis craſſior.* 4. *Longius a Joviali Diſco Intervallum : ad Obſervationum* ἀκρ*ι*βεί*αν conducit.* 1. *Motus Satellitum velocior.* 2. *Penumbra Jovis anguſtior.*

Hæc omnia nobiſcum meditati, ſubducta benè ſingulorum Ratione, Satellitum intimum & penextimum ad Rem noſtram præ cæteris accomodatos; atque adeo, cum ſatis frequentes ſint ipſorum Eclipſes, ſolos adhibendos eſſe judicamus.

Extimum omninò negligimus, utpotè minimum omnium & obſcuriſſimum ; præſertim verò quod tantâ nonnunquam ſit Latitudine præditus, ut Umbra Jovis ipſum Aphelium neutiquam attingat.

Penintimus autem nullâ gaudet ex ſuprà recenſitis Prærogativâ, quæ alterutri ſaltem eorum, quos jam prætulimus, potiori Jure non debeatur.

Maxima Satellitum in Umbra incidentium a Limbo

A a *Diſci*

Difci Jovialis Diftantia, unâ aut alterâ, poft priorem Solis & Jovis Quadraturam, Hebdomadâ contingit.

Eftque ea penextimi Sefquidiametro Jovis ferè æqualis : Intimi verò Semidiametro ejufdem non multò major, fextâ ante memoratam Quadraturam Hebdomadâ. Penextimus Umbram ingrediens Diametro Jovis à Difco abeft: Augendâ indè ufque ad maximam Diftantiâ, Incremento non uniformi, fed continuè decrefcente.

Hinc iifdem reciprocè paffibus (Decremento fc. fenfim increfcente) diminuitur iftiufmodi Intervallum, ad bimeftre ufque Tempus à dictâ Quadraturâ elapfum, quando iterum Diametro Joviali æquatur.

Poftea autem ufque ad ipfa Acronychia, penextimus Umbram fubiturus, æquabili ferè Gradu (fingulis nempe Hebdomadis Quadrante Diametri) promotus, ad Limbum Jovis accedit. Intimi, pro diverfo Jovis ad Solem Situ, Diftantia eâdem planè ratione variatur : ejus enim, quam ubique obtinet, penextimus, Trienti ferè perpetuo eft æqualis.

Menfe circiter poft Jovem Soli oppofitum, penextimus (Intimi poft 8 ☉ ♃, Immerfiones obfervari non poffe fupra innuimus) fimul ac Corporis Jovialis Limbum orientalem tranfierit, occidentalem Umbra continuo intrabit.

Inde augetur paulatim penextimi evanefcentis Diftantia, donec unâ aut alterâ ante pofteriorem Quadraturam Hebdomadâ, maxima evadat ; quando à Difci Jovialis Margine Semidiametro ejufdem removetur.

Poftquam autem hucufque diminutâ fenfim Velocitate, Umbra Jovis ab ipfius Difco receffit : hinc, Motu continuè accelerato, ad eundem redit.

Per bimeftre ante & poft Jovis cum Sole Conjunctionem Spatium, in Locis Longitudine multum differentibus, eadem Eclipfis apparere nequit: adeoque tunc

I   *Temporis*

Temporis Obfervationes inftituere non eft Operæ Pre-tium.

Quæ cum ita fint, Tempus quadrimeftre, à Sextili priori ufque ad ipfa ferè Acronychia numerandum, utri-que Satelliti obfervando erit unice opportunum : Pe-nextimi autem foli, infuper trimeftre, ab altero poft Oppofitionem menfe ad Sextilem pofteriorem.

Intra tempora jam definita, octoginta circiter utriuf-que fimul Satellitis fient Eclipfes ; penextimi fc. fere triginta, intimi autem quinquaginta.

Has cum non ubivis terrarum, fed aliæ aliis in locis fint confpiciendæ,in fex Claffes digeremus.

1. *In Europâ & Africâ.*
2. *In Afiâ.*
3. *In Americâ.*
4. *In Europa Africa & Afia.*
5. *In Europa Africa & America.*
6. *In Afia Orient.& America Occident.*

} *Eclipfes ob-fervandas compre-hendet.*

Non opus eft fortè ut moneamus in Infulis

Oceani { *Æthiopici / Atlantici / Pacifici* } *obfervandam effe claffem* { 4am. / 5am. / 6am.

Calculus Eclipfium à nobis exhibendus in ipfo fortaf-fe Loco ad quem inftituitur,plus Horâ integrâ nonnun-quam à vero obfervabit, ob variam fc. in Satellitum motu ἀνομαλίαν, ab Excentricitate (ut verifimile eft) & propriarum ipfis Orbitarum ad Jovis Orbitam In-clinatione oriundam.

Alibi autemTerrarum multo minusCalculo fidendum, propter incertam infuper in plerifque Locis Meridiano-

rum Differentiam; quæ tamen ut fiat, Reductio Temporis aliqua utcunque adhibenda est.

Longam itaque futuram sæpiuscule Eclipsium harum Expectationem præmonemus, assiduamque interim Attentionem, nec (ob καιρὸν admodum ʼὀξὺν) unquam fere interruptam, esse continuandam: primum enim, quum Visu assequi possumus Luminis Diminutionem, brevissimâ (præsertim in intimo) interpositâ Morulâ, mox insequitur perfecta ejus Extinctio.

Molestum autem in observando Tædium, summa Τηρήσεων ἀκριβεία abunde compensabit, idemque plurimum minuit, Sociorum mutuas operas tradentium, ubi suppetit, Præsentia.

Ad Momenta Temporis accuratissime notanda (quod in hujusmodi Observationibus est Palmarium) perutile erit Horologium Oscillatorium, ab ingeniosissimo & candidissimo Hugenio feliciter excogitatum.

APPENDIX.

L Ongitudinis Scientiam Nauticam vix unquam de Cælo expectandam, suprà asseruimus; siqua tamen ejusmodi aliquando futura est, non aliud Fundamentum, quam Lunarium Motuum præcisam Cognitionem, habitura videtur. Horum autem Restitutionem a Parallaxi inchoandam, solertissime monuit Keplerus. Parallaxeως verò indagandæ, & à Lunæ latitudine (cui semper ferè complicatur) distinguendæ, optima (si non sola) Methodus est, quæ, in Regionibus longe dissitis & sub eodem Meridiano positis, Altitudinum Lunæ meridianarum, per singulas Orbitæ Partes simul observatarum Serie innititur: inde enim, Polorum Elevatione solum præcognitâ, certissima innotescit Globi Lunaris à Terrestri Distantia.*

I

*Proponimus itaque nos Africæ Promontorium Cap.
Bonæ Spei, vel in Oceano Atlantico Sanctæ Helenæ Insulam, cum Locis in Europâ iis respondentibus, Satellitum
Ope, ut docuimus, determinandis, in quibus istiusmodi
Observationes commodissimè instituantur.*

Upon the reading of these last *Directions*, Mr.
Rook the Author of them being dead, I cannot forbear saying something of that excellent Man, which
his incomparable *Modesty* would not have permitted me to write, if he had been living. He was indeed a Man of a profound *Judgment*, a vast *Comprehension*, prodigious *Memory*, solid *Experience*. His *Skill*
in the *Mathematicks* was reverenc'd, by all the Lovers
of those Studies; and his *Perfection* in many other
Sorts of Learning deserves no less Admiration. But
above all, his *Knowledge* had a right Influence on the
Temper of his Mind, which had all the Humility,
Goodness, Calmness, Strength, and Sincerity of a
sound and unaffected *Philosopher*. This is spoken, not
of one who liv'd long ago, in praising of whom it were
easie to *feign* and to exceed the *Truth*, where no Man's
Memory could confute me: but of one who is lately
dead, who has many of his Acquaintance still living,
that are able to confirm this *Testimony*, and to join
with me, in delivering down his Name to Posterity,
with this just Character of his *Virtues*. He died in the
year sixty two, shortly after the Establishment of the
Royal Society, whose *Institution* he had zealously promoted. And it was a deplorable Accident in his
Death, that he deceas'd the *very Night* which he had
for some Years expected, wherein to finish his accurate Observations on the *Satellites* of *Jupiter*: however this *Treasure* will not be lost, for the *Society* has
refer'd

refer'd it to fome of the beft *Aftronomers* of *Europe*, to bring his Beginnings to Conclufion.

Sect. XXXI.
Their Pro-
pofals and
Recommen-
dations.

To many of thefe *Queries* they have already re-ceiv'd good *Returns*, and *Satisfaction* ; and more fuch *Accounts* are daily expected from all Coafts.   Befides thefe, there have been feveral great and profitable *Attempts*, relating to the Good of Mankind, or the *Englifh Nation*, propounded to them by many publick Bodies, and private Perfons; which they have again recommended, to be examin'd apart by diverfe of their own *Number*, and by other Men of *Ability* and *Inte-grity*, who have accepted of their *Recommendations* of this Kind : The principal that I find recorded in their *Regifters*, are thefe.

They have propounded the compofing a *Catalogue* of all *Trades, Works*, and *Manufactures*, wherein Men are employ'd; in order to the collecting each of their Hiftories, by taking notice of all the phyfical Re-ceipts or Secrets, the Inftruments, Tools, and Engines, the manual Operations or Slights, the Cheats and ill Practices, the Goodnefs, Bafenefs, and different *Value* of Materials, and whatever elfe belongs to the Ope-rations of all *Trades*.

They have recommended the making a *Catalogue* of all the Kinds of *natural Things* to be found in *Eng-land*.   This is already in a very good Forwardnefs : And for its better completing, many *Expedients* for the preferving, drying, and embalming of all living Creatures have been profecuted.

They have fuggefted the making a perfect *Survey*, *Map*, and *Tables*, of all the fix'd Stars within the *Zo-diac*, both vifible to the naked Eye, and difcoverable by a fix-foot *Telefcope*, with a large Aperture ; towards
the

the obferving the apparent Places of the Planets, with a *Telefcope,* both by Sea and Land. This has been approv'd, and begun, feveral of the *Fellows* having their Portions of the Heavens allotted to them.

They have recommended the advancing of the *Manufacture* of *Tapeftry* : the improving of *Silk-making* : the propagating of *Saffron:* the melting of *Lead-Oar* with Pit-coal : the making Iron with Sea-c   : the ufing of the Duft of black Lead inftead of ('n Clocks : the making *Trials* on *Englifh* Earths, to   : if they will not yield fo fine a Subftance as *China,* for the perfecting of the Potter's Art.

They have *propounded* and *undertaken* the comparing of feveral *Soils* and *Clays,* for the better making of *Bricks* and *Tiles:* the Way of turning *Water* into *Earth*; the obferving of the Growth of Pebbles in Waters : the making exact *Experiments* in the large *Florentine* Loadftone : the Confideration of the *Bononian* Stone : the examining of the Nature of *petrifying Springs:* the ufing an *Umbrella Anchor,* to ftay a Ship in a Storm : the Way of finding the *Longitude* o Places by the *Moon:* the Obfervation of the Tides about *Lundy,* the Southweft of *Ireland,* the *Bermudas,* and diverfe parts of *Scotland:* and in other Seas and Rivers, where the ebbing and flowing is found to be irregular.

They have ftarted, and begun to practife, the Propagation of *Potatoes*; the planting of *Verjuyce Grapes* in *England*; the chymical Examination of *French* and *Englifh* Wines; the gradual Obfervation of the Growth of *Plants,* from the firft Spot of Life; the increafing of *Timber,* and the planting of Fruit-Trees; which they have done by fpreading the Plants into many Parts of the Nation, and by publifhing a

large

large *Account* of the beft Ways of their Cultivation.

They have propounded, and attempted with great
Effeƈt, the making *Experiments* with *Tobacco Oil*;
the anatomifing of all amphibious Creatures, and
examining their Lungs ; the obferving the Manner
of the *Circulation* of the Blood in Fiſhes ; the Ways
of tranfporting Fiſh from one Place to another for
Breed ; the *collecting Obfervations* on the *Plague* ;
the examining of all the feveral Ways to breed *Bees* ;
the altering the Tafte of the Fleſh of *Animals*, by altering their Food ; the Probability of making *Wine*
out of *Sugar-Canes :* Which laft I will fet down as
one Example.

A

A

PROPOSAL
For making WINE.

By Dr. *GODDARD*.

IT is recommended to the Care of *some* skilful *Plan-ters in* Barbadoes, *to try whether good Wine may not be made out of the Juice of Sugar-canes. That which may induce them to believe this Work to be possible, is this Observation, that the Juice of Wine, when it is dried, does always granulate into Sugar, as appears in Raisins, or dried Grapes : and also that in those Vessels wherein a cute, or unfermented Wine is put, the Sides are wont to be cover'd over with a Crust of Sugar. Hence it may be gather'd, that there is so great a Likeness of the Liquor of the Cane, to that of the Vine, that it may probably be brought to serve for the same Uses. If this Attempt shall succeed, the Advantages of it will be ve-ry considerable. For the English being the chief Masters of the Sugar Trade, and that falling very much in its Price of late Years, while all other outlandish Producti-ons are risen in their Value ; it would be a great Benefit to this Kingdom, as well as to our Western Plantati-ons, if Part of our Sugar, which is now in a manner a meer Drug, might be turn'd into Wine, which is a foreign Commodity, and grows every Day dearer ; espe-cially seeing this might be done, by only bruising and pres-sing the Canes, which would be a far less Labour and Charge, than the Way by which Sugar is now made.*

B b   Thefe

These are some of the most advantageous *Proposals* they have scatter'd and incouraged in all Places, where their Interest prevails. In these they have recommended to many distinct and separate *Trials*, those Designs, which some private Men had begun, but could not accomplish, by reason of their *Charge*; or those which they themselves have devis'd, and conceiv'd capable of Success; or even those of which Men have hitherto seem'd to despair. Of these, some are already brought to a hopeful Issue; some are put in Use, and thrive by the Practice of the publick; and some are discover'd to be feasible, which were only before thought imaginary, and fantastical. This is one of the greatest *Powers* of the true and unwearied *Experimenter*, that he often rescues Things from the Jaws of those dreadful Monsters, *Improbability*, and *Impossibility*. These indeed are two frightful Words to weaker Minds, but by diligent and wise Men, they are generally found to be only the Excuses of *Idleness* and *Ignorance*. For the most part, they lie not in the Things themselves, but in Men's false *Opinions* concerning them; they are rais'd by *Opinions*, but are soon abolish'd by *Works*. Many *Things*, that were at first improbable to the Minds of Men, are not so to their Eyes: many that seem'd impracticable to their *Thoughts*, are quite otherwise to their *Hands:* many that are too difficult for their naked Hands, may be soon perform'd by the same Hands, if they are strengthen'd by *Instruments*, and guided by *Method:* many that are unmanageable by a few Hands, and a few Instruments, are easie to the joint Force of a Multitude: many that fail in one *Age*, may succeed by the renew'd Endeavours of *another*. It is not therefore the Conceit or Fancy of Men alone, that is of sufficient

cient Authority to condemn the moſt unlikely Things for *impoſſible*; unleſs they have been often attempted in vain, by many *Eyes,* many *Hands,* many *Inſtruments,* and many *Ages.*

    This is the *Aſſiſtance* and *Information* they have given to others to provoke them to enquire, and to order and regulate their *Inquiſitions.* To theſe I will add the *Relations* of the Effects of *Nature* and *Art,* which have been communicated to them. Theſe are infinite in number : And though many of them have not a ſufficient Confirmation to raiſe *Theories,* or *Hiſtories* on their *Infalibillity* ; yet they bring with them a good Aſſurance of Likelihood, by the Integrity of the *Relators* ; and withal they furniſh a judicious *Reader* with admirable Hints to direct his Obſervations. For I will once more affirm, that as the Minds of Men do often miſtake *Falſhoods* for *Truths,* though they are ever ſo circumſpect; ſo they are often drawn by uncertain, and ſometimes erroneous *Reports,* to ſtumble on *Truths* and *Realities.* Of this vaſt Heap of *Relations,* which is every where ſcatter'd in their *Entry Books,* I will only take notice of theſe occaſional *Accounts.*

Sect. XXXII
The Relations of Things of Nature and Art, they have receiv'd.

    Relations of two new Kinds of *Stars,* obſerv'd in the Year ſixty ſix, the one in *Andromeda,* the other in *Cygnus,* in the ſame Place where they appear'd ſixty Years ſince, and have ever ſince diſappear'd ; of ſeveral Obſervations of *Cœleſtial Bodies* made in *Spain*; of Obſervations of ſeveral of the *Planets* made at *Rome,* and in other Parts, by extraordinary *Glaſſes* ; of the comparative Goodneſs of *Glaſſes* us'd in other Countries; of ſeveral *Eclipſes* obſerv'd in diverſe Parts of the World.

    Relations of *Parhelii,* and other ſuch Appearances

feen in *France* ; of the Effects of *Thunder* and *Light-ning* ; of *Hurricanes*, and *Spouts* ; of the Bigness, Fi-gure, and Effects of *Hailftones* ; of *Fifh*, and *Frogs* faid to be rain'd ; of the raining of Duft out of the *Air*, and of the Diftance it has been carried by great *Fires* and *Earthquakes* ; of Changes of Weather, and a Way of predicting them ; of the Vermination of the *Air* ; of the fuppos'd raining of *Wheat* in *Glocefterfhire*, which being fown was found to be nothing but *Ivy Berries.*

Relations of a *Spring* in *Lancafhire*, that will pre-fently catch Fire on the Approach of a Flame ; of *Burning-glaffes* performing extraordinary Effects ; of *Burning glaffes* made with Ice ; of *Fire-balls* for Fuel ; of a more convenient Way of ufing *Wax-Candles* ; of the kindling of certain Stones, by their being moi-ften'd with Water ; of ufing ordinary Fuel to the beft Advantage.

Relations of the Times of the rifing and difappear-ing of *Springs* ; of Artificial *Springs* ; of the Natures of feveral of our *Englifh Springs*, and of other *olea-ginous* and *bituminous Springs* : of the Fitnefs and Unfitnefs of fome Waters for the making of *Beer* or *Ale* ; of brewing Beer with *Ginger* inftead of *Hops* ; of *Tides* and *Currents* ; of *petrifying Springs* ; of the Water-blafts of *Tivoly* ; of *floating Iflands* of *Ice* ; of the fhining of *Dew* in a Common of *Lancafhire*, and elfewhere ; of *Divers*, and *Diving*, their Habit, their long holding their Breath, and of other notable *Things* obferv'd by them.

Relations of the Effects of *Earthquakes*, and the moving and finking of Earths ; of deep *Mines*, and deep *Wells* ; of the feveral Layers of Earth in a Well at *Amfterdam* ; of the fhining Cliffs in *Scotland* ; of the Layers of Earth obferv'd in diverfe Cliffs ; of *Screw-*
                                                              Stones,

Stones, Lignum Foffile, Blocks buried in *Exeter* River, Trees found under Ground in *Chefhire, Lincolnfhire,* and elfewhere; of a Coal-Mine wrought half a Mile from the Shoar, under the Sea; of the fatal Effects of *Damps* on *Miners,* and the Ways of recovering them.

Relations of the extraordinary Strength of fome fmall *Loadftones,* taking up above 150 Times their own Weight; of feveral *Englifh Loadftones*; of the Variation of the *Loadftone* obferv'd in two *Eaft-India* Voyages, and other Places; of the growing of *Pebbles* inclos'd in a Glafs of Water; of feveral excellent *Englifh* Clays; of Gold found in little Lumps in a Mine in *England*; of the moving Sands in *Norfolk*

Relations about refining *Lead,* and *Tin-Oar*; of hardning *Steel* fo as to cut *Porphyry* with it, and foftning it fo much, as to make it eafie to be wrought on; of impregnating *Lead Oar* with *Metal,* after it has been once freed; of *petrify'd Teeth,* and a petrify'd human *Fœtus*; of feveral Ways of fplitting Rocks; of living Mufcles found in the midft of Rocks at *Leghorn*; of the Way of making *Quick-filver*; of Things obfervable at the Bottom of the Sea; of a foft Metal, which hardens after it has taken off the Impreffion, and the Way of reducing fuch Impreffions into as fmall a Proportion as is defir'd.

Relations about *Agriculture*; of ordering of *Vines*; of the fetting and planting of Trees feveral Ways; of *Elms* growing from Chips, of new Trees fprung from rotten Roots; of feveral Kinds of Trees, growing one out of another, and in the Place of others; of the beft Ways of Pruning; of making a Kind of Silk with *Virginia* Grafs; of a Kind of Grafs making ftronger Ropes than the common Hemp; of a new Way of ordering *Mulberry* Trees in

2 *Virginia;*

Virginia; of a *Locuſt*-Tree *Bow* ſtanding bent ſix Months without loſing its *Spring* ; of a Way of improving the Planting of *Tobacco*.

Relations of the Uſefulneſs of changing Seed yearly ; of the ſteeping, liming, ſowing it ſeveral Ways ; of freeing it from Worms; preſerving it long (as *eighty Years*) of freeing it from *Smut* ; of the Cauſes and firſt Signs of *Smut* ; of the *Inſtrument* and Way of chopping Straw, for the feeding of *Horſes* ; of Plants growing in *meer Water*; of others growing in *meer Air* ; of ſeveral *Indian* Woods ; of the growing of the divided Parts of *Beans*, of the growing of chop'd Stalks of *Potatoes*; of ordering *Melons* ; of keeping their Seed, and producing extraordinary good ones without *Tranſplanting*.

Relations of the Growth, Breeding, Feeding, and Ordering of *Oiſters* ; of a *Sturgeon* kept alive in Saint *James's-Park* ; of the moveable Teeth of *Pikes* ; of young *Eeles* cut alive out of the old ones Belly ; of the tranſporting Fiſh ſpawn, and *Carps* alive from one Place to another ; of the ſtrange Increaſe of *Carps* ſo tranſported ; of *Snake-Stones* and other *Antidotes* ; of *Frogs, Frog-ſpawn, Toads, Newts, Vipers, Snakes, Rattle-Snakes*.

Relations of ſeveral Kinds of *Poiſons*, as that of *Maccaſſar*, and *Florence* ; of *Craw-fiſhes* ; of the Generation, Growth, Life, and Tranformation of *Ants* ; of *Cheeſe Worms* leaping like *Fleas* ; of living Worms found in the Entrails of *Fiſhes*; of *Inſects* found in the ſheathing of Ships ; of the Generation of *Inſects* out of dead *Cantharides* ; of *Inſects* bred in Men's Teeth, Gums, Fleſh, Skin ; of great Quantities of *Flies* living in Winter, though frozen ; of the Ways of ordering *Silk-Worms* in *France, Italy, Virginia* ; and of their not being hurt in *Virginia* by Thunder.

Rela-

Relations of *Swallows* living after they had been frozen under Water ; of *Barnacles* and *Solan Geefe*, of a new Way of hatching *Pigeons* ; of the Way of hatching *Chickens* in *Egypt* ; of *Eggs* proving fruitful, after they had been frozen ; of recovering a *tir'd Horfe* with *Sheep's Blood*.

Relations of feveral Monfters with their Anatomies ; of the Meafure of a Giant-Child ; of Stones found in feveral Parts of the Body ; of an unufual Way of cutting the Stone out of the *Bladder* ; of a Woman's voiding the *Bones* of a *Child* out of her Side, eighteen Years after her having been *with Child* ; of grafting Teeth, and making the Teeth of one Man grow in the Mouth of another.

Relations of feveral *Chirurgical* Operations ; of renewing the beating of the Heart, by blowing into the *Receptaculum Chyli* ; of the *Art* of perfectly reftoring Nerves tranfverfly cut, practis'd in *France* ; of a *Mummy* found in the Ruins of St. *Paul's*, after it had lain buried above 200 Years ; of breaking the Nerve to the *Diaphragm*, and of its Effects ; of cutting a *Stetoma* out of a Woman's Breaft ; of making the Blood florid with *Volatile*, and *coagulating* with *Acid* Salts.

Relations of fympathetick Cures and Trials ; of the Effects of *Tobacco Oil* for cafting into Convulfion Fits ; of *Moors* killing themfelves by holding their Breaths ; of walking on the Water by the Help of a Girdle filled with Wind ; of *Pendulum* Clocks ; of feveral rare Guns, and Experiments with them ; of new *Quadrants* and *Aftronomical* Inftruments ; of Experiments of *Refraction* made by the *French Academy* ; of a Way to make ufe of Eggs in Painting, inftead of Oil ; of the Ifland *Hirta* in *Scotland* ; of the *whifpering Place* at *Glocefter* ; of the *Pike* of *Tenariff*. .   2   A

A

RELATION

OF THE

𝒫*ICO TENERIFFE.*

RECEIV'D FROM

Some confiderable Merchants and Men
worthy of Credit, who went to the Top
of it.

"   HAving furnifhed our felves with a Guide, Ser-
"   vants, and Horfes to carry our Wine and
" Provifions, we fet out from *Oratava,* a Port Towu
" in the Ifland of *Teneriffe,* fituated on the *North* of
" it, two Miles diftant from the main Sea. We tra-
" velled from twelve at Night till eight in the Morn-
" ing, by which Time we got to the Top of the firft
" Mountain towards the *Pico de Terraira ;* here, un-
" der a very great and confpicuous Pine-Tree, we
" brake our Faft, dined and refrefh'd our felves till
" two in the Afternoon; then we procceded through
" much fandy Way, over many lofty Mountains, but
" naked and bare, and not cover'd with any Pine
" Trees, as our firft Night's Paffage was. This expofed
" us to exceffive Heat, till we arrived at the Foot of
" the *Pico* ; where we found many huge Stones,
" which feem'd to have been fallen down from fome
" upper Part.

                                                " About

" About fix a Clock this Evening, we began to af-
" cend up the *Pico*, but being now a Mile advanced,
" and the Way no more paflable for our Horfes, we
" quitted and left them with our Servants: In this
" Mile's Afcent fome of our Company grew very faint
" and fick, diforder'd by Fluxes, Vomitings, and aguifh
" Diftempers, our Horfes Hair ftanding upright like
" Briftles ; but calling for fome of our Wine, which
" was carried in fmall Barrels on a Horfe, we found
" it fo wonderfully cold, that we could not drink it
" till we had kindled a Fire to warm it, although yet
" the Temper of the Air was very calm and mode-
" rate.   But when the Sun was fet, it began to blow
" with that Violence, and grew fo cold, that taking
" up our Lodging under certain great Stones in the
" Rocks, we were conftrained to keep great Fires be-
" fore the Mouths of them all Night.

" About four in the Morning we began to mount
" again, and being come about a Mile up, one of the
" Company fail'd, and was able to proceed no far-
" ther.   Here began the black Rocks.   The reft of
" us purfued our Journey till we came to the *Sugar-*
" *loaf*, where we began to travel again in a white
" Sand, being fore-fhod with Shoes whofe fingle Soles
" are made a Finger broader than the upper Leather,
" to encounter this difficult and unftable Paffage ;
" being afcended as far as the black Rocks, which
" are all flat, and lie like a Pavement, we climbed
" within a Mile of the Top of the *Pico*, and at
" laft we gained the *Summit*, where we found no fuch
" Smoak as appeared a little below, but a continual
" breathing of a hot and fulphurous Vapour, which
" made our Faces extremely fore.

" In this Paffage we found no confiderable Altera-
C c
" tion

" tion of Air, and very little Wind; but being at the
" top, it was fo impetuous, that we had much ado to
" ftand againft it, whilft we drank the King's Health,
" and fired each of us a Piece. Here we alfo brake
" Faft, but found our Strong-water had quite loft its
" Force, and was become almoft infipid, whilft our
" Wine was rather more fpirituous and brisk than
" it was before.

" The Top on which we ftood, being not above a
" Yard broad, is the Brink of a Pit called the *Caldera*,
" which we judged to be about a Musket-fhot over,
" and near fourfcore Yards deep, in Shape like a *Cone*,
" within hollow like a Kettle or Cauldron, and all
" over cover'd with fmall loofe Stones mixt with
" Sulphur and Sand, from amongft which iffue diverfe
" Spiracles of Smoak and Heat, when ftirred with any
" thing puffs and makes a noife, and fo offenfive, that
" we were almoft ftifled with the fudden Emanation
" of Vapours upon the removing of one of thefe
" Stones, which are fo hot as they are not eafily to be
" handled. We defcended not above four or five
" Yards into the *Caldera*, in regard of its fliding from
" our Feet and the Difficulty. But fome have ad-
" ventured to the Bottom. Other obfervable Mate-
" rials we difcover'd none, befides a clear fort of *Sul-*
" *phur*, which looks like Salt upon the Stones.

" From this famous *Pico*, we could ken the *Grand*
" *Canaria*, fourteen Leagues diftant, *Palma* eighteen,
" and *Gomera* feven Leagues, which Interval of Sea
" feem'd to us not much larger than the River of
" *Thames* about *London:* We difcerned alfo the *Her-*
" *ro*, being diftant above twenty Leagues, and fo to the
" utmoft Limits of the Sea much farther.

" So foon as the Sun appeared, the Shadow of the
" *Pico*

" *Pico* feemed to cover, not only the whole Ifland,
" and the *Grand Canaries*, but the Sea to the very
" *Horizon*, where the Top of the *Sugar-loaf* or *Pico*
" vifibly appeared to turn up and caft its Shade into
" the Air it felf, at which we were much furprized :
" But the Sun was not far afcended, when the Clouds
" began to rife fo faft, as intercepted our Profpect
" both of the Sea, and the whole Ifland, excepting
" only the Tops of the fubjacent Mountains, which
" feem'd to pierce them through : Whether thefe
" Clouds do ever furmount the *Pico* we cannot fay,
" but to fuch as are far beneath, they fometimes feem
" to hang above it, or rather wrap themfelves about
" it, as conftantly when the North-weft Wind blows ;
" this they call the *Cappe*, and is a certain Progno-
" ftick of enfuing Storms.

" One of our Company, who made this Journey
" again two Years after, arriving at the Top of the
" *Pico* before Day, and creeping under a great Stone
" to fhrowd himfelf from the cold Air (after a little
" Space) found himfelf all wet, and perceived it to
" come from a perpetual trickling of Water from the
" Rocks above him. Many excellent and very
" exuberant Springs we found iffuing from the Tops
" of moft of the other Mountains, gufhing out in
" great Spouts, almoft as far as the huge Pine-Tree
" which we mention'd.

" Having ftay'd fome time upon the Top, we all
" defcended by the fandy Way till we came to the
" Foot of the *Sugar-loaf*, which being fteep, even
" to almoft a Perpendicular, we foon paffed. And here
" we met a Cave of about ten Yards deep, and fifteen
" broad, being in Shape like an Oven or *Cupola*, having
" a Hole at the Top which is near eight Yards over ;

" by

" by this we defcended by a Rope, which our Ser-
" vants held at the Top, whilft the other end being
" faftned about our Middles, we fwing our felves,
" till being over a Bank of Snow, we flide down and
" light upon it.   We were forced to fwing thus in
" the Defcent, becaufe in the middle of the Bottom
" of this Cave, oppofite to the Overture at the Top, is
" a round Pit of Water, refembling a Well, the Sur-
" face whereof is about a Yard lower than the Snow,
" but as wide as the Mouth at Top, and is about fix
" Fathom deep. We fuppofe this Water not a Spring,
" but diffolv'd Snow blown in, or Water trickling
" through the Rocks.

   " About the Sides of the Grot, for fome height,
" there is Ice and Icicles hanging down to the Snow.
" But being quickly weary of this exceffive cold
" Place, and drawn up again, we continued our De-
" fcent from the Mountains by the fame Paffages we
" went up the Day before, and fo about five in the
" Evening arrived at *Oratava*, from whence we fet
" forth, our Faces fo red and fore, that to cool them,
" we were forced to wafh and bath them in Whites
" of Eggs, *&c.*

   " The whole Height of the *Pico* in perpendicular
" is vulgarly efteem'd to be two Miles and a half. No
" Trees, Herbs, or Shrubs in all the Paffage but Pines,
" and amongft the whiter Sands a kind of Broom,
" being a bufhy Plant; and at the fide where we lay
" all Night, a kind of *Cordon*, which hath Stems of
" eight Foot high, the Trunk near half a Foot thick,
" every Stem growing in four Squares, and emerging
" from the Ground like Tuffets of Rufhes; upon the
" Edges of thefe Stems grow very fmall red Buttons
" or Berries, which being fqueezed produc'd a poy-

                    +   " fonous

" fonous Milk, which lighting upon any Part of a
" Horfe, or other Beaft, fetches off the Hair from
" the Skin immediately ; of the dead Part of this we
" made our Fires all Night.   This Plant is alfo uni-
" verfally fpread over the Ifland, and is perhaps a
" Kind of *Euphorbium.*

    " Of the Ifland *Teneriffe* it felf, this Account was
" given by a judicious and inquifitive Man, who liv'd
" twenty Years in it as a Phyfician and Merchant.
" His Opinion is, that the whole Ifland being a Ground
" mightily impregnated with Brimftone,   did in for-
" mer Times take Fire, and blow up all or near upon
" all at the fame Time, and that many Mountains of
" huge Stones calcin'd and burnt, which appear every
" where about the Ifland, efpecially in the South-
" weft Parts of it, were rais'd and heav'd up out of
" the Bowels of the Earth, at the Time of that ge-
" neral Conflagration; and that the greateft Quanti-
" ty of this Sulphur lying about the Center of the
" Ifland, raifed up the *Pico* to that Height at which
" it is now feen.   And he fays, that any one upon the
" Place that fhall carefully note the Situation and
" Manner of thefe calcin'd Rocks how they lye, will
" eafily be of that Mind : For he fays, that they lye
" for three or four Miles almoft round the Bottom of
" the *Pico*, and in fuch Order one above the other al-
" moft to the very *Sugar Loaf* (as 'tis called) as if
" the whole Ground fwelling and rifing up together
" by the Afcenfion of the Brimftone, the Torrents
" and Rivers of it did with a fudden Eruption rowl
" and tumble them down from the reft of the Rocks,
" efpecially (as was faid before) to the South-weft :
" For on that fide, from the very top of the *Pico* al-
                                moft

" moſt to the Sea-ſhoar, lye hugeHeaps of theſe burnt
" Rocks, one under another.   And there remain to
" this time the very Tracts of the Rivers of Brim-
" ſtone, as they ran over all this Quarter of the Iſland,
" which hath ſo waſted the Ground beyond Recovery,
" that nothing can be made to grow there but
" Broom : But on the North ſide of the *Pico,* few or
" none of theſe Stones appear.   And he concluded
" hence, that the *Volcanio* diſcharg'd it ſelf chiefly to
" the South-weſt.   He adds farther , that Mines of
" ſeveral Metals were broken and blown up at the
" ſame time.   Theſe calcin'd Rocks reſembling ſome
" of them Iron-Oar, ſome Silver, and others Copper.
" Particularly at a certain Place in theſe South-weſt
" Parts called the *Azuleios,* being very high Moun-
" tains, where never any *Engliſh* Man but himſelf
" (that ever he heard of) was.   There are vaſt Quan-
" tities of a looſe blewiſh Earth intermixt with blue
" Stones, which have on them yellow Ruſt as that
" of Copper and Vitriol : And likewiſe many little
" Springs of vitriolate Waters, where he ſuppoſes was
" a Copper Mine.   And he was told by a Bell-foun-
" der of *Oratava,* that out of two Horſe Loads of
" this Earth, he got as much Gold as made two large
" Rings. And a *Portugueze* told him, who had been
" in the *Weſt Indies,* that his Opinion was, there were
" as good Mines of Gold and Silver there as the beſt
" in the *Indies.*   There are likewiſe hereabout ni-
" trous Waters and Stones covered with a deep Saf-
" fron-colour'd Ruſt, and taſting of Iron.   And far-
" ther he mentions a Friend of his, who out of two
" Lumps of Earth or Oar, brought from the top of
" this ſide the Mountain, made two Silver-ſpoons. All
this

" this he confirms from the late Inftance of the *Palme*
" Ifland eighteen Leagues from *Tenariffa,* where a
" *Volcanio* was fired about twelve Years fince, the
" Violence whereof made an Earthquake in this Ifland
" fo great, that he and others ran out of their Houfes,
" fearing they would have fallen upon their Heads.
" They heard the Noife of the Torrents of flaming
" Brimftone like Thunder, and faw the Fire as plain
" by Night, for about fix Weeks together, as a Candle
" in the Room : And fo much of the Sand and Afhes,
" brought from thence by the Wind with Clouds,
" fell on his Hat, as fill'd a Sand Box for his Ink-
" horn.

   " In fome Part of this Ifland there grows a crooked
" Shrub which they call *Legnan,* which they bring
" for *England* as a fweet Wood : There are likewife
" Abricots, Peaches, *&c.* in Standard, which bear
" twice a Year, Pear-Trees alfo which are as pregnant :
" Almonds of a tender Shell ; Palms, Plantains, Oran-
" ges and Lemmons, efpecially the *Pregnadas* which
" have fmall ones in their Bellies, from whence they
" are fo denominated. Alfo they have Sugar-Canes,
" and a little Cotton. *Colloquintida, &c.* The Rofes
" blow at *Chriftmas.* There are good Carnations, and
" very large ; but Tulips will not grow or thrive there :
" Sampier cloaths the Rocks in Abundance, and
" a kind of Clover the Ground. Another Grafs
" growing near the Sea, which is of a broader Leaf,
" fo lufcious and rank, as it will kill a Horfe that eats
" of it, but no other Cattle. Eighty Ears of Wheat
" have been found to fpring from one Root, but it
" grows not very high. The Corn of this is tranfpa-
" rent and bright like to the pureft yellow Amber, and
one

" one Bufhel hath produc'd one hundred and thirty
" in a feafonable Year.

    " The Canary Birds (which they bring to us in
" *England*) breed in the *Barancos* or *Gills*, which
" the Water hath fretted away in the Mountains, be-
" ing Places very cold. There are alfo Quails, Par-
" tridges, larger than ours and exceeding beautiful,
" great Wood-pigeons, Turtles at Spring, Crows,
" and fometimes from the Coaft of *Barbary* appears
" the Falcon. Bees are carried into the Mountains,
" where they profper exceedingly.

    " They have wild Goats on the Mountains, which
" climb to the very top of the *Pico* fometimes: Alfo
" Hogs and Multitudes of Conies.

    " Of Fifh they have the Cherna, a very large and
" excellent Fifh, better tafted than any we have in
" *England*; the Mero, Dolphin, Shark, Lobfters
" without the great Claws, Mufcles, Periwinkles,
" and the Clacas, which is abfolutely the very beft
" Shell-Fifh in the World; they grow in the Rocks
" five or fix under one great Shell, through the top
" Holes whereof they peep out with their Nebs,
" from whence (the Shells being broken a little more
" open with a Stone) they draw them forth. There
" is likewife another Fifh like an Eel, which hath
" fix or feven Tails of a Span in Length united to
" one Head and Body, which is alfo as fhort. Be-
" fides thefe, they have Turtles and Cabridos which
" are better than our Trouts.

    " The Ifland is full of Springs of pure Water taft-
" ing like Milk. And in *Lalaguna* (where the Wa-
" ter is not altogether fo limpid and clear) they per-
" colate it through a kind of fpungy Stone cut in
" Form of a Bafon.   " The

" The Vines which afford thofe excellent Wines,
" grow all about the Ifland within a Mile of the Sea;
" fuch as are planted farther up are nothing efteem'd,
" neither will they thrive in any of the other Iflands.
" For the *Guanchios* or antient Inhabitants he
" gives this full Account.

" *September* the third, about twelve Years fince, he
" took his Journey from *Guimar* (a Town inhabited
" for the moft Part by fuch as derive themfelves from
" the old *Guanchios*) in the Company of fome of them,
" to view their Caves and the Bodies buried in them.
" This was a Favour they feldom or never permit to
" any (having in great Veneration the Bodies of their
" Anceftors, and likewife being moft extremely a-
" gainft any Moleftation of the Dead) but he had
" done feveral *eleemofynary* Cures amongft them (for
" they are generally very poor, yet the pooreft thinks
" himfelf too good to marry with the beft *Spaniard*)
" which indeared him to them exceedingly; other-
" wife it is Death for any Stranger to vifit thefe
" Caves or Bodies.

" Thefe Bodies are fowed up in Goat-skins with
" Thongs of the fame, with very great Curiofity, par-
" ticularly in the incomparable Exactnefs and Even-
" nefs of the Seams, and the Skins are made very loofe
" and fit to the Body. Moft of thefe Bodies are in-
" tire, the Eyes clofed, Hair on the Head, Ears, Nofe,
" Teeth, Lips, Beard, all perfect, only difcoloured and
" a little fhrivel'd, likewife the *Pudenda* of both Sexes;
" He faw about three or four hundred in feveral
" Caves, fome of them are ftanding, others lie on Beds
" of Wood, fo hardned by an Art they had (which the
" *Spaniards* call *Curar*, to cure a piece of Wood) as
D d   " no

" no Iron can pierce or hurt it. He fays, that one Day
" being hunting a Ferret (which is much in ufe there)
" having a Bell about his Neck, ran after a Coney in-
" to a Hole, where they loft the Sound of the Bell;
" the Owner being afraid he fhould lofe his Ferret,
" feeking about the Rock and Shrubs, found the
" Mouth of a Cave, and entring in, was fo affrighted,
" that he cried out. It was at the Sight of one of
" thefe Bodies, very tall and large, lying with his Head
" on a great Stone, his Feet fupported with a little
" Wall of Stone, the Body refting on a bed of Wood
" (as before was mention'd.) The Fellow being now a
" little out of his Fright entred it, and cut off a great
" Piece of the Skin that lay on the Breaft of this Body,
" which, the Doctor fays, was more flexible and pli-
" ant than ever he felt any Kids-leather Glove, and
" yet fo far from being rotten, that the Man ufed it
" for his Flail many Years after.

" Thefe Bodies are very light, as if made up of
" Straw, and in fome broken Limbs he obferv'd the
" Nerves and Tendons, and alfo fome Strings of the
" Veins and Arteries very diftinctly.

" His great Care was to enquire of thefe People
" what they had amongft them of Tradition con-
" cerning the Embalming and Prefervation of thefe
" Bodies: from fome of the eldeft of them (above
" a hundred and ten Years of Age) he received this
" Account, That they had of old one particular
" Tribe of Men that had this Art amongft themfelves
" only, and kept it as a thing facred, and not to be
" communicated to the Vulgar: Thefe mixt not with
" the reft of the Inhabitants, nor married out of their
" own Tribe, and were alfo their Priefts and Minifters
                                        " of

" of Religion : That upon the Conqueſt of the *Spa-*
" *niards* they were moſt of them deſtroy'd, and the
" Art loſt with them, only they held ſome Traditions
" yet of a few Ingredients, that were made uſe of
" in this Buſineſs. They took Butter of Goats Milk
" (ſome ſaid Hogs Greaſe was mingled with it) which
" they kept in the Skins for this purpoſe; in this they
" boiled certain Herbs; firſt a ſort of wild Laven-
" der, which grows there in great Quantities on the
" Rocks: Secondly, an Herb called Lara, of a very
" gummy and glutinous Conſiſtence, which now
" grows there under the Tops of the Mountains only :
" Thirdly, a kind of Cyclamen or Sow-bread : Fourth-
" ly, wild Sage, growing plentifully in this Iſland :
" Theſe with others bruiſed and boiled in the Butter,
" render'd it a perfect Balſam. This prepared, they
" firſt unbowelled the Corps (and in the poorer ſort,
" to ſave Charges, they took out the Brain behind,
" and theſe poor were alſo ſew'd up in Skins with
" the Hair on, whereas the richer ſort were, as was
" ſaid before, put up in Skins ſo finely and exactly
" dreſſed, as they remain moſt rearly pliant and gen-
" tle to this Day.) After the Body was thus order-
" ed, they had in Readineſs a *Lixivium* made of the
" Bark of Pine-trees, with which they waſht the Bo-
" dy, drying it in the Sun in Summer, and in Stoves
" in Winter, this repeating very often. Afterward
" they began their Unction with the Balſam, both
" without and within, drying it again as before. This
" they continued till the Balſam had penetrated in-
" to the whole Habit, and the Muſcles in all parts ap-
" peared through the contracted Skin, and the Body
" became exceeding light : Then they ſew'd them

" up

" up in the Goat-skins, as was mention'd already. He
" was told by thefe antient People, that they have
" above twenty Caves of their Kings and great Per-
" fons, with their whole Families, yet unknown to any
" but themfelves, and which they will never difcover.
" Laftly, he fays, that Bodies are found in the Caves
" of the *Grand Canaria* in Sacks, and quite confumed,
" not as thefe in *Teneriffa*. Thus far of the Bodies
" and embalming.

 " Antiently when they had no Knowledge of Iron,
" they made their Lances of Wood hardned as be-
" fore, fome of which the Doctor hath feen. He hath
" alfo feen Earthen-pots fo hard, that they cannot be
" broken ; of thefe fome are found in the Caves and
" old *Bavances*, and ufed by the poorer People that
" find them, to boil Meat in. Likewife they had *Cu-*
" *ror* Stone it felf, that is to fay, a Kind of Slate called
" now *Tobona*, which they firft formed to an Edge or
" Point as they had Occafion to ufe it, either as Knives
" or Lancets to let Blood withal.

 " Their Food is Barley roafted, and then ground
" with little Mills, which they made of Stone, and
" mixt with Milk and Honey : This they ftill feed
" on, and carry it on their Backs in Goat-skins.

 " To this Day they drink no Wine, nor care for
" Flefh. They are generally very lean, tall, active
" and full of Courage.

 " He himfelf hath feen them leap from Rock to
" Rock, from a very prodigious Height, till they
" came to the Bottom, fometimes making ten Fathom
" deep at one leap.

 " The manner is thus :

 " Firft they *teritate* their Lance (which is about
" the

" the Bignefs of a half Pike) that is, they poife it
" in their Hand, then they aim the Point of it at any
" Piece of a Rock, upon which they intend to light
" (fometimes not half a Foot broad.)   At their going
" off they clap their Feet clofe to the Lance, and fo
" carry their Bodies in the Air.   The Point of the
" Lance firft comes to the Place, which breaks the
" Force of their Fall; then they flide gently down
" by the Staff, and pitch with their Feet upon the
" very Place they firft defigned, and from Rock to
" Rock till they come to the Bottom.   Their
" Novices fometimes break their Necks in learn-
" ing.

" He added feveral Stories to this Effect of their
" great Activity in leaping down Rocks and Cliffs.
" And how twenty eight of them made an Efcape
" from the Battlements of an extraordinary high Ca-
" ftle in the Ifland, when the Governor thought he
" had made fure of them.

" He told alfo (and the fame was ferioufly con-
" firm'd by a *Spaniard*, and another *Canary* Mer-
" chant then in the Company) That they whiftle fo
" loud as to be heard five Miles off: And that to be
" in the fame Room with them when they whiftle,
" were enough to indanger breaking the *Tympanum*
" of the Ear, and added; that he (being in Compa-
" ny of one that whiftled his loudeft) could not hear
" perfectly for fifteen Days after, the Noife was fo
" great.

" He affirms alfo, That they throw Stones with a
" Force almoft as great as that of a Bullet, and now
" ufe Stones in all their Fights as they did antiently.

*   When

When my *Reader* shall behold this large Number of *Relations*; perhaps he will think, that too many of them seem to be incredible Stories, and that if the *Royal Society* shall much busy themselves, about such wonderful and uncertain *Events*, they will fall into that Mistake, of which I have already accus'd some of the *Antients*, of framing *Romances*, instead of solid *Histories* of Nature. But here, though I shall first confirm what I said before, that it is an unprofitable, and unsound Way of *Natural Philosophy*, to regard nothing else, but the prodigious and extraordinary *Causes* and *Effects*; yet I will also add, that it is not an unfit Employment for the most judicious *Experimenter*, to examine and record the most unusual and monstrous Forces, and Motions of *Matter*. It is certain that many things, which now seem *miraculous*, would not be so, if once we come to be fully acquainted with their *Compositions* and *Operations*. And it is also as true, that there are many *Qualities*, and *Figures*, and *Powers* of things, that break the common Laws, and transgress the standing Rules of *Nature*. It is not therefore an Extravagance, to observe such *Productions*, as are indeed *admirable* in themselves, if at the same time we do not strive to make those appear to be *admirable*, that are groundless and false. In this there is a near Resemblance between *Natural* and *Civil History*. In the *Civil*, that way of *Romance* is to be exploded, which heightens all the Characters and Actions of Men, beyond all Shadow of *Probability*; yet this does not hinder, but the great and eminent *Virtues* of extraordinary Men of all Ages, may be related and propos'd to our Example. The same is to be affirm'd of *Natural History*. To make that only to consist of strange, and delightful Tales, is to render it

nothing

nothing elfe but *vain* and *ridiculous Knight-Errantry.*
Yet we may avoid that Extreme, and ftill leave room
to confider the fingular and irregular *Effects,* and to
imitate the unexpected and monftrous *Exceffes,* which
Nature does fometimes practife in her *Works.* The firft
may be only compar'd to the Fables of *Amadis,* and
the *Seven Champions ;* the other to the real *Hiftories*
of *Alexander, Hannibal, Scipio,* or *Cæfar :* in which
though many of their Actions may at firft furprife
us ; yet there is nothing that exceeds the *Truth* of
Life, and that may not ferve for our *Inftruction,* or
Imitation.

If this Way of general receiving all credible Accounts of *Natural,* and *Artificial Productions,* fhall feem
expos'd to overmuch Hazard and Uncertainty : that
Danger is remov'd by the *Royal Society's* reducing
fuch Matters of Hear-fay and Information, into real
and impartial *Trials,* perform'd by their own *Hands :*
Of the Exactnefs, Variation, and accurate Repetition
of their *Experiments,* I have already difcours'd : I will
now go on to lay down in fhort Compafs thofe Parts
of the vifible World, about which they have chiefly
beftow'd their *Pains.*

Sect. XXXIII.
*The Expe-
riments they
have try'd.*

The firft kind that I fhall mention, is of *Experi-* *Of Fire.*
ments about *Fire,* and *Flame,* of thefe many were
made in order to the Examination of a *Theory* propounded to them, that there is no fuch thing, as an
elementary Fire of the *Peripatetics ;* nor *fiery Atoms*
of the *Epicureans :* but that *Fire* is only the Act of the
Diffolution of heated *fulphureous Bodies,* by the *Air*
as a *Menftruum,* much after the fame manner as *Aqua
Fortis,* or other fharp *Menftruums* do work on diffoluble.

luble Bodies, as *Iron, Tin, Copper :* that Heat and
Light are two infeparable Effects of this Diffolution, as
Heat and Ebullition are of thofe Diffolutions of *Tin,*
and *Copper :* that *Flame* is a Diffolution of *Smoak,*
which confifts of combuftible Particles, carried up-
ward by the Heat of rarified *Air :* and that *Afhes* are
a Part of the *Body* not diffoluble by the *Air.*

Of this Sort, they have made *Experiments;* to find
the lafting of the burning of a Candle, Lamp, or
Coals, in a cubic Foot of common, rarified, and *condens'd Air :* to exhibit the fudden Extinction of Candles, Lamps, and lighted Coals, when they are put into *fatiated Air :* to fhew the fpeedy Extinction of
kindled Charcoals, by blowing on them with Bellows,
that *Air* which had before been fatiated with burning : to fhew that the greateft and moft lafting Heat,
without a Supply of frefh *Air,* is unable to burn
Wood, Sulphur, and moft other combuftible Matters :
to find the comparative Heat of all Kinds of *Fires,*
and *Flames* of feveral Materials, as of Sulphur, Camphire, Spirit of Wine, Oyl, Wood, Coal, Seacoal,
Iron : to find at what Degree of Heat, Lead, Tin,
Silver, Brafs, Copper, Gold will melt.

Experiments of the Tranfparency, and Refracted-
nefs of *Flames :* of difcerning the Strength of feveral
Kinds of Gunpowder, *Pulvis Fulminans, Aurum Fulminans :* of Gunpowder in the exhaufting Engine : of
bending Springs by the Help of Gunpowder : of
melting Copper immediately, by the Help of a Flux-
powder : of the recoyling of Guns.

Experiments of Candles, and Coals, extinguifh'd by
the Damps of a deep Well : of the burning of Lamps
under Water : of burning Spirit of Wine and Camphire together, and the Diverfity of their *Flames :* of
reducing

reducing Copper to a very combuftible Subftance : of
heating the *Air*, by blowing it through a red-hot
earthen *Pipe*, fo as to burn Wood: of the Brightnefs
of the *Flame* of *Niter* and *Sulphur:* of the burning
and flaming of Tin Filings by the Help of *Niter :* of
kindling Bodies, in common rarified and condens'd
Air, by the Help of a *Burning-glafs :* of the comparative Heat caft by a *Burning-glafs*, in the Morning, and
at Noon : of burning with a *Lens* made of Ice : of cal-
cining *Antimony* in the Sun with Lofs: to find whether
Aurum Fulminans or *Putris Fulminans* do flame upon
Explofion : of hatching *Eggs* with a Lamp Furnace.

Their fecond Sort of *Experiments* is of thofe that *Of Air.*
have been made in order to find out the Nature, Properties, and Ufes of *Air :* Such as thefe.

Experiments for determining the Height of the
Atmofphere, for finding the Preffure of the *Atmofphere :* on the Tops of Mountains, on the Surface
of the Earth, and at the Bottoms of very deep Pits
and Mines, by the Help of *Quick-filver*, and other Contrivances : for finding the Preffure of the *Atmofphere,*
both in the fame Place, and Places very far remov'd.

Experiments to determine the poffible Bounds of
Expanfion and Condenfation of the *Air*, by Heat and
Cold, by exhaufting and compreffing : to determine
the Strength of *Air* under the feveral Degrees of *Rarefaction* and *Condenfation :* of the Force of condens'd
Air in Wind-Guns , to ftate the comparative Gravity
of the *Air* to other fluid and folid Bodies : to difcover the refractive Power of the *Air*, under the feveral
Degrees of *Rarefaction* and *Condenfation :* to manifeft
the inflective Veins of the *Air :* to produce a Kind of
Opacity of the *Air :* of the falling of Smoak in reri-

E e   fied

fied *Air* : to make *Glaſs Bubbles* ſwim in *Air* very much condens'd: of *Glaſs-balls* riſing in a heavy or condens'd *Air*, and falling in a lighter and more rarified.

Experiments of the Propagation of Sounds through common rarified and condens'd *Air* : of the Congruity or Incongruity of *Air*, and its Capacity to penetrate ſome Bodies, and not others: of generating *Air* by corroſive *Menſtruums* out of fermenting Liquors, out of Water and other Liquors, by Heat and by Exhauſtion: of the returning of ſuch *Air* into the *Water* again: of the vaniſhing of *Air* into *Water* exhauſted of *Air* : of the maintaining and increaſing a *Fire* by ſuch *Airs* : of the Fitneſs and Unfitneſs of ſuch *Air* for Reſpiration: of the Uſe of *Air* in breathing.

Experiments of keeping Creatures many Hours alive, by blowing into the *Lungs* with Bellows, after that all the *Thorax* and *Abdomen* were open'd and cut away, and all the Entrails, ſave the *Heart* and *Lungs*, remov'd: of reviving *Chickens*, after they have been ſtrangled, by blowing into their *Lungs:* to try how long a Man can live, by exſpiring and inſpiring again the ſame *Air:* to try whether the *Air* ſo reſpired, might not by ſeveral Means be purified or renew'd: to prove that it is not the Heat, nor the Cold of this reſpired *Air*, that choaks.

Experiments of the reſpiring of *Animals* in *Air* much rarified, and the fatal Effects: of the long Continuance of ſeveral *Animals* very well in *Air* as much condens'd, as it will be under Water, at two hundred Fathoms deep, that is about eight Times: of the Quantity of freſh *Air* requiſite for the Life of a reſpiring *Animal*, for a certain Space of Time: of making *Air* unfit for Reſpiration, by ſatiating it, by ſuffering Candles,

dles or Coals to burn in it, till they extinguish themselves.

Experiments of including living *Animals*, and kindled Coals, and Candles, in a large Glafs, to obferve which of them will be firft exftinguifh'd: of a Man's living half an Hour, without any Inconvenience, in a *Leaden Bell*, at diverfe Fathoms under Water: of the Quantity of *Air* refpir'd at once by a Man: of the Strength a Man has to raife Weights by his Breath.

Experiments of the fwelling of an Arm put into the rarifying Engine, by taking off the Preffure of the *Ambient Air:* of the fwelling of Vipers and Frogs, upon taking off the Preffure of the *Ambient Air:* of the Life, and free Motion of Fifhes in Water, under the Preffure of *Air* eight Times condens'd: of Infects not being able to move in exhaufted *Air:* of the Refiftance of *Air* to Bodies mov'd through it: of the not growing of Seeds for want of *Air:* of the growing of Plants hung in the *Air*, and of the Decreafe of their Weight: of the living of a Cameleon, Snakes, Toads, and diverfe Infects, in a free *Air*, without Food: of conveying *Air* under Water to any Depth: of condenfing *Air* by *Water*, and by the Expanfion of freezing *Water:* of the fwelling of *Lungs* in the rarifying Engine: of the Velocity and Strength of feveral *Winds*.

The third Kind, are thofe which have been made *Of Water.* about the Subftance and Properties of *Water:* Such are,

Experiments about the comparative Gravity of *falt Water* and *frefh*, and of feveral *Medicinal Springs* found in this Nation: of the different Weight of the *Sea-water*, in feveral Climates, and at feveral Seafons:

of the Weight of *Diftill'd-water, Snow-water, May-
dew, Rain-Water, Spring-water* : of augmenting the
Weight of *Liquor*, by diffolving *Salts* : of the greater
Thicknefs of fuch *Water* at Bottom than at the Top :
of weighing afcending and defcending Bodies in
Water ; of the Preffure of the *Water* at feveral Depths
under its Surface.

Experiments of the Heat and Cold of the *Water*, at
feveral Depths of the *Sea* : of propagating Sounds
through the *Water* : of founding the Depth of the
Sea without a Line : of fetching up *Water* from the
Bottom of the Sea : of fetching up Earth, Sand, Plants,
from the Bottom of the Sea.

Experiments of the Refiftance of *Water* to Bodies
mov'd on its Surface, of feveral Figures, and by feveral
Degrees of Force : of the Refiftance of *Water* to Bodies
mov'd through its Subftance, afcending and defcending : of the Expanfion and Condenfation of *Water* by
Heat and Cold : of the Condenfation of *Water* by feveral Ways of Preffure : of converting *Water* into
a vaporous *Air*, lafting fome time in that Form : the
Torricellian Experiment tried with *Water* in a *Glafs-
Cane* thirty fix and forty Foot high, in a leaden *Tube*
alfo with a Glafs at the Top : the fame tried with Oyl,
and other Liquors.

Experiments of the rifing of *Water* in fmall *Tubes*,
and many others about its Congruity : of Filtration,
or of the rifing of *Water* to a great Height in Sand, &c.
of the fwimming of Fifhes : of *Water*'s being able to
penetrate through thofe Pores, where *Air* will not : of
opening Bellows at a Depth under *Water*, and blowing
up Bladders, to find the Preffure of the *Water* : of
Water not fubfiding in a high Glafs-Cane upon removing the ambient Preffure, after it had been well ex-

*   h=ufted

haufted of the *Air-bubbles* that lurk'd in it; of forcing *Water* out of a Veffel by its own Vapors.

Experiments of the different Weight and Refraction of warm *Water* and cold; of the paffing of *Water* through the Coats of a Man's Stomach; of the living of Fifh in *Water*, the *Air* being exhaufted; of clofing up a Fifh in a Glafs of *Water*; of the dying of Fifhes in *Water*, upon taking off the Preffure of the *Air*, in the rarifying Engine; of *Hydroftaticks*, and making a Body fink by pouring more *Water* upon it; of raifing *Water* above its Standard by fucking; of the fubfiding of *Water* in the Stem, upon putting the Bolt-head into warm *Water*; of the fhrinking of *Water* upon cooling.

The fourth Kind are about *Mines, Metals, Oars, Stones, &c.* Such as. *Of Metals and Stones.*

Experiments of *Coppelling* made at the Tower; of diffolving many Salts in one Liquor; of the *Oculus Mundi*; of *Rufma*; of the Tenacity of feveral *Metals* examin'd by Weights; of the Rarefaction and Condenfation of Glafs; of the volatifing *Salt of Tartar*, with burnt Alom, with Vinegar and Spirit of Wine; on the *Bononian Stone*; on *Diamonds*, of their fhining by rubbing; on *Copper-Oar*; of the Diftillation of *Coal*; of refining feveral Kinds of *Lead-Oar*; of extracting a much greater Quantity of *Silver* out of that Oar, than is commonly done; of feveral Ways of reducing *Letharges* into *Lead*; of changing *Gold* into *Silver*.

Experiments Magnetical, of the beft Form of capping *Loadftones*; of the beft Forms of *Needles*, of feveral Lengths and Bigneffes; of various Ways of touching *Needles* on the *Loadftone*; of making the fame.

fame Pole of the *Loadstone* both attract and chafe the fame End of the *Needle*, without touching it; to find the Variation of the *Loadstone* here at *London*.

Experiments with the dipping *Needle*; of the extraordinary Strength in Proportion to its Bulk of a fmall *Loadstone*; to meafure the Strength of the *Magnetical* attractive Power, at feveral Diftances from the *Stone*; to examine the Force of the attractive Power, through feveral *Mediums*, as Water, Air, Wood, Lead, and Stone; to divert the attractive Power, by interpofing Iron; to find the directive Virtue of the *Loadstone* under Water.

Experiments to manifeft, by the Help of Steel-duft, the Lines of the directive Virtue of the *Loadstone* to be oval, in a contrary Pofition to what *Des Cartes's Theory* makes them; to manifeft thofe Lines of Direction by the Help of *Needles*; to difcover thofe Lines of Direction, when the Influence of many *Loadstones* is compounded; to find what thofe Lines are incompaffing a *Sphærical Loadstone*, what about a Square, and what about a regular Figure; to bore through the *Axis* of a *Loadstone*, and fill it up with a *Cylindrical Steel*; *Experiments* on *Loadstones* having many Poles, and yet the *Stones* feeming uniform.

Of Vegetables. The fifth Kind is of the Growth of *Vegetables* in feveral Kinds of Water; as *River-water, Rain-Water, Diftill'd Water, May Dew*; of hindring the Growth of Seed Corn in the Earth, by extracting the Air, and furthering their Growth, by admitting it; of fteeping Seeds of feveral Kinds; of inverting the Pofitions of *Roots* and *Plants* fet in the Ground, to find whether there are Valves in the Pores of the Wood, that only open one Way; of the Decreafe of the Weight
of

of *Plants* growing in Air; of *Lignum Foſſile*; of
the growing of ſome Branches of *Roſemary,* by only
ſprinkling the Leaves with Water; of *Camphire Wood*;
of Wood brought from the *Canaries*; of a ſtinking
Wood brought out of the *Eaſt Indies*; of the Re-
union of the *Bark* of *Trees* after it had been ſeparated
from the *Body.*

The ſixth are *Experiments Medicinal* and *Anato-* *Medicinal*
mical; as of cutting out the Spleen of a Dog; of the *and Anatomi-*
Effects of Vipers biting Dogs; of a *Camæleon,* and *cal.*
its Diſſection; of preſerving *Animals* in Spirit of Wine,
Oil of Turpentine, and other Liquors; of injecting
various Liquors, and other Subſtances into the Veins
of ſeveral Creatures.

Experiments of deſtroying *Mites* by ſeveral Fumes;
of the equivocal Generation of *Inſects*; of feeding a
Carp in the Air; of making Inſects with Cheeſe, and
Sack; of killing Water-Newts, Toads, and Sloworms
with ſeveral Salts; of killing Frogs, by touching their
Skin with Vinegar, Pitch, or Mercury; of a Spider's
not being inchanted by a Circle of *Unicorns Horn,* or
Iriſh Earth, laid round about it.

Experiments with a poiſon'd *Indian* Dagger on ſeveral *Animals*; with the *Maccaſſer* Poiſon; with
Florentine Poiſon, and ſeveral *Antidotes* againſt it; of
making Fleſh grow on, after it has been once cut off;
of the grafting a *Spur* on the Head of a *Cock,* and its
growing; of the living of Creatures by factitious
Air; of the reviving of *Animals* ſtrangled, by
blowing into their *Lungs*; of Fleſh not breeding
Worms, when ſecur'd from Fly-blowing; of the Suffo-
cation of *Animals* upon piercing the *Thorax*; of hatching Silk-Worm's Eggs in rarified Air; of transfuſing
the Blood of one *Animal* into another.

*

The

The seventh Sort are about those which are call'd *sensible Qualities*; as of Freezing; of Cold, and Heat; of freezing Water freed from Air; of the Time and Manner of the Contraction in freezing luke-warm Water; of the Temperature of several Places, by seal'd *Thermometers*; as of several Countries; of the Bottoms of deep Mines, Wells, Vaults, on the Tops of Hills, at the Bottom of the Sea.

Experiments of the Contraction of Oil of *Vitriol*; and diverse other Oils by *freezing*; of *freezing* bitter Tinctures; of *freezing* several ting'd Liquors, and driving all the Tincture inward to the Center; of shewing Ice to be capable of various Degrees of Cold, greater than is requisite to keep it Ice; of producing Cold by the Dissolution of several Salts; of *freezing* Water without *Blebs*; of a membranous Substance separable from the Blood by *freezing*; of a *Thermometer* in rarified and condens'd Air; of very easie *freezing* of Oil of Anifeeds; of making a Standard of Cold by *freezing* distill'd Water.

The eighth are of *Rarity, Density, Gravity, Pressure, Levity, Fluidity, Firmness, Congruity,* &c. as of the Nature of *Gravity*; of the Cohæsion of two flat Marbles; of compressing the Air with *Mercury* to find its Spring; of the Weights of Bodies, solid and fluid; of Rarefaction and Condensation by the Help of *Mercury*; of the Tenacity of several Bodies; of the turning of two very fluid Liquors into one solid Mass, by mingling them together.

Experiments for examining, whether the Gravity of Bodies alter, according as they are carried a good Way above or below the Surface of the Earth; of the

standing

ftanding of *Mercury* well exhaufted, many Inches, nay many Feet, above its ufual ftanding; of a *Wheel-Barometer*, of the Expanfion, and Contraction of Glafs and Metals by Heat and Cold; of Spirit of Wine, and feveral ting'd Liquors, by the Help of a Glafs Tube; the Examination of *Monfieur Pafchal's* Experiment by many others.

The ninth are *Experiments* of *Light*, *Sound*, *Co-lours*, *Tafte*, *Smell*; as of two tranfparent Liquors producing an opacous one: of Echoes and reflected *Sounds*; of mufical *Sounds* and *Harmonies*; of Colours; of the greater Refraction of Water than of Ice; of Refraction in a new Engine; of the Refraction of Glafs of various Shapes under Water; of deftroying the fhining of Fifh by Oil of *Vitriol*; of making a great Light by rubbing two Chryftals hard one againft the other; of making a *deaf* and *dumb* Man to fpeak. *Of Light, Sound, &c.*

The tenth are *Experiments* of *Motion*: as of Glafs Drops feveral Ways order'd and broken; of the Velocity of the Defcent of feveral Bodies of diverfe Fafhions through feveral Liquors; of determining the Velocity of Bodies falling through the Air, tried by many Ways; of the *fwift Motion* of Sounds; of the irregular *Motion* of the Oil of Turpentine on Spirit of Wine; of the Strength of falling Bodies, according to the feveral Heights, from which they fall; of proportioning the Shapes of Bodies, fo as to make them fall together in the fame Time through differing *Mediums*. *Of Motion.*

Experiments of the Swiftnefs of a Bullet fhot with extraordinary Powder; of the beft Figure of the Weight

of a *Pendulum* for *Motion* ; of the *Motion* of pen-
dulous Bodies of various Figures ; to determine the
Length of *Pendulums*, to find the Velocity of the
Vibrations of a founding String ; to find the Velocity of *Motion*, propagated by a very long extended
Wire ; for explaining the Inflection of a ftrait Motion into a circular, by a fupervening attractive Power
towards the Center, in order to the explaining of
the *Motion* of the Planets.

Experiments of the circular and complicated *Motion* of *Pendulums*, to explain the *Hypothefis* of the
Moons moving about the Earth ; of comparing the
Motions of a circular *Pendulum*, with the *Motion*
of a ftrait one ; of the Propagation of *Motion* from
one Body to another; of the Reflection of *Motion* ;
of the vibrating *Motion* of *Quick-filver* in a crooked
Pipe, imitating the *Motion* of a *Pendulum* ; of communicating of the Strength of Powder for the bending of Springs ; and thereby for making artificial
Mufcles, to command what Strength we defire.

Chymical and Mecha-nical.   The eleventh are *Experiments Chymical, Mechanical, Optical* ; as of reducing the Flefh of Animals in-
to a Liquor like Blood, by diffolving it in a certain
Menftruum ; of a great Facility of raifing Water in
Pipes of a large Bore ; of brewing Beer with Bread,
Barley, Oats, Wheat, and without melting ; of pre-
cipitating Tartar out of *Wine* by feveral Expedients ;
of a *chymical* Extraction of a volatile Spirit, and Salt
out of Spunges ; of examining *Aurum fulminans* after
Explofion ; of the Diffolution of *Manna* in Water,
and of a chryftallifing it again out of it, by Evapora-
tion.

Experiments of *volatifing* Salt of *Tartar* many
Ways;

Ways; of examining the *mucilaginous* Matter call'd *Star-shoot*; of examining our *English Telescopes*, and *Microscopes*, and comparing them with such as have been made at *Rome*; of making a volatile Salt with Oil of *Turpentine*, and Sea-salt; of the Quantity of Spirits in *Cyder*; of the Strength of several Springs; of examining a Pump made with Bellows; of dying Silk with several *Jamaica* Woods; of finding the Strength of Wood of several Kinds, for bearing; of finding the Flexibility of various Woods, and determining the utmost Extent of their yielding and bending.

Experiments about the Gravity of Bodies made on the Top of St. *Paul*'s Steeple, *Westminster Abby*, and several other high Places; and in a Well of seventy Fathoms Depth; examined about the *Virgula Divina*, wherein the common Assertions were found false; of the various Refractions of several Liquors, in a new refractive Engine of common Oil of *Tobacco*, made by Distillation in a Glass Retort; of making the object Glass of a *Microscope* to bear as large an Aperture as is desir'd.

Of this their Way of Experimenting I will here produce these Examples.

The HISTORY of
EXPERIMENTS
Of the Weight of Bodies increased in the FIRE:

Made at the Tower, *and the Account brought in by my Lord* BROUNCKER.

1 *Copper and* Lead.

	d.	gr.
THe Copel weighed	10	8 $\frac{1}{32}$
Lead	4	9
Copper	0	6
Into the Fire all three	14	23 $\frac{1}{32}$
Out of the Fire	15	4 $\frac{8}{32}$
Gained	0	5 $\frac{1}{02}$

Besides what the Copel lost in Weight, supposed to be about three Grains.

2 *Copper and* Lead.

	d.	gr.
Copel	10	2
Lead	4	9.$\frac{3}{4}$
Copper	0	6
Into the Fire all three	14	17 $\frac{3}{4}$
Out of the Fire	15	1 $\frac{19}{32}$
Gained	0	7 $\frac{27}{32}$

3 *Lead*

3. *Lead alone.*

	d.	gr.	
Copel ————	10	3	$\frac{29}{32}$
Lead — — ——	4	9	
Into the Fire both	14	12	$\frac{29}{32}$
Out of the Fire ——	14	3	$\frac{19}{32}$
Gained ——	0	10	$\frac{22}{32}$

4. *Lead alone.*

	d.	gr.	
Copel ————	10	10	$\frac{7}{8}$
Lead ————	4	9	
Into the Fire both	14	19	$\frac{7}{8}$
Out of the Fire ——	15	1	$\frac{5}{64}$
Gained——	0	5	$\frac{13}{64}$

5 *Copel alone.*

	d.	gr.	
Into the Fire ——	10	5	
Out of the Fire ——	10	1	$\frac{3}{8}$
Loft —	0	3	$\frac{5}{8}$

6 *Copel alone.*

	d.	gr.	
Into the Fire ——	10 wanting	7	$\frac{3}{4}$
Out of the Fire ——	10 wanting	9	
Loft—0 ——	1	$\frac{1}{4}$	

EXPE-

The HISTORY *of*

EXPERIMENTS

Of a Stone called

OCULUS MUNDI

Made by Dr. GODDARD.

A Small Stone of the Kind, called by some Authors Oculus Mundi, *being dry and cloudy, weighed* ———5 gr. $\frac{200}{256}$

The same being put under Water, for a Night and somewhat more, became transparent, and the Superficies being wiped dry, weighed ——————— 6 gr. $\frac{3}{256}$

The Difference between these two Weights ——— 0. $\frac{50}{256}$

The same Stone kept out of Water one Day and becoming cloudy again, weighed ——— ——— —— 5. $\frac{225}{256}$

which was more than the first Weight ——— —— 0. $\frac{25}{256}$

The same being kept dry two Days longer, weighed —— —— 5. $\frac{202}{256}$

which was less than at first —— —— —— 0. $\frac{7}{256}$

Being put under Water for a Night and becoming again transparent, and wiped dry, the weight was 6. $\frac{2}{256}$ *the same with the first, after putting in Water, and more than the last Weight, after keeping of it dry* —— 0. $\frac{57}{256}$

Being kept dry some longer, it did not grow sensibly lighter.

Another Stone of the same Kind, being variegated with milky, white, and grey, like some Sort of Agates, while it lay under Water, was always invironed with little Bubbles, such as appear in Water before boyling, next the Sides of the Vessel.

*

There

There were also some of the like Bubbles on the Surface of the Water just over it ; as if either some Exhalations came out of it, or that it did excite some Fermentation in the Parts of the Water contiguous to it.

There was little sensible Difference of Transparency in this Stone, before the putting under Water, and after : To be sure the milky white Parts continued as before, but more different in Weight, than in the former. For whereas, before the putting into the Water, the weight was ———— 18 gr. $\frac{97}{128}$ after it had lyen in about twenty four Hours the Weight was 20 gr. $\frac{37}{128}$; so the Difference was ———— 1 gr. $\frac{68}{128}$.

The same Stone was infused in the Water scalding hot, and so continued for a while after it was cold, but got no more Weight, than upon infusing in the cold; neither was there any sensible Difference in the Weight both Times.

A

An Account of a Dog dissected,

By Mr. *HOOK*.

IN Prosecution of some Inquiries into the Nature of Respiration in several Animals; a Dog was dissected, and by means of a Pair of Bellows, and a certain Pipe thrust into the Wind-pipe of the Creature, the Heart continued beating for a very long while after all the Thorax and Belly had been open'd, nay after the Diaphragm *had been in great Part cut away, and the* Pericardium *remov'd from the Heart. And from several Trials made, it seem'd very probable, that this Motion might have been continued, as long almost as there was any Blood left within the Vessels of the Dog; for the Motion of the Heart seem'd very little chang'd, after above an Hour's time from the first displaying the* Thorax *; though we found, that upon removing the Bellows, the Lungs would presently grow flaccid, and the Heart begin to have convulsive Motions; but upon removing the Motion of the Bellows, the Heart recover'd its former Motion, and the Convulsions ceased. Though I made a* Ligature *upon all the great Vessels that went into the lower Parts of its Body, I could not find any Alteration in the Pulse of the Heart; the Circulation, it seems, being perform'd some other Way. I cou'd not perceive any thing distinctly, whether the Air did unite and mix with the Blood; nor did in the least perceive the Heart to swell upon the Extension of the Lungs; nor did the Lungs seem to swell upon the Contraction of the Heart.*

E X-

Fig: 1.

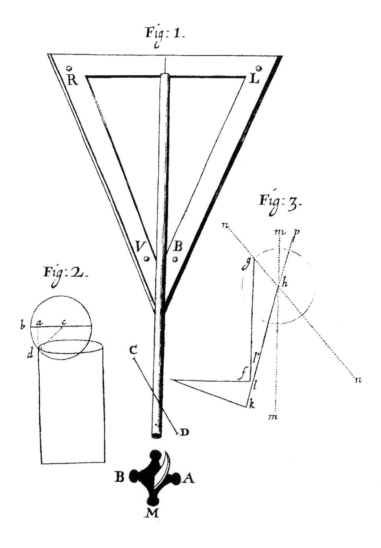

Fig: 3.

Fig: 2.

EXPERIMENTS
of the Recoiling of
G U N S
By the Lord *BROUNCKER.*

WHen *I was commanded by this Society, to make*   Fig.   1.
some Experiments of the Recoiling of Guns :
In order to the discovery of the cause thereof, I caused
this Engine that lies here before you to be prepared,
and with it (assisted by some of the most eminent of
this Society) I had divers shots made in the Court of
this Colledge, near the length thereof from the mark,
with a full charge (about a fourpenny weight) of
Powder ; But without any other success, then that
there was nothing Regular in that way, which was
by laying it upon a heavy Table, unto which it was
sometimes fastned with Screws at all the four places
R, L, V, B, sometimes only at R or L, having wheels
affixed at L and V or R, and B, that it might the
more easily recoil.

This uncertainty I did then conceive might arise
from one or more of these three causes, viz.

1. *The violent trembling motion of the Gun, whence*
the Bullet might casually receive some literal impulse
from the nose of the peece at the parting from it.

2. *The yielding of the Table which was sensible.*

3. *The difficulty of aiming well by the Sight and*
Button so far from the Mark.

*

G g   *Therefore*

Therefore to avoid all thefe, the Experiments I caus'd to be made before you in the Gallery of this Colledge, you may be pleafed to remember were performed, firft, taking only eight grains of Powder for the charge. Secondly, laying the Engine upon the floor, and thirdly, aiming by a thread at M, *a mark about an Inch and* ¼ *from the mouth of the Gun (the edge of a knife being put for the mark the better to difcern the line that was fhot in) and they thus fucceeded.*

When the peece was faftned to the floor both at R *and* L *the Bullet then did fo fully hit the mark, that it was divided by it into two parts, whofe difference in weight was lefs than ten grains (about the thirty third part of the whole Bullet) although the leffer part was a little hollow, and that from which the neck of Lead was a little too clofe pared off : But when hindred from Recoiling only at* R, *the Bullet mift the mark towards* L *or* A, *for the whole Bullet, lefs than two grains excepted, went on that fide : And in like manner when hindred from Recoiling at* L, *the Bullet mift the mark towards* R *or* B, *the whole Bullet, lefs than two grains excepted, paffing the knife on that fide thereof.*

I had the honour to make other Experiments with the fame Engine, lately at White-Hall *before his Majefty and his Highnefs Royal within the* Tilt-yard *Gallery, where there is the hearth of a chimny raifed a little above the floor, about the diftance of thirteen feet from the oppofite wall, againft which I caufed a plank to be placed, and the Engine to be laid firft againft the middle of the Hearth, that it might not recoil at all, and that part of the board to be marked againft which 'twas levelled, known by a line ftretch-*
ed.

ed from the Breech of the Peece unto the Board, directly over the fight and button, and the fire being
given (the charge being but eight grains of Powder
as before) the Bullet did fully hit the mark. Secondly,
the Peece (charged and levelled in the same manner)
was laid at the end of the Hearth next the Park, so
that very little of the corner R rested against it, and
then the Bullet mifs'd the mark about an inch and a
quarter towards the Park or A. The like being done
at the other end of the Hearth, the Bullet then
mifs'd the mark as much the other way; and afterwards with double that charge something more, as
before I had found it lefs with a smaller charge.

Since this (at first defigning only to experiment the
several distances that the Bullet is carried wide of
the mark with different charges of Powder) I made
these Experiments following.

In the first Colume whereof you have the corner
stopt from recoiling.

In the second the grains of Powder with which
the Peece was charged.

In the third the distance the Bullet was shot wide
from the mark in inches, tenths, and parts of tenths.

In the fourth the side on which the Bullet was
carried.

In the last the distance of the mark from the muzzle of the Gun in feet.

B	16	0.	N	9	L	48	0. 5	L	9	R	39	0. 3½	L	9	R	48	0. 0	N	9
L	16	1. 7½	R	9	L	56	0. 8	L	9	R	39	0. 2	L	9	R	48	0. 1	L	9
R	16	1. 5	L	9	L	96	1. 2½	L	9	R	40	0. 2	L	9	R	48	0. 0¼	R	9
R	12	1. 5	L	9	L	96	1. 5	L	9	R	40	0. 0	L	9		4	1. 6	R	9
L	12	1. 7½	R	9	L	40	0. 5	L	9	R	40	0. 2	L	9		4	1. 5½	L	9
L	8	1. 6	R	9	L	46	0. 9	R	9	R	96	0. 6½	R	9		4	1. 6	L	9
R	8	1. 1	L	9	B	8	0. 2	R	9	L	96	1. 0¼	L	9		8	1. 8	L	9
R	4	1. 0	L	9	R	96	0. 6	R	9	L	96	1. 0¼	L	9		8	1. 8	R	9
L	4	1. 1¼	R	9	L	96	0. 9	L	9	R	96	0. 7½	R	9		12	2. 0	R	9
L	24	1. 1½	R	9	L	40	0. 1¾	L	9	R	96	1. 0	R	9		12	2. 1	L	9
L	32	0. 6	R	9	L	38	0. 1½	R	9	R	40	0. 8	L	9		16	1. 7½	L	9
L	40	0. 1	R	9	L	39	0. 0½	L	9	R	40	0. 5	R	9		16	1. 8	R	9
L	48	0. 4½	L	9	R	39	0. 1	L	9	L	48	0. 1	R	9		20	1. 5	R	9
R	20	1. 0½	L	9	R	12	0. 6	L	2	L	48	0. 0¼	L	2		20	0. 2	R	
R	20	1. 4	L	9	R	12	0. 9¼	L	4		12	1. 7	R	9		24	0. 2¾	L	
K	64¾	0. 7¾	R	9	R	12	1. 2	L	6		12	0. 2¼	R	9		28	0. 1	R	
L	64¾	0. 9	L	9	R	12	1. 5½	L	8		12	0. 6½	R	2		32	0. 1½	R	
L	96	1. 1	L	9	R	12	1. 9	L	9		12	1. 0	R	4		36	0. 1¼	R	
R	96	0. 7	R	9	B	12	0. 1	L	9		12	1. 1¾	R	6		40	0. 1	R	
R	96	0. 8	R	9	R	12	0. 3	L			48	0. 0¾	L			44	0. 0¾	R	
L	96	1. 3	L	9	L	12	0. 3½	R			48	0. 1½	L	2		48	0. 0¾	R	
L	96	1. 3½	L	9	L	96	0. 0½	R			48	0. 2½	L	4		52	0. 0¾	R	
R	12	0. 3¼	L	6	R	96	0. 0½	L			48	0. 5½	L	6		56	0. 0¾	R	
R	12	1. 3	L	9	R	96	0. 2	R			4	0. 1½	R			60	0. 0⅞	R	
L	12	0. 6¾	L	2	L	96	0. 2	R			4	0. 1½	R			64	0. 0⅞	R	
L	12	1. 0¾	R	4	L	48	0. 1½	L			8	0. 3¼	R			96	0. 0	L	
L	12	1. 2	R	6	L	48	0. 0	N			12	0. 3	R			96	1. 1	L	
L	12	1. 4¼	R	8	R	48	0. 1¼	N			16	0. 2¼	R						

Whence

Whence you may be pleased to observe:

First, That the recoil of the Peece being hindred only at R or L, whatsoever be the charge of the Powder, the Bullet still misses the mark, placed at the mouth of the Gun, on the same side that the recoil is made.

Secondly, That about twelve grains of Powder shoots widest from the mark at all distances abovementioned, on the same side that the recoil is made.

Thirdly, That above forty eight grains of Powder shoots wide from the mark, placed at nine foot from the muzzle of the Peece, on the contrary side to that on which the recoil is made.

The cause of the *first* I cannot doubt to be the recoil of the Peece (from the force of the Powder) before the Bullet be parted from it.

The *second* is, as I conceive, because with less than twelve grains the Peece ceaseth to recoil before the Bullet be parted from it. And with more than twelve grains the Bullet is parted from the Peece before it hath recoiled so far: A greater power not moving a greater weight swifter (horizontally) in the same proportion that it doth the lesser.

And for the *third* I have this to offer, viz. Because the mouth of the Gun is moving sidewards whilst the Bullet is going out; Therefore the mouth of the Peece must be contiguous (at least) unto the Bullet on the contrary side to that on which the Peece recoils, some time after the separation made on the other side, and therefore the last impulse of the Bullet from the force of the Powder is on that side the Peece recoils, wherefore the Bullet must necessarily cross the Axis of the Peece, and that with a greater or lesser Angle, according to the force of the Powder, and when this Angle therefore is greater than the Angle of recoil,

then

then muſt the Axis of that Cylinder in which the Bullet moves croſs the Axis of the mark, beyond which interjection the mark being placed, the Bullet muſt be carried neceſſarily wide of the mark on the contrary ſide to the recoil of the Peece.

Fig. 2.

Let a d = a.

and d c = r.

and therefore a b = r --- $\sqrt{} : r^2 a^2$

Therefore $\overline{a b. a d :: r ---}$ $\sqrt{} : r^2 a^2 a :: 1. x$ (x *being any given quantity.*)

Wherefore a = x r -- x $\sqrt{} : r^2 a^2 :$

$\overline{and x \sqrt{} : r^2 a^2 :}$ = x r -- a.

Therefore $x^2 r^2 x^2 a^2 x^2 r^2 ... 2 x r a + a.$

therefore 2 x r a = $x^2 a^2 + a^2.$

therefore $\dfrac{2 x r}{x^2 + 1}$ = a

Quod &c.

f c k = f l p = p h m = *the Angle of Recoil* p h n *the Angle of Reflexion made at the parting of the Bullet from the Peece. When* p h n ⊳ p h m (m h *being always parallel to* f g) *then muſt* h n *interſect* f g *if continued.*

Some other Experiments I have alſo made with another Peece (about the ſame length, but of a bore neer two tenths of an inch leſs) and ordered in the ſame manner, and do find, that with a ſmall charge the Bullet is ſhot (thence too) wide of the mark on the ſame ſide on which the Recoil is made, and with a full charge wide the contrary ſide.

I

Fig. 3.

I caufed befides two Piftol barrels of about five inches long to be placed upon Carriages with four Wheels, and loaded with lead, that they might not overturn when difcharged, and both of equal weight, and an Iron Cylinder *of the length of both their bores, and of the fame diameter with a piece of Lead of weight equal to it.   So that the piece of Lead affixed to either of thefe Guns (which of them I fhould pleafe to charge) might equally poife the other with the Iron* Cylinder.   *And thus indifferently charging either with eight grains more or lefs of* Powder, *and putting the Iron* Cylinder *home into both, the piece of Lead being affixed to that which held the Powder, and then both fo fet upon the floor and the Powder fired, I could not thereby difcover, that the charged* Peece, *or the other, either of them, did certainly recoil more or lefs than the other, they rather feemed ftill to be equal.*

Thefe few Experiments I have made fince, the Barrel being firft cut at the muzzle, parallel to a vertical plain paffing the line C D.

B	48	0. 8	L	R	48	1. 2	L
B	48	0. 9	L	L	48	0. 2	L
B	16	0. 1	R	L	48	0.3	L
B	8	0. 2	R				
B	8	0. 0	N				

Befides thefe, there is another that I fhall mention, and that is the Experiment it felf, or the Double-Bottom'd Ship, invented by Sir *William Petty* : of this I will venture to add a few Words, and I think I may do it, without tranfgrefling that Rule I had fix'd to my felf, of not enlarging on the praife of particular Names, or Defigns.   For fince the *Experiment* it felf is loft, I hope I may fecurely fpeak of its advantages : feeing Men are wont out of common humanity to allow the commendations of dead Men, I truft I may commend a *wreck'd Ship,* without any fear of the envy that may thence arife to the *Author*. In brief therefore I will fay this of it, that it was the moft confiderable *Experiment,* that has been made in this *Age* of *Experiments :* if either we regard the great charge of the work, or the wonderful change it was likely to make in *Navigation,* or the great fuccefs, to which this firft *Attempt* was arriv'd. Tho' it was at firft confronted with the doubts, and Objections of moft *Seamen* of our *Nation,* yet it foon confuted them by *Experience.*   It appear'd very much to excel all other forms of *Ships,* in fayling, in carriage, in fecurity and many other fuch benefits. Its firft *Voyage* it perform'd with admirable *fwiftnefs.* And tho' it mifcarried after its return, yet it was deftroyed by a common fate, and by fuch a dreadful *tempeft,* as overwhelm'd a great *Fleet* the fame Night : fo that the Antient Fabricks of *Ships* have no reafon to triumph over that new *Model,* when of threefcore and ten Sail that were in the fame *Storm,* there was not one efcap'd to bring the News.

In a word, though this *Invention* fucceeded not, while it was only fupported by *private Purfes* ; it will undoubtedly produce great effects, if ever it fhall
be

be retriev'd upon the *publick Stock* of a *Nation:* which will be able to fuftain the firft hazards, and loffes that muft be allow'd to happen in the beginnings of all extraordinary *Trials.*

To their *Experiments* I will fubjoin their *Obferva-* §. XXXIV *tions,* which differ but in name from the other, the *Their Obfer-* fame fidelity and truth, being regarded in collecting *vations.* them both.

Obfervations of the *fix'd Stars* for the perfecting of *Aftronomy,* by the help of *Telefcopes:* of the *Comets* in 1665, and 1666. which were made both in *London,* and elfewhere ; and particularly of the firft *Comet,* for above a month after, it difappear'd to the naked eye, and became Stationary, and Retrograde.

Obfervations about *Saturn,* of the proportion, and pofition of its *Ring,* of the motion and Orbit of its *Lunale,* of the fhadow of the *Ring* on the *Body,* and of the *Body* on the *Ring* ; and of its *Phafes, &c.* of *Jupiters Belts,* and of its fpots, and verticity about its *Axis,* of its eclipfing its *Satellites,* and being eclips'd by them ; of the Orbs, Inclinations, Motions, *&c.* of the *Satellites,* together with *Tables,* and *Epheme-rides* of their motions.

Obfervations of the Spots, about the Body of *Mars,* and of its whirling motion about its Center : of feveral Eclipfes of the *Sun,* and *Moon,* and fome of them as were not taken notice of, by *Aftronomers,* or Tables commonly us'd : of the Spots in the *Moon,* and of the feveral appearances in the Phafes of it : of the *Moon* at the fame time, by *Correfpondents* in feveral parts of the World, towards the finding her Parallax, and diftance.

Obfervations of the Eliptical and waved Figures

of the *Planetary Bodies*, near the *Horizon* from the refraction of the *Hemisphere* : of the effects of *Lightning* : of the various pressure of the *Atmosphere*, by a *Wheel-barometer* for several years, and of its usefulness for predicting the changes of Weather.

Observations on frozen *Beer* : on the Figures of *Snow*, frozen *Water*, *Urine* congeal'd : on the suspension of *Mercury* at a great height : on *Mines* and *Minerals* : on the Concretions of *Wood*, *Plants*, *Shells*, and several *Animals* Substances : on the effects of Earthquakes, Fiery Eruptions, and Inundations : on Lakes, Mountains, Damps, subterraneous Fires : on Tides, Currents, and the Depth of the Sea.

Observations of the liming of *Ground*, for improvement of the Bodies of *Sheep*, but spoiling their Wool : of several ways for preventing smutty *Corn* : of the importance of changing *Seed-Corn* : of the alteration of the *Horns* of *Sheep*, and other *Cattel*, by the change of Pasture : of the Pores and Valves in *Wood* : the Anatomy of *Trees* : of the sensitive, and humble *Plant*.

Observations on the *Bills* of *Mortality* : on the leaves of *Sage* : on small living *Flies* in the Powder of *Cantharides* : of Insects bred in *Dew* : of *Virginian* Silk-Bottoms : of the Parts, and Anatomy of *Fishes* : of the Teeth of *Lupus Marinus*, that they are the same thing with the *Toad stones* set in *Rings* : of the Respiration of *Fishes* : of *Bernacles* : of the calcin'd Powder of *Toads* : of an Outlandish *Deer-Skin*, and Hair : of the Parts of *Vipers* : of Stones taken out of the Heart of a *Man* : of young *Vipers* : that they do not eat holes through their old ones Bellies, as is commonly affirm'd.

For Examples of this *Head*, I will only refer my
Reader

Reader to thofe which Mr. *Graunt* has publifh'd on the *Bills of Mortality*; wherein the *Author* has fhewn, that the meaneft and moft trivial Matters may be fo cultivated, as to bear excellent Fruit, when they come under the Managment of an accurate, and prudent *Obferver*: For, from thofe *Papers*, which went about fo many years, through every Tradefmans hands, without any manner of Profit, except only to the Clerks that collected them, he has deduc'd many true Conclufions, concerning the graveft, and moft weighty Parts of *Civil Government*, and *humane Nature*.

As I am now paffing away from their *Experiments*, and *Obfervations*, which have been their proper, and principal work: there comes before me an *Objection*, which is the more to be regarded, becaufe it is rais'd by the *Experiments* themfelves. For it is their common complaint, that there is a great *nicety*, and *contingency*, in the making of many *Experiments*: that their fuccefs is very often various, and inconftant, not only in the hands of *different*, but even of the fame *Triers*. From hence they fuggeft their fears, that this continuance of *Experimenters*, of which we talk fo much, will not prove fo advantageous, though they fhall be all equally cautious in *obferving*, and faithful in recording their *Difcoveries*: becaufe it is probable, that the *Trials* of Future Ages will not agree with thofe of the prefent, but frequently thwart, and contradict them.

§. XXXV. *An Objection anfwered concerning the uncertainty of Experiments.*

The *Objection* is ftrong, and material: and I am fo far from diminifhing the weight of it, that I am rather willing to add more to it. I confefs many *Experiments* are obnoxious to failing; either by reafon of

fome

some *circumstances*, which are scarce discernable, 'till the work be over : or from the diversity of *Materials*, whereof some may be *genuine*, some *sophisticated*, some *simple*, some *mix'd*, some *fresh*, some may have lost their *virtue*. And this is chiefly remarkable, in *Chymical Operations*, wherein if the dissolvents be ill prepar'd, if the *Spirits* be too much, or too little purify'd, if there be the least alteration, in the degrees of *Fire*, the quantity of *Matter*, or by the negligence of those that attend it, the whole course will be overthrown, or chang'd from its first purpose.

But what is now to be concluded from hence ? shall this *instability*, and *Casualty* of *Experiments*, deter us from labouring in them at all ? or should it not rather excite us to be more curious and watchful in their *process ?* It is to be allow'd that such *undertakings* are wonderfully hazardous and difficult ; why else does the *Royal Society* indeavour to preserve them from degenerating, by so many *forewarnings*, and *Rules*, and a *Method* so severe ? It is granted, that their *event* is often uncertain, and not answerable to our expectations. But that only ought to admonish us, of the indispensible necessity of a jealous, and exact *Inquiry*. If the uncertainty proceeded from a constant irregularity of *Nature*, we had reason then to despair : but seeing it for the most part arises only from some defect or change in our progress, we should thence learn, first to correct our own miscarriages, before we cease to hope for the *success*.

Let then the *Experiment* be often renew'd. If the same kinds and proportions of *Ingredients* be us'd, and the same circumstances be punctually observ'd, the *effect* without all question will be the same. If some little variation of any of these, has made any alteration.

tion, a judicious, and well practis'd *Trier* will soon be able to difcern the *caufe* of it; and to rectifie it, upon the next repetition. If the difference of *time*, or *place*, or *matter*, or *Inftruments*, will not fuffer the product to be juft the fame in all points: yet fomething elfe will refult, that may prove perhaps as beneficial. If we cannot always arrive at the main end of our *Labours*, fome lefs unfought *Curiofities* will arife. If we cannot obtain that which fhall be ufeful for practice, there may fomething appear that may inftruct.

It is ftranger that we are not able to inculcate into the minds of many men, the neceffity of that *diftinction* of my Lord *Bacon's*, that there ought to be *Experiments* of *Light*, as well as of *Fruit*. It is their ufual word, *What folid good will come from thence?* They are indeed to be commended for being fo fevere *Exactors* of *goodnefs*. And it were to be wifh'd, that they would not only exercife this vigour, about *Experiments*, but on their own *lives*, and *actions*: that they would ftill queftion with themfelves, in all that they do; what *folid good* will come from thence? But they are to know, that in fo large, and fo various an *Art* as this of *Experiments*, there are many degrees of ufefulnefs: fome may ferve for real, and plain *benefit*, without much *delight*: fome for *teaching* without apparent *profit*: fome for *light* now, and for *ufe* hereafter; fome only for *ornament*, and *curiofity*. If they will perfift in contemning all *Experiments*, except thofe which bring with them immediate *gain*, and a prefent *harveft*: they may as well cavil at the Providence of God, that he has not made all the feafons of the year, to be times of *mowing*, *reaping*, and *vintage*.

Of

§. XXXVI.   Of the variety, and excellence of the *Inſtruments*,
The Inſtru- with which this Age abounds, for their help in *Philo-*
ments they *ſophical* matters, I have already diſcourſed in the for-
have inven- mer Part.   I will now go on to mention thoſe new
ted.
ones, which they themſelves, or ſome of their Members, have either *invented*, or *advanc'd*, for the eaſe,
ſtrength, and direction of their *Senſes*, in the motions
of *Nature*, and *Art :* of this kind are theſe that follow.

An *Inſtrument* for finding a ſecond of Time by
the Sun : another for finding the Celeſtial Refractions.

Three ſeveral *Quadrants* made after three new
contrivances, which though they are not above eighteen Inches in Diameter, and ſo are manageable in
any Window, or Turret, are yet far more exact, than
the beſt, that have been hitherto us'd, for *Aſtrono-*
mical Obſervations, or taking Angles at Land.

A new *Inſtrument* for taking Angles by reflection ;
by which means the Eye at the ſame time ſees the two
Objects, both as touching in the ſame point, though
diſtant almoſt to a Semicircle : which is of great uſe
for making exact *Obſervations* at Sea.

A new kind of *Back-ſtaff* for taking the Sun's Alti-
tude by the Shadow, and Horizon : which is ſo contriv'd, that though the Shadow be at three foot diſtance, or as much more as is deſir'd, yet there ſhall
not be the leaſt *Penumbra :* and the Shadow may be
eaſily diſtinguiſh'd to the fourth part of a minute.

A *Hoop* of all the fix'd Stars in the *Zodiac*, for the
ſpeedy finding the Poſition of the *Ecliptic*, and for
knowing the Extent of the *Conſtellations*.

A *Copernican Sphere*, repreſenting the whirling
Motion

Motion of the Sun, and the Motion of the feveral Planets.

A great many new ways of making *Inftruments*, for keeping time very exactly, both with *Pendulums*, and without them; whereby the intervals of time may be meafur'd both on the *Land*, and *Sea*.

A univerfal *Standard*, or meafure of *Magnitudes*, by the help of a *Pendulum*, never before attempted.

A new kind of *Pendulum Clock*, wherein the *Pendulum* moves circularly, going with the moft fimple, and natural motion, moving very equally, and making no kind of noife.

A *Pendulum Clock* fhewing the æquation of Time.

Three new ways of *Pendulums* for *Clocks*, and feveral ways of applying the motion of the Watchwork to them.

Several new kinds of *Pendulum Watches* for the Pocket, wherein the motion is regulated, by Springs, or Weights, or Loadftones, or Flies moving very exactly regular.

Several forts of *Inftruments* for comprefing, and rarefying the Air: A *Wheel-Barometer*, and other *Inftruments* for finding the preffure of the Air, and ferving to predict the changes of the Weather.

A new kind of *Scales*, for examining the gravity of Bodies in all places; to fee whether the attraction of the *Earth*, be not greater in fome parts of the *Earth*, than in others, and whether it do not decreafe, at farther diftances from the furface of the *Earth*, either upwards into the *Air*, or downwards under the *Earth*.

A very exact pair of *Scales*, for trying a great number of *Magnetical Experiments*.

Several

Several very accurate *Beams*, for trying many *Statical Experiments*, and for finding the moft exact gravity of feveral kinds of Bodies.

A great number of *Magnetical Inftruments*, for making *Experiments* about *Loadftones*.

Several new kinds of *Levels* for finding the true Horizon, where, by one of not above a foot length, the Horizontal line may be found, without the error of many feconds.

A new kind of *Augar* for boring the ground, and fetching up whatever it meets with in the right order.

A new *Inftrument* for fetching up any Subftance from the bottom of the Sea, whether Sand, Shells, Clay, Stones, Minerals, Metals.

A new *Bucket* for examining and fetching up whatever Water is to be found at the bottom of the *Sea*, or at any depth, and for bringing it up without *mixing* with the other Water of the *Sea*, through which it paffes.

Two new ways of founding the depth of the *Sea* without a Line, for examining the greateft depth of the *Ocean*, in thofe parts of it, that are moft remote from the *Land*.

Several *Inftruments* for finding the velocity of fwimming Bodies of feveral Figures, and mov'd with divers ftrengths, and for trying what *Figures* are leaft apt to be overturn'd, in order to the making a true *Theory*, of the *Forms* of *Ships*, and *Boats* for all ufes.

An *Inftrument* of great height, with Glafs windows on the fides, to be fill'd with Water, for examining the velocity of Bodies of feveral Subftances, Figures and Magnitudes, by their defcent.

An

An *Inftrument* for meafuring, and dividing the time of their Defcent, to the accuratenefs of two, or three thirds of time, ferving alfo for examining the fwift-nefs of Bodies defcending through the Air, and of Bodies fhot by a Gun, or Bow.

A *Bell* for diving under water to a great depth, wherein a man has continued at a confiderable depth under water, for half an hour, without the leaft in-convenience.

Another *Inftrument* for a *Diver*, wherein he may continue long under water, and may walk to and fro, and make ufe of his ftrength and limbs, almoft as freely as in the Air.

A new fort of *Spectacles*, whereby a *Diver* may fee any thing diftinctly under Water.

A new way of conveighing the *Air* under Wa-ter, to any Depth, for the ufe of *Divers*.

An *Inftrument* for meafuring the fwiftnefs, and ftrength of the *Wind*.

An *Inftrument* for raifing a continual ftream of *Water*, by turning round a moveable valve, within the hollow of a clofe *Cylindrical* Barrel.

Several kinds of *Thermometers* for difcovering the heat, and cold of the *Air*, or any other Liquors: a *Thermometer* for examining all the degrees of heat in Flames, and Fires, made of feveral Subftances; as al-fo the degrees of heat requifite to melt Soder, Lead, Tin, Silver, Brafs, Iron, Copper, Gold.

A *Standard* for Cold feveral ways.

An *Inftrument* for planting of Corn.

Four feveral forts of *Hygrofcopes* made with feveral Subftances, for difcovering the drowth, and moifture of the Air.

Several kinds of ways to examine the goodnefs, and badnefs of *Waters*.   I i   Se-

Several *Engines* for finding, and determining the force of *Gun-powder*, by Weights, Springs, Sliding, &c.

An *Inftrument* for receiving, and preferving the force of *Gun-powder*, fo as to make it applicable, for the performing of any motion defir'd.

Several *Inftruments* for examining the recoiling, true carriage, and divers other proporties of Guns.

Several kinds of *Otocoufticons*, or *Inftruments* to improve the fenfe of hearing.

Several Models of *Chariots*, and other *Inftruments*, for Progreffive Motion.

A *Chariot-way-wifer*, meafuring exactly the length of the way of the *Chariot*, or *Coach* to which it is apply'd.

An *Inftrument* for making Screws with great difpatch.

A way of preferving the moft exact impreffion of a *Seal*, *Medal*, *Sculpture*; and that in a Metal harder than Silver.

An *Inftrument* for grinding *Optick-glaffes* : a double *Telefcope* : feveral excellent *Telefcopes* of divers lengths of fix, twelve, twenty eight, thirty fix, fixty foot long, with a convenient *Apparatus* for the managing of them : and feveral contrivances in them for meafuring the Diameters, and parts of the *Planets*, and for finding the true pofition, and diftance of the fmall fix'd *Stars*, and *Satellites*.

Towards the exactnefs of all manner of thefe *Optick-glaffes*, the *Englifh* have got a great advantage of late years, by the *Art* of making *Glafs*, finer, and more ferviceable for *Microfcopes*, and *Telefcopes*, than that of *Venice*. This Invention was brought into our Coun-

try,

try, and practis'd here, by the care, and expence of the
Duke of *Buckingham*; whom the Author of thefe
Papers ought to mention with all honour ; both for
his Skill and Zeal in advancing fuch *Experimental
Studies* of which I am writing : and alfo becaufe it
has been by the favour of fo great a *Patron,* that I
have injoy'd the leifure, and convenience of compofing this *Hiftory.*

As foon as they were reduc'd into a *Fix'd Affembly,* §. XXXVII.
one of the Principal Intentions they propos'd to ac- *Their Repo-*
complifh, was a General Collection of all the Effects *fitory and*
of *Arts,* and the Common, or Monftrous *Works* of Na- *Library.*
ture. This they at firft began by the cafual *Prefents,*
which either *Strangers,* or any of their own *Members*
beftow'd upon them. And in fhort time it has increas'd fo faft, by a contribution from all Parts, and
chiefly by the bounty of Mr. *Colwal,* that they have
already drawn together into one Room, the greateft
part of all the feveral kinds of things, that are fcatter'd throughout the *Univerfe.* The Keeping,
and Ranging of thefe into order, is committed to
Mr. *Hook,* who had alfo the honour of being made
the firft *Curator* of the *Royal Society* by election.
This *Repofitory* he has begun to reduce under its feveral heads, according to the exact Method of the
Ranks of all the *Species* of *Nature,* which has been
compos'd by Dr. *Wilkins,* and will fhortly be publifh'd in his *Univerfal Language :* A Work wherein
this excellent Man has undertaken a Defign, that
very well fits the temper of his own Mind; for it
well became him to teach a *Communion* of Speech a-
mongft all *Philofophers;* whofe chief ftudy it has always been, to promote a general agreement, and

cor-

correspondence amongst all virtuous and wise Men.

This *Book* had sooner seen the light, if part of it had not perish'd in the *Fire*. Of its use and accurate composition there is no man can doubt, that has ever heard the name of the *Author* : of whom, if I had not at first restrain'd my self from particular commendations, I might have said very much in his praise, which deserves to be known to all the World, and to be the first *Experiment* of his own *Universal Language*.

Their Library. Having well succeeded in this their purpose of *collecting* divers patterns of all *Natural,* and *Artificial* things : they have also (amongst others) appointed a *Committee,* whose chief employment shall be to read over whatever *Books* have been written on such subjects. By this means they hope speedily to observe, and digest into *Manuscript volumes,* all that has been hitherto try'd, or propounded in such studies. This is the only help that an *Experimenter* can receive from *Books :* which he may still use, as his *Guides,* though not as his *Masters*. For this end they have begun a *Library* consisting only of such *Authors,* as may be serviceable to their *Design*. To this there has been lately made a great Addition, by the Munificent Gift of Mr. *Henry Howard* of *Norfolk,* who has bestow'd on the *Society* the whole *Arundelian Library,* containing several hundreds of choice *Manuscripts,* besides some thousands of other *Books* of all kinds. And because many of them belong'd to other *Professions,* this Noble Benefactor has given them with a free permission of changing them for others, that shall be more proper for their *Work :* Whereby they will shortly be able to shew a compleat *Collection* of all that has been

publish'd

publifh'd in the Ancient, or Modern Tongues, which either regards the productions of *Nature*, or the effects of all *Manual Arts.*

Nor is this the only bounty which this Illuftrious *Perfon* has conferr'd on the *Royal Society* ; fince by the firing of *London*, the firft place of their meeting has been reftored to its original ufe, and made an *Exchange*, he has afforded them a retreat in his own houfe, where they affemble at this prefent : By which favour he has added a new honour to the antient *Nobility* of his *Race* : one of his *Anceftors* had before adorn'd that place with many of the beft Monuments of *Antiquity :* and now by entertaining thefe new difcoveries under his Roof, his *Family* deferves the double Praife of having cherifh'd both the old, and new *Learning* ; fo that now methinks in *Arundel* houfe, there is a perfect reprefentation, what the real *Philofophy* ought to be: As there we behold new *Inventions* to flourifh amongft the *Marbles*, and *Images* of the *Dead :* fo the prefent *Arts*, that are now rifing, fhould not aim at the deftruction of thofe that are paft, but be content to thrive in their company.

It will not I hope be expected, that I fhould prefent my *Reader* an *Index* of all the feveral *Writings*, which have at any time been publifh'd by the *Members* of the *Royal Society.* I fhall omit thofe, which either were printed before the beginning of this *Inftitution*, or which treat of matters, that have no relation to their *Defign.*   Only I will fay in general, that there is fcarce any *Art*, or *Argument*, which has ever been the fubject of humane *Wit*, of which I might not produce Inftances, that fome *Fellows* of this *Society* have given good proofs of their labours in it : of thofe *Difcourfes,*

*Sect.
XXXVIII.
Their Difcourfes and
Theories.*

ses, which have been since compos'd by some of their *Body*, or read before their weekly *Assemblies*, and directly concern the advancement of their *Work*, these are the principal.

Several *Hypotheses* explaining the divers *Phases* and *Motions*, and other *Phænomena* of the *Comets*.

Several *Hypotheses* of *Saturn*, and its *Satellites*.

An *Hypothesis* of the cause of the *Rugosity* of the *Moons* surface.

An *Hypothesis* of the motion of the *Moon*, and of the *Sea* depending upon it.

An *Hypothesis* of the motion of the *Planets*, and of Circular *Motion* in general.

Several *Hypotheses* for the *Æquation* of Time.

A *Discourse* about the possibility of the Retardation of *Cælestial Motions*, and of their going slower, and slower, the longer they last.

A *Discourse* of making the several *Vibrations* of a *Pendulum æqual*, by making the weight of it move in a *Cycloid* instead of a *Circle*.

Several *Discourses*, and *Hypotheses* about the length of a *Pendulum*, for moving once in a second of Time.

A *Discourse* of the most convenient length of a *Pendulum*, for making a Standard for a universal Measure.

Several *Astronomical Discourses* of Mr. *Hortex* retriv'd, and digested for the Press.

Uleg Beg translated, about the places of the fix'd Stars, and several other Astronomical *Observations*.

A *Discourse* about the possibility of the change of the attractive power of the *Earth*, and consequently of the variation of the vibrative motion of *Pendulums*.

A *Discourse* about short inclining *Pendulums*, and of other *Pendulums* counterpois'd above the Center of
Motion,

Motion, and of others lying *Horizontal* in the manner of a Beam.

An *Hypothesis* about *Fire,* and *Flame.*

An *Hypothesis,* and discourse of the gravity, pressure, and spring of the *Air.*

A *Discourse* of an *Air Register.*

Several *Discourses* Mathematical, and Philosophical, upon the *Experiment* of raising great weights by the *Breath.*

A *Discourse* and Demonstration against a propos'd Method of doubling the *Cube,* and of finding two mean *Proportionals.*

Several *Discourses* about *Thermometers, Hygroscopes, Baroscopes,* and other *Weather-wifers.*

An *Hypothesis* and *Discourse* of the *Inflection* and inflective veins of the *Air,* and of the fitness, and unfitness of the *Air* for *Cælestial Observations.*

An *Hypothesis* of the Form, and Spring of the *Air.*

A *Discourse* of the different parts of the same Water, and of the difference of Waters.

A *Discourse* and *Hypothesis* of Filtration, and of the Congruity, and Incongruity of *Bodies.*

A *Discourse* of the possible height of the *Air,* and of its proportionable rarefaction upwards.

An *Hypothetical Discourse* about the suspension of the Clouds, and their pressure.

An *Hypothesis,* and *Discourse* of *Earthquakes.*

A *Discourse* of Petrifactions, and an *Hypothesis* for explaining the several varieties of such Bodies.

Several *Discourses* about the *Loadstone,* and an *Hypothesis* for salving its appearances.

A *Discourse* about the Pores of Stones.

A *Discourse* about Eggs.

A *Discourse* concerning the Glass-drops.

A

A *Difcourfe* and *Hypothefis* of annealing, and tem-
pering Steel.

Difcourfes about Cyder, and Coffee.

A *Difcourfe* of the original of Forms.

An *Hypothefis* of Light.

A *Difcourfe* and *Hypothefis* of the Nature and Pro-
prieties of Colours.

A *Difcourfe* about improving Wood for Dying,
and for fixing Colours.

A *Difcourfe* about the improvement of Mufick.

A *Difcourfe* of the differing Heat of Summer,
and Winter.

A *Difcourfe*, and *Hypothefis* about Fluidity.

Difcourfes upon feveral *Mercurial Experiments*.

Difcourfes of *Hydroftaticks*.

Difcourfes about the force of falling Bodies.

A *Treatife* of the motion of the Mufcles.

A *Difcourfe* of the Ufefulnefs of Experimental
Philofophy.

A *Treatife* of the vanity of Dogmatizing.

The Sceptical Chymift.

Eflays about Salt-peter.

The *Parallel* of the Ancient, and Modern Architecture.

Microfcopical Obfervations.

Micrographia, or a *Difcourfe* of things difcover'd
by a *Microfcope*.

Three *Books* of *Fevers*, of the Brain, and of the
Scurvy, which I will alledge as the great Inftances of
this head : Wherein the famous *Author* has with accurate Diligence made prodigious improvements in
all the parts of Phyfick, and fhewn that the largenefs
of his *Knowledge* in it, is equal to the happy fuccefs
of his *practice*.

** 　　　　　　　　　　　　　in

In this Collection of their *Difcourfes*, and *Treatifes,* my Reader beholding fo many to pafs under the name of *Hypothefes*, may perhaps imagine that this confifts not fo well with their Method, and with the main purpofe of their *Studies*, which I have often repeated to be chiefly bent upon the *Operative*, rather than the *Theoretical Philofophy*. But I hope he will be fatisfied, if he fhall remember, that I have already remov'd this doubt, by affirming that whatever *Principles*, and *Speculations* they now raife from things, they do not rely upon them as the abfolute end, but only ufe them as a means of farther *Knowledge*. This way the moft fpeculative *Notions*, and *Theorems* that can be drawn from matter, may conduce to much profit. The light of *Science*, and *Doctrines* of caufes, may ferve exceeding well to promote our *Experimenting* ; but they would rather obfcure, than illuminate the mind, if we fhould only make them the perpetual Objects of our *Contemplation* : as we fee the light of the Sun, is moft beneficial to direct our footfteps in walking, and our hands in working, which would certainly make us blind, if we fhould only continue fix'd, and gazing on its Beams.

The *Hiftories* they have gather'd, are either of *Nature*, *Arts*, or *Works*. Thefe they have begun to collect by the plaineft Method, and from the plaineft Information. They have fetch'd their Intelligence from the conftant and unerring ufe of *experienc'd Men* of the moft unaffected, and moft unartificial kinds of life. They have already perform'd much in this way, and more they can promife the world to accomplifh in a very fhort fpace of time.

There are already brought in to them the *Hiftory*

§. XXXIX. *The Hiftories they have collected.*

K k   of

of *Comets* in general, and efpecially of the two laft: The Hiftory of *Englifh Mines,* and *Oars:* And particularly two feveral *Hiftories* of *Tinneries* and *Tin-working*.

The *Hiftories* of *Iron-making:* of *Lignum Foffile:* of *Saffron:* of *Alkermes:* of *Verdigreace:* of *whiting* of *Wax:* of *Cold:* of *Colours:* of *Fluidity,* and *firmnefs*.

The *Hiftories* of Refining: of making Copperas: of making Allum: of Salt-peter: of making Latten: of Lead: of making Salt out of Sea-water: of refining Gold: of making Pot-afhes: of making Cerufe: of making Brafs: of Painting, and Limning: of Calcography: of Enamelling: of Varnifhing: of Dying.

The *Hiftories* of making Cloath: of Worfted-Combers: of Fullers: of Tanners, and Leather-making: of Glovers, and Leather-drcffing: of Parchment, and Vellum-making, and the way of making tranfparent Parchment: of Paper-making: of Hatters: of making Marble Paper: of the Rowling-Prefs.

The *Hiftories* of making Bread: of Malt: of brewing Beer and Ale in feveral places: of Whale-fifhing: of the Weather for feveral years: Wind-mills, and other Mills in *Holland:* of Mafonry: of Pitch and Tar: of Maiz: of Vintners: of Shot: of making Gun-powder: and of making fome, that is twenty times as ftrong as the common Piftol-powder.

The two laft of thefe were communicated to the *Royal Society* by the favour of *Prince Rupert;* whom I take the boldnefs to mention here, for his excellent Knowledge, and ufe in all manner of Mechanical Ope-

Operations. But his name will be recorded in all the *Histories* of this time, for greater works, for many glorious Enterprises by Sea and Land, and for the Immortal Benefits whereby he has oblig'd the *English Nation.*

The Instances that I shall give of this their manner of collecting *Histories,* shall be, of *Works,* that of *Saltpetre*; of *Arts,* that of *Dying* ; of *Nature,* that of *Oysters*: which last may perhaps seem a subject too mean to be particularly alledg'd : but to me it appears worthy to be produc'd. For tho' the *British Oysters* have been famous in the World, ever since this Island was discover'd, yet the skill how to order them a-right, has been so little consider'd amongst our selves, that we see at this day, it is confin'd to some few narrow *Creeks* of one single County.

THE

T H E

HISTORY

Of the Making of

SALT-PETER,

By *Mr.* H E N S H A W.

" WHether the *Nitre* of the Antients be of the
" same species with the Salt which is com-
" monly known by the name of *Salt-peter*, is variouf-
" ly difputed by very learned Authors amongft the
" modern Pyfitians: on the negative fide are *Ma-*
" *thiolus* and *Bellonius* ; the latter of which had the
" advantage, by the opportunity of his travels in *E-*
" *gypt*, to have often feen and handled them both, and
" is fo pofitive as to pronounce, that in all *Chriften-*
" *dom* there is not one grain of *Nitre* to be found, un-
" lefs it be brought from other parts, although at the
" time of his being in *Grand Caire* (which was about
" the year 1550.) it was fo common there (as he
" fays) that ten pounds of it would not coft a
" *Moidin.* Among thofe that hold the affirmative,
" the moft eminent are *Cardan* and *Longius* ; and it
" fhould feem the general vote of learned Men hath
" been moft favourable to that Opinion, by reafon
" that in all Latine Relations and Prefcriptions, the
" word *Nitrum* or *Halinitrum* is moft commonly uf-
" ed for *Salt-peter.*

" E

" I have often enquired, amongſt our *London*
" Drugſters, for *Egyptian Nitre,* and if I had been ſo
" fortunate as to have found any, I doubt not but I
" ſhould have been able to have put an end to that
" Queſtion by a Demonſtration ; that is, by turning
" the greateſt part of it into *Salt-peter.* However,
" the Obſervations I have made in my own private
" Experiments, and in the practice of *Salt-peter-men*
" and Refiners of *Salt-peter,* ſeem to give me ſuffici-
" ent ground to ſuſpect, that the confidence of thoſe,
" who hold them to be ſeveral Salts, proceedeth
" chiefly from their being unacquainted with the
" various Φαινόμενα of *Salt-peter* in the marking and
" refining of it : and alſo their comparing double re-
" fined *Salt-peter* (of which Gunpowder is made)
" with that deſcription of *Nitrum* and *Aphronitrum*
" in the tenth chapter of the one and thirtieth Book
" of *Plinies Natural Hiſtory* (the only tolerable ac-
" compt of that Salt that hath been handed to us
" from Antiquity) where he tells us, That *Aphroni-*
" *trum* was *Colore pene purpureo,*and *Egyptian Nitre*
" *Fuſcum & Lapidoſum,* adding afterward, *Sunt ibi*
" *Nitrariæ in quibus rufum exit a colore terræ,*which
" is ſufficient to have hinted to any one but mode-
" rately verſed in the modern way of ordering *Salt-*
" *peter,*that the Antients were not at all skilled in re-
" fining their *Nitre* from the Earth and common Salt
" that is uſually mingled with it, nor from that foul
" yellow Oyl, which, it ſeems, did accompany their
" *Nitre,* as well as it doth our *Salt-peter,* in great
" abundance ; for *Pliny* takes notice of it, when he
" mentions the removing the *Nitre* (after it is grain-
" ed) out of the *Nitraria,* ſaying, *Hic quoque natura*
" *olei intervenit, ad ſcabiem animalium utilis :* And
                                    " indeed

" indeed this greafy Oyl (which the Workmen call
" *Mother of Salt-peter,* and perhaps is but the crude
" and unripe part of it) doth by nature fo wonder-
" fully adhere to every part elfe of the *Peter* (it
" may be ordained for the nutriment and augmenta-
" tion of it) that the feparation of it, is the fole caufe
" of the great charge and labour that is required to
" the refining of *Peter* : otherwife the *Peter* will be
" yellow, or brown, or fome other dark colour. And
" *Scaliger* in his 104. *Exercit. fect.* 15. faith, *Sublu-*
" *ſtris purpuræ quaſi ſplendor quidem in ſalis-petræ*
" *terris ſæpenumero eſt a novis obſervatus* ; and he
" that fhall boil a Lixivium paft through a *Salt-peter-*
" earth, up to a confiftence, without filtring it
" through afhes, or giving the Salt leave to Chry-
" ftallize, may perhaps find fomething not unlike
" the *Nitre* of the Antients.

"   To make this doubt yet clearer, it will require
" your patience to obferve a few fhort remains out of
" the fame *Pliny,* concerning the production of *Ni-*
" *tre* ; faith he, *Exiguum Nitri fit apud Medos, can-*
" *defcentibus ſiccitate convallibus quod vocant Hal-*
" *mirhaga : minus etiam in Thracia juxta Philippos*
" *ſordidum Terra quod appellant Agrium.*

"   This agrees very exactly with what I have been
" informed by a Refiner of *Salt-peter,* that near
" *Sophia, Santa-Cruz,* and feveral other places in *Bar-*
" *bary,* he hath feen *Salt-peter* fhoot out of the ground
" (as thick and white as a hoar froft) on many barren
" and defart Lands ; only he adds, that this hap-
" pens not till the begining of the rains of *Auguſt,* or
" *September* ; and that it is the falling of the frefh-
" water that caufes the *Salt-peter* to fhoot out into
" little Chryftals ; and that the people of the Coun-
"   try

" try do no more but take it off the ground as clean
" as they can, and fell it to Merchant-ſtrangers. This
" is, ſays he, the *Barbary Peter,* which the Refiners
" buy commonly at twenty ſhillings *per Cent.*

" Much after the ſame manner (by the relation of
" on *India* Merchant) is that great quantity of *Pe-*
" *ter* produced, which of late years hath been
" brought into *England,* and other parts of *Chriſten-*
" *dom,* from about *Pegu* in *Eaſt-India,* ſaving that the
" Natives do refine it once, before they ſell it to the
" Merchants : But being not ſo skilful, to diſcharge
" it from the common Salt, which attends *Peter,* our
" Workmen do refine it again, before it be fit for
" Gun-powder.

" The next remarque out of *Pliny,* is, *Aquæ vero*
" *Nitroſe pluribus in locis reperiuntur, ſed ſine viribus*
" *Denſandi* (he means the heat of the Sun in thoſe
" places) *Optimum Copioſumque in Clytis Macedoniæ*
" *quod vocant Chalaſtricum candidum purumque pro-*
" *ximum ſali. Lacus eſt Nitroſus, exiliente è medio*
" *dulci fonticulo, ibi ſit Nitrum circa Canis ortum,*
" *novenis diebus, totidemque ceſſat, & rurſus innatat*
" *& deinde ceſſat, iis autem diebus quibus gignitur*
" *ſi fuere imbres ſalſius Nitrum faciunt, Aquilones*
" *deterius quia Validius commovent limum. In E-*
" *gypto autem conficitur multò abundantius ſed dete-*
" *rius, nam fuſcum lapidoſumque eſt, fit penè eodem*
" *modo quo Sal : niſi quod Salinis mare infundunt,*
" *Nilum autem Nitrariis.*

" How ſuch great plenty of *Nitre* ſhould be found
" in the Waters above mention'd will be no difficulty
" to conjecture, if we conſider that Lakes are the re-
" ceptacles of Land floods, and that great Rains may
" eaſily bring it to the Lake in *Macedonia,* from the
"   " higher

" higher parts in the Country about it- And for the
" River *Nile*, there muft needs be lefs fcruple con-
" cerning it, if we call to mind that once in a year, it
" fweeps with an impetuous overflow the burnt and
" barren Defarts of *Africa* under the *Torrid Zone*;
" where by the relation of Travellers, thofe Sands
" are vifibly full of *Nitre*, and thofe few Springs and
" Wells that are to be found there, are by that rea-
" fon fo bitter, that the *Mores* and their Camels are
" forced to make a hard fhift with them in their long
" journeys.

 " But when he comes to defcribe the *Aphronitrum*,
" he comes more home, both to the name and nature
" of our *Salt-peter*, in thefe words, *Proxima ætas Me-*
" *dicorum tradidit, Aphronitrum in Afia Colligi in*
" *fpeluncis & molibus diftillans, dein fole ficcant.* And
" *Scaliger* fpeaking of *Salt-peter*, fays, *Eft quædam*
" *Nitri fpecies inhærens Rupibus, in quibus infolatur,*
" *ac propterea Salpetra dicitur.* And, I myfelf, for my
" own fatisfaction in the point, have drawn very
" good *Rock-peter* out of thofe *Stiriæ*, which are
" ufually found hanging like Icycles in Arched-cel-
" lars and Vaults; and have been told, that a Phy-
" fitian in *Shropfhire* did perform great Cures by ver-
" tue of *Sal-prunellæ*, which he made only of Flower
" of Brimftone and thofe *Stiriæ*.

 " But to fteer more directly upon our immediate
" fubject *Salt-peter*; tho' it be likely, that the Air
" is every where full of a volatile kind of *Nitre*,
" which is frequently to be feen coagulated into fine
" white Salt, like Flower of Wheat (but by the ve-
" ry tafte may be eafily known to be *Peter*) fticking
" to the fides of Plaftred-walls, and in Brick-walls
" to the Mortar between the Bricks, (in dry wea-
            " ther,

" ther, or where the wall is defended from the rain)
" for Lime doth ſtrongly attract it ; though Dew and
" Rain do conveigh much of it to the Earth, and the
" Clouds ſeem to be ſpread out before the face of the
" Sun either to imbibe ſome part of his influence, or
" to have a Salt generated in them, for to advance the
" fertility of the Earth, and certainly they return not
" without a bleſſing ; for I have more than once ex-
" tracted *Salt-peter* out of Rain and Dew, but from
" the latter more plentifully, and yet even there, is
" *Salt-peter* accompanied with a greazy purple Oyl,
" in great plenty : Though (as I have found upon
" tryal) that moſt ſtanding waters, and even deep
" Wells have ſome ſmall quantity of *Salt-peter* in
" them ; though the face of the Earth, if it were not
" impregnated with this Salt, could not produce Ve-
" getables ; for Salt (as the Lord *Bacon* ſays) is the
" firſt Rudiment of Life ; and *Nitre* is as it were the
" Life of Vegetables : Yet to be more ſure of it, I
" made Experiment likewiſe there too, and found
" ſome little of it in fallows, and the Earth which
" Moles caſt up in the Spring : Though I ſay the Air
" and Water want it not, yet it is not there to be had
" in any proportion, anſwerable to the charge in get-
" ting it : And though the Earth muſt neceſſarily have
" great quantities thereof, generated or infuſed into
" it ; yet in theſe temperate Countreys of *Europe,*
" it is no ſooner dilated by Rain-water, or the Moi-
" ſture of the Earth, but it is immediately applyed
" to the production or nutriment of ſome Plant, In-
" ſect, Stone, or Mineral ; ſo that the Artiſt will find
" as little of it here to ſerve his turn, as in the other
" two Elements.

   " The only place therefore, where *Salt-peter* is to
" be

" be found in thefe Northern Countries, is in Stables,
" Pigeon-houfes, Cellars, Barns, Ware-houfes, or in-
" deed any place, which is covered from the Rain,
" which would diffolve it, and (as I have faid) make
" it vegetate ; as alfo from the Sun, which doth rarify
" it, and caufed it to be exhaled into the Air ; (For
" the fame reafon Husbandmen alfo might make dou-
" ble or treble the profit they ufually do of their
" Muck, if they will lay it up under a Hovel, or
" fome covered place, until they carry it out upon
" their Land.)   And I have been told by an experi-
" enced Workman, that no Man yields *Peter* fo plen-
" tifully, as the Earth in Churches, were it not an
" impiety to difturb the Afhes of our Anceftours, in
" that facred Depofitory.

" Provided always, that the Earth be of good
" mould, and the better the mould is, the more *Pe-*
" *ter* is produc'd, for in Clay or fandy Earth, little
" or none is to be found : The freer ingrefs the Air
" hath into a place, is ftill of more advantage, fo that
" the Sun be excluded ; And let the Earth be never fo
" good, if it be laid on a brick or boarded floor, it
" will not be fo rich in *Peter*, as if it have free com-
" munication with the Exhalations of the lower parts
" of the Earth.

" In any place thus qualified, you cannot mifs of
" good quantities of *Peter*, if it have not been drawn
" out in fome Years before ; which a Workman will
" quickly find, after he hath digged the firft fpadeful
" of Earth, by laying a little of it on the end of his
" tongue, and if it taft bitter, he is fure of good ftore
" of mineral, (as they love to call it) that is, *Salt-*
" *peter* ; if the Ground be good, it continues rich, to
" fix or eight foot deep, and fometimes, but not often,
" to ten.   " After

" After the *Salt-peter* is extracted, if the Earth be
" laid wet in the fame place again, it will be twenty
" Years e're any confiderable quantity grow there of
" it; but if the Earth be well dryed, it will come in
" twelve or fourteen : and if they mingle, with the
" dryed Earth ftore of Pigeons-dung, and mellow
" Horfe-dung, and then temper it with Urine (as
" was ufual before we were fupplyed with *Peter* from
" *India*) it will be fit to dig again in five or fix Years.
" He that fhall caft Water upon a Ground fit to dig
" for *Peter*, will only fink the Mineral deeper into
" the Earth; but he that throws Soap-fuds on it, will
" quite deftroy the *Peter*, (as the Workmen have a
" Tradition) and it very well deferves a further En-
" quiry.

" That *Salt-peter*, and the way of drawing it out
" of the Earth, now in ufe, was a modern Invention,
" is generally concluded by all Authors; but whether
" we owe it to chance, or the fagacity of fome great
" Wit, is as unknown, as the time when it was firft
" difcovered.

" It feems to have many Years preceeded the Inven-
" tion of Gun-powder, which by the *Germans* is afcri-
" bed to *Conftantine Autlitzer*, or *Berthold Schwertz*
" a Monk of *Friburgh*, and was, in all probability, not
" long difcovered, when the Inventor (*Polydore Vir-
" gil* tells us) taught the ufe of Guns, to the *Veneti-
" ans*, at the Battel of *Foffa Claudia*, when they ob-
" tain'd that notable Victory over the *Genouefes*, *An-
" no* 1380. For there is mention made, both of *Salt-
" peter* and *Aqua-fortis*, in the Writings of *Geber*, a
" *Spanifh More*, and an *Alchymift*; but at what time
" he lived is unknown, though it be certain, fome
" hundreds of Years before *Raimund Lully*; who a-

" bout

" about the Year 1 3 3 3, publithed fome of his Books,
" wherein he treats of *Salt-peter* and *Aqua-fortis*.
" It is no ill conjecture of *Maierus*, that the forefaid
" Monk, being a skilful Alchymift, had a defign to
" draw a higher Spirit from *Peter* than the common
" *Aqua-fortis*, and that he might better open the Bo-
" dy of *Peter*, he ground it with Sulphur and Char-
" coal, by which Compofure he foon became the In-
" venter of Gun-powder.

The manner of making

SALT-PETER.

" IN the firft place you muft be provided of eight
" or ten Tubs, fo large, that they may be able to
" contain about ten Barrows full of Earth, each of
" them.   Thefe Tubs muft be all open at the top ;
" but in the bottom of every one of them, you muft
" make a hole near to that fide you intend to place
" outermoft, which hole you muft fit very well with
" a Tap and Spigot on the outfide downward.   On
" the infide of the Tub, near the tap-hole, you muft
" carefully place a large wad of ftraw, and upon that
" a fhort piece of board, which is all to keep the earth
" from ftopping up the tap-hole.   When you have
" placed your Tubs on their ftands, at fuch a diftance
" one from the other, that you may come with eafe
" between them, then fill them up with fuch *Peter-*
" *earth* as you have chofen for your work, leaving
" only void about a fpans breadth between the Earth
" and the edge of the Tub ; then lay on the top of
                                                    " the

" the Earth in each Tub, as near as you can to the
" middle, a rundle of Wicker, like the bottom of a
" Basket, and about a foot in diameter, and by it ſtick
" into the Earth a good ſtrong Cudgel, which muſt
" be thruſt pretty near the bottom ; the Wicker is to
" keep the Water, when it is poured on, from hollow-
" ing and diſordering the Earth, and the Cudgel is to
" be ſtirred about, to give the Water ingreſs to the
" Earth upon occaſion : Then pour on your Earth
" common cold Water, till it ſtand a hands breadth
" over the Earth : When it hath ſtood eight or ten
" hours looſen the Spigots, and let the Water rather
" dribble, than run into half Tubs, which muſt be ſet
" under the taps : This *Lixivium* the Workmen call
" their Raw-liquor ; and note that if it come not
" clear at the firſt drawing, you muſt pour it on again,
" and after ſome little time draw it off, till it come
" clear, and of the colour of Urine.

" If you are curious to know how rich your Li-
" quor is before boyling, you may take a Glaſs-vial,
" containing a quart, fill it with the common Water
" you uſe, then weigh it exactly ; next fill the ſame
" Glaſs with your Liquor, and find the difference of
" weight, which compared with the quantity of all
" your Liquors, will give you a very near gueſs, how
" much *Salt-peter* you are like to make by that boyl-
" ing.

" Then pour on again, on the ſame Earth, more
" common Water, that it may bring away what is
" remaining in the Earth of the former Liquor. This
" ſecond Liquor is of no other uſe, but to be poured
" on new Earth, inſtead of common Water; be-
" cauſe it contains ſome quantity of *Salt-peter* in
" it.

" When

" When this is done, turn out the ufelefs infipid
" Earth out of the Tubs, which you muft fill with
" new Earth, and continue this Operation, till you
" have in the fame manner lixiviated all the Earth :
" Then fill your Copper with your Liquor, which
" Copper, for one of the Profeffion, muft be about
" two hundred weight, and fet ftrongly in a Furnace
" of brick-work ; befides, on one fide of your Fur-
" nace you are to place a Tub full of your Liquor,
" which at a tap below may dribble as faft into the
" Copper, as the force of the Fire doth waft your
" Liquor, which Invention is only to fave charges in
" Fewel. When you have boyled it up to that height,
" that a little of it, flirted off the finger on a live
" Charcoal, will flafh like Gun-powder (which for
" the moft part falls out to be about two Days and a
" Nights boyling) at what time, upon tryal, a hun-
" dred weight of the Liquor contains about five
" and thirty pound weight of *Peter.*   But the Work-
" men feldom make ufe of any further indication,
" than by finding the Liquor hang like oyl on the
" fides of the Brafen fcummer, when 'tis dipped into
" it, which is a fign it is fit to be paffed through the
" Afhes, which is done in this manner.

" You muft prepare two Tubs fitted after the man-
" ner of the firft, where you put your Earth, faving
" that at the bottom of thefe Tubs, you muft lay
" Reeds or Straw a foot high ; over them place loofe
" boards, pretty near one another, over them, a little
" more Straw (which is to keep the Afhes from the
" top, and to give the Liquor room to drein the
" better from them:) Then fill up your Tubs with
" any fort of Wood-afhes to half a foot of the top ;
" Then pour on the forefaid Liquor, as it comes fcal-

**   " ding

" ding hot out of the Copper, on the Aſhes contain-
" ed in the firſt Tub ; then after a while draw it off
" at the top : and ſo continue putting on and draw-
" ing off, firſt at one Tub of Aſhes, then at the other,
" till your Liquor grow clear, and loſe the thick tur-
" bid colour it had when it went on.

" When all the Liquor hath in this manner paſt
" through the Aſhes of both Tubs, that by this means
" all its greaſie oyl is left behind in the Aſhes, you
" muſt keep it for the ſecond boyling in a Veſſel by it
" ſelf : in the mean time pour upon your Aſhes a ſuffi-
" cient quantity of common Water very hot, once
" or twice, to bring away what is remaining of the
" Liquor in the Aſhes.

" When you begin the ſecond boyling, put firſt
" into the Copper the Water that went laſt through
" your Aſhes, and as that waſteth, let your ſtrong Li-
" quor drop into the Copper, out of the Tub above
" deſcribed, ſtanding on the ſide of the Furnace, till
" the Liquor in the Copper be ready to ſhoot or
" chryſtalliſe.

" *Note*, That toward the end of your boyling, there
" will ariſe great ſtore of Scum and Froth, which
" muſt be carefully taken off with a great braſs Scum-
" mer, made like a Ladle, full of little holes, and uſu-
" ally about that time it lets fall ſome common Salt
" to the bottom, which you muſt take up with the
" ſaid Scummer, and lay it aſide for another uſe.

" To know when the Liquor is ready to ſhoot into
" *Peter*, you need but drop a little of it on a knife, or
" any other cold thing that hath a ſmooth ſuperfi-
" cies, and if it coagulate, like a drop of tallow, and
" do not fall off the knife when it is turned down-
" ward, which alſo may be judged by its hanging like
" oyl

" oyl to the fides of the Scummer. When the Li-
" quor is brought to this pafs, every hundred weight
" of it containeth about threefcore and ten pound
" weight of *Peter*.

 " When you find your Liquor thus ready to fhoot,
" you muft with great Iron Ladles lade it out of the
" Copper into a high narrow Tub for that purpofe,
" which the Workmen call their fettling Tub; and
" when the Liquor is grown fo cold, that you can en-
" dure your finger in it, you fhall find the common or
" cubick Salt begin to gravulate and ftick to the fides
" of the Tub, then at the tap, placed about half a
" foot from the bottom, draw off your Liquor into
" deep wooden Trays, or Brafs-pans, and the cooler
" the place is where you let them ftand to fhoot in,
" the better and more plentifully will the *Salt-peter*,
" be produc'd; but it will be of no good colour till
" it be refined, but will be part white, part yellow,
" and fome part of it blackifh.

 " The Salt which fticketh to the fides and bottom
" of the fetling Tub is (as I have faid) of the na-
" ture of common Salt; and there is fcarce any *Pe-*
" *ter* to be found but is accompanied with it, though
" no doubt fome of this is drawn out of the Afhes
" by the fecond Liquors: If it be foul they refine it
" by it felf, and about *London* fell it at good rates to
" thofe that falt Neat Tongues, Bacon, and Collar-
" Beef; for befides a favory tafte, it gives a pleafing red
" colour to moft Flefh that is falted with it. *Pliny*
" fays, *Nitrum obfonia alba & deteriora reddit Olera*
" *viridiora*, whether *Salt-peter* doth fo, I have not
" yet tryed.

 " When the Liquor hath ftood two Days and two
" Nights in the Pans, that part of the Liquor which is
          " not

" not coagulated but fwims upon the *Peter,* muft be
" carefully poured off, and being mingled with new
" Liquors muft again pafs the Afhes before it be boil-
" ed, elfe it will grow fo greafy it will never generate
" any Salt.

To Refine

SALT-PETER.

" After you have made your Copper very clean,
" " put in as much Water as you think will dif-
" folve that quantity of *Peter* you purpofe to Refine,
" when the Water is very hot caft in the *Peter* by lit-
" tle and little, ftirring it about with a Ladle, that it
" may the fooner diffolve, then increafe the Fire till
" your Liquor begin to boile : In the mean time feel
" with the Scummer, whether there be at the bottom
" any Salt undiffolv'd and take it out, for it is Com-
" mon-Salt, and doth not fo foon diffolve as the *Peter* ;
" then as the water boils fcim off the Froth that fwims
" at the top of it as faft as it rifeth ; when it hath
" boiled to the height that a drop of it will coagu-
" late on a Plate, (as hath been faid above in the ma-
" king of *Salt-peter,*) then caft in by degrees either
" a Pint of the ftrongeft Wine-vinegar, or elfe four
" Ounces of Allom beaten to powder (fome choofe
" burnt Allom,) and you fhall obferve a black Scum
" to rife on the top of the Liquor, which when you
" have allowed fome time to thicken, you may eafily
" take off with the Scummer; repeat this fo often till
" no more Scum arifes. Some do ufe to throw in a
" Shovel full of quick-Lime, and fay it makes *Peter*

" the

" the whiter, and Rock the better ; you muſt take
" great care all this while the Fire be not too ſtrong,
" for while this is doing, the Liquor will be apt to
" boil over, and will not eaſily be appeaſed without
" your great loſs.

" When this is done, lade out the Liquor into a
" ſetling Tub, and cover it over with a Cloth, that it
" cool not too ſoon, and within an hour or two, a
" thick yellow Fæces will fall to the bottom of the
" Tub, then quickly draw off the Liquor while it is
" hot, into the ſhooting Trays or Pans, and do as you
" did in making *Peter*, ſaving, that you muſt cover the
" Trays with a Cloth, for then the Liquor will begin
" to ſhoot at the bottom, which will make the *Peter-*
" *Rock* into much fairer Chryſtals, than otherwiſe it
" would : When no more *Peter* will ſhoot (which is
" commonly after two days,) pour off the Liquor
" that ſwims at the top, and put the *Peter* into a
" Tub with a hole at the bottom for to drain, and
" when it is dry, it is fit for uſe.

" The Figure of the Chryſtals is Sexangular, and
" if it hath rightly ſhot, is fiſtulous and hollow like
" a Pipe.

" Before I proceed to tell you, how this darling
" of Nature (the very Baſis and Generation of Nu-
" triment) is converted into Gun-powder (the moſt
" fatal Inſtrument of Death that ever Mankind was
" truſted withal) I will crave leave to acquaint you
" with a few Speculations I have of this Salt, which
" if I could clearly make out, would lead us into
" the knowledge of many noble Secrets in Nature ;
" as alſo to a great improvement in the Art of ma-
" ing *Salt-peter*.

" Firſt, then you are to obſerve, that though *Peter*
" go

" go alway in Gun-powder, yet if you fulminate it
" in a Crucible, and burn off the volatile part with
" Powder of Coal, Brimftone, Antimony or Meal,
" there will remain a Salt, and yet fo fixed (very
" unlike Common-Salt) that it will endure the force
" of almoft the ftrongeft Fire you can give it ; which
" being diffolved into Water and Spirit of *Nitre* drop-
" ped into it, till it give over hiffing (which is the
" fame with the volatile Part that was feparated
" from it in the fulmination) it will be again reduced
" to Chryftals of *Peter*, as it was at firft, which noble
" Experiment the World hath already been taught
" by an honourable Member of this Society ; with a
" train of fuch important Obfervations, as never be-
" fore were raifed from one Experiment.

" That which I aim at then is, that if the Spirit of
" the volatile Salt of Soot, or of the Urine, Blood,
" Horns, Hoofs, Hair, Excrements, or indeed any part
" of Animals, (for all abound with fuch a volatile
" Salt fixed, and Oyl as *Peter* doth) could by the
" fame way or any like it, be reduc'd to *Peter* or
" fome *Nitrous* Salt not much differing from it : It
" would excellently make out a Theory that I am
" much delighted with, till I am convinced in it ;
" which is, that the Salt which is found in Vegetables
" and Animals, is but the *Nitre* which is fo univer-
" fally diffufed through all the Elements, (and muft
" therefore make a chief Ingredient in their Nutri-
" ment, and by confequence of their Generation)
" a little altered from its firft Complexion : And that
" the reafon why Animals that feed on Vegetables
" are obliged by Nature, to longer meals than thofe
" that feed on other Animals ; is, becaufe Animals
" are fuller of that Salt than Vegetables : And in-

" deed

" deed fuch Animals are but Caterers of it for Man;
" and others whom Natures bounty gratifies with a
" more lufty and delicious Diet.

    " I confefs I have been the more confirmed in this
" fancy, fince I have often feen a Friend of mine,
" with a Natural and Facile Ἐχαεἰα convert the
" greater part of *Peter*, into a Salt fo like the Vola-
" tile Salt of Urine, that they are fcarce to be diftin-
" guifhed by fmell or taft, and yet he adds nothing
" to it that can poffibly be fufpected to participate of
" that Nature: But indeed all Volatile Salts are fo
" alike, that it is not eafy to diftinguifh them in any
" refpect.

THE

THE
HISTORY
Of Making
GUN-POWDER.

" THE materials of *Gun-powder* are *Salt-peter,*
" *Brimstone,* and *Coal* ; the *Peter* and *Brim-*
" *stone* must be both refined if you mean to make
" good *Powder,* and the Coal must be *Withy* and *Al-*
" *der* equal parts ; for *Withy* alone is counted too
" soft, and some do commend *Hazle* alone to be as
" good as the other two.

" The whole Secret of the Art consists in the pro-
" portion of the Materials, the exact mixture of them,
" that in every the least part of *Powder* may be found
" all the Materials in their just proportion ; then the
" Corning or making of it into Grains ; and lastly the
" Drying and Dusting of it.

" The proportion is very differently set down by
" several Authors ; *Baptista Porta* tells us the ordina-
" ry *Powder* is made of four Parts of *Peter,* one of
" *Sulphur,* and one of *Withy* Coal : But the best *Pow-*
" *der* of 6, or 8. of *Peter,* and one a piece of the other,
" which agrees pretty well with *Bonfadini* a late *Ita-*
" *lian* Writer, in his Book of the Art of *Shooting flying,*
" where to make the best *Gun-powder* he prescribes
" seven Parts of *Peter,* one of *Brimstone,* and of *Ha-*
" *zel* Coal an ounce less in every pound : *Cardan*
" says ; *Constat ex tribus Halinitri partibus, duabus*
" *Saligni*

" *Saligni Carbonis atque una Sulphuris, Convenitque*
" *magnis Machinis ; Sed Medioeribus Halinitri par-*
" *tes decem, Saligni carbonis tres, Sulphuris duas, par-*
" *vis vero Halinitri partes decem ; Carbonis ligni nu-*
" *cis Avellonæ fine nodis, tum Sulphuris partem unam*
" *fingularem : Langius* appoints three of *Peter*, two
" of *Withy* Coal, and one of *Brimftone :*   The *Eng-*
" *lifh* Author of Fire-works fays, that the proportions
" in *England* to make good, indifferent, and ordinary
" *Powder* is 5. 4. and 3. parts of *Peter*, to two of
" Coal, and one *Brimftone.*   Our *Englifh* Workmen
" are generally fo curious of their fecret, that I could
" not obtain the proportion of them without a pro-
" mife of Secrecy : But when all is done their fecret
" is not fo much the way to make the beft *Powder*,
" as the beft way to get moft mony by it ; by fubftract-
" ing from the *Peter*, and making up weight with
" the Coal ; when indeed there is fo great a Latitude,
" that Provided the Materials be perfectly mixt, you
" make good *Powder* with any of the proportions
" above mention'd ; but the more *Peter* you allow
" it, it will ftill be the better, till you come to obferve
" eight Parts.
    " The next thing after the proportion, is the mix-
" ture, about which moft of the workmens time and
" pains is beftowed : For firft in a Horfe-mill with
" two ftones (like that with which they grind their
" Materials at the *Glafs-houfe*) moving upon a Mar-
" ble bottom, which is edged with boards fet floap-
" ing, that what flips from under the ftones may flide
" back again.
    " They grind the Brimftone and Coal each of them
" apart by themfelves as fine as poffibly they can ;
" then they fift each of them apart by themfelves :
          **   " The

" The Brimſtone is ſifted thorow Tiffany in a Bolt-
" ing-mill, ſuch as the Bakers uſe for wheat flower :
" the Coal is ſifted thorow Lockram, in a bag made
" like a ſhirt ſleeve ; for the convenience of the
" Work-man it is done in a cloſe Bin, with only two
" holes for him to put his arms in, and ſhake the bag
" about. Whatſoever of each material is not ſmall
" enough to ſift thorow, is brought again to the Mill
" to be new ground.

" As for the *Peter*, that muſt in the Copper be diſſol-
" ved in as much water as will juſt take it up, and then
" the water muſt be boiled away till the *Peter* comes
" to the thickneſs of haſty-pudding. The reaſon of
" this operation is becauſe when the *Peter* is thus ſoft,
" the other materials will the eaſilier incorporate
" with it, and in the next place it will not wear the
" wooden peſtles ſo much when it comes to the Mill,
" as when it is hard and dry.

" When the Materials are in this readineſs, they
" are weighed (only the *Peter* is weighed before it is
" put to diſſolve in the Copper) and by proportion
" are carried to the mingling Trough, which is made
" of boards, like a great Cheſt without a cover, being
" about eight foot long, four broad, and three foot
" high. The Coal is laid in firſt, the Brimſtone next,
" and the *Peter* at top of all ; Then two men with
" ſhovels ſtir and mingle them together for an hour,
" and then 'tis ready for the Mill.

" The Powder-mills are ſeldom made to move
" with any thing but water: The great water-wheel
" is made like that of an ordinary water-wheel, ei-
" ther over-ſhot or under-ſhot, according to the
" quantity of water they have : to the *axis* of this
" wheel, a little way within the Mill is faſtened a
" leſſer

" lefler wheel called the Spar-wheel, with ftrong
" Cogs, which in their motion round take hold of
" the round ftaves of another wheel of about the
" fame diameter, fet a little way above it, and faftned
" to the end of a beam of 15 or 16 foot long, laid
" parallel to the Horizon, with an iron gudgeon at
" the other end of it, to facilitate its motion round :
" This beam is called the round beam ; out of it
" come a certain number of arms of about nine inch-
" es long, and three inches broad, which in their go-
" ing round meet with other leffer arms (called
" Tapes) coming out of the Peftles (for fo they call
" certain fmall quarters of Timber placed perpendi-
" cular to the Horizon, about nine foot long and four
" inches broad ; they are fet in a flight frame to keep
" them fteady) ; by thefe fmall arms the Peftles are
" lifted up about two foot and a half, and then let
" fall into a ftrong wooden Trough fet under them,
" wherein the Powder is put to be pounded.

" Every Mill hath two Troughs, and about fixteen
" Peftles : every Peftle hath faftned to the lower end
" of it a round piece of *Lignum Vitæ*, of about five
" inches long and three and a half diameter ; and in-
" to the bottom of the Trough juft where the Peftle
" is to fall, is let in another piece of *Lignum Vitæ*, of
" the fafhion and bignefs of an ordinary Bowl,
" fplit according to its longeft diameter : The Peftles
" are not lifted up all together, but alternatively, to
" make the Powder turn the better in the working ;
" and for the fame reafon round Troughs are counted
" better than fquare.

" To make excellent Powder it ought to be
" wrought thus thirty hours ; but of late they will
" not afford it above eighteen or twenty hours : once
                                                    " in

" in eight hours they ufe to moiften the Powder with
" a little fair Water ; others who are more curious,
" put Water fomething thickned with quick-lime; o-
" thers ufe White-wine Vinegar, others *Aqua vitæ :*
" But if it be not moiftned with fomething once in
" eight hours, the Powder will grow dry, and in half
" an hour after it will take fire. As foon as the Pow-
" der grows dry, you may find it, though at a di-
" ftance, by the Noife of the Mill ; for then the Peftles
" will rebound from the bottom of the Trough and
" make a double ftroak. The only danger to the
" Mill is not from the Trough ; for many times the
" iron Gudgeons grow hot for want of greafing and
" then the Duft that flies about will be apt to fire, and
" fo the Mill blows up.

   " From the Mill the Powder is brought to the
" Corning-houfe, of a middle temper between moift
" and dry. The way of corning it is with two hair
" Sieves join'd together, the upper Sieve inclofing
" fome part of the Hoop of the lower Sieve : The
" upper Sieve hath holes of the fize you will have
" the Powder grained at ; the holes of the lower
" Sieve are much leffer : The upper Sieve they call
" their corning Sieve, the lower their wet Dufter :
" They lay the Powder upon the upper Sieve fome
" two inches thick ; upon that a Peice of heavy
" wood made like a Trencher, of about eight inches
" diameter and two and a half in thicknefs, called a
" Runner, which when the Sieve is moved, by its
" weight and motion, forces the Powder thorow the
" upper Sieve, and that corns it. Then the lower
" Sieve receives the Powder, and lets the duft go
" thorow the Bin, over which the Sieve is fhaken
" called the Dufting-Bin.

      " When

" When the Powder is thus corned, it is laid about
" an inch and half thick on the drying Sieves, which
" are made of coarse Canvas fastned to flight
" frames of Deal about an Ell long, and some twenty
" inches broad; and thus it is carried into Stoves to
" dry.

" The Stove is commonly a little Room about
" eighteen or twenty foot square, with ranges of small
" Firr poles about two foot one above another, to lay
" the drying Sieves upon, but only on that side the
" fire is made. Besides a glass window to give light,
" there must be a small lover hole at the top of the
" Room, to let out the steam, else the Powder will
" not only be the longer a drying, but often by the re-
" turn of the steam on the Sieves, the top of the Pow-
" der will be so crusted that the lower part will not dry.
" The Room is heated by an Iron about a yard high
" and half a yard broad, cast in the form of an Arch,
" equal to a semi-quadrant, and placed in the back
" of a Chimney, the fore part whereof is like a Fur-
" nace; and to avoid danger, opens into another
" little Room apart called the Stoke-hole.

" The Powder is brought into the Stove before it
" be heated, and is not taken out again till the Stove
" be cold; and about eight hours is required to the
" drying of it. In hot Countries the Sun is the best
" Stove, and a great deal of danger and charges that
" way avoided.

" After the Powder is dried, it is brought again to
" the Corning-house, where it is again sifted over
" the dusting Bin in other double Sieves, but without
" any Runners. These Sieves have both of them
" smaller holes than the former: The upper Sieve is
" called the Separater, and serves to divide the great
" corns

" corns from the leffer; the great corns are put by
" themfelves, and ferve for Cannon Powder. The
" lower Sieve is called the dry Dufter, and retains
" the fmall corns (which ferve for Mufquet and Piftol)
" and lets fall the duft into the bin, which is to be
" mingled with frefh Materials, and again wrought
" over in the Mill.

" So that good Powder differs from bad (befides
" the well working and mingling of the Materials)
" in having more *Peter* and lefs Coal; and laftly, in
" the well dufting of it.

" The laft Work is to put the Powder into Barrels;
" every Barrel is to contain five fcore weight of Pow-
" der, and then 'tis ready for fale.

N n 2　　　A N

A N

APPARATUS

TO THE

HISTORY

Of the Common Practices of

D Y I N G.

By Sir *WILLIAM PETTY.*

" I T were not incongruous to begin the History
"   with a Retrospect into the very nature of
" Light it felf (as to inquire whether the fame be a
" Motion or elfe a Body ;) nor to premife fome The-
" orems about the Sun, Flame, Glow-worms, the
" Eyes of fome Animals, fhining Woods, Scales
" of fome Fifhes, the dafhing of the Sea, ftroaks
" upon the Eyes, the *Bolonian* Slate (called by fome
" the Magnet of Light) and of other light and lucid
" Bodies.

" It were alfo not improper to confider the very
" effentials of Colour and Tranfparencies (as that the
" moft tranfparent Bodies, if fhaped into many an-
" gles, prefent the eye with very many colours;)
" That bodies having but one fingle fuperficies, have
" none at all, but are fufcipient of every colour laid

" before

" before them; That great depths of Air make a
" Blew, and great Depths of Water a Greenish co-
" lour; That great Depths or thicknesses of colour-
" ed Liquors do all look Blackish (red Wine in a
" large conical Glass being of all reddish colours
" between black at the top and white at the Bot-
" tom.

    " That most Vegetables, at one time or other, are
" greenish; and that as many things passing the Sun
" are blackned, so many others much whitened by
" the same: Other things are whitened by acid
" Fumes, as red Roses and raw Silks by the smoak
" of Brimstone.

    " Many Mettals, as Steel and Silver, become of
" various colours and Tarnish by the Air, and by se-
" veral Degrees of heat.

    " We might consider the wonderful variety of co-
" lours appearing in Flowers, Feathers; and drawn
" from Mettals, their Calces and Vitrifications; and
" of the Colours rising out of transparent Liquors
" artificially mixed.

    " But these things, relating to the abstracted nature
" of Colours, being too hard for me, I wholly de-
" cline; rather passing to name (and but to name)
" some of the several Sorts of Colorations now com-
" monly used in Humane affairs, and as vulgar Trades
" in these Nations; which are these: *viz.*

    1. " There is a whitening of Wax, and several
" sort of Linnen and Cotton Cloaths, by the Sun,
" Air, and by reciprocal effusions of Water.

    2. " Colouring of Wood and Leather by Lime,
" Salt, and Liquors, as in Staves, Canes, and Marble
" Leathers.

    3. Colouring of Paper, *viz.* Marbled Paper, by
                " distemper-

" diftempering the colours with Ox-gall, and apply-
" ing them upon a ftiff gummed Liquor.

    4. " Colouring, or rather difcolouring the Colours
" of Silks, Tiffanies, &c. by Brimftone.

    5. " Colouring of feveral Iron and Copper work,
" into Black, with Oyl.

    6. " Colouring of Leather into Gold-colour, or
" rather Silver leaves into Gold by Varnifhes, and in
" other cafes by Urine and Sulphur.

    7. " Dying of Marble and Alabafter with heat
" and coloured Oyls.

    8. " Colouring Silver into Brafs with Brimftone
" or Urine.

    9. " Colouring the Barrels and Locks of Guns in-
" to Blew and Purple with the temper of Small-coal
" heat.

    10. " Colouring of Glafs (made of Sands, Flints,
" &c.) as alfo of Chryftals and Earthen Ware, with
" the rufts and folutions of Metals.

    11. " The colouring of live Hair, as in *Poland,*
" Horfe and Man's Hair; as alfo the colouring of
" Furrs.

    12. " Enameling and Anealing.

    13. " Applying Colours as in the Printing of
" Books and Pictures, and as in making of playing
" Cards; being each of them performed in a feveral
" way.

    14. " Guilding and Tinning with *Mercury, Block-*
" *Tin, Sal-Armoniack.*

    15. " Colouring Metals, as Copper with *Calamy*
" into Brafs, and with *Zink* or *Spelter* into Gold, or
" into Silver with *Arfenick:* And of Iron into Cop-
" per with *Hungarian Vitriol.*

    16. " Making Painters Colours by preparing of
" Earth,

" Earth, Chalk, and Slates; as in *Umber, Oker, Cul-*
" *len earth, &c.* as also out of Calces of Lead, as
" *Ceruse* and *Minium* ; by Sublimates of Mercury and
" Brimstone, as in *Vermilion* ; by tinging of white
" Earths variously, as in *Verdeter,* and some of the
" *Lakes* ; by concrete Juyces or *Fæculæ,* as in *Gam-*
" *brugium, Indico, Pinks, Sap-green,* and *Lakes :*
" As also by Rusts, as in *Verdegreafe, &c.*

17. " The applying of these colours by the adhe-
" sion of Ox-gall, as in the Marble Paper aforesaid ;
" or by Gum-water, as in Limning ; or by clammy
" drying Oyls, (such as are the Oyls of Linseed,
" Nuts, Spike, Turpentine, *&c.*)

18. " Watering of *Tabbies.*

19. " The last I shall name is the colouring of
" Wool, Linnen, Cotton, Silk, Hair, Feathers, Horn,
" Leather, and the Threads and Webbs of them with
" Woods, Roots, Herbs, Seeds, Leaves, Salts, Limes,
" Lixiviums, Waters, Heats, Fermentations, Macera-
" tions, and other great variety of Handling : An ac-
" count of all which is that History of Dying we in-
" tend. All that we have hitherto said being but a
" kind of remote and scarce pertinent Introduction
" thereunto.

" I begin this History by enumerating all the seve-
" ral Materials and Ingredients which I understand
" to be or to have been used in any of the last afore-
" mentioned Colorations, which I shall represent in
" various Methods, *viz.* out of the *Mineral* Family.
" They use Iron and Steel, or what is made or comes
" from them, in all true Blacks (called *Spanish* Blacks)
" though not in *Flanders* Blacks ; *viz.* they use Cop-
" peras, Steel-filings, and Slippe; which is the stuff
" found in the Troughs of Grind-stones, whereon
" Edge.

" Edge-tools have been ground.   They alfo ufe Pew-
" ter for Bow-dye, Scarlet, *viz*. they diffolve Bars of
" Pewter in the *Aqua fortis* they ufe ; and make alfo
" their Dying-kettles or Furnace of this Mettal.

" *Litharge* is ufed by fome, though acknowledged
" by few, for what neceffary reafon I cannot learn, o-
" ther than to add weight unto Dyed Silk ; *Litharge*
" being a calx of Lead, one of the heavieft and moft
" colouring Mettals.

" I apprehend *Antimony* much ufed to the fame
" purpofe, though we know there be a very tingent
" Sulphur in their Mineral, which affordeth variety of
" Colour by the precipitations and other operations
" upon it.

" *Arfenick* is ufed in Crimfon upon pretence of
" giving Luftre, although thofe who pretend not to
" be wanting in giving Luftre to their Silks, do utter-
" ly difown the ufe of *Arfenick*.

" *Verdegreafe* is ufed by Linnen Dyers in their
" Yellow and Greenifh Colours, although of it felf
" it ftrike not deeper colour than of pale Straws.

" Of *Mineral Salts* ufed in *Dying* ; the chief is
" Allum ; the very true ufe thereof feems to me ob-
" fcure enough, notwithftanding all the Narrations
" I could get from Dyers about it : For I doubt,

" 1. Whether it be ufed to make Common water
" a fit *Menftruum*, wherewith to extract the Tingent
" particles of feveral hard Materials ; for I find Al-
" lum to be ufed with fuch Materials as fpend eafy
" enough, as Brafill, Logwood, *&c.* And withal,
" that the Stuffs to be dyed are firft boyled in Allum-
" Liquors, and the Allum afterwards (as they fay)
" cleared from the faid Stuff again, before any Co-
" lour at all be apply'd.

" 2. Whether it be ufed to fcour the *Sordes*, which
"   " may

" may interpose between the *Coloranda*, and the Dy-
" ing Stuff; and so hinder the due adhesion of the
" one unto the other : The boyling of several things
" first in Allum seeming to tend this way. But I find
" this work to be done in Cloth, and Rugs, by a
" due scouring of the same in the Fulling mills with
" Earth, and in Silk with Soaps, by which they boyl
" out the Gums and other *Sordes*, hindring or vitia-
" ting the intended Colours.

" 3. Whether Allum doth intenerate the Hairs of
" Wool, and Hair-stuff, as Grograins, *&c.* Whereby
" they may the better, receive and imbibe their Co-
" lours? Unto which opinion I was led by the Dy-
" ers ; saying, that after their Stuffs were well boyled
" in Allum, that they then cleared them of the Al-
" lum again : But we find the most open Bodied Cot-
" tons and Silks, to have Allum used upon them ; as
" well as the harder Hairs. Nor is Allum used in
" many Colours, *viz.* In no Woad or Indico Blews ;
" and yet the Stuffs Dyed Blew, are without any
" previous inteneration quickly tinged ; and that
" with a slight and short immersion thereof into the
" Blew fat.

" 4. Whether it contribute to the Colour it self,
" as Copperas doth to Galls, in order to make a black ;
" or as Juice of Lemmons doth to Cochenel in the
" *Incarnadives* ; or as *Aqua-Fortis* impregnated with
" Pewter, doth in the Bow-Scarlet, changing it from
" a red Rose-Crimson to flame Colour. This use is
" certainly not to be denyed to Allum in some cases ;
" but we see in other cases, that the same Colours may
" be Dyed without Allum, as well as with it, though
" neither so bright and lively, nor so lasting.

" 5. Wherefore Fifthly, I conclude (as the most
O o   " probable

" probable opinion) that the ufe of Allum is to be a
" *Vinculum* between the Cloth and the Colour, as
" clammy-Oyls and Gum-waters are in Painting and
" Limming ; Allum being fuch a thing, whofe parti-
" cles and *Aculei* diffolved with hot Liquors will ftick
" to the Stuffs, and pitch themfelves into their Pores ;
" and fuch alfo, as on which the particles of the Dy-
" ing Drugs will alfo catch hold, as we fee the parti-
" cles of Copperas and other Cryftallizing materials,
" do of Boughs and Twigs in the Veffel, where fuch
" Cryftallization is made. A fecond ufe I imagine
" of Allum in Dying, to be the extracting or drying
" up of fome fuch particles, as could not confift with
" the Colour to be fuperinduced, for we fee Allum
" is ufed in the dreffing of *Alutas* or white Leather,
" the which it dryeth, as the Salt of Hen-dung doth
" in Ox-hides, and as common Salt doth in preferva-
" tion of Flefh-meats ; for we know, a Sheep skin
" newly flayed could not be Colour'd as Brafils are,
" unlefs it were firft dreffed into Leather with Allum,
" *&c.* which is neceffary to the Colour, even although
" the Allum be, as it is, cleared out of the Leather
" again, before the faid Colouration, with Bran,
" yelks of Eggs, *&c.* Wherefore as Allum, as it
" were by accident, makes a wet raw skin to take a
" bright Colour by extracting fome impedimental
" particles out of it ; fo doth it alfo out of other ma-
" terials, though perhaps lefs difcernably.

" Another ufe I fuppofe of Allum, which is to
" brighten a Colour : For as we fee the fineft and
" moft Glaffie materials to make the moft orient
" Colours, as Feathers, Flowers, *&c.* So certainly
" if by boyling Cloth in Allum, it become incrufta-
" ted with particles, as it were of Glafs, the tinging
                                                    " of

" of them yields more brightnefs, than the tinging of
" a Scabrous matter, (fuch as unallumed Cloth is) can
" do. *Analogous* hereunto I take the ufe of Bran, and
" Bran-liquors in Dying to be; for Bran yielding a
" moft fine flower (as we fee in the making of white
" Starch ;) I conceive that this flower entring into
" the pores of the Stuff, levigates their *Superficies*, and
" fo makes the Colour laid on it, the more beautiful,
" juft as we fee, that all woods, which are to be guild-
" ed are firft fmoothned over with white Colours,
" before the Gold be laid on.

" And indeed all other Woods are filled, not only
" as to their greater holes and Afperities, with *Putty*;
" but alfo their fmaller Scabrities are cured by pri-
" ming Colours, before the Ultimate Colour intend-
" ed be laid thereon.

" The next Mineral Salt is *Salt-Peter*, not ufed by
" ancient Dyers, and but by few of the modern.
" And that not till the wonderful ufe of *Aqua-fortis*
" (whereof *Salt-Peter* is an ingredient) was obferv-
" ed in the Bow-fcarlet: Nor is it ufed now, but to
" brighten Colours by back-boyling them; for which
" ufe *Argol* is more commonly ufed. Lime is much
" ufed in the working of blew-fats, being of Lime-
" ftone calcined and called *Calke*, of which more
" hereafter.

" Of the *Animal* family are ufed about Dying,
" Cochineel (if the fame be any part of an *Animal*)
" Urine of labouring Men, kept till it be ftale and
" ftinking; Honey, Yelks of Eggs, and Ox-gall. The
" three latter fo rarely; and as the conceits of par-
" ticular Work-men, and for Collateral ufes (as to
" increafe weight, promote fermentation, and to
" fcour, &c.) That I fhall fay very little more of them

" in

" in this place, only faying of Urine that it is ufed to
" fcour, and help the fermenting and heating of
" Woad; it is ufed alfo in the blew-fats inftead of
" Lime: It difchargeth the yellow (of which and
" blew, moft Greens are compounded) and there-
" fore is always ufed to fpend *Weld* withal. Laftly,
" the ftale Urine, or old mudd of piffing places, will
" colour a well fcoured fmall piece of Silver, into a
" Golden colour, and it is with this (and not at all
" with the Bath-water) wherewith the Boys at *Bath*
" colour fingle pence; although the generality be-
" lieve otherwife. Laftly it feems to me, that Urine
" agreeth much in its Nature with *Tartarous Lixi-*
" *via*; not only becaufe Urine is a Lye made of Ve-
" getables in the body of *Animals*; nor becaufe in
" the Receptacles of Urine, *Tartarous* ftones are bred
" like as in Veffels of Wine; nor becaufe Urine dif-
" charges and abrades Colours as the *Lixivia* of *Tar-*
" *tar*, or the deliquated Salts of *Tartar* do; but be-
" caufe *Tartar* and *Sulphur-Lixivia* do colour the
" fuperficies of Silver, as we affirmed of Urine; and
" the difference I make between Urine and *Tarta-*
" *rous-Lixivia* is only this, that though the Salts of
" both of them feem by their effects in Dying, in a
" manner the fame; yet that Urine is made and con-
" fifts of Salt and Sulphur both.

" Before we enter upon the *Vegetable* materials for
" Dying, we may interpofe this Advertifement, That
" there are two forts of Water ufed by Dyers, *viz.*
" River-water and Well-water: By the latter I mean
" in this place the Pump-water in great Cities and
" Towns, which is a harfh Water wherewith one can
" fcarce wafh ones hands, much lefs fcour them clean;
" nor will Soap diffolve in it, but remains in rolls and
" lumps:

" lumps: moreover the Flesh boyled in it becomes
" hard and reddith.   The Springs rising out of large
" covered spaces (such as are great Cities) yield this
" Water, as having been percolated thorow more
" ground than other Water, and consequently been
" divested of its fatty earthy particles, and more im-
" pregnated with saline substances in all the way it
" hath passed.   The Dyers use this Water in Reds,
" and in other colours wanting restringency, and in
" the Dying of Materials of the slacker Contextures,
" as in Callico, Fustian, and the several species of Cot-
" ton-works.   This Water is naught for Blews, and
" makes Yellows and Greens look rusty.

   " River-water is far more fat and oylie, sweeter,
" bears Soap; that is, Soap dissolves more easily in it,
" rising into froth and bubbles, so as the Water thick-
" ens by it.   This Water is used in most cases by Dy-
" ers, and must be had in great quantities for washing
" and rinsing their Cloaths after Dying.

   " Water is called by Dyers White Liquor; but
" there is another sort of Liquor called Liquor abso-
" lutely, and that is their Bran-liquor, which is one
" part of Bran and five of River-water, boyled toge-
" ther an hour, and put into leaden Cisterns to settle.
" This Liquor when it turns sour is not good; which
" sournefs will be within three or four Days in the
" Summer-time.   Besides the uses afore-named of
" this Liquor, I conceive it contributes something to
" the holding of the Colour; for we know Starch,
" which is nothing but the flower of Bran, will make
" a clinging Paste, the which will conglutinate some
" things, tho' not every thing; *viz.* Paper, tho' nei-
" ther Wood nor Metals.   Now Bran-liquors are
" used to mealy dying Stuffs, such as *Mather* is, being
                                           " the

" the Powder or *fecula* of a Root ; So as the flower
" of the Bran being joyned with the *Mather*, and
" made clammy and glutinous by boyling, I doubt
" not but both sticking upon the *villi* of the Stuff
" Dyed, the *Mather* sticks the better by reason of the
" starchy pastiness of the Bran-flower joyned with it.

   " Gums have been used by Dyers about Silk, *viz.*
" *Gum Arabick, Gum Dragant, Mastick,* and *San-*
" *guis Draconis.* These Gums tend little to the
" tincture of the said Silk, no more than Gum doth
" in ordinary writing Ink, which only gives it a con-
" sistence to stay just where the Pen delivers it, with-
" out running abroad uncertainly : So Gum may
" give the Silk a glassiness, that is, may make it
" seem finer, as also stiffer ; so as to make one believe
" the said stiffness proceeded from the quantity of
" Silk close woven : And lastly to increase weight ;
" for if an ounce of Gum, worth a peny, can be in-
" corporated into a pound of Silk, the said peny in
" Gum produceth three Shillings, the price of an
" ounce of Silk.   Wherefore we shall speak of the
" use of each of the said four Gums, rather when
" treat of Sising and Stiffening, than now; in a Dis-
" course of Dying, where also we may speak of Ho-
" ney and Molasses.

   " We refer also the Descriptions of Fullers-earth,
" Soaps, Linseed-oyl, and Ox-galls, unto the head of
" Scouring, rather than to this of Dying.

   " Wines and *Aqua vitæ* have been used by some
" particular Artists ; but the use of them being nei-
" ther constant nor certain, I omit further mention
" of them.   The like I say of Wheaten-flower and
" Leaven.

   " Of *Cummin-feed, Fenugreek-feed, Senna,* and *A-*
                                                     " *garick,*

"*garick*, I have as yet no satisfactory accompt.

" Having spoken thus far of some of the Dying
" stuffs, before I engage upon the main, and speak
" more fully of those which have been but slightly
" touched upon already, I shall more Synoptically
" here insert a Catalogue of all Dying Materials, as
" well such as I have already treated upon, as such as
" I intend hereafter to describe.

" The three peculiar Ingredients for Black are Cop-
" peras, filings of Steel, and Slippe.

" The Restringent binding Materials are Alder
" Bark, Pomegranet Pills, Wallnut rinds and roots,
" Oaken Sapling Bark, and Saw-dust of the same ;
" Crab-tree Bark, Galls, and Sumach.

" The Salts are Allum, Argol, Salt-peter, *Sal Ar-*
" *moniack*, Pot-ashes, and Stone-Lime ; unto which
" Urine may be enumerated as a liquid Salt.

" The Liquors are Well-water, River-water, Wine,
" *Aqua-vitæ*, Vinegar, juyce of Lemmon, and *Aqua-*
" *fortis :* There is Honey used, and Molasses.

" Ingredients of another *Classis* are Bran, Wheat-
" en-flower, Yelks of Eggs, Leaven, Cummin-seed,
" Fenugreek-seed, Agarick, and Senna.

" Gums are *Gum Arabick, Dragant, Mastick,* and
" *Sanguis Draconis.*

" The Smecticks or Absterfives are Fullers-earth,
" Soap, Linseed-oyl, and Ox-gall.

" The other Metals and Minerals are Pewter, Ver-
" degrease, Antimony, Litharge, and Arsenick.

" But the *Colorantia colorata* are of three sorts, *viz.*
" Blew, Yellow, and Red ; of which Logwood, old
" Fustick, and Mather, are the *Polycaresta* in the pre-
" sent and common practices, being one of each sort.
" The Blews are Woad, Indico, and Logwood : The Yel-

" lows.

" lows are Weld, Wood-wax, and old Fuſtick, as alſo
" Turmerick now ſeldom uſed : The Reds are Red-
" wood, Brazel, Mather, Cochineel, Safflowrs, Ker-
" mes-berries, and Sanders; the latter of which is
" ſeldom uſed, and the Kermes not often. Unto theſe
" *Arnotto* and young Fuſtick making Orange-colours,
" may be added, as often uſed in theſe times.

　" In Cloth Dying wood-ſoot is of good uſe.

　" Having preſented this Catalogue, I come now to
" give or enlarge the Deſcription and Application of
" ſome of the chief of them, beginning with Cop-
" peras.

　" Copperas is the common thing us'd to dye Blacks
" withal, and it is the ſalt of the *Pyrites* ſtone, where-
" with old Iron (having been diſſolved in it) is incor-
" porated.　The filings of Steel, and ſuch ſmall par-
" ticles of Edge-tools as are worn away upon the
" Grindſtone, commonly called Slipp, is uſed to the
" ſame purpoſe in dying of Silks (as was ſaid before)
" which I conceive to be rather to increaſe the weight
" than for any other neceſſity ; the particles of Cop-
" peras being not ſo heavy and craſs as theſe are : for
" elſe why ſhould not theſe later-named Materials be
" as well uſed about Cloth, and other cheaper Stuffs ?

　" We obſerve, That green Oaken-boards by affri-
" ction of a Saw become black ; and that a green ſour
" Apple, cut with a knife, becomes likewiſe black ;
" and that the white greaſe wherewith Coach-wheels
" are anointed becomes likewiſe black, by reaſon of
" the Iron boxes wherewith the Nave is lined, beſides
" the uſtulation or affriction between the Nave and
" the Axel-tree.　Moreover we obſerve, That an
" Oaken-ſtick, by a violent affriction upon other
" wood in a Turning-Lath, makes the ſame black.

" From

" From all which we may obferve, That the whole
" bufinefs of Blacking lies in the Iron, as if the falt of
" the *Pyrites*-ftone in Copperas ferved only to ex-
" tract the fame; and withal it feems to lie in a kind
" of findging and uftulation, fuch as rapid affrictions
" do caufe : For Allum feems to be of the fame na-
" ture with Vitriol ; and yet in no cafe that I know
" of, is ufed for black colours : And in the black co-
" lour upon earthen Ware is made with fcalings of
" Iron vitrified.   Note, That where-ever Copperas is
" ufed, either Galls, Sumach, Oak Sapling-barks,
" Alder-bark, Wallnut-rinds, Crabtree-bark, or green
" Oak faw-duft, muft be ufed with it ; All which
" things Phyficians call Auftere and Stiptick.

" Red-wood muft be chopt into fmall pieces, then
" ground in a Mill between two heavy ftones, as corn
" is.   It is ufed alfo in Dying of Cloth and Rugs,
" and thofe of the Courfer fort : The colour is ex-
" tracted with much and long boyling, and that with
" Galls.   The colour it makes is a kind of Brick-co-
" lour Red ; it holdeth much better than Brafil.   The
" Cloth it dyeth is to be boyled with it : Wherefore
" only fuch matters as are not prejudiced by much
" boyling are dyed herewith.

" Brafil is chopt and ground like as the Red-wood :
" It dyeth a Pink-colour or Carnation, imitating the
" colour of Cochineil the neareft : It is ufed with
" Allum for the ordinary colour it dyeth ; and with
" addition of Pot-afhes, when it is ufed for Purples.

" Brafil fteept in Water giveth it the colour of Clar-
" ret-wine, into which a drop or two of Juyce of
" Lemmons or Vinegar being put, turneth it into the
" colour of Canary-Sack ; in which particular it a-
" greeth with Cochineil.   This colour foon ftaineth,

P p   " as

" as may appear by the eafie change which fo fmall a
" quantity of acid liquor makes upon it.   A drop of
" Spirit of Vitriol turneth the infufion of Brafil into a
" purplifh violet-colour, even although it hath been
" made yellow before, by the addition of Juyce of
" Lemmons or Vinegar; and is the fame effect which
" Pot-afhes alfo produce, as we faid before.

" *Mather* is a Root cultivated much in *Flanders* :
" There be of it two forts; *Pipe-Mather*, which is
" the coarfeft; and *Bale-Mather*, otherwife called
" *Crap-Mather* : This *Mather* ufed to the beft advan-
" tage, dyeth on Cloth a colour the neareft to our
" Bow dye, or the new Scarlet; the like whereof
" Safflowr doth in Silk, infomuch as the colours cal-
" led Baftard-Scarlets are dyed with it.   This colour
" indures much boyling, and is ufed both with Allum
" and Argol : it holdeth well.   The brighteft colours
" dyed with this material are made by over-dying the
" fame, and then by difcharging part of it by back-
" boyling it in Argol.

" *Mather* is ufed with Bran-liquor, inftead of
" White-liquor or ordinary Water.

" *Cochineel* is of feveral forts, *viz. Silvefter* and
" *Meftequa* : This alfo is ufed with Bran-liquor in Pew-
" ter-Furnaces, and with *Aqua-fortis*, in order to the
" Scarlet-dye. It is the colour whereof the like quan-
" tity effecteth moft in Dying; and Colours dyed
" with it, are faid to be dyed in Grain.   Rags dyed
" in the dregs of this colour is called *Turnfole*, and 'tis
" ufed to colour Wines; *Cochineel* being counted fo
" far from an unwholefome thing, that it is efteemed a
" Cordial.   Any acid Liquor takes off the intenfe
" Rednefs of this colour, turning it towards an O-
" range, Flame, or Scarlet colour : With this colour
                                                    " alfo

" alſo the *Spaniſh* Leather and Flocks are dyed which
" Ladies uſe. The extract or *fecula* hereof makes the
" fineſt *Lake*.

" *Arnotto* dyeth of it ſelf an Orange-colour, is
" uſed with Pot-aſhes upon Silk, Linnen, and Cot-
" tons, but not upon Cloth, as being not apt to pene-
" trate into a thick ſubſtance.

" *Weld*, called in Latin *Luteola* ; when 'tis ripe
" (that is to ſay, in the flower) it dyeth (with the
" help of Pot-aſhes) a deep Lemmon colour, like un-
" to *Ranunculus*, or Broom flower ; and either by
" the ſmallneſs of proportion put into the Liquor, or
" elſe by the ſlighter tincture, it dyeth all Colours
" between White and the Yellow aforeſaid.

" In the uſe of this material, Dyers uſe a croſs,
" driven down into their Furnace with a ſcrew to
" keep it down, ſo as the Cloth may have liberty in
" the ſupernatant Liquor, to be turned upon the
" Winch and kept out with the ſtaves : This weed is
" much cultivated in *Kent*, for the uſe of the *Lon-*
" *don* Dyers, it holdeth ſufficiently well but againſt
" Urine and *Tartarous* Liquors. Painters Pinke is
" made of it.

" *Wood wax*, or *Geniſta Tinctoria* (commonly cal-
" led Graſing-weed by the Dyers,) produces the ſame
" effect with *Luteola*, being uſed in greater quanti-
" ties : It is ſeldom made uſe of as to Silk, Linnen,
" or Cottons, but only as to coarſe-Cloths : It is
" alſo ſet with Pot-aſhes or Urine, called by the Dy-
" ers *Sigge fuſtick* ; of it there be two ſorts, the *young*
" and the *old*. *Fuſtick* is chopt and ground, as the
" other Woods above-mentioned are.

" The *young Fuſtick* Dyeth a kind of Reddiſh-
" Orange-colour ; the *old*, a Hair colour with ſeveral

" degrees

" degrees of yellownefs between : It is ufed with
" flacked Lime. The colours Dyed with *old Fuftick*
" hold extreamly ; and are not to be difcharged, will
" fpend *with* Salts or *without*, and will work hot
" or cold.

 " *Soot of Wood.* *Soot* containeth in it felf both a
" Colour and Salt ; wherefore there is nothing added
" to it to extract its Colour, nor to make it ftrike up-
" on the Stuff to be Dyed ; the natural Colour which
" it Dyeth of it felf, is the Colour of Honey ; but
" is the foundation of many other Colours upon
" Wool and Cloth ; for to other things 'tis not ufed.
" *Woad* is made of a Weed, fown upon ftrong new-
" broken Land, perfectly cleered from all ftones
" and weeds, cut feveral times by the top leaves,
" then ground, or rather chopt with a peculiar Mill
" for that purpofe ; which being done feveral times,
" it is made up in Balls and dryed in the Sun ; the
" dryer the year is, the better the Woad,

 " When it is made up in Balls, it is broken again
" and laid in heaps, where if it heat too faft, it is
" fprinkled with ordinary water : but if it heat too
" flowly, then they throw on it a quantity of Lime,
" or Urine. But of the perfect cultivating and cu-
" ring of Woad, we fhall fpeak elfe-where.

 " *Englifh Woad* is counted the ftrongeft, it is com-
" monly tryed by ftaining of white Paper with it, or
" a white Limed wall, and if the Colour be a French-
" green it is good.

 " *Woad* in ufe is ufed with Pot-afhes commonly
" called Ware, which if it be double refin'd, is called
" hard Ware (which is much the fame with Kelp) or
" Sea-weeds, calcin'd and burnt into the hardnefs of
" a ftone, by reiterated Calcinations.

" Lime

"*Lime* or *Calke* which is ſtrong Lime, is uſed to
"accelerate the fermentation of the Woad, which
"by the help of the ſame Pot-aſhes and warm liquors
"kept always ſo, in three or four Days will come
"to work like a Kive of Beer, and will have a blew
"or rather greeniſh froth or flowry upon it, anſwer-
"ing to the Yeſt of the Kive. Now the over quan-
"tity of Ware, fretting too much upon the Woad, is
"obtunded or dulled by throwing in Bran ſometimes
"looſe, ſometimes in Bags.

"The making and uſing Woad, is one of the moſt
"myſterious, nice, and hazardous operations in Dy-
"ing: It is one of the moſt laſting Colours that is
"Dyed: An intenſe Woad-Colour is almoſt black,
"that is to ſay, of a Damſon colour; this Colour is
"the foundation of ſo many others in its degree, that
"the Dyers have a certain Scale, or number of Stalls,
"whereby to compute the lightneſs and deepneſs
"of this Colour.

"*Indico* is made of a Weed of the ſame Nature
"with Woad, but more ſtrong; and whereas Woad
"is the whole ſubſtance of the Herb, Indico is only
"a mealy concrete juice or *fæcula* dryed in the Sun,
"ſometimes made up in flat Cakes, ſometimes into
"round-balls, there be ſeveral ſorts of Indico.

"*Logwood* is chopt and ground like other of the
"Woods above-mentioned, it maketh a purpliſh-
"blew; may be uſed without Allum: It hath been
"eſteemed a moſt falſe and fading Colour; but
"now being uſed with Galls, is far leſs complain-
"ed of.

General

General Obſervations upon

D Y I N G.

" F Irſt, that all the materials (which of themſelves
"   " do give Colour) are either Red, Yellow, or
" Blew, ſo that out of them, and the primitive fun-
" dumental Colour, white; all that great variety
" which we ſee in Dyed Stuffs doth ariſe.

" 2. That few of the Colouring materials (as
" Cochineel, Soot, Wood wax, Woad,) are in their
" outward and firſt appearance of the ſame Colour,
" which by the ſleighteſt diſtempers and ſolutions in
" the weakeſt *Menſtrua*, the Dye upon Cloth, Silk,
" &c.

" 3. That many of the Colouring materials will
" not yield their Colours without much grinding,
" ſteeping, boyling, fermenting, or corroſion by pow-
" erful *Menſtrua*; as Red-wood, Weld, Woad, Ar-
" notto, &c.

" 4. That many of the ſaid Colouring materials
" will of themſelves give no Colouring at all, as
" Copperas, or Galls, or with much diſadvantage,
" unleſs the Cloth or other Stuff to be Dyed, be as
" it were, firſt covered or incruſtated with ſome
" other matter, though Colour-leſs, aforehand, as
" Mather, Weld, Braſil with Allum.

" 5. That ſome of the ſaid Colouring materials
" by the help of other Colour-leſs Ingredients, do
" ſtrike different Colours from what they would
" alone, and of themſelves; as Cochineel, Braſil,
" &c.

" 6. That

" 6. That fome Colours, as Mather, Indico, and
" Woad, by reiterated tinctures, will at laft become
" black.

" 7. That although Green be the moft frequent and
" common of natural Colours, yet there is no fimple
" ingredient, which is now ufed alone, to dye Green
" with upon any Material; *Sap green* (being the con-
" denfated juyce of the *Rhamnous Berry*) being the
" neareft; the which is ufed by Country People.

" 8. There is no black thing in ufe which dyes
" black; tho' both the Coal and Soot of moft things
" burnt or fcorched be of that colour; and the
" blacker, by how much the matter before it was
" burnt was whiter, as in the famous inftance of
" *Ivory black.*

" 9. The tincture of fome Dying Stuffs will fade
" even with lying, or with the Air, or will ftain even
" with Water; but very much with Wine, Vinegar,
" Urine, &c.

" 10. Some of the Dyers Materials are ufed to bind
" and ftrengthen a Colour, fome to brighten it, fome
" to give luftre to the ftuff, fome to difcharge and take
" off the colour either in whole or in part, and fome
" out of fraud, to make the Material Dyed (if coftly)
" to be heavyer.

" 11. That fome Dying Ingredients or Drugs, by
" the coarfenefs of their Bodies, make the thread of
" the dyed Stuff feem coarfer; and fome by fhrink-
" ing them, fmaller, and fome by levigating their A-
" fperities, finer.

" 12. Many of the fame colours are dyed upon fe-
" veral Stuffs with feveral Materials; as *Red wood* is
" ufed in Cloth, not in Silks; *Arnotto* in Silks, not
" in Cloth; and may be dyed at feveral prizes.

" 13. That

" 13. That Scowering and Wafhing of Stuffs to be
" dyed, is to be done with fpecial Materials ; as fome-
" times with Ox-galls, fometimes with Fullers earth,
" fometimes with Soap : This latter being pernicious
" in fome cafes, where Pot-afhes will ftain or alter the
" colour.

" 14. Where great quantities of Stuffs are to be
" dyed together, or where they are to be done with
" great fpeed, and where the pieces are very long,
" broad, thick, or otherwife, they are to be diffe-
" rently handled, both in refpect to the Veffels and
" Ingredients.

" 15. In fome Colours and Stuffs the Tingent Li-
" quor muft be boyling ; in other cafes blood-warm ;
" in fome it may be cold.

" 16. Some Tingent Liquors are fitted for ufe by
" long keeping ; and in fome the vertue wears away
" by the fame.

" 17. Some Colours or Stuffs are beft dyed by re-
" iterated Dippings ever into the fame Liquor at fe-
" veral diftances of time ; and fome by continuing
" longer, and others leffer whiles therein.

" 18. In fome cafes the matter of the Veffel where-
" in the Liquors are heated, and the Tinctures prepared,
" muft be regarded ; as the Kettles muft be Pewter for
" Bow-dye.

" 19. There is little reckoning made how much
" Liquor is ufed in proportion to the dying Drugs ;
" the Liquor being rather adjufted to the bulk of the
" Stuff, as the Veffels are to the breadth of the fame :
" The quantity of dying Drugs being proportioned
" to the colour higher or lower, and to the Stuffs
" both ; as likewife the Salts are to dying Drugs.

" Concerning the weight which Colours give to
" Silk

" Silk (for in them 'tis moſt taken notice of, as being
" ſold by weight, and being a Commodity of great
" price:) It is obſerved, That one pound of raw Silk
" loſeth four ounces by waſhing out the Gums and
" natural *Sordes.*

" That the ſame ſcowred Silk may be raiſed to
" above thirty ounces from the remaining twelve, if
" it be dyed black with ſome Materials.

" The reaſon why Black colour may be moſt heavy
" dyed, being becauſe all gravitating Drugs may be
" dyed black, being all of colours lighter than it :
" whereas perhaps there are few or no Materials
" wherewith to increaſe the weight of Silk, which
" will conſiſt with fair light colours ; ſuch as will, ha-
" ving been uſed, as white Arſenick to Incarnadives.
" Of a thing truly uſeful in Dying, eſpecially of Blacks,
" nothing increaſes weight ſo much as Galls, by reaſon
" whereof Black Silks are reſtored to as much weight
" as they loſt by waſhing out their Gum : Nor is it
" counted extraordinary, that Blacks ſhould gain a-
" bout four or ſix ounces in the Dying upon each
" pound.

" Next to Galls old Fuſtick increaſes the weight
" about $1\frac{1}{2}$ in 12.

" Mather about one ounce.

" Weld half an ounce.

" The Blew-fat, in deep Blews of the fifth ſtall,
" gives no conſiderable weight.

" Neither doth Logwood, Cochineel, nor Arnotto:
" Nor doth Copperas it ſelf, where Galls are not.

" I conceive much light would be given to the
" Philoſophy of Dying, by careful Experiments of
" the weight added by each Drug or Salt in Dying of
" every colour.

Slipp

" *Slipp* adds much to the weight, and giveth a
" deeper Black than *Copperas* it felf; which is a good
" excufe for the Dyers that ufe it.

" I have hitherto but mentioned the feveral Colo-
" rations ufed in Humane Affairs, enumerated the
" feveral Materials ufed in one of them, namely, Dy-
" ing; and imperfectly defcribed the feveral ufes and
" applications of them in Dying. I have alfo fet
" down fome general Obfervations relating to that
" whole Trade. It remains now that we defcribe
" the feveral Veffels, Tools, and Utenfils ufed in the
" fame. And particularly to fhew how any Colour
" affigned may be fuperinduced upon any kind of Ma-
" terial, as Wool, Linnen, Hair, Feathers, Cotton or
" Silk : And with what Advantages or Difadvantages
" of Lafting, Brightnefs, Cheapnefs, and Variety, &c.
" each may be performed. But this being infinite,
" and almoft unteachable by words, as being incom-
" parably more difficult, than how to imitate and
" compofe any Colour affigned, out of the few, ufu-
" ally furnifhing a Painters palat; I leave the whole
" to the further confideration of this Learned So-
" ciety.

THE

THE

HISTORY

Of the Generation and Ordering of

GREEN OYSTERS,

Commonly called

Colchester-Oysters.

" IN the Month of *May* the *Oysters* cast their Spaun
" (which the Dredgers call their Spat;) it is
" like to a drop of Candle, and about the bigness of
" an half-penny.

 " The Spat cleaves to Stones, old Oyster-shells,
" pieces of Wood, and such like things, at the bot-
" of the Sea, which they call Cultch.

 " 'Tis probably conjectured, that the Spat in twen-
" ty four hours begins to have a Shell.

 " In the Month of *May*, the Dredgers (by the Law
" of the Admiralty Court) have liberty to catch all
" manner of *Oysters*, of what size soever.

 " When they have taken them, with a knife they
" gently raise the small brood from the Clutch, and
" then they throw the Cultch in again, to preserve
" the ground for the future, unless they be so newly
" Spat that they cannot be safely severed from the
" Cultch, in that case they are permitted to take the
" stone or shell, *&c.* that the Spat is upon, one Shell
" having many times 20 Spats.

" After the Month of *May* it is Felony to carry a-
" way the Cultch, and punifhable to take any other
" *Oyfters*, unlefs it be thofe of fize (that is to fay) a-
" bout the bignefs of an half Crown piece, or when
" the two fhells being fhut, a fair fhilling will rattle
" between them.

" The places where thefe *Oyfters* are chiefly catcht,
" are called the *Pont-Burnham*, *Malden*, and *Colne-*
" Waters; the latter taking its name from the River
" of *Colne*, which paffeth by *Colne-Chefter*, gives the
" name to that Town, and runs into a Creek of the
" Sea at a place called the *Hythe*, being the Suburbs
" of the Town.

" This Brood and other *Oyfters* they carry to
" Creeks of the Sea at *Brickel-Sea*, *Merfey*, *Langno*,
" *Fringrego*, *Wivenho*, *Tolesbury*, and *Salt-coafe*, and
" there throw them into the Channel, which they
" call their Beds or Layers, where they grow and fat-
" ten, and in two or three years the fmalleft Brood
" will be *Oyfters* of the fize aforefaid.

" Thofe *Oyfters* which they would have green,
" they put into Pits about three foot deep, in the
" Salt-Marfhes, which are overflowed only at Spring-
" tides, to which they have Sluices, and let out the
" Salt water until it is about a foot and half deep.

" Thefe Pits from fome quality in the Soil co-ope-
" rating with the heat of the Sun, will become green,
" and communicate their colour to the *Oyfters* that
" are put into them in four or five days, though they
" commonly let them continue there fix Weeks, or
" two Months, in which time they will be of a dark
" green.

" To prove that the Sun operates in the greening,
" *Tolesbury* Pits will green only in Summer; but that

" the Earth hath the greater power, *Brickle fea* Pits
" green both Winter and Summer : and for a further
" proof, a Pit within a foot of a greening Pit will not
" green ; and thofe that did green very well, will in
" time lofe their quality.

" The *Oyfters* when the Tide comes in, lie with
" their hollow fhell downwards, and when it goes
" out they turn on the other fide ; they remove not
" from their place unlefs in cold weather, to cover
" themfelves in the Oufe.

" The reafon of the fcarcity of *Oyfters*, and confe-
" quently of their dearnefs, is, becaufe they are of
" late years bought up by the *Dutch.*

" There are great penalties by the Admiralty-
" Court, laid upon thofe that fifh out of thofe grounds
" which the Court appoints, or that deftroy the
" Cultch, or that take any *Oyfters* that are not of
" fize, or that do not tread under their feet, or throw
" upon the fhore, a Fifh which they call a *Five finger,*
" refembling a Spur-rowel, becaufe that fifh gets into
" the *Oyfters* when they gape, and fucks them out.

" The reafon why fuch a penalty is fet upon any
" that fhall deftroy the Cultch, is becaufe they find
" that if that be taken away the Oufe will increafe,
" and then *Mufcles* and *Cockles* will breed there, and
" deftroy the *Oyfters*, they having not whereon to
" ftick their Spat.

" The *Oyfters* are fick after they have Spat ; but in
" *June* and *July* they begin to mend, and in *Auguft*
" they are perfectly well : The *Male-Oyfter* is black-
" fick, having a black Subftance in the Fin ; the Female
" white-fick (as they term it) having a milky Sub-
" ftance in the Fin. They are falt in the Pits, falter
" in the Layers, but falteft at Sea.

In

In Compoſing *Hiſtories* after this manner, they reſolve to proceed, till they have not only obtain'd an *Account* of all the Great, and moſt ſubſtantial *Trades*; but alſo of all the leſs *Works*, and Private *Productions*, which are confin'd to ſome particular *Soyls*, or *Corporations*, or *Families*. As this Stock ſhall increaſe, they purpoſe to make it of General uſe; either by continuing *Printing* the moſt remarkable of them, or by freely expoſing them to the view of all, that deſire ſuch *Informations*; provided, that at the ſame time they receive ſome, they will alſo Communicate others: And they have aſſured grounds of *confidence*, that when this attempt ſhall be compleated, it will be found to bring innumerable benefits to all practical *Arts*: When all the ſecrets of *Manufactures* ſhall be diſcover'd, their *Materials* deſcrib'd, their *Inſtruments* figur'd, their *Products* repreſented: It will ſoon be determin'd, how far they themſelves may be promoted, and what new conſequences may thence be deduc'd. Hereby we ſhall ſee whether all the parts of the moſt obvious *Crafts* have been brought to perfection; and whether they may not aſſiſt each other, more than has been hitherto endeavour'd: Hereby we ſhall diſcern the compaſs, the power, the changes, the degrees, the ages of them all; and ſpeedily underſtand, whether their effects have been large enough, and the ways of producing them ſufficiently compendious. In ſhort, by this help the worſt *Artificers* will be well inſtructed, by conſidering the *Methods*, and *Tools* of the beſt: And the greateſt *Inventors* will be exceedingly inlighten'd; becauſe they will have in their view the labours of many men, many places, and many times, wherewith to compare their own. This is the ſureſt, and

moſt

moft effectual means, to inlarge the *Inventions:* whofe Nature is fuch, that it is apt to increafe, not only by mens beholding the *Works* of greater, but of equal, nay of lefs Wits than themfelves.

In the whole progrefs of this *Narration,* I have been cautious to forbear commending the labours of any Private *Fellows* of the *Society*. For this, I need not make any *Apology* to them; feeing it would have been an inconfiderable Honour, to be prais'd by fo mean a Writer: But now I muft break this *Law,* in the particular cafe of Dr. *Chriftopher Wren:* For doing fo, I will not alledge the excufe of my *Friend-fhip* to him; though *that* perhaps were fufficient; and it might well be allow'd me to take this occafion of Publifhing it: But I only do it on the meer confi-deration of Juftice: For in turning over the *Regifters* of the *Society,* I perceiv'd that many excellent things, whofe firft *Invention* ought to be afcrib'd to him, were cafually omitted: This moves me to do him right by himfelf, and to give this feparate Account of his indeavours, in promoting the Defign of the *Royal Society,* in the fmall time wherein he has had the opportunity of attending it.

Sect. XL. *The Conclu-fion of this Part.*

The firft inftance I fhall mention, to which he may lay peculiar claim, is the *Doctrine of Motion,* which is the moft confiderable of all others, for eftablifh-ing the firft *Principles* of *Philofophy,* by *Geometrical Demonftrations* This *Des Cartes* had before begun, having taken up fome *Experiments* of this kind upon Conjecture, and made them the firft *Foundation* of his whole *Syftem* of *Nature:* But fome of his Con-clufions feeming very queftionable, becaufe they were only deriv'd from the grofs Trials of Balls

meeting

meeting one another at *Tennis*, and *Billiards :* Dr.
Wren produc'd before the *Society*, an *Inſtrument* to
repreſent the effects of all ſorts of *Impulſes*, made between two hard globous Bodies, either of equal, or
of different bigneſs, and ſwiftneſs, following or meeting each other, or the one moving, the other at reſt.
From theſe varieties aroſe many unexpected effects;
of all which he demonſtrated the true *Theories*, after
they had been confirm'd by many hundreds of *Experiments* in that *Inſtrument*. Theſe he propos'd as
the Principles of all *Demonſtrations* in *Natural Philoſophy :* Nor can it ſeem ſtrange, that theſe *Elements*
ſhould be of ſuch Univerſal uſe; if we conſider that
Generation, Corruption, Alteration, and all the Viciſ-
ſitudes of *Nature*, are nothing elſe but the effects
ariſing from the meeting of little Bodies, of differing
Figures, Magnitudes, and Velocities.

The Second *Work* which he has advanc'd, is the
Hiſtory of *Seaſons :* which will be of admirable benefit to Mankind, if it ſhall be conſtantly purſued,
and deriv'd down to Poſterity. His propoſal therefore
was, to comprehend a *Diary* of Wind, Weather,
and other conditions of the *Air*, as to Heat, Cold,
and Weight; and alſo a *General Deſcription* of the
Year, whether contagious or healthful to Men or
Beaſts; with an Account of *Epidemical Diſeaſes*, of
Blaſts, Mill-dews, and other accidents, belonging
to Grain, Cattle, Fiſh, Fowl, and Inſects. And
becauſe the difficulty of a conſtant *Obſervation* of
the *Air*, by Night and Day, ſeem'd invincible, he
therefore devis'd a *Clock* to be annex'd to a Weather-
Cock, which mov'd a rundle, cover'd with Paper,
upon which the Clock mov'd a black lead-Penſil;
ſo that the Obſerver by the Traces of the Pencil on
the

the Paper, might certainly conclude, what Winds had blown in his abſence, for twelve hours ſpace : After a like manner he contriv'd a *Thermometer* to be its own *Regiſter:* And becauſe the uſual *Thermometers* were not found to give a true meaſure of the extenſion of the *Air,* by reaſon that the accidental gravity of the liquor, as it lay higher or lower in the Glaſs, weigh unequally on the *Air,* and gave it a farther contraction or extenſion, over and above that which was produc'd by heat and cold ; therefore he invented a *Circular Thermometer,* in which the liquor occaſions no fallacy, but remains always in one height moving the whole *Inſtrument,* like a Wheel on its *Axis.*

He has contriv'd an *Inſtrument* to meaſure the quantities of *Rain* that falls : This as ſoon as it is full, will pour out it ſelf, and at the years end diſcover how much Rain has fallen on ſuch a ſpace of Land, or other hard ſuperficies, in order to the *Theory* of *Vapours, Rivers, Seas,* &c.

He has devis'd many ſubtil ways for the eaſier finding the gravity of the *Atmoſphere,* the degrees of drought and moiſture, and many of its other accidents. Amongſt theſe *Inſtruments* there are *Balances* which are uſeful to other purpoſes, that ſhew the weight of the *Air* by their ſpontaneous inclination.

Amongſt the new Diſcoveries of the *Pendulum,* theſe are to be attributed to him, that the *Pendulum* in its motion from reſt to reſt ; that is, in one deſcent and aſcent, moves unequally in equal times, according to a line of ſines : That it would continue to move either in *Circular,* or *Eliptical* Motions ; and ſuch *Vibrations* would have the ſame Periods with thoſe that are reciprocal ; and that by a complication of feveral *Pendulums* depending one upon another, there might be reprefented motions like the planetary *Helical Motions*, or more intricate : And yet that thefe *Pendulums* would difcover without confufion (as the *Planets* do) three or four feveral *Motions*, acting upon one Body with differing *Periods*; and that there may be produc'd a Natural ftandard for Meafure from the *Pendulum* for vulgar ufe.

He has invented many ways to make *Aftronomical Obfervations* more acurate and eafy : *He* has fitted and hung *Quadrants*, *Sextants*, and *Radii*, more commodioufly than formerly : *He* has made two *Telefcopes*, to open with a joynt like a Sector, by which Obfervers may infallibly take a diftance to half minutes, and find no difference in the fame Obfervation reiterated feveral times ; nor can any warping or luxation of the Inftrument hinder the truth of it.

He has added many forts of *Retes, Screws*, and other devifes to *Telefcopes*, for taking fmall diftances and apparent Diameters to Seconds. He has made apertures to take in more or lefs light, as the Obferver pleafes, by opening and fhutting like the Pupil of the Eye, the better to fit Glaffes to *Crepufculine Obfervations : He* has added much to the Theory of *Dioptrics* ; much to the Manufacture it felf of grinding good Glaffes. *He* has attempted, and not without fuccefs, the making of Glaffes of other forms than Spherical : *He* has exactly meafur'd and delineated the Spheres of the Humours in the *Eye*, whofe proportions one to another were only ghefs'd at before. This accurate difcuffion produc'd the Reafon, why we fee things erected, and that *Reflection* conduces as much to *Vifion* as *Refraction*.

He difcours'd to them a Natural and eafy *Theory of*
Re-

Refraction, which exactly anſwer'd every *Experiment.*
He fully demonſtrated all *Dioptrics* in a few Propoſi-
tions, ſhewing not only (as in *Keplers Dioptrics*) the
common properties of Glaſſes, but the Proportions
by which the individual Rayes cut the *Axis,* and
each other ; upon which the Charges (as they are
uſually called) of *Teleſcopes,* or the Proportion of the
Eye-glaſſes and *Apertures* are demonſtrably diſcover'd.

He has made conſtant Obſervations on *Saturn* ; and
a Theory of that Planet, truly anſwering all *Obſervations,* before the printed Diſcourſe of *Hugonius* on
that Subject appear'd. *He* has eſſay'd to make a true *Selenograpy* by mea-
ſure ; the *World* having nothing yet but Pictures, ra-
ther than Surveighs or Maps of the *Moon.* *He* has
ſtated the *Theory* of the Moon's Libration, as far as his
Obſervations could carry him. *He* has compos'd a
Lunar Globe, repreſenting not only the Spots, and various degrees of whiteneſs upon the Surface, but the
Hills, Eminencies, and Cavities moulded in ſolid Work.
The Globe thus faſhioned into a true Model of the
Moon, as you turn it to the Light, repreſents all the
Menſtrual phaſes, with the variety of Appearances
that happen from the Shadows of the Mountains and
Valleys. *He* has made Maps of the *Pleiades,* and
other *Teleſcopical* Stars ; and propos'd Methods to de-
termine the great doubt of the Earth's motion or reſt,
by the ſmall Stars about the Pole to be ſeen in large
Teleſcopes.

In order to *Navigation he* has carefully purſu'd many *Magnetical Experiments* ; of which this is one of
the nobleſt and moſt fruitful *Speculation.* A large *Terella*
is plac'd in the midſt of a Plane Board, with a hole in-

to which the *Terella* is half immers'd, till it be like a *Globe* with the *Poles* in the *Horizon*. Then is the Plane dufted over with fteel-filings equally from a Sieve : The Duft by the *Magnetical* virtue is immediatly figur'd into Furrows that bend like a fort of *Helix*, proceeding as it were out of one *Pole*, and returning into the other : And the whole Plane is thus figur'd like the Circles of a *Planifphere*.

It being a Queftion amongft the Problems of *Navigation*, very well worth refolving, to what Mechanical powers the Sailing (againft the wind efpecially) was reducible ; he fhew'd it to be a Wedge : And he demonftrated how a tranfient Force upon an oblique Plane, would caufe the motion of the Plane againft the firft Mover. And he made an *Inftrument*, that *Mechanically* produc'd the fame effect, and fhew'd the reafon of Sailing to all Winds.

The *Geometrical Mechanics* of *Rowing*, he fhew'd to be a *Vectis* on a moving or cedent *Fulcrum*. For this end he made *Inftruments*, to find what the expanfion of Body was towards the hindrance of Motion in a Liquid *Medium* ; and what degree of impediment was produc'd, by what degree of expanfion : With other things that are the neceffary Elements for laying down the *Geometry* of *Sailing, Swimming, Rowing, Flying,* and the Fabricks of *Ships.*

He has invented a very curious and exceeding fpeedy way of *Etching*. *He* has ftarted feveral things towards the emendation of *Water-works*. *He* has made *Inftruments* of *Refpiration,* and for ftraining the breath from fuliginous vapours, to try whether the fame breath fo purify'd will ferve again.

He was the firft *Inventor* of drawing Pictures by *Microfcopical Glaffes*. *He* has found out perpetual, at
leaft

leaſt long liv'd Lamps, and Regiſters of Furnaces, and the like, for keeping a perpetual temper, in order to various uſes; as hatching of Eggs, Inſects, production of Plants, Chymical Preparations, imitating Nature in producing Foſſils and Minerals, keeping the motion of Watches equal, in order to *Longitudes* and *Aſtronomical uſes*, and infinite other advantages.

He was the firſt Author of the Noble *Anatomical Experiment* of *Injecting Liquors into the Veins of Animals*. An *Experiment* now vulgarly known; but long ſince exhibited to the Meetings at *Oxford*, and thence carried by ſome *Germans*, and publiſh'd abroad. By this *Operation* divers Creatures were immediatly purg'd, vomited, intoxicated, kill'd, or reviv'd, according to the quality of the Liquor injected: Hence aroſe many new *Experiments*, and chiefly that of *Transfuſing Blood*, which the *Society* has proſecuted in ſundry Inſtances, that will probably end in extraordinary Succeſs.

This is a ſhort account of the principal *Diſcoveries* which Dr. *Wren* has preſented or ſuggeſted to this *Aſſembly*. I know very well, that ſome of them *he* did only ſtart and deſign; and that they have been ſince carry'd on to perfection, by the Induſtry of other hands. I purpoſe not to rob them of their ſhare in the honour: Yet it is reaſonable, that the original *Invention* ſhould be aſcrib'd to the true *Author*, rather than the *Finiſhers*. Nor do I fear that this will be thought too much, which I have ſaid concerning him: For there is a peculiar reverence due to ſo much excellence, cover'd with ſo much modeſty. And it is not Flattery but honeſty, to give him his juſt praiſe; who is ſo far from uſurping the fame of other men,

that

that he indeavours with all care to conceal his own.

I have now perform'd my *Promise*, and drawn out of the Papers of the *Society*, an *Epitome* of the chief *Works* they have conceiv'd in their minds, or reduc'd into Practice. If any shall yet think they have not usefully employ'd their time, I shall be apt to suspect, that they underſtand not what is meant by a *diligent* and *profitable labouring* about *Nature*. There are indeed ſome men who will ſtill condemn them for being idle ; unleſs they immediately profeſs to have found out the Squaring the Circle, or the *Philoſophers Stone*, or ſome other ſuch mighty *Nothings*. But if theſe are not ſatisfied with what the *Society* has done, they are only to blame the extravagance of their own Expectations. I confeſs I cannot boaſt of ſuch pompous *Diſcoveries :* They promiſe no Wonders, nor endeavour after them : Their Progreſs has been equal, and firm, by Natural degrees, and thorow ſmall things, as well as great : They go leiſurably on ; but their ſlowneſs is not caus'd by their idleneſs, but care. They have contriv'd in their thoughts, and couragiouſly begun an *Attempt*, which all *Ages* had deſpair'd of. It is therefore fit that they alone, and not others, who refuſe to partake of their burden, ſhould be Judges by what ſteps, and what pace, they ought to proceed.

Such men are then to be intreated not to interrupt their *Labours* with impertinent rebukes ; they are to remember, that the *Subject* of their *Studies* is as large as the *Univerſe :* and that in ſo vaſt an *Enterpriſe,* many intervals and diſappointments muſt be recon'd upon. Though they do not behold that the *Society* has already fill'd the world with *perfect Sciences* ;
yet

yet they are to be inform'd, that the nature of their *Work* requir'd that they fhould firft begin with *imme-thodical Collections* and *indigefted Experiments*, before they go on to finifh and compofe them into *Arts*. In which Method they may well be juftified, feeing they have the *Almighty Creator* himfelf for an *Example* : For he at firft produc'd a confus'd and fcatter'd Light ; and referv'd it to be the *work* of another day, to gather and fafhion it into beautiful *Bodies*.

The End of the Second Part.

THE

HISTORY

OF THE

ROYAL SOCIETY.

The THIRD PART.

Hough it be certain, that the promoting of *Experiments* according to this *Idea*, cannot injure the Virtue, or Wifdom of men's minds, or their former *Arts*, and mechanical Practices; or their eftablifh'd ways of life : Yet the perfect innocence of this defign, has not been able to free it from the Cavil of the *Idle*, and the *Malicious* ; nor from the jealoufies of private Interefts. Thefe groundlefs prejudices of the particular *Profeffions*, and *Ranks* of Men, I am now in the laft Place to remove ; and to fhew that there is no Foundation for them : To fufpect the *Change*, which can be made by this *Inftitution*; or the new things it is likely to produce.

Sect. I. *The Subject and Divifion of this Third Part.*

That it will probably be the Original of many *new things*, I am fo far from denying, that I chearfully acknowledge it. Nor am I frighted at that, which is wont to be objected in this Cafe, the hazard of *alteration*, and *Novelty*. For if all things that are

S f

new

new be *deſtructive*, all the ſeveral means, and degrees, by which Mankind has riſen to this perfection of *Arts*, were to be condemn'd. If to be the *Author* of *new things*, be a crime; how will the firſt Civilizers of *Men*, and makers of *Laws*, and Founders of *Governments* eſcape? Whatever now delights us in the Works of *Nature*, that excells the rudeneſs of the firſt Creation, is *New*. Whatever we ſee in Cities, or Houſes, above the firſt wildneſs of Fields, and meaneſs of Cottages, and nakedneſs of Men, had its time, when this imputation of *Novelty*, might as well have bin laid to its charge. It is not therefore an offence, to profeſs the introduction of *New things*, unleſs that which is introduc'd prove pernicious in it ſelf; or cannot be brought in, without the extirpation of others, that are better.

And the *Experimental Knowledge*, will not expoſe us to theſe dangers, I am next to declare, in a Univerſal *Apology* for its intentions, and effects. This was the Third Portion, which I at firſt reſerv'd, for the Concluſion of my Diſcourſe. Yet caſting my eyes back, I find, that I have already on ſeveral occaſions prevented myſelf; and ſaid many things as I came along, which would have bin more proper for this place. But I deſire that my Reader would interpret this to have proceeded from the Nature of my Subject, of which it is hard to Write a plain *Hiſtory*, without falling ſometimes unawares into its *Praiſe*. And now I will proceed to a fuller, and more ſolemn *Defence*: In which, I will try to prove, that the increaſe of *Experiments* will be ſo far from hurting, that it will be many ways advantageous, above other *Studies*, to the wonted Courſes of *Education*; to the Principles, and inſtruction of the minds of

**   Men

Men in general ; to the *Chriſtian Religion*, to the Church of *England* ; to all Manual *Trades* ; to *Phyſic* ; to the *Nobility*, and *Gentry* ; and the Univerſal Intereſt of the whole *Kingdom*.

In all which *Particulars*, I hope I ſhall repreſent this *Model*, to be inoffenſive to all the various ways of Living, already in uſe : And thereby I ſhall ſecure all the Ancient *Proprietors* in their *Rights :* A work as neceſſary to be done, in raiſing a new *Philoſophy*, as we ſee it is in building a *new London*.

The Firſt prejudice I am to wipe away, concerns the uſual ways of *Education*. For it is an obvious doubt ; whether ſo great a change in *Works*, and in *Opinions*, may not have ſome fatal conſequence, on all the former Methods of *Teaching*, which have bin long ſettled, and approv'd by much Cuſtom. And here many Good Men of ſevere, and ancient manners, may ſeem to have reaſon, when they urge a-gainſt us ; that the Courſes of Training up of Youth, ought to be ſtill the ſame ; that if they be ſubverted, or multiply'd, much confuſion will follow ; and that this our *Univerſal Inquiry* into things hitherto un-queſtion'd, can never be made, without diſturbing ſuch eſtabliſh'd *Rules* of *Diſcipline*, and *Inſtruction*.

For a *General Anſwer* to this, it might ſuffice to declare, that in this *Inſtitution*, Men are not ingag'd in theſe *Studies*, till the Courſe of *Education* be fully compleated : That the *Art* of *Experiments*, is not thruſt into the hands of Boys, or ſet up to be per-form'd by Beginners in the School ; but in an Aſ-ſembly of Men of Ripe years : Who while they be-gin a *new Method* of Knowledge, which ſhall con-ſiſt of *Works*, and is therefore moſt proper for Men :

Sect. II. Experiments will not injure Educa-tion.

S ſ 2   They

they ftill leave to Learners, and Children, the old talkative *Arts* which beft fit the younger Age. From hence it muft follow, that all the various manners of *Education*, will remain undifturb'd; becaufe the practifes of them, and the labours of this, are not appointed to meet in the fame *Age*, or *Perfons*. But if this will not fatisfy our *Adverfaries*, let us proceed to confider the different Parts of *Education*: and then we fhall be able to make the furer Conjectures, what manner of Influence, *new Experiments* will have upon it.

Education confifts in divers Rules, and Practifes, whereby men are furnifh'd for all the feveral Courfes of Life, to which they may apply themfelves. Of thefe præparatory *Arts*, fome concern the *Body*, fome the *Mind*. Thofe of the *Body* have no relation to my prefent *Argument* : Of thofe of the *Mind*, fome intend the Purity and Ornament of *Speech* : Some the Knowledge of the Actions of former, and prefent *Times* : Some the Government, and Virtue of our Lives : Some the *Method* of reafoning : Some the skill in the motions and meafures of the *Heavens*, and the *Earth*, and all this great Frame of *Vifible* things.

Grammar- and Rhe- toric.   Firft then I will make no fcruple to acquit *Experimental Philofophy*, from having any ill effects, on the ufual *Arts*, whereby we are taught the Purity, and Elegance of *Languages*. Whatever difcoveries fhall appear to us afrefh, out of the hidden things of *Nature*, the fame words, and the fame waies of Expreffion will remain. Or if perhaps by this means, any change fhall be made herein ; it can be only for the better ; by fupplying mens Tongues, with very many *new things*, to be nam'd; and adorn'd, and defcrib'd in their difcourfe.   N o r

Nor can there be any more jealoufy concerning *Moral Phi-* the *Moral*, and *Political* Rules of ordering mens lives. *lofophy.* But they may ftill have the fame influence, and authority, and may be propos'd to our imitation, by the fame præcepts, and arguments, of perfuafion.

It is alfo as manifeft, that the *Art* of teaching the *Hiftory.* *Actions* of former Ages; can from hence receive no dammage, or alteration. This cannot be otherwife; feeing the Subjects of *Natural*, and *Civil Hiftory* do not crofs each other; nor does the *New Philofophy* of Nature, more interfere with the *Hiftories* of *Men*, and *Government*, than the *Old*, of which this doubt was never rais'd.

Thus far then we are fecure. Thefe great, and fundamental Parts of *Education*, the Inftruments of mens Expreffing, and Ruling their own minds, and fearching into the Actions of others, will be unalter'd, whatever new changes of Opinions may arife about *Natural Things*. Let us next go on to confider the *Arts* of *Demonftration*, and *Argumentation*, in which confifts one of the moft weighty Parts of youthful Studies.

Firft for all the *Mathematical Sciences*, they will *The Mathe-* ftill remain the fame, and ftill continue to be learn'd, *matics.* and taught, in the fame *Syftemes*, and *Methods* as before. Nothing that can now be difcover'd will fubvert, but rather Confirm what is already well built on thofe immoveable principles. As they came down to us without detriment, through all the corrupt Times of *Learning*; fo they will certainly now continue *uncorrupt*, at this prefent, when *Learning* is reftor'd.

Seeing

Seeing they could not be deftroy'd in the *Ignorant Ages*, they will be in no fear, at this time, by this *Inftitution*, which defigns not only to inlarge them, but to promote the fame rigid way of *Conclufion*, in all other *Natural things*, which only the *Mathematics* have hitherto maintain'd.

Metaphyfics and Logic.   Now then, this whole controverfy is reduc'd to the alteration, which the *Logic*, and *Phyfics* of the Ancients, may receive by this change. As for their *Metaphyfics*, they fcarce deferve to have a place allow'd them in this confideration.

Nor does that prevail with me, which the Lovers of that *Cloudy Knowledge* are wont to boaft, that it is an excellent inftrument to refine, and make fubtil the minds of men. For there may be a greater Excefs in the fubtilty of mens wits, than in their thicknefs: As we fee thofe threads, which are of too fine a fpinning, are found to be more ufelefs, than thofe which are home-fpun, and grofs.

Logic is the *Art* of *Conceiving*, *Arguing*, and *Method*. And notwithftanding all the progrefs which may happen in *Natural Knowledge*, all the feveral parts of Reas'ning, which it teaches in all manner of bufinefs, will continue the fame. The operations, and powers of the *mind* will ftill be the fame: They will ftill be fubject to the fame errors: They will ftill ufe the fame degrees of Arguing from particular things, to *propofitions*, and *conclufions*; and therefore they will ftill require the fame means, and exercifes for *direction*. It is not the complaint of the promoters of *Experiments*, that men have been wanting to themfelves, in regulating, difpofing, or judging of their own *thoughts*. Nay they rather condemn them, for being wholly
im-

imploy'd about the *productions* of their own *minds*, and neglecting all the works of *Nature*, that are without them. It cannot therefore be suspected that these *Inquisitive Men*, should busy themselves, about altering the *Art of Discours*, wherein they judge that mankind has bin already rather too curious, than negligent.

The last Part that I shall mention, of the *Learning* that is taught, is the *Systeme* of *Natural Philosophy*. And it is in this alone, that I can allow, there will be any alteration made, by this reformation of *Knowledge*. But yet the change will be so advantageous, that I have no reason to dissemble it. I grant indeed that the greatest part of the former Body of *Physics*, may hereby chance to fall to the ground. But to what sum will the damage amount? What can we lose, but only some few *definitions* and idle *questions*, and empty *disputations*? Of which I may say, as one did of *Metaphors*, *Poterimus vivere sine illis*. Perhaps there will be no more use of Twenty, or Thirty obscure Terms, such as *Matter*, and *Form*, *Privation*, *Entelichia*, and the like. But to supply their want, an infinit variety of *Inventions*, *Motions*, and *Operations*, will succeed in the place of words. The Beautiful Bosom of *Nature* will be expos'd to our view: We shall enter into its *Garden*, and tast of its *Fruits*, and satisfy our selves with its *plenty*: Instead of Idle talking, and wandring under its fruitless shadows; as the *Peripatetics* did in their first institution, and their Successors have done ever since.

Natural Philosophy.

Thus

Thus far I have briefly examin'd the influence of *new Experiments*, or all the chief Parts of *Education*. And after all the *Innovation*, of which they can be suspected, we find nothing will be indanger'd, but only the *Physics* of *Antiquity:* wherein we also behold, that many things of greater concernment, will arise, to supply the place of what shall be cut away. By this discours, I hope, I have said enough, to manifest the innocence of this *Design* in respect of all the present *Schools of Learning* ; and especially our own *Universities.* And it was but just, that we should have this *tenderness*, for the Interest of those magnificent *Seats* of *humane Knowledge*, and *divine*; to which the *Natural Philosophy* of our Nation, cannot be injurious without horrible *ingratitude* ; seeing in them it has been principally cherish'd, and reviv'd. From hence the greatest part of our *Modern Inventions* have deduc'd their *Original.* It is true such *Experimental Studies* are largely dispers'd at this time : But they first came forth thence, as the *Colonies* of old did from *Rome :* and therefore as those aid, they should rather intend the strength, than the destruction of their *Mother Cities.*

I confess there have not been wanting some forward *Assertors* of *new Phylosophy*, who have not us'd any kind of *Moderation* towards them : But have presently concluded, that nothing can be well-done in *new Discoveries*, unless all the *Ancient Arts* be first rejected, and their Nurseries abolish'd. But the rashness of these mens proceedings, has rather prejudic'd, than advanc'd, what they make to shew promote. They have come as furiously to the purging of *Philosophy*, as our *Modern Zealots* did to the
Reformation

reformation of *Religion.* And the one Party is as juftly to be condemn'd, as the other. Nothing will fuffice either of them, but an utter *Deftruction, Root* and *Branch*, of whatever has the face of *Antiquity*. But as the *Univerfities* have withftood the fiercenefs of the one's Zeal without Knowledge ; fo there is no doubt, but they will alfo prevail againft the Violence of the other's pretences to *Knowledge* without *Prudence.*

BUT now after I have fhewn that all the receiv'd Forms of *Education* will be fafe, I fhall make no Scruple to add my *Conjecture*, that it could be no hindrance to the *minds* of Men, if befides thofe courfes of Studies which are now follow'd, there were alfo trial made of fome other more practical Ways, to prepare their *Minds* for the World, and the Bufineffes of human Life. It is not enough to urge againft this, that the multiplicity of *Methods* would hinder and confound the Spirits of young Men ; for it is apparent that nothing more fuppreffes the *Genius* of *Learners*, than the *Formality*, and the *Confinement* of the Precepts, by which they are inftructed. To this purpofe I will venture to propofe to the *Confideration* of wife Men, whether this way of *Teaching* by *Practice* and *Experiments*, would not at leaft be as beneficial, as the other by *Univerfal Rules* ; Whether it were not as profitable to apply the Eyes, and the Hands of Children, to fee, and to touch all the feveral kinds of *fenfible Things*; as to oblige them to learn, and remember the difficult *Doctrines* of general *Arts* ? In a word, Whether a *Mechanical Education* would not excel the *Methodical* ?

This certainly is no new Device: For it was that

Sect. IV. The Advantage of an Experimental Education.

T t

which

which *Plato* intended, when he injoin'd his *Scholars* to begin with *Geometry*; whereby, without queſtion, he deſign'd, that his *Diſciples* ſhould firſt handle *Material Things*, and grow familiar to viſible Objects, before they enter'd on the retir'd *Speculations* of other more abſtracted *Sciences*.

According to this Counſel of the *Father* of *Philoſophers*, it would not be amiſs, if before young Scholars be far ingag'd in the beaten Tracks of the Schools, the Myſteries of *Manual Arts*, the Names of their *Inſtruments*, the Secrets of their *Operations*, the Effects of Natural Cauſes, the ſeveral kinds of *Beaſts*, of *Birds*, of *Fiſhes*, of *Plants*, of *Stones*, of *Minerals*, of *Earths*, of *Waters*, and all their common Virtues and Qualities, were propoſed to be the Subjects of their firſt Thoughts and Obſervations. It may be here ſuggeſted, That the vaſt Number of ſuch Particulars will ſoon overwhelm their tender Minds, before they are well eſtabliſh'd by Time, and Uſe. But on the contrary it is evident, that the *Memories of Youth* are fitter to retain ſuch ſenſible Images, than thoſe of a fuller Age. It is *Memory* that has moſt Vigour in Children, and *Judgment* in Men : Which if rightly conſider'd, will confirm what I ſaid, that perhaps we take a præpoſterous Courſe in *Education*, by teaching *General Rules*, before *Particular Things :* And that therein we have not a ſufficient Regard to the different Advantages of *Youth* and *Manhood*. We load the Minds of Children with Doctrines, and Præcepts, to apprehend which they are moſt unfit, by reaſon of the weakneſs of their Underſtandings ; whereas they might with more Profit be exercis'd in the Conſideration of *viſible* and *ſenſible Things* ; of whoſe Impreſſions they are moſt capable, becauſe of the Strength

of

of their *Memories*, and the Perfection of their *Senses*.

THE firſt Years of Men being thus freed from any Apprehenſions of Miſchief by new *Experiments :* I will now proceed more boldly to bring them in amidſt the Throngs, and Crowds of human Buſineſs ; and to declare to all Profeſſions, and practical Lives, that they can receive no ill Impreſſions from them, but that they will be the moſt beneficial and proper *Studies,* for their Preparation and Direction.   And to this Purpoſe, I will treat of their uſefulneſs, both in reſpect of Mens public Practice, and the private Government of their own Minds. *Sect. V. The uſe of Experiments to a practical Life.*

As to the firſt, it has been an old Complaint, that has been long manag'd by Men of Buſineſs, againſt many ſorts of *Knowledge,* that our Thoughts are thereby infected with ſuch Conceptions as make them more unfit for Action, than they would have been, if they were wholly left to the force of their own *Nature.*   The common Accuſations againſt *Learning* are ſuch as theſe ; That it inclines Men to be unſettled, and *contentious* ; That it takes up more of their time, than Men of Buſineſs ought to beſtow ; That it makes them *Romantic,* and ſubject to frame more perfect Images of Things, than the Things themſelves will bear ; That it renders them overweening, unchangeable, and obſtinate ; That thereby Men become averſe from a practical Courſe, and unable to bear the Difficulties of Action ; That it employs them about Things, which are no where in uſe in the World ; and, that it draws them to neglect and contemn their own preſent Times, by doting on the paſt. But now I will maintain, that in every one of theſe Dangers *Experimental Knowledge Experiments free from the faults of other ſorts of Learning.*

T t 2   *ledge*

ledge is lefs to be fufpeded than any other ; That in moft of them (if not all) it is abfolutely innocent ; nay, That it contains the beft Remedies for the Diftempers, which fome other forts of Learning are thought to bring with them.

Sect. VI.
The firft
Objection
againft
Learning,
That it
makes Men
too Difpu-
tative.

THE firft *Objection* againft *Knowledge*, of which I fhall take notice in the active part of Life is this, That it makes Men too plentiful in their *Thoughts*; too inventive, and cavilling in their *Arguments*; and fo rather teaches them to be witty in *Objecting*, than ready in *Refolving*, and diligent in *Performing*. I confefs the Ancient *Philofophy* will hardly be able to vindicate it felf from this Charge: For its chief Purpofe is to enlarge the Fancy, and to fill the Head with the Matter and Artifice of Difcourfe. But this cannot any way touch the *Art* of *Experiments*: That confifts not in *Topicks* of Reas'ning, but of Working: That indeed is full of doubting and inquiry, and will fcarce be brought to fettle its Affent ; but it is fuch a doubting as proceeds on *Trials*, and not on *Arguments*: That does neither practife nor cherifh this humour of Difputing, which breaks the force of Things by the fubtilty of Words ; as *Seneca* was faid to do by his Style: It weakens Mens Arms, and flackens all the Sinews of Action: For fo it commonly happens, that fuch earneft Difputers evaporate all the ftrength of their Minds in arguing, queftioning, and debating ; and tire themfelves out before they come to the *Practice*.

Sect. VII.
The fecond,
That it takes
up too much
time.

THE next Accufation is, That fo many intricate Paths, and fpacious Windings of *Learning*, will require more time than can be fpar'd by Men of active and
busy

bufy Lives. The Belief of this has always made a wide Divorce between Men of *Knowledge* and *Action*; while both have Thought, that they muft either be wholly *Scholars*, or wholly Men of *Bufinefs*; and that an Excellence in both thefe Courfes can never be obtain'd by human Wit. 'Tis true indeed, there is no *Knowledge* or *Science* that can be acquitted from being too large, if their *Profeffors* have not the Difcretion to know how far to proceed, and what Moderation is to be us'd in every *Study*. There is in the leaft *Art* enough Matter, about which if Men fhall refolve to trouble their Brains all their Lives, one *Queftion* and *Difficulty* will perpetually beget another, and fo (as one of the *Antients* fays) *Ipfa tractatio, & quæftio quotidiè ex fe gignet aliquid, quod cum defidiosâ delectatione veftiges.*

To this Danger perhaps *Experiments* may feem moft expos'd, by reafon of the infinite multitude of Particulars, and innumerable variations of Inquiries, that may be made. But the *Royal Society* has prevented this Mifchief, by the Number and Succeffion of thofe that fhall undertake the *Work*. They require not the whole time of any of their *Members*, except only of their *Curators*: From the reft they expect no more but what their *Bufinefs*, nay even their very *Recreations* can fpare. It is the Continuance and Perpetuity of fuch *Philofophical Labours*, to which they principally truft; which will both allow a fufficient Relaxation to all the particular *Labourers*, and will alfo give good affurance of the happy Iffue of their *Work* at the laft: For though that be true, which the Great Phyfician laments, *That Art is long, and Life is fhort:* yet many Lives of ftudious and induftrious Men in one *Age*, and the Succeffion of many Lives of fuch Men in all
future

future *Ages*, will undoubtedly prove as long as *Art* it felf.

Seƈ. VIII.
The third
Objeƈion,
That it
makes our
Minds Ro-
mantic.

THEY farther objeƈt againſt *Learning*, That it makes our Minds too *Lofty* and *Romantic*, and inclines them to form more perfeƈt Imaginations of the Matters we are to praƈtiſe, than the Matters themſelves will bear. I cannot deny, but a mere comtemplative Man is obnoxious to this Error: He converſes chiefly in his Cloſet, with the Heads and Notions of Things, and ſo diſcerns not their Bottoms near and diſtinƈly enough: And thence he is ſubjeƈt to overlook the little Circumſtances, on which all human Aƈtions depend. He is ſtill reducing all Things to ſtanding *Do-* *ƈrines*; and therefore muſt needs be liable to negleƈt the Opportunities, to ſet upon Buſineſs too ſoon, or too late; to put thoſe Things together in his Mind, which have no agreement in *Nature*. But this above all is his greateſt Danger, that thinking it ſtill becomes him to go out of the *ordinary Way*, and to refine and heighten the Conceptions of the Vulgar, he will be ready to diſdain all the *natural* and *eaſy* ways of *Praƈtice*, and to believe that nothing ought to be done, though never ſo common, but by ſome device of *Art*, and trick of unuſual *Wiſdom*.

From theſe Inconveniences the *Experimenter* is ſecure: He invents not what he does out of himſelf; but gathers it from the Footſteps and Progreſs of *Nature*. He looks on every Thing ſtanding equal to it, and not as from a higher Ground: He labours about the plain and undigeſted Objeƈts of his Senſes, without conſidering them as they are joyn'd into common *Notions*. He has an Opportunity of underſtanding the moſt natural Ways by which all Things are produc'd.

t

duc'd. He clearly beholds all the secret Accidents and Turnings, Advantages and Failings of *Nature*. He endeavours rather to know, than to admire; and looks upon *Admiration*, not as the End, but the Imperfection of our *Knowledge*.

THE next hindrance of *Action*, is *an obstinacy of Resolution*, and a want of *Dexterity* to change our apprehensions of Things according to Occasions. This is the more destructive, because it carries with it the most solemn appearance of *Wisdom*. There is scarce any thing that renders a Man so useless, as a perverse sticking to the same things in *all times*, because he has sometimes found them to have been in Season. But now in this, there is scarce any *Comparison* to be made, between him who is only a *thinking Man*, and a *Man of Experience*. The first does commonly establish his constant Rules, by which he will be guided : The later makes none of his *Opinions* irrevocable. The one if he mistakes, receives his Errors from his *Understanding*; the other only from his *Senses*; and so he may correct, and alter them with more ease. The one fixes his *Opinion* as soon; the other doubts as long as he can. The one chiefly strives to be unmovable in his Mind ; the other to enlarge, and amend his *Knowledge* : And from hence the one is inclin'd to be *præsumptuous*, the other modest in his *Judgment*.

Sect. IX. The fourth Objection, That it makes Men presumptuous and obstinate.

THE next Pretence, on which Men of *Learning* are wont to be vilified, is, that they use to be so much affected with the pleasant Musings of their own Thoughts, as to abhor the Roughness, and Toyl of *Business*. This Accusation, I confess, is not altogether groundless. The solitary Imaginations of *Speculative*

Sect. X. The fifth Objection, that 'tis Pleasure draws Men off from Business.

culative Men are of all other the moſt eaſy : There a
Man meets with little ſtubbornneſs of Matter : He may
'chooſe his Subject where he likes ; he may faſhion and
turn it as he pleaſes : Whereas when he comes abroad
into the World, he muſt endure more *Contradiction :*
More *Difficulties* are to be overcome ; and he cannot
always follow his own *Genius :* So that it is not to be
wonder'd, that ſo many *great Wits* have deſpis'd the
labour of a practical Courſe ; and have rather choſen
to ſhut themſelves up from the *Noiſe* and *Preferments*
of the *World,* to converſe in the Shadow with the
pleaſant *Productions* of their own *Fancies.*

And this perhaps is the reaſon why the moſt *extraordinary Men* of *Arts* in all Ages, are generally obſerv'd to be the greateſt *Humoriſts :* They are ſo full
of the ſweetneſs of their own *Conceptions,* that they
become Moroſe, when they are drawn from them, they
cannot eaſily make their minds ductil and pliable to
others Tempers, and ſo they appear untractable, and
unskilful in *Converſation.*

From this I ſhall alſo free the *Experimental Philoſopher.* The Satisfaction that he finds, is not *imaginary,* but *real :* It is drawn from Things that are not out
of the World, but in it : It does not carry him farther
off, but brings him nearer to *Practice.* 'Tis true,
that *Knowledge* which is only founded on Thoughts
and Words, has ſeldom any other end, but the *breeding* and *increaſing* of more Thoughts and Words : But
that which is built on *Works* (as his will be) will naturally deſire to diſcover, to augment, to apply, to
communicate it ſelf by more *Works.*

Nor can it be thought, that his *Mind* will be made
to languiſh by this pleaſure of *Obſervation,* and to
have any Averſion from the difficulty and tedſiouſneſs
of

of human Affairs; feeing his way of *Obfervation* it felf
is fo *laborious*. It is a good Precept, which is wont to
be given in refpect of all forts of *Exercifes*, that they
fhould be at leaft as hard and toilfome, as that *Art*
which we ftrive to gain by them. And by this Rule
Experiments are an excellent preparation towards any
habit or faculty of Life whatfoever. For what Thing,
which can be effected by *mortal Induftry*, can feem impoffible to him who has been ingag'd in thefe *Studies*,
which require fuch an indefatigable Watchfulnefs?
What can overcome his Diligence, who has been able
to fuftain with Patience the *Efcapes*, the *Delays*, the
Labyrinths of *Nature*; whom the Repetition of fo
many *Labours*, fo many Failings, with which he meets,
and fo long attendance could not tire?

A N O T H E R principal Mifchief to be avoided, is the
Conformity of our *Actions* to Times paft, and not the
prefent. This Extravagance is generally imputed to
ftudious Men; and they cannot be wholly acquitted
from it. For while they continue heaping up in their
Memories the Cuftoms of paft *Ages*, they fall infenfibly to imitate them, without any manner of Care how
fuitable they are to *Times* and *Things*. The Grounds of
this Miftake will be worth our difcovering, becaufe
in Mens Opinions it does fo much Prejudice to the
Learned part of the *World*. In the ancient *Authors*
which they turn over, they find Defcriptions of Ver-
tues more perfect than indeed they were: The *Governments* are reprefented better, and the Ways of
Life pleafanter than they deferv'd. Upon this, thefe
Bookifh wife Men ftrait compare what they read with
what they fee: And here beholding nothing fo heroi-
cally tranfcendent, becaufe they are able to mark all

Sect. XI.
*The fixth
Objection,
That it
makes Men
regard the
Times paft,
and neglect
the prefent.*

U u   the

the *Spots*, as well as *Beauties* of every Thing, that is
fo clofe to their Sight, they prefently begin to difpife
their own *Times*, to exalt the paft, to contemn the
Virtues, and aggravate the *Vices* of their *Country*; not
endeavouring to amend them, but by fuch Examples as
are now unpracticable, by reafon of the Alteration of
Men and *Manners*.

For this Defect, *Experiments* are a foveraign Cure :
They give us a perfect Sight of what is before us ;
they bring us home to our felves ; they make us live
in *England*, and not in *Athens* or *Sparta*, at this prefent time, and not three thoufand Years ago : Though
they permit us to reflect on what has been done in *former Ages* ; yet they make us chiefly to regard and contemplate the Things that are in our *View*. This certainly is comformable to the *Defign* of *Nature* it felf ;
which though it has fram'd our Bodies in that manner, that we may eafily upon occafion turn about to
look behind us ; yet it has plac'd the *Eyes*, the chief
Inftruments of Obfervation, not in our *Backs*, but in
our *Foreheads*.

Sect. XII.   THE laft Failing which is wont to be imputed to
The feventh *Learned Men*, is want of *Ufe*, and fear of *Practice*, and
Objection, a converfing with Things in their *Studies*, which they
That it hin- meet with no where elfe. It may now perhaps be
ders ufe. thought, that an *Experimenter* is as inclinable to thefe
Weaknefles, as he that only contemplates ; becaufe
they both keep out of the way, in the Shadow ; the
one in his *Library, arguing, objecting, defending, concluding* with himfelf ; the other in his *Workhoufe*, with fuch
Tools and Materials, whereof many perhaps are not
publickly in ufe. Let us then confider which of them
is moft to be blam'd for converfing with Matters unlike

like thofe that we meet with in *Civil Affairs* ? And which moft abounds with *Fears* and *Doubts*, and miftaken in Ideas of *Things*.

It cannot be denied, but the Men of *Reading* do very much bufy themfelves about fuch *Conceptions*, which are no where to be found out of their own Chambers. The *Senfe*, the *Cuftom*, the *Practice*, the *Judgment* of the World, is quite a different Thing from what they imagine it to be in private. And therefore it is no wonder, if when they come abroad into Bufinefs, the fight of Men, the Tumult and Noife of Cities, and the very brightnefs of Day it felf affright them : Like that *Rhetorician*, who having been us'd to declaim in the fhade of a *School*, when he came to plead a true Caufe in the open *Air*, defir'd the Judges to remove their Seat under fome Roof, becaufe the *Light* offended him.

But now on the other fide, the Men of *Works* and *Experiments* perhaps do not always handle the very fame *Subjects* that are acted on the Stage of the *World*; yet they are fuch as have a very great refemblance to them. It is *Matter*, a vifible and fenfible *Matter*, which is the Object of their *Labours* : And the fame is alfo us'd by Men of practical Lives. This Likenefs of their *Imployments* will foon make the one excel in the other. For it is far eafier for him who has been converfant in one fort of *Works*, to apply himfelf to any other ; than for him who has only thought much, to turn a Man of *Practice* : As he that can paint the Face of a Man or a Lion, will much fooner come to draw any other Creature, than he who has all the *Rules* of *Limning* in his Head, but never yet us'd his Hand to lay on a *Colour*.

And as for the *Terrors* and *Mifapprehenfions* which

com-

commonly confound weaker Minds, and make Mens Hearts to fail and boggle at Trifles; there is fo little hope of having them remov'd by *Speculation* alone, that it is evident they were firft produc'd by the moft *contemplative* Men amongft the *Antients*; and chiefly prevail'd of late Years, when that way of *Learning* flourifh'd. The *Poets* began of old to impofe the Deceit. They to make all Things look more venerable than they were, devis'd a thoufand falfe *Chimæras*; on every *Field, River, Grove*, and *Cave*, they beftow'd a *Fantafm* of their own making: With thefe they amaz'd the World; thefe they cloath'd with what Shapes they pleas'd; by thefe they pretended, that all Wars, and Counfels, and Actions of Men were adminiftred. And in the modern *Ages* thefe *Fantaftical Forms* were reviv'd and poffefs'd *Chriftendom*, in the very height of the *Schoolmens* time: An infinite Number of *Fairies* haunted every Houfe; all Churches were fill'd with *Apparitions*; Men began to be frighted from their *Cradles*, which Fright continu'd to their *Graves*, and their Names alfo were made the Caufes of fcaring others. All which Abufes if thofe acute *Philofophers* did not promote, yet they were never able to overcome; nay, even not fo much as King *Oberon* and his invifible *Army*.

But from the time in which the *real Philofophy* has appear'd, there is fcarce any whifper remaining of fuch *Horrors:* Every Man is unfhaken at thofe Tales at which his *Anceftors* trembled: The courfe of Things goes quietly along in its own true Channel of *Natural Caufes* and *Effects*. For this we are beholden to *Experiments*; which though they have not yet compleated the Difcovery of the true World, yet they have already vanquifh'd thofe wild Inhabitants of the falfe

Worlds,

Worlds, that us'd to aftonifh the Minds of Men. A Bleffing for which we ought to be thankful, if we remember, that it is one of the greateft Curfes that God pronounces on the Wicked, *that they fhall fear where no fear is.*

From what I have faid may be gather'd, That *Experimental Philofophy* will prevent Mens fpending the ftrength of their Thoughts about *Difputes,* by turning them to *Works:* That it may well be attended by the united *Labours* of many, without wholly devouring the time of thofe that *labour:* That it will cure our Minds of *romantic Swelling,* by fhewing all Things familiarly to them, juft as large as they are: That it will free them from *Perverfity,* by not permitting them to be too peremptory in their *Conclufions:* That it accuftoms our Hands to Things which have a near refemblance to the bufinefs of Life; and, that it draws away the Shadows which either inlarge or darken *human Affairs.* And indeed of the ufual Titles by which Men of Bufinefs are wont to be diftinguifh'd, the *Crafty,* the *Formal,* and the *Prudent*; the *Crafty* may anfwer to the *Empyric* in *Philofophy*; that is, he is fuch a one who has a great Collection of particular *Experiences,* but knows not how to ufe them but to bafe and low Ends. The *Formal* Man may be compar'd to the meer *Speculative Philofopher:* For he vainly reduces every Thing to grave and folemn general *Rules,* without Difcretion, or mature Deliberation. And laftly, the *Prudent* Man is like him who proceeds on a conftant and folid courfe of *Experiments.* The one in Civil Life neither wholly rejects the Wifdom of *Ancient* or *Modern* times: The other in *Philofophy* has the fame reverence for *former Ages,* and regard for the *prefent.* The one does not reft upon
empty

empty *Prudence*, but designs it for Action : The other
does the same with his *Discoveries* : Upon a just, fevere, and deliberate Examination of Things, they both
raise their *Observations*, which they do not suffer to
lie idle, but use them to direct the *Actions*, and supply the *Wants* of *human Life.*

Sect. XIII.   BESIDES what I have said of the help which *Expe-*
Experi-   *riments* will bring to our public *Duties*, and civil
ments use-   *Actions*, I promis'd to add something concerning the
ful for the   Assistance that they are able to give towards the Ma-
cure of Mens nagement of the private *Motions*, and *Passions* of our
Minds.   *Minds* : Of this I need say the less, because there is
amongst the *Philosophers* a particular Science appointed for this Purpose, to prescribe Rules for calming our
Affections, and conquering our *Vices*. However, I
will not wholly pass it over in Silence : but I will try
in few Words to make appear, that the *real Philoso-*
phy will supply our Thoughts with excellent *Medi-*
cines against their own *Extravagancies*, and will
serve in some sort, for the same ends, which the *Mo-*
ral professes to accomplish.

If we shall cast an Eye on all the *Tempests* which
arise within our Breasts, and consider the Causes, and
Remedies of all the violent *Desires*, malicious *Envies*,
intemperate *Joys*, and irregular *Griefs*, by which
the Lives of most Men become *miserable*, or *guilty* ;
we shall find, that they are chiefly produc'd by *Idle-*
ness, and may be most naturally cur'd by *Diversion*.
Whatever *Art* shall be able to busy the *Minds* of Men,
with a constant course of *innocent Works*, or to fill
them with as vigorous and pleasant Images, as those
ill *Impressions*, by which they are deluded ; it will
certainly have a surer effect in the composing and
purifying

purifying of their Thoughts, than all the rigid Præcepts of the Stoical, or the empty Diftinctions of the *Peripatetic Moralifts.*

Now then it is requir'd in that *Study,* which fhall attempt, according to the force of *Nature,* to cure the Difeafes of the Mind, that it keep it from *Idlenefs,* by full and earneft *Employments*; and that it poffefs it with innocent, various, lafting, and even fenfible *Delights.*

How active and induftrious the *Art* of *Experiments* ought to be, may be concluded from the whole tenour of my Difcourfe : wherein I have often prov'd, that it can never be finifh'd by the perpetual *Labours* of any one Man, nay fcarce by the fucceffive force of the greateft *Affembly.*

That therefore being taken for granted, that it will afford eternal *Employments :* it is alfo as true, that it's Labours will contain the moft *affecting,* and the moft *diverting Delights :* And that thence it has Power enough to free the *Minds* of Men from their Vanities and Intemperance, by that very way which the greateft *Epicure* has no reafon to reject, by oppofing Pleafure againft Pleafure.

And I dare challenge all the corrupt *Arts* of our *Senfes,* or the Devices of voluptuous Wits, to provide fuller, more changeable, or nearer Objects, for the Contentment of Mens *Minds.* It were indeed to be wifh'd, that fevere Virtue it felf, attended only by its own *Authority,* were powerful enough to eftablifh its Dominion. But it cannot be fo. The Corruptions, and Infirmities of *Human Nature* ftand in need of all manner of Allurements, to draw us to Good, and quiet Manners. I will therefore propofe for this End this Courfe of *Study,* which will not affright us
with

with rigid Præcepts, or four Looks, or peevish Commands, but confifts of fenfible *Pleafure*, and befides will be moft lafting in its Satisfaction, and innocent its Remembrance.

What *Raptures* can the moft *voluptuous* Men fancy, to which thefe are not equal ? Can they relifh nothing but the *Pleafures* of their *Senfes* ? They may here enjoy them without Guilt or Remorfe. Are they affrighted at the Difficulties of *Knowledge* ? Here they may meet with a *Study*, that as well fits the moft *negligent* Minds, as the moft *induftrious*. This confifts of fo many *Works*, and thofe fo obvious, and facil, that the moft laborious will never find Caufe to be idle, and the moft idle may ftill have fomething to do with the greateft Eafe. In this they need not weary themfelves by fearching for *Matter* : whatever they feel, or fee, will afford them *Obfervations*. In this there is no tedious Preparation requir'd to fit them for fuch Endeavours : as foon as they have the ufe of their *Hands*, and *Eyes*, and common *Senfe*, they are fufficiently furnifh'd to undertake them. Though we cannot comprehend the *Arts* of Men without many prævious *Studies*, yet fuch is the Indulgence of *Nature*, that it has from the Beginning, out of its own Store, fufficiently provided every Man with all Things, that are needful for the Underftanding of it felf.

Thus neither the *fenfual Mind*, has any occafion to contemn *Experiments* as unpleafant, nor the idle as burdenfome, or intolerable, nor the virtuous as unworthy of his *Labours*. And the fame Influence they may have on all other *moral* Imperfections of *human Nature*. What room can there be for low and little *Things* in a *Mind* fo ufefully and fuccefsfully employ'd ?
What

What *ambitious Difquiets* can torment that Man, who has fo much Glory before him, for which there are only requir'd the delightful *Works* of his *Hands?* What dark or melancholy Paffions can overfhadow his *Heart*, whofe *Senfes* are always full of fo many various *Productions*, of which the leaft Progrefs, and Succefs, will affect him with an *innocent Joy?* What Anger, Envy, Hatred, or Revenge, can long torment his Breaft, whom not only the greateft, and nobleft Objects, but every Sand, every Pible, every Grafs, every Earth, every Fly can divert? To whom the return of every Seafon, every Month, every Day, do fuggeft a Circle of moft pleafant *Operations?* If the *Antients* prefcrib'd it as a fufficient *Remedy*, againft fuch *violent Paffions*, only to repeat the Alphabet over; whereby there was Leifure given to the *Mind*, to recover itfelf from any fudden Fury: Then how much more *effectual Medicines*, againft the fame *Diftempers*, may be fetch'd from the whole Alphabet of *Nature*, which reprefents itfelf to our *Confideration*, in fo many infinite *Volumes!*

I will now proceed to the weightieft, and moft folemn Part of my whole *Undertaking*; to make a Defence of the *Royal Society*, and this new *Experimental Learning*, in Refpect of the *Chriftian Faith*. I am not ignorant, in what a flippery Place I now ftand; and what a tender Matter I am enter'd upon. I know that it is almoft impoffible without Offence, to fpeak of things of this *Nature*, in which all *Mankind*, each *Country*, and now almoft every *Family*, do fo widely difagree among themfelves. I cannot expect that what I fhall fay will efcape Mifinterpretation, though it be fpoken with the greateft Simplicity,

Sect. XIV. *Experiments not dangerous to the Chriftian Religion.*

X x

plicity, and submiffion, while I behold that moft
Men do rather value themfelves, and others, on the
little Differences of *Religion*, than the main Subftance
itfelf; and while the Will of God is fo varioufly diftracted, that what appears to be *Piety* to fome *Chriftians*, is abhorr'd as the greateft Superftition and
Herefy by others.

However to fmooth my Way as much as I can, and
to prepare all our feveral *Spiritual Interefts*, to read
this Part with fome tolerable *Moderation*; I do here,
in the beginning, moft fincerely declare, that if this
Defign fhould in the leaft diminifh the *Reverence*, that
is due to the *Doctrine of Jefus Chrift*, it were fo far
from deferving *Protection*, that it ought to be abhorr'd by all the *Politic* and *Prudent*; as well as by
the devout Part of Chriftendom. And this, I profefs,
I think they were bound to do, not only from a juft
Dread of the *Being*, the *Worfhip*, the *Omnipotence*,
the *Love of God*, all which are to be held in the
higheft Veneration, but alfo out of a Regard to the
Peace and Profperity of Men. In Matters that concern our *Opinions* of another *World*, the leaft Alterations are of wonderful Hazard: how mifchievous then
would that Enterprize be, whofe Effects would abolifh
the *Command of Confcience*, the Belief of a *Future
Life*; or any of thofe Heavenly *Doctrines*, by which
not only the *Eternal Condition* of Men is fecur'd,
but their *Natural Reafon*, and their *Temporal Safety*
advanc'd? Whoever fhall impioufly attempt to fubvert
the Authority of the *Divine Power*, on falfe Pretences to better *Knowledge*, he will unfettle the ftrongeft
Foundations of our *Hopes*: he will make a terrible
Confufion in all the Offices and Opinions of Men: he
will deftroy the moft prevailing *Argument* to *Virtue*:
he

he will remove all *Human Actions*, from their firmeſt Center : he will even deprive himſelf of the Prerogative of his *Immortal Soul* ; and will have the ſame Succeſs, that the *Ancient Fables* make thoſe to have had, who contended with their *God*, of whom they report, that many were immediately turn'd into *Beaſts*.

With theſe Apprehenſions I come to examine the *Objections*, which I am now to ſatisfy : and having calmly compar'd the *Arguments* of ſome devout Men againſt *Knowledge*, and chiefly that of *Experiments* ; I muſt pronounce them both, to be altogether inoffenſive. I did before affirm, that the *Royal Society* is abundantly cautious, not to intermeddle in *Spiritual Things :* But that being only a general Plea, and the Queſtion not lying ſo much on what they do at preſent, as upon the probable Effects of their Enterprize ; I will bring it to the Teſt through the chief Parts of *Chriſtianity* ; and ſhew that it will be found as much averſe from *Atheiſm*, in its Iſſue and Conſequences, as it was in its original Purpoſe.

The publick Declaration of the *Chriſtian Religion*, is to propoſe to Mankind an infallible Way o *Salvation.* Towards the Performance of this happy End, beſides the *Principles* of *Natural Religion*, which conſiſts in the Acknowledgment and Worſhip of a *Deity* it has offer'd us the Merits of a glorious *Saviour :* By him, and his *Apoſtles Miniſtry*, it has given us ſufficient *Examples*, and *Doctrines*, to acquaint us with *Divine Things*, and carry us to *Heaven*. In every one of theſe, the *Experiments* of *Natural Things*, do neither darken our Eyes, nor deceive our Minds, nor deprave our Hearts.

X x 2. FIRST

Sect. XV.   FIRST there can be no juft Reafon affign'd, why an
Experi-   *Experimenter* fhould be prone to deny the Effence,
ments will   and Properties of *God*, the univerfal Sovereignty of
not deftroy his *Dominion*, and his *Providence* over the *Creation*.
the Doctrine He has before him the very fame Argument, to con-
of the God- firm his Judgment in all thefe ; with which he himfelf
hee l.   is wont to be abundantly fatisfy'd, when he meets
with it in any of his *Philofophical Inquiries*. In every
thing that he tries, he believes, that this is enough
for him to reft on, if he finds, that not only his own,
but the *univerfal Obfervations* of Men of all Times
and Places, without any mutual Confpiracy have con-
fented in the fame *Conclufion*. How can he then re-
frain from embracing this common *Truth*, which is
witnefs'd by the unanimous Approbation of all *Countries*, the Agreement of *Nations*, and the fecret Acknowledgment of every Man's Breaft ?

'Tis true his *Employment* is about *material Things*.
But this is fo far from drawing him to oppofe invifible *Beings*, that it rather puts his Thoughts into an
excellent good Capacity to believe them. In every
Work of *Nature* that he handles, he knows that there
is not only a grofs Subftance, which prefents itfelf
to all Mens Eyes ; but an infinite fubtilty of *Parts*,
which come not into the fharpeft Sence. So that what
the *Scripture* relates of the Purity of *God*, of the
Spirituality of his *Nature*, and that of *Angels*, and
the *Souls* of Men, cannot feem incredible to him, when
he perceives the numberlefs Particles that move in
every Man's *Blood*, and the prodigious Streams
that continually flow unfeen from every *Body*. Having found that his own *Senfes* have been fo far affifted by the *Inftruments* of *Art*, he may fooner admit,

mit, that his Mind ought to be rais'd higher, by a heavenly Light, in thofe things wherein his *Senfes* do fall fhort. If (as the *Apoftle* fays) the invifible things of *God* are manifefted by the vifible ; then how much ftronger Arguments has he for his Belief, in the *eternal Power*, and *Godhead*, from the vaft Number of Creatures, that are invifible to others, but are expos'd to his View by the help of his *Experiments ?*

THUS he is prepar'd to admit a *Deity*, and to embrace the Confequences of that Conceffion. He is alfo from his *Experiments* as well furnifh'd with Arguments to adore it : He has always before his Eyes the *Beauty*, *Contrivance*, and *Order* of *God's Works* : From hence, he will learn to ferve him with all Reverence, who in all that he has made, confulted *Ornament*, as well as *Ufe*.

Sect. XVI. *Experiments not injurious to the worfhip of God.*

From hence he will beft underftand the infinite Diftance between *himfelf* and his *Creator*, when he finds that all things were produc'd by him : Whereas he by all his Study, can fcarce imitate the leaft Effects, nor haften, or retard the common Courfe of *Nature*. This will teach him to *worfhip* that *Wifdom*, by which all things are fo eafily fuftain'd, when he has look'd more familiarly into them, and beheld the Chances and Alterations, to which they are expofed. Hence he will be led to admire the wonderful Contrivance of the *Creation* ; and fo to apply, and direct his Praifes aright : which no doubt, when they are offer'd up to *Heaven*, from the Mouth of one, who has well ftudied what he commends, will be more fuitable to the *Divine Nature*, than the blind Applaufes of the Ignorant. This was the firft Service that *Adam* perform'd to his *Creator*, when he obey'd him in mu-
ftring

ſtring, and naming, and looking into the *Nature* of all the *Creatures*. This had been the only *Religion* if Men had continued innocent in *Paradiſe*, and had not wanted a *Redemption*. Of this the *Scripture* itſelf makes ſo much Uſe, that if any devout Man ſhall re-ject all *Natural Philoſophy*, he may blot *Geneſis*, and *Job*, and the *Pſalms*, and ſome other Books out of the *Canon* of the *Bible*. God never yet left himſelf with-out Witneſs in the *World*: And it is obſervable, that he has commonly choſen the dark and ignorant *Ages*, wherein to work Miracles; but ſeldom or never the Times when *Natural Knowledge* prevail'd: For he knew there was not ſo much need to make uſe of ex-traordinary Signs, when Men were diligent in the Works of his Hands, and attentive on the Impreſſions of his Foot-ſteps in his *Creatures*.

It is almoſt a *proverbial* Speech, *that the moſt* Learn-ed Ages *are ſtill the moſt* Atheiſtical, *and the* Ignorant *moſt* Devout. Whoever devis'd this Diſtinction at firſt, the true *Piety* is little beholden to him for it; for inſtead of obeying the *Jewiſh Law*, which for-bids us to offer up to *God* a Sacrifice that has a Ble-miſh, he has beſtow'd the moſt excellent of all the Race of Men on the Devil; and has only aſſign'd to *Religion* thoſe *Men* and thoſe *Times*, which have the greateſt Blemiſh of *Human Nature*, even a Defect in their *Knowledge* and *Underſtanding*.

If there can be found any Colour for this *Obſerva-tion*, that the *Light* of *Reaſon* ſhould produce a *Spiri-tual Darkneſs*; it can only then hold good, when the *Knowledge* of Men, and not that of *Nature* abounds. Whether the firſt be true, or no, let the *Politicians* conſider: But of the ſecond, this is a ſufficient Con-viction, that in moſt Countries God has been worſhipp'd

fhipp'd in a Form proportionable to that kind of *Natural Philofophy* in which they excell'd. In *Perfia*, where the Skill of the *Heavenly Motions* firft began, they had their Temples on the Tops of Hills, and open to the Air. In *Ægypt* they had the beft Opportunities of ftudying the Nature of *living Creatures* ; by reafon of that variety which their River and their Land produc'd. And their *Religious Myfteries* were contain'd in *Hieroglyphicks* which were moft of them borrow'd from Beafts. And why fhould *Natural Philofophy* be now condemn'd for contempt of all *Divinity*, when of old it did rather incline them to *Superftition*, which is the other extreme? It is true indeed, by that *Knowledge* which they had of many Creatures, they were drawn to adore them ; but that was only becaufe it was imperfect : If they had underftood them throughly, they had never done it : So true is that Saying of my Lord *Bacon*, *That by a little Knowledge of Nature Men become Atheifts*; *but a great deal returns them back again to a found and religious Mind.* In brief, if we rightly apprehend the Matter, it will be found that it is not only Sottifhnefs, but Prophanefs, for Men to cry out againft the underftanding of *Nature* ; for that being nothing elfe but the Inftrument of *God*, whereby he gives Being and Action to *Things* : the *Knowledge* of it deferves fo little to be efteem'd impious, that it ought rather to be reckon'd as *Divine*.

BUT the chief Part of our *Religion*, on which the Certainty of all the reft depends, is the *Evangelical Doctrine* of *Salvation* by *Jefus Chrift*. In this there is nothing from which he that converfes much with *Nature*, can be thought to be more averfe than others : nay,

Sect. XVII. *Experiments not prejudicial to the Doctrine of the Gofpel.*

nay, to which he may not be concluded to be more inclinable, on this very Account; seeing it has all been prov'd to him his own Way. Had not the appearance of *Chrift* been ftrengthen'd by undeniable Signs of *Almighty Power*, no Age nor Place had been oblig'd to believe his Meffage. And thefe *Miracles* with which he afferted the *Truths* that he taught (if I might be allow'd this Boldnefs in a Matter fo facred) I would even venture to call *Divine Experiments* of his *Godhead*.

What then can there be in all this *Doctrine*, at which a real and impartial *Inquirer* into *natural Things*, fhould be offended? Does he demand a Teftimony from *Heaven*? He has it: He reads Effects produc'd, that did exceed all mortal Skill and Force: And of this he himfelf is a better Judge than others: For to underftand aright what is *Supernatural*, it is a good Step firft to *know* what is according to *Nature*.

Does he require that this fhould be teftified, not by Men of *Craft* or *Speculation*; but rather by Men of *Honefty*, *Trades*, and *Bufinefs*? The *Apoftles* were fuch. Will he not confent to any Man's *Opinions*, unlefs he fees the *Operations* of his Hands agree with them? *Chrift* himfelf requires no more of any of his *Followers*: For he commanded his *Difciples* not to believe him, but the *Works* that he did. Does he think that it is the moft honorable Labour to ftudy the Benefit of Mankind? to help their Infirmities? to fupply their Wants? to eafe their Burdens? He here may behold the whole *Doctrine* of *Future Happinefs*, introduc'd by the fame Means; by feeding the Hungry, by curing the Lame, and by opening the Eyes of the Blind: All which may be call'd *Philofophical Works*, perform'd by an *Almighty Hand*.

What

What then can hinder him from loving and admi-
ring this *Saviour*, whose *Design* is so comfortable to
his own, but his *Ability* so much greater ? What Jealousy can he have of an Imposture in this *Messias* ?
Who though his *Doctrine* was so pure and venerable,
though his *Life* was so blameless, though he had the
Power of *Heaven* and *Earth* in his Hands, though he
knew the Thoughts of Men and might have touch'd
and mov'd them as he pleas'd ; did yet not rely on his
Doctrine, on his *Life*, on the irresistible Assistance of
Angels, or on his own *Divinity* alone ; but stoop'd
to convince Men by their *Senses*, and by the very
same Course by which they receive all their *Natural
Knowledge*.

THE last *Doctrinal* Part of our *Religion*, I shall
mention, consists of those *Doctrines* which have been
long since deduc'd by Consequences from the *Scripture*, and are now settled in the Body of that *Divinity*,
which was deliver'd down to us by the *Primitive
Church*, and which the generality of *Christendom* em-
braces. It may here be suggested, that the sensible
Knowledge of *Things* may in time abolish most of
these, by insinuating into Men's Minds that they cannot stand before the Impartiality of *Philosophical Inquisitions*. But this Surmise has no manner of Foundation. These Superstructures are of two Sorts : Either
those of which a Man may have a clear Apprehension
in his Thoughts, upon a rational Account, and which
are intelligible to any ordinary Reader ; or else such
as exceed the common Measures of our *Reason* and
Senses. There will be no Fear that an *Experimenter*
should reject the first, seeing they may be conceiv'd
by the meanest Capacity, and have that Stamp upon

§. XVIII.
*Experi-
ments will
not over-
throw the
Doctrine of
the Primi-
tive Church.*

Y y   them,

them, which he for the most part esteems the Character of *Truth*, that they are vulgar. But now towards the consenting to the last, there is nothing better than to believe them in gross; and for this he is
as well prepar'd as any other *Philosopher*. If we suppose him sufficiently convinc'd of the Authority of
the Deliverer, (as I have already shewn he may be)
he cannot be suspected for disavowing his Word,
though never so mystical, or for resisting the Voice
of him whose Arm he has found to be Omnipotent.
This Submission of his *Judgment* he may make, not-
withstanding the Severity of his *Inquiries*; and the
most subtil speculative Man in the World can do no
more. After all his acute *Arguings* in *Divinity*, he
can never render any one Point, which is the proper
Object of *Faith*, to be plain, and equal, and expressi-
ble to our *Reason*. What good can he then do? seeing
he is not able to make it any way fitter for our *Faith*,
by all his *Transcendental Notions*, than it was before
on the bare Account of the *wondrous Works* of the
Author.

This is the Place in which the *Peripatetic Philosophy* has long triumph'd; but I cannot imagine on
what Right. The spiritual and supernatural Part of *Christianity* no *Philosophy* can reach; and in the plain things
there is no need of any at all; so that it is excluded
on both Accounts. In some *Doctrines* it is useless, by
reason of their Sublimity; in others, because of their
Commonness. How small Assistance it brings, may be
seen in those very Points in which its Empire seems
most to be plac'd, in *God's Decrees*, his *Immateriality*,
his *Eternity*, and the holy Mystery of the *Trinity:*
in all which we are only brought into a more learned Darkness by it; and in which unfathomable
                                                      Depths

Depths a plain *Believing* is at laſt acknowledg'd by all to be our only Refuge. The Truth is, notwith-ſtanding the great Stir they have made about *Religion*, if we had only follow'd their Light, we had ſtill worſhipp'd the *Creator* and *Redeemer* of the *World*, under the ſame Title by which their Predeceſſors did formerly at *Athens*, as the *unknown God*.

This I have urg'd ſo far, becauſe I am confident that the reducing of *Chriſtianity* to one particular Sect of *Philoſophy*, and confining it to that, is one of the moſt deſtructive Engines that ever was manag'd againſt it. Of this the Church of *Rome*, for her Share, has already found the ill Effects: And the Danger is apparent: For by this means the Benefit of *Religion* will become very narrow, ſeeing where *Reaſon* takes Place it will only convince them who are of the ſame Opinions in *Philoſophy* with thoſe that convert them: And alſo, (that which is worſe) if ever by any Fate of *Times*, or Change of *Governments*, or Succeſſion of new *Arts*, that Sect ſhall chance to be quite broken, the *Doctrine* of *Chriſt*, relying upon it, were inevitably ruin'd, unleſs *God* were pleas'd to ſupport it a ſupernatural Way, or to reſtore it again by new *Miracles*. *Religion* ought not to be the Subject of *Diſputations:* It ſhould not ſtand in need of any Devices of *Reaſon:* It ſhould in this be like the temporal Laws of all Countries, towards the obeying of which there is no need of *Syllogiſms* or *Diſtinctions*; nothing elſe is neceſſary but a bare Pro-mulgation, a common Apprehenſion, and Senſe enough to underſtand the Grammatical Meaning of ordinary Words. Nor ought *Philoſophers* to regret this Divorce; ſeeing they have almoſt deſtroy'd themſelves by keeping *Chriſtianity* ſo long under their Guard; by fetching *Religion* out of the *Church*

and

and carrying it Captive into the *Schools,* they have
made it fuffer Banifhment from its proper Place : And
they have withal thereby very much corrupted the
Subftance of their own *Knowledge* : They have done
as the *Philiftines* by feizing on the *Ark* ; who by the
fame Action depriv'd the People of *God* of their *Religion,* and alfo brought a Plague amongft themfelves.

Sect. XIX.   THUS far I truft it will be confefs'd, that *Experi-*
Experi-   *ments* are unblameable. But yet there is much more
ments will   behind, of which many pious Men are wont to exprefs
not hinder   their Jealoufy. For though they fhall be brought
the Practice to allow, that all thefe *Doctrines,* which I have
of Religion. nam'd, may feem to remain fafe amidft the Studies
of *Natural Things* : Yet they ftill whifper, that they
may chance by degrees, to make the Sincerity of Devotion appear ridiculous, and to bring the Strictnefs
of holy Life out of Fafhion : And that fo they will
filently, and by Peice-meals, demolifh *Religion* which
they dare not openly encounter. I will therefore
next endeavour the Removal of thefe Scruples, though
I fufficiently underftand, that it is a very *difficult
Work,* to confute fuch popular and plaufible Errors,
which have the Pretence of the Caufe of *God* to confirm them.

The chief Subftance of real and fober *Piety,* is
contain'd in the devout Obfervation of all thofe Ways
whereby *God* has been pleas'd to manifeft his Will ;
and in a right Separation of our Minds from the Lufts
and Defires of the *World.* The moft remarkable Means,
whereby he has made known his Pleafure, are thofe
which have been fix'd and reveal'd in his *Word* ; or
elfe the extraordinary Signs of his Authority, and
Command.

                                                    Con-

Concerning our Acknowledgment of his *reveal'd Will* in the *Scripture*, I have already spoken. And our Obedience to the latter, confifts chiefly of two Kinds : an humble Submiffion to *Divine Prophecies*, and a careful Obfervance of all *remarkable Providences*. In both which *Experimental Philofophy* may well be juftify'd. It may perhaps correct fome Exceffes which are incident to them : But it declares no Enmity againft the things themfelves

The Sum of all the whole *Doctrine* of *Prophecies* is this, that the *great Creator* of the World has the Prerogative of forefeeing, appointing, and predicting all future Events : That he has often, in former Ages, made ufe of this Power, by the Vifions and Raptures of holy Men infpir'd from above ; that his *infinite Wifdom* has ftill the like Ability to do the fame ; that whenever fuch Predictions are accompanied, with undeniable Teftimonies of their being fent from *Heaven*, they ought to be preferr'd before all *human Laws*.

The true Foundation of *divine Prodigies*, is much of the fame Nature with the other. It relies on thefe Suppofitions, that all the Creatures are fubject to *God's Word*, by which they were made ; that he can alter their *Courfes*, exalt or deftroy, their *Natures*, and move them to different Ends from their own, according to his Pleafure ; that this he has often done heretofore ; that ftill his Arm is not weakn'd, nor the fame *Omnipotence* diminifh'd ; that ftill he may change the wonted Law of the *Creation*, and difpofe of the *Beings* and *Motions* of all Things, without controul ; and that when this is done it is with a peculiar Defign of punifhing, or rewarding, or forewarning Mankind.

To

To the Belief and Affertion of thefe *Doctrines*, we are oblig'd by the very end of *Religion* itfelf. But yet their counterfeit Colours have feduc'd many virtuous Minds into manifold Mifchiefs.

The Miftakes about *Prophecies* may arife either from our abufing of the old, or a vain fetting up of new. We err in the firft, when we tranflate the ancient *Prophecies* from thofe Times and Countries, which they did properly regard, to others, which they do not concern. And we offend in the fecond, when we admit of new *Prophetical Spirits* in this Age, without the uncontroulable Tokens of *Heavenly Authority*.

We are guilty of falfe Interpretations of *Providences* and *Wonders*, when we either make thofe to be *Miracles* that are none, or when we put a falfe Senfe on thofe that are real; when we make general Events to have a private Afpect, or particular Accidents to have fome univerfal Signification. Though both thefe may feem at firft to have the ftricteft Appearance of *Religion*, yet they are the greateft Ufurpations on the Secrets of the *Almighty*, and unpardonable Prefumptions on his high *Prerogatives* of *Punifhment* and *Reward*.

Sect. XX.
Experiments will not deftroy the Doctrine of Prophecies, and Prodigies.

AND now if a moderating of thefe Extravagancies muft be efteem'd Prophanenefs, I profefs, I cannot abfolve the *Experimental Philofopher*. It muft be granted, that he will be very fcrupulous, in believing all manner of Commentaries on *Prophetical Vifions*, in giving Liberty to new *Predictions*, and in affigning the Caufes, and marking out the Paths of *God's Judgments* amongft his *Creatures*.

He cannot fuddenly conclude all extraordinary

Events

Events to be the immediate Finger of *God*, becaufe
he familiarly beholds the inward Workings of Things;
and thence perceives that many Effects, which ufe
to affright the *Ignorant*, are brought forth by the
common *Inftruments* of *Nature.* He cannot be fuddenly inclin'd to pafs Cenfure on Mens eternal Condition, from any *Temporal Judgments* that may
befal them; becaufe his long Converfe with all Matters, Times, and Places, has taught him the Truth of
what the *Scripture* fays, that *all things happen alike
to all.* He cannot blindly confent to all Imaginations
of devout Men, about future *Contingencies*; feeing
he is fo rigid in examining all particular Matters of
Fact: he cannot be forward to affent to *Spiritual
Raptures* and *Revelations*; becaufe he is truly acquainted with the Tempers of Mens Bodies, the Compofition of their Blood, and the Power of Fancy;
and fo better underftands the Difference between
Difeafes and *Infpirations.*

But in all this he commits nothing that is *irreligious.* 'Tis true, to deny that *God* has heretofore
warn'd the World of what was to come, is to contradict the very Godhead itfelf; but to reject the Senfe,
which any private Man fhall faften to it, is not to difdain the Word of *God*, but the Opinions of Men like
ourfelves. To declare againft the Poffibility, that
new *Prophets* may be fent from *Heaven*, is to infinuate
that the fame infinite Wifdom, which once fhew'd
itfelf that Way, is now at an end. But to flight all
Pretenders that come without the help of *Miracles*,
is not a Contempt of the Spirit, but a juft Circumfpe-
ction, that the *Reafon* of Men be not over-reach'd.
To deny that God directs the Courfe of human Things,
is Stupidity; but to hearken to every *Prodigy*, that
Men

Men frame againſt their Enemies, or for themſelves, is not to reverence the *Power* of *God*, but to make that ſerve the Paſſions, and Intereſts, and Revenges of Men.

It is a dangerous Miſtake, into which many good Men fall ; that we neglect the *Dominion of God over the World*, if we do not diſcover, in every Turn of human Actions, many ſupernatural *Providences* and miraculous *Events*. Whereas it is enough for the Honour of his *Government*, that he guides the whole Creation, in its wonted Courſe of *Cauſes* and Effects : As it makes as much for the Reputation of a Prince's Wiſdom, that he can rule his Subjects peaceably, by his known and ſtanding Laws, as that he is often forc'd to make uſe of extraordinary Juſtice to puniſh, or reward.

Let us then imagine our *Philoſopher*, to have all ſlowneſs of Belief, and rigour of Trial, which by ſome is miſcall'd a blindneſs of Mind, and hardneſs of Heart. Let us ſuppoſe that he is moſt unwilling to grant that any thing exceeds the Force of *Nature*, but where a full Evidence convinces him. Let it be allow'd, that he is always alarm'd, and ready on his Guard, at the Noiſe of any *miraculous Event* ; leſt his Judgment ſhould be ſurpriz'd by the Diſguiſes of *Faith*. But does he by this diminiſh the *Authority* of *ancient Miracles* ? Or does he not rather confirm them the more, by confining their Number, and taking care that every Falſhood ſhould not mingle with them? Can he by this undermine *Chriſtianity*, which does not now ſtand in need of ſuch extraordinary Teſtimonies from *Heaven* ? or do not they rather indanger it, who ſtill venture all its Truths on ſo hazardous a Chance ? Who require a Continuance of

Signs,

Signs and *Wonders*, as if the Works of our *Saviour* and his *Apostles* had not been sufficient : who ought to be esteem'd the most carnally minded ? The *Enthusiast*, that pollutes his *Religion*, with his own Passions ; or the *Experimenter*, that will not use it to flatter and obey his own Desires, but to subdue them ; who is to be thought the greatest Enemy of the *Gospel*? He that loads Mens *Faiths*, by so many improbable Things, as will go near to make the Reality itself suspected ; or he that only admits a few *Arguments*, to confirm the *Evangelical Doctrines*, but then chuses those that are *unquestionable* : It cannot be an ungodly purpose to strive to abolish all *Holy Cheats*, which are of fatal Consequence, both to the Deceivers and those that are deceiv'd : To the Deceivers, because they must needs be *Hypocrites*, having the Artifice in their keeping : To the deceiv'd, because if their Eyes shall be ever open'd, and they chance to find, that they have been deluded in any one Thing, they will be apt not only to reject that, but even to despise the very *Truths* themselves, which they had before been taught by those Deluders.

It were indeed to be confess'd, that this Severity of *Censure* on *Religious Things*, were to be condemn'd in *Experimenters*, if while they deny any Wonders that are falsely attributed to the *True God*, they should approve those of Idols or false *Deities*. But that is not objected against them. They make no Comparison between his Power, and the Works of any others, but only between the several ways of his own manifesting himself. Thus if they lessen one Heap, yet they still increase the other : In the main they diminish nothing of his Right. If they take from the *Prodigies*, they add to the ordinary *Works* of the ·

Z z   same

fame *Author.* And thofe ordinary *Works* themfelves, they do almoft raife to the height of *Wonders,* by the exact Difcovery, which they make of their Excellencies : While the *Enthufiafts* goes near to bring down the Price of the true, and primitive *Miracles,* by fuch a vaft, and fuch a negligent augmenting of their Number.

Sect. XXI. *On this account Experiments are fit for the prefent Temper of our Nation.* By this I hope it appears, that this inquiring, this fcrupulous, this incredulous Temper, is not the Difgrace, but the Honour of *Experiments.* And therefore I will declare them to be the moft feafonable Study, for the prefent *Temper* of our *Nation.* This wild amufing Mens Minds, with *Prodigies,* and Conceits of *Providences,* has been one of the moft confiderable Caufes of thofe fpiritual Diftractions, of which our Country has long been the *Theatre.* This is a Vanity to which the *Englifh* feem to have been always fubject above others. There is fcarce any *Modern Hiftorian,* that relates our Foreign Wars, but he has this *Objection* againft the *Difpofition* of our Countrymen, that they us'd to order their Affairs of the greateft Importance, according to fome obfcure *Omens,* or *Prædictions,* that pafs'd about amongft them, on little or no Foundations. And at this time, efpecially this laft Year, this gloomy, and ill-boding humour has prevail'd. So that it is now the fitteft Seafon for *Experiments* to arife, to teach us a Wifdom, which fprings from the depths of *Knowledge,* to fhake off the Shadows, and to fcatter the Mifts, which fill the Minds of Men with a vain Confternation. This is a *Work* well-becoming the moft *Chriftian Profeffion.* For the moft apparent Effect, which attended the *Paffion* of *Chrift,* was the putting of an eternal filence

on

on all the falfe Oracles, and diffembled Infpirations of *ancient Times.*

There have been, 'tis true, fome peculiar Occafions wherein *God* was pleas'd to convince the World from *Heaven* in a vifible manner. But if we confider the *Arguments* that us'd to move him to it, we may conclude that fuch wonderful Signs are not often now to be expected.

He has either done it, in Times of grofs Ignorance, or in the beginning of a new way of *Religion,* or for the peculiar Punifhment of fome prevailing Wickednefs : Upon the account of the two firft, we have no reafon to expect Wonders in this *Age :* Becaufe all forts of *Knowledge* do fo much abound ; and becaufe we have a *Religion* already eftablifh'd, againft which the Gates of Hell fhall never prevail.

The third time has been, when *God* has taken to himfelf, the *Exemplary Punifhment* of fome heinous Sin. From this indeed our *Age* is no more exempted, than it is free from thofe Vices, that are wont to provoke the *Divine Vengeance.* This then we confefs, that even at this prefent *God* may declare himfelf againft the Iniquities of Men, by the fupernatural Tokens of his Difpleafure. But yet the Interpretation of fuch Punifhments ought to be handled with the greateft tendernefs. For as it is faid of the laft and general Judgment, *that no Man knows the time when it fhall happen* ; fo we may alfo affirm of thefe particular *Judgments* ; That there is no Man who underftands the Circumftances, or Occafions of their Infliction, but they are one of the deepeft parts of *God*'s unfearchable Councils.

Whenever therefore a heavy Calamity falls from *Heaven* on our *Nation,* an *univerfal Repentance* is required ;

quir'd; but all particular Applications of private Men, except to their own Hearts, is to be forborn. Every Man muſt bewail his own *Tranſgreſſions*, which have increas'd the *Publick Miſery*. But he muſt not be too haſty in aſſigning the Cauſes of *Plagues*, or *Fires*, or *Inundations*, to the Sins of other Men. Whoever thinks that way to repent, by condemning the Miſcarriages of thoſe Parties, that differ from his own, and by reproving them, as the *Authors* of ſuch *Miſchiefs*, he is groſsly miſtaken : For that is not to repent, but to make a Satire : That is not an Act of Humiliation, but the greateſt *Spiritual Pride*.

It is indeed a Diſgrace to the Reaſon and Honour of Mankind, that every fantaſtical *Humoriſt* ſhould preſume to interpret all the *ſecret Ordinances* of *Heaven*; and to expound the Times, and Seaſons, and Fates of Empires, though he be never ſo ignorant of the very common *Works* of *Nature*, that lye under his Feet. There can be nothing more injurious than this, to Mens publick or private Peace. This withdraws our Obedience from the true Image of *God*, the rightful Sovereign, and makes us depend on the vain Images of his Pow'r, which are fram'd by our own *Imaginations*. This weakens the Conſtancy of human Actions. This affects Men with Fears, Doubts, Irreſolutions, and Terrors. It is uſually obſerv'd, that ſuch *Preſaging*, and *Prophetical Times*, do commonly fore-run great *Deſtructions* and *Revolutions* of human Affairs. And that it ſhould be ſo is natural enough, though the *Preſages* and *Prodigies* themſelves did ſignifie no ſuch Events. For this *melancholy*, this *frightful*, this *Aſtrological* humour diſarms Mens Hearts, it breaks their Courage, it confounds their Councils, it makes them help to bring
                                                             ſuch

such *Calamities* on themselves : First, they fancy that such ill Accidents must come to pass ; and so they render themselves fit Subjects to be wrought upon ; and very often become the *Instruments*, to bring those Effects about, which they fondly imagin'd were inevitably threaten'd them from *Heaven.*

§. XXII. *Experiments not prejudicial to Mortification.*

The last *Accusation* concerns that which is necessary to a *holy Life*, the *mortifying* of our *Earthly Desires*. And here the Men of a retir'd and severe Devotion are the loudest : For they tell us, that we cannot conquer and despise the *World* while we study it so much ; that we cannot have sufficient leisure to reflect on another Life, while we are so taken up about the Curiosities of this ; that we cannot be strict enough in correcting the Irregularities of our own Thoughts, while we give them so much liberty to wander, and so pleasant a Road wherein to travel ; and that it is in vain to strive after the *Purity* and *Holiness* of our Minds, while we suffer them to spend so much Time, on the Labours of our *Senses.* This *Objection* appears at first sight somewhat terrible : But I come the more boldly to answer it, because there are involv'd in the same Indictment, all the most innocent *Arts*, and civil *Actions* of Men, which must either stand, or fall with *Experiments* in this Trial.

First then I will alledge, that if this sort of *Study*, should be acknowledg'd not to be proper, for the promoting of the severer Offices of *Christianity*, yet it would sufficiently recompence for that, by the Assistance it may bring to some other kinds of *Christian Virtues :* If it shall not fill our Minds with the most mortifying Images, which may rise from the Terrors

of

of *God's Justice*, yet it will make amends for that, by inclining us to adore his *Goodness*. If it fits us not so well for the Secrecy of a *Closet*; it makes us serviceable to the *World*. If it shall not seem to contribute towards *Godly Sorrow*, or *Contrition*; it will give us more Opportunities of *Charity, Affability, Friendship*, and *Generosity*, which are all of them *Divine Graces*, as well as *Faith*, and *Repentance*.

It is a great Error to think that *Religion* does only consist in one sort of *Duties*. It is as various as the Dispositions, the Qualities, the Conditions of Men : With some, the severe, the strict, the retir'd are best : with others, the bountiful, the affable, the cheerful, the friendly : Of both which kinds I will not say whether is to be preferr'd : But this is true, that while the first are chiefly limited to the regulating of our own *Hearts*, the influence of the last extends much farther ; to spread the Fame of the *Gospel* in the *World*; to make it appear lovely in the Eyes of all Beholders ; and to allure them to submit to the honourableness, the gentleness, the easiness of its Yoke. And this methinks is evident in our *Saviour's* Life : For whenever he intended to convert any to his *Faith*, he did it by some visible *good Work*, in the sight of the Multitude. But he never gain'd any *Disciple* by the Conflicts, which he was pleas'd to undergo in his own Mind ; for he perform'd his *Fast*, and his *Agony* alone, in the *Wilderness*, and the *Garden*.

In the next place I will affirm, That it is improbable that even the hardest and most rigorous parts of *Mortification* itself should be injur'd by these *Studies* more than others; seeing many Duties of which it is compos'd, do bear some resemblance to the Qualifications

cations that are requisite in *Experimental Philosophers*. The spiritual *Repentance* is a careful survey of our former Errors, and a Resolution of amendment. The spiritual *Humility* is an Observation of our Defects, and a lowly Sense of our own Weakness. And the *Experimenter* for his part must have some Qualities that answer to these: He must judge aright of himself; he must misdoubt the best of his own Thoughts; he must be sensible of his own Ignorance, if ever he will attempt to purge and renew his Reason: So that if that be true, which is commonly observ'd, that Men are wont to prove such kinds of *Christians* as they were Men before; and that Conversion does not destroy, but only exalt our *Tempers*; it may well be concluded, that the doubtful, the scrupulous, the deligent *Observer* of *Nature*, is nearer to make a modest, a severe, a meek, an humble *Christian*, than the Man of *Speculative Science*, who has better thoughts of himself and his own *Knowledge*.

But I need not take so great a Compass in this Vindication, when it may be fairly maintain'd, that the true and unfeign'd *Mortification* is not at all inconsistent with Mens consulting of their Happiness in this World, or being employ'd about earthly Affairs. The honest pursuit of the Conveniencies, Decencies, and Ornaments of a mortal Condition, by just and regular ways, is by no means contradictory to the most real and severe Duties of a *Christian*. It is true indeed, the irregular Prosecution of such Things is an offence to *Religion*: but so it is also to *right Reason*, and *Nature* itself.

It is a wrong Conception of the State of *Grace*, if Men believe, that when they enter upon it, they must presently cast away all the Thoughts and Desires of of *Humanity.* If this were fo, to fanctifie our *Natures,* were not to renew, but to deftroy them. When we are commanded to *put off the old Man,* we are not enjoin'd to renounce our Faculties of *Reafon.* When we are bidden *not to think our own Thoughts,* it is not intended that we fhould forbear all *Natural Actions* and *Inclinations.* Such *Scriptures* as thefe are to be underftood in a moderate Senfe : By fuch Expreffions the Irregularity of the *Luft,* and not the *Natural De-fire* is condemn'd : The *Piety* and *Innocence* of our *Lives,* and not the utter Change of our *Eftate,* is re-commended. Seeing the *Law* of *Reafon* intends the Happinefs and Security of Mankind in this Life ; and the *Chriftian Religion* purfues the fame Ends, both in this and a future Life ; they are fo far from being op-pofite one to another, that *Religion* may properly be ftyl'd the beft and the nobleft Part, the Perfection and the Crown of the Law of *Nature.*

I will therefore firft demand, whether it be not lawful for the ftricteft *Chriftian* to provide for the Neceffities of this Life ? This Requeft is modeft e-nough : For if they deny it, they will reduce Man-kind into a Condition which is literally worfe than that of the Beafts that perifh ; feeing to them it is natural to feek out for all the ways of their own Prefervation. I will go on to ask them, whether it be a Breach of the *Law of Chriftianity,* to labour for the Advantages of Living, which are enjoy'd by others ? If this be re-fus'd me, we fhall not deprive it of that Honour which now juftly belongs to it, that there is little Civility at prefent amongft Men without the Pale of the *Chriftian Church.*

But, in few Words, let them tell me, whether it be indifpenfably neceffary for us to be always thinking

of

of heavenly Things? If so, how far short were the very *Apostles* of this Character of *Sanctity*, which these Men would prescribe us? What Traffick, what Commerce, what Government, what secular Employment could be allow'd? Where should we at last make an end of refining? What would become of all the Men of Trade themselves, of whom this *Age* has shewn so many Pretenders to the purest *Religion*.

Let it only therefore be granted, that we are *Men*, and not *Angels*: Let it be confefs'd, that there may be an *Excefs*, as well as *Defect*, in Men's Opinions of Holinefs: And then I will make no fcruple to fay, that the *Philofopher* defiles not his Mind when he labours in the *Works* of *Nature*; that the Diverfion they give him, will ftand with the greateft Conftancy, and the Delight of purfuing them, with the Truth and Reality of *Religion*. But to fay no more, How can it be imagin'd to be a finful and carnal Thing, to confider the Objects of our *Senfes*; when *God*, the moft *fpiritual Being*, did make them all? Since they firft were conceiv'd in his unfpotted Mind, why may they not innocently enter into ours? For if there be any Pollution which neceffarily flows from thinking of them, it might as well be concluded to ftick on the *Author*, as on the *Souls* of them that only obferve them.

AND now having infifted fo long on the Parts of the *Chriftian Religion* in General, it will be lefs needful that I fhould be large in vindicating this *Defign* from the Imputation of being prejudicial to the *Church of England*: For this has the fame Intereft with that, and differs in nothing from its primitive Pattern, but only in the addition of fome Circumftances, which make it fit for this *Age* and this *Place*: And therefore

§. XXIII. *Experiments not dangerous to the Church of England.*

A a a   they

they will both be ftrengthen'd by the fame Benefits,. and weaken'd by the fame Mifchiefs.

What I have then to add concerning our *Church*, fhall be compriz'd in thefe Particulars : That it can never be prejudic'd by the Light of *Reafon*, nor by the Improvements of *Knowledge*, nor by the Advancement of the *Works* of Mens Hands.

For the proof of the Firft, it will be fufficient to confider its *True Defign*, what O*pinions* it principally encounters, and by what *Arguments* it ought to defend itfelf.

The true and certain Intereft of our *Church* is to derive its *Doctrine* from the plain and unqueftion'd parts of the *Word of God*, and to keep itfelf in a due Submiffion to the *Civil Magiftrate.* The Extremes which it oppofes, are *implicit Faith*, and *Enthufiafm :* And it is a great Miftake, if Men think it cannot be maintain'd againft thefe, but by the mutual *Arguments* of its Enemies ; that it cannot withftand the *Separatifts*, but by the Authority of the *Church of Rome* ; nor diffent from the *Church of Rome*, but on the *Tenents* of the *Separatifts.* The Grounds on which it proceeds are different from both ; and they are no other but the Rights of the *Civil Power*, the Imitation of the firft uncorrupt *Churches*, and the *Scripture* expounded by *Reafon :* From whence may be concluded, that we cannot make War againft *Reafon*, without undermining our own Strength, feeing it is the conftant Weapon we ought to employ.

From this I will farther urge, That the *Church of England* will not only be fafe amidft the Confequences of a *Rational Age*, but amidft all the Improvements of *Knowledge*, and the Subverfion of old Opinions about *Nature*, and Introduction of new ways

of

of reafoning thereon. This will be evident, when we behold the Agreement that is between the prefent *Defign* of the *Royal Society*, and that of our *Church* in its Beginning. They both may lay equal claim to the word *Reformation*; the one having compafs'd it in *Religion*, the other purpofing it in *Philofophy*. They both have taken a like courfe to bring this about; each of them paffing by the *corrupt Copies*, and referring themfelves to the *perfect Originals* for their Inftruction; the one to the *Scripture*, the other to the large Volume of the *Creatures*. They are both unjuftly accus'd by their Enemies of the fame Crimes, of having forfaken the *Ancient Traditions*, and ventur'd on *Novelties*. They both fuppofe alike, that their *Anceftors* might err; and yet retain a fufficient Reverence for them. They both follow the great Precept of the *Apoftle*, of *trying all Things*. Such is the Harmony between their *Interefts* and *Tempers*. It cannot therefore be fufpected, that the *Church of England*, that arofe on the fame Method, though in different Works; that heroic ally pafs'd through the fame Difficulties, that relies on the fame *Sovereign's Authority*, fhould look with jealous Eyes on this *Attempt*; which makes no change in the Principles of Mens Confciences, but chiefly aims at the Increafe of *Inventions* about the *Works* of their Hands.

This was the laft Particular in this Subject which I undertook to make good; That our *Church* can never be impair'd by the Growth of the ufeful *Arts* of *Life*. But now I come nearer to it, I find that I may fafely omit it : For the thing itfelf is fo manifeft, that there can be no ground of raifing a Queftion about it. If our *Church* fhould be an Enemy to Commerce, Intelligence, Difcovery, Navigation, or any fort of *Mecha-*

nics :

nics; how could it be fit for the present *Genius* of this *Nation?* What greater Advantage could its Adverfaries have againft it ? How fhould we be able to reconcile thefe two Titles, which fo juftly belong to our *King*, of *Defender of the Faith*, and *Patron of Experimental Knowledge.*

But in this I am not only encourag'd to promife, that our *Church* will be out of all Danger ; but to recommend this *Enterprize* to it, as that which will become its other *Excellencies*, and is moft worthy of its *Protection*. And I fhall moft humbly reprefent to its Confideration, that this is not only an honourable *Work*, but even a neceffary *Duty*, to which it is oblig'd by *Natural Affection*. The prefent *inquiring Temper* of this *Age* was at firft produc'd by the Liberty of Judging, and Searching, and Reafoning, which was us'd in the firft *Reformation*. Though I cannot carry the Inftitution of the *Royal Society* many Years back, yet the Seeds of it were fown in King *Edward* the Sixth's and Queen *Elizabeth*'s Reign : And ever fince that time *Experimental Learning* has ftill retain'd fome vital Heat, though it wanted the Opportunities of ripening it felf, which now it enjoys. The *Church of England* therefore may juftly be ftyl'd the *Mother* of this fort of *Knowledge* ; and fo the Care of its *Nourifhment* and *Profperity* peculiarly lies upon it.

And indeed this is an Honour which feems referv'd for it alone. For all the feveral forts of *Enthufiafts*, I fear, there cannot much help be expected towards fuch *Works*, till they fhall have left off to abhor them under the Title of *vain Philofophy*.

The *Reformed Churches* of other Countries, though they have given us many Men, who have been eminent in this way, yet are not in a Condition to promote

mote it by themfelves: For either they have not the Encouragement of the *Magiftrate*; or thofe that have, are cut fo fhort in their Revenue, that they have fcarce enough to fupport the Decence of their own Publick Worfhip.

The *Church of Rome* has indeed of late look'd more favourably upon it. They will now condemn no Man for afferting the *Antipodes*: The Severity with which they handled *Galileo*, feems now very much abated: They now permit their *Jefuits* to beftow fome Labours about *Natural Obfervations*, for which they have great Advantages by their Travels; and their *Clergy* may juftly claim fome fhare in this Honour, as long as the immortal Names of *Merfennus* and *Gaffendus* fhall live.

But ftill it is a queftion, whether that *Church* does not rather connive at, than really intend its Progrefs. They have indeed feiz'd on fome parts of *New Philofophy*; but perhaps it is only with the fame Policy that we often fee great *Monarchs* ufe, in retaining fome out-Province of their *Empire*; who, though they find that the Benefit does not countervail the Charge of the keeping it, yet will not wholly quit their Intereft in it, left their *Neighbours* fhould get Poffeffion, and fortify it againft them. Thus it is likely they have cherifh'd fome *Experiments*, not out of Zeal to the continuance of fuch *Studies*, but that the *Proteftants* might not carry away all the Glory, and thence withal get new Strength to oppofe them.

This Undertaking therefore is wholly caft on the *Church of England*, which can have no Jealoufie of its Effects, to which *Ignorance* is not a Support, but anEnemy; which aims not at the Captivity, but the Freedom of Mens Minds; which is lately return'd to

a

a profperous Condition, and having fuffer'd with the *Crown* in its Misfortunes, does now partake of the happy Fruits of its *Refloration.*

Nor will *Experimental Philofophy* be unthankful for the Affiftance it fhall receive : For it will enable us to provide before hand, againft any Alterations in *Religious Affairs,* which this *Age* may produce. If we compare the Changes to which *Religion* has been always fubject, with the prefent face of Things, we may fafely conclude, That whatever Viciffitude fhall happen about it in our time, it will probably neither be to the Advantage of *implicit Faith,* nor of *Enthufiafm,* but of *Reafon.* The Fiercenefs of *violent Infpirations* is in good meafure departed : The Remains of it will be foon chas'd out of the World, by the remembrance of the terrible Footfteps it has every where left behind it. And though the *Church of Rome* ftill preferves its Pomp, yet the real Authority of that too is apparently decaying. It firft got by degrees into *Temporal Power,* by the means of its *Spiritual;* but now it only upholds fome Shadow of the *Spiritual,* by the Strength of the *Temporal Dominion* it has obtain'd.

This is the prefent State of *Chriftendom.* It is now impoffible to fpread the fame Clouds over the World again : The univerfal Difpofition of this *Age* is bent upon a *rational Religion :* And therefore I renew my affectionate Requeft, that the *Church of England* would provide to have the chief fhare in its firft Adventure ; that it would perfift, as it has begun, to incourage *Experiments,* which will be to our *Church,* as the *Britifh Oak* is to our *Empire,* an Ornament, and Defence to the Soil wherein it is planted.

Thus I have finifh'd what I intended concerning
Religion;

Religion; wherein I defire it might not be thought that I have defended every particular *Searcher* into *Nature*. That could not be juftly expected from me; for there is no Man that makes an *Apology* for any general way, who will take upon him to make good all the Actions of. all private Men who profefs it. It is enough for my Purpofe, if it fhall be granted, that however fome *Experimenters* may be inclinable to Irreligion ; yet this rather proceeds from their own *Genius*, than from any Corruption that could be contracted from thefe *Studies*; and that if the fame Men had profefs'd *Phyfic*, or *Law*, or even *Divinity* itfelf, they would have been in like manner difaffected towards heavenly Things.

I cannot deny, but that fome *Philofophers*, by their Carelefsnefs of a future Eftate, have brought a Difcredit on *Knowledge* itfelf : But what Condition of Men is free from fuch Accufations? Or why muft we ftrait believe that their Impiety proceeds from their *Philofophy* ? It is eafy for Men to fall into grofs Errors, and to miftake the wrong Caufes for the true, in the Judgement which they make of others Opinions and Inclinations : When they behold them addicted to fuch or fuch Vices, and to have withal fome good Qualities, in which they themfelves do not excel, they prefently are apt to imagine the *bad* to arife from the *good*, and fo condemn both together ; whereas perhaps it fprung from fome other hidden Caufe, of which they took no notice.

But let it be a true *Obfervation*, That many *Modern Naturalifts* have been negligent in the *Worſhip of God* : yet perhaps they have been driven on this Prophanenefs by the late extravagant Exceffes of *Enthufiafm*. The infinite Pretences to *Infpiration*, and *immediate Commu-*

nion with God, that have abounded in this *Age*, have carry'd several Men of Wit so far, as to reject the whole Matter ; who would not have been so exorbitant, if the others had kept within more moderate Bounds. This is natural enough to be suppos'd ; for so it has commonly happen'd, that the greatest Degrees of all *contrary Opinions* have met in the same *Age*, and have still heighthen'd and increas'd each other.

From hence it may be gather'd, That the way to reduce a *real* and *sober* Sense of *Religion*, is not by indeavouring to cast a Veil of Darkness again over the Minds of Men; but chiefly by allaying the Violence of *spiritual Madness :* and that the one Extreme will decrease proportionably to the less'ning of the other.

It is apparent to all, That the Influence which *Christianity* once obtain'd on Mens Minds, is prodigiously decay'd. The Generality of *Christendom* is now well-nigh arriv'd at that fatal Condition, which did immediately precede the Destruction of the Worships of the ancient World; when the Face of *Religion* in their public *Assemblies*, was quite different from that Apprehension which Men had concerning it in private : In public they observ'd its Rules with much Solemnity, but in private regarded it not at all. It is difficult to declare by what Means and Degrees we are come to this dangerous Point : But this is certain, that the *Spiritual Vices* of this *Age* have well-nigh contributed as much towards it, as the *Carnal :* And for these, the most efficacious *Remedy* that Man of himself can use, is not so much the sublime part of *Divinity* as its intelligible, and natural, and practicable *Doctrines*. The *Medicines* for *Religious Distempers* must be changeable according to the *Diseases :* And in this
we

we may imitate *Chrift* himſelf in his Method of healing Mens Bodies: Some Cures he perform'd by his Voice, ſome by Prayer, but ſome by the touch of his Hands, and even by his Spittle mingled with Earth. In a groſs and ſenſual *Age*, the deepeſt Myſteries of our *Religion* may be proper to purify the Stupidity of Mens Spirits; but there muſt be an Application of quite different and more ſenſible Preſcriptions, in a ſubtile, refin'd, and enthuſiaſtical Time.

Such is the preſent Humour of the *World*; and ſuch muſt be the Courſe of its Cure. Men muſt now be told, that as *Religion* is a *heavenly Thing*, ſo it is not utterly averſe from making uſe of the Rules of *Human Prudence:* They muſt be inform'd, that the *true Holineſs* is a Severity over ourſelves, and not others: They muſt be inſtructed, that it is not the beſt Service that can be done to *Chriſtianity*, to place its chief Precepts ſo much out of the way, as to make them unfit for Men of Buſineſs. They muſt remember, that the chief of the *Apoſtles became all Things to all Men, that he might gain ſome.* But above all, there muſt be caution given, that Men do not ſtrive to make themſelves and their own Opinions ador'd, while they only ſeem zealous for the Honour of *God*. This is a Fault which is very incident to Men of *Devotion*; for when they have once form'd in themſelves a *perfect Model* of the *Will of God*, and have long confirm'd their Minds by continual thinking upon it, they are apt to contemn all others that agree not with them in ſome Particulars. Upon this, they have ſtraight the reproachful Term of *Atheiſts* to caſt upon them; which though it be a Title that ought only to be employ'd againſt the bold and inſolent Defiers of *Heaven* in their *Words* and *Actions*, yet it is too frequently us'd to expreſs

B b b ·the

the Malice of any eager and cenforious Spirit, that has the Confidence to object it.

This, and all other the like *Principles* of *Vncharitablenefs*, are to be oppos'd by afferting the Duties of the *Law* of *Nature*, by the ufe of paft and prefent *Times*, by the *Analogy* of human Things, by *Moral* Virtue, by the Offices of *Society*, by the Comtemplation of *God's vifible Works*, and fuch eafy and rational *Arguments*. Next to the Succour of *Divine Power*, this is the moft probable way to preferve the *Chriftian Faith* amongft us; if *God* has not in his Wrath refolv'd to tranfplant it into fome other quarter of the *Earth*, which has not fo much neglected his Goodnefs. This indeed were a Revolution, which cannot be thought on without Horrour. The Subverfion of all *Europe* would attend it. The Departure of the *Chriftian Profeffion* would be accompanied with as frightful Effects, as thofe which follow'd on the Death of its *Founder*; when the *Heavens* were darken'd, the *Temple* fhook, the Vail was rent, the Earth trembled, and the *Philofopher* had reafon to cry out, *That either Nature was diffolving, or the God of Nature dying.*

§. XXIV. *Experiments Advantageous to Manual Arts.*   I will now enter on the next Member of my *Divifion*, to confider the Purpofe of the *Royal Society*, and the probable Effects of *Experiments*, in refpect of all the *Manual Trades*, which have been heretofore found out and adorn'd. And I will difpatch this *Argument* in the Refolution of thefe four Queftions.

Whether the *Mechanic Arts* are ftill improveable by human *Induftry*?

Whether it be likely, that they may be advanc'd by any others, befides the *Mechanic Artifts* themfelves?

ı

Whe-

Whether there be any ground of hope from *Experiments*, towards this Work?

And whether if such *Arts* shall hereby happen to multiply, they will not ruine those *Trades* that are already settled?

If in these Particulars I shall answer my Readers Doubts, I trust it will be granted me, that it is not a vain or impossible Design, to indeavour the increase of *Mechanic Contrivances*; that the Enterprize is proper for a mixt *Assembly*; that the Course which they observe towards it will be effectual; and that the increase of such *Operations* will be inoffensive to others of the same kind, that have been formerly discover'd.

Before I examine these several *Heads* apart, perhaps it will not be an impertinent Labour, to take one general Survey of the principal Degrees and Occasions, by which the several *Manufactures* have risen, which beautify the face of the *Earth*, and have brought forth so much Pleasure and Plenty amongst Men.

The first of all human Race, when they were dispers'd into several Lands, were at first sustain'd by the *Fruits* of the *Earth*, which fell to their Share. These at first they cherish'd, and us'd, not by any *Rules* of *Art*, but by that *Natural Sagacity*, which teaches all Men to endeavour their own Preservation. For the peaceable Enjoyment of these, they combin'd into Families, and little Leagues, which were the Beginnings of *Civil Government*. But finding that all Places did not bring forth all Things for Cloathing, Food, and Defence; they either violently seiz'd on what their Neighbours possess'd, or else they fairly agreed on a *mutual Exchange* of the Productions of their Soils. This Traffick was at first made in Kind;

and the *Fruits* that were thus barter'd, were either spent, or planted in other Grounds. By this means Mankind was maintain'd; and several *Earths* were furnish'd by *Labour*, with what *Nature* bestow'd not upon them. For this *Commutation* of their *Fruits*, and of the rude Effects of their first Industry, they began to devise the Conveniencies of *Carriage* by Land and Water; and to make it still easier, and larger, they agreed on some common Things, to be the universal Standard of *Value* and *Price*; whence arose the use of *Money*.

This was the first Original of *Trade*, which from a narrow Commerce between the Hills, the Vallies, the Woods, the Plains and the Rivers that border'd one upon another, is since extended to the whole Compass of the *Earth*. For in course of Time, the small Clans, and natural Commonwealths, were devour'd by the Strength of the greater; or else some of the wiser Men reduc'd the rude Multitude into one Place, and perswaded them to live quietly under the *Laws*. From thence Mankind began to have the face of *Civility*, which arose at first, by that which is the best Means of preserving it now, by the *greatness* and *enlargement* of *Dominion*.

The first, all the Differences of *Living*, and the Advantages of *Strength* and *Empire* did shew themselves. Then some took on them to *Rule*, some to Assist, or Council those that Rul'd, and some were forc'd to be subject to their Power. Thus the *Riches* and *Dominion* that were at first in common, were unequally divided: The Great, the Wise, or the Strong, obtain'd a principal Share; and either perswaded, or constrain'd all the rest to serve them with their Bodies. Thence sprung all the *Arts* of *Convenience*,

ence and *Pleafure*, while the one part of Men would
not be content to live according to the firſt Plainneſs
of *Nature :* And the other were compell'd to work
with their Hands, for the Eaſe and Pleaſure of their
Maſters Lives, and the Support of their own. From
theſe Beginnings the Inventions of *Peace* and *War*, the
Delights of *Cities* and *Palaces*, the Delicacies of *Food*,
the Curioſities of *Cloathing*, the Varieties of *Recrea-*
tions took their Riſe. And theſe have ſtill continued
to increaſe, either by ſome caſual Diſcoveries, or by
Luxury, or elſe as Men have been driven by ſome new
Neceſſities, to paſs on farther to attempt new ways of
maintaining themſelves.

THIS is the moſt *natural Method* of the Foundation §. XXV.
and Progreſs of *Manual Arts.* And they may ſtill be *The Manu-*
advanc'd to a higher Perfection, than they have yet *al Arts are*
obtain'd, either by the Diſcovery of new *Matter*, to *ſtill im-*
imploy Mens Hands, or by a new *Tranſplantation* of *proveable.*
the ſame *Matter*, , or by handling the old Subjects of
Manufactures after a new way, in the ſame Places.

And firſt, we have reaſon to expect; that there may
ſtill ariſe new *Matter* to be manag'd by *Human Art*
and *Diligence* ; and that from the parts of the *Earth*
that are yet unknown ; or from the new diſcover'd
America ; or from our own Seas and Land, that have
been long ſearch'd into, and inhabited:

If ever any more *Countries*, which are now hidden *Firſt by new*
from us, ſhall be reveal'd, it is not to be queſtion'd, *Matter*
but there will be alſo opened to our *Obſervation*, very *from new*
many kinds of *living Creatures*, of *Minerals*, of *Plants*, *Lands.*
nay, of *Handicrafts*, with which we have been hi-
therto unacquainted. This may well be expected
if

if we remember, that there was never yet any *Land* difcover'd, which has not given us divers new forts of *Animals*, and *Fruits* of different Features and Shapes, and Virtues from our own, or has not fupply'd us with fome new artificial *Engine*, and *Contrivance*.

And that our *Difcoveries* may ftill be inlarg'd to farther *Countries*, it is a good Proof, that fo many fpacious Shores and Mountains, and Promontories, appear to our *Southern* and *Northern Sailors*; of which we have yet no Account, but only fuch as could be taken by a remote Profpect at Sea. From whence, and from the Figure of the *Earth*, it may be concluded, that almoft as much fpace of Ground remains ftill in the *Dark*, as was fully known in the times of the *Affyrian* or *Perfian Monarchy*. So that without affuming the vain prophetic Spirit, which I lately condemn'd, we may foretel, that the *Difcovery* of another *new World* is ftill behind.

To accomplifh this, there is only wanting the *Invention of Longitude*, which cannot now be far off, feeing it is generally allow'd to be feafible, feeing fo many Rewards are ready to be heap'd on the *Inventors*; and (I will alfo add) feeing the *Royal Society* has taken it into its peculiar care. This, if it fhall be once accomplifh'd, will make well-nigh as much alteration in the World, as the Invention of the *Needle* did before : And then our *Pofterity* may outgo us, as much as we can travel farther than the *Antients*; whofe *Demy Gods* and *Heroes* did efteem it one of their chief Exploits, to make a Journey as far as the *Pillars of Hercules*. Whoever fhall think this to be a defperate Bufinefs, they can only ufe the fame *Arguments*, wherewith *Columbus* was at firft made ridiculous, if he had been difcourag'd by the Raillery of
his

his Adverfaries, by the Judgment of moft *Aftronomers* of his time, and even by the Intreaties of his own *Companions*; but three Days before he had a fight of *Land*, we had loft the Knowledge of half the *World* at once.

And as for the new difcover'd *America*; 'tis true, that has not been altogether ufelefs to the *Mechanic Arts*: But ftill we may guefs, that much more of its Bounty is to come, if we confider, that it has not yet been fhewn above *two hundred Years*; which is fcarce enough time to travel it over, defcribe, and meafure it, much lefs to pierce into all its Secrets. Befides this, a good part of this Space was fpent in the *Conqueft* and *fettling* the *Spanifh Government*, which is a Seafon improper for *Philofophical Difcoveries*. To this may be added, that the chief Defign of the *Spaniards* thither, has been the Tranfportation of *Bullion*; which being fo profitable, they may well be thought to have overfeen many other of its *Native Riches*. But above all, let us reflect on the Temper of the *Spaniards* themfelves. They fuffer no Strangers to arrive there: they permit not the *Natives* to know more than becomes their Slaves. And how unfit the *Spanifh* humour is to improve *Manufactures*, in a Country fo diftant as the *Weft-Indies*, we may learn by their Practice in *Spain* itfelf, where they commonly difdain to exercife any *Manual Crafts*, and permit the Profit of them to be carry'd away by Strangers.

From all this, we may make this *Conclufion*, That if ever that vaft Tract of *Ground* fhall come to be more familiar to *Europe*, either by a *free Trade*, or by *Conqueft*, or by any other *Revolution* in its Civil Affairs, *America* will appear quite a new Thing to us; and

§. XXVI.
Mechanics improveable by new Matter from America.

and many furnish us with an abundance of *Rarities*, both Natural and Artificial ; of which we have been almoſt as much depriv'd by its preſent *Maſters*, as if it had ſtill remain'd a part of the *unknown World.*

§ XXVII. *By new Matter from the World.* But Laſtly to come nearer home,we have no ground to deſpair, but very much more *Matter*, which has been yet unhandled, may ſtill be brought to Light, even in the moſt civil and moſt peopled Countries ; whoſe *Lands* have been throughly meaſur'd by the Hands of the moſt *exact Surveyors* ; whoſe underground *Riches* have been accurately pry'd into ; whoſe Cities, Iſlands, Rivers, and Provinces, have been deſcrib'd by the Labours of *Geographers*. It is not to be doubted, but ſtill there may be an infinite Number of *Creatures* over our Heads, round about us, and under our Feet, in the large Space of the *Air*, in the Caverns of the *Earth*, in the Bowels of *Mountains*, in the Bottom of *Seas*, and in the Shades of *Foreſts* : which have hitherto eſcap'd all *mortal Senſes*. In this the *Microſcope* alone is enough to ſilence all Oppoſers. Before that was invented, the chief help that was given to the *Eyes* by *Glaſſes*, was only to ſtrengthen the dim Sight of old *Age* ; but now by the means of that excellent *Inſtrument*, we have a far greater Number of different kinds of Things reveal'd to us, than were contain'd in the viſible Univerſe before ; and even this is not yet brought to *Perfection* : The chief Labours that are publiſh'd in this way, have been the *Obſervations* of ſome *Fellows* of the *Royal Society*, nor have they as yet apply'd it to all Subjects, nor tried it in all Materials and Figures of *Glaſs*.

To the *Eyes* therefore there may ſtill be given a vaſt addition of *Objects :* And proportionably to all the all the other Senfes. This Mr. *Hook* has undertaken to make out, that *Tafting, Touching, Smelling,* and *Hearing,* are as improveable as the *Sight* ; and from his excellent *Performances* in the one, we may well rely on his *Promife* in all the reft.

THE next *Increafe* of *Manual Arts* which is probable to fucceed, may happen by the farther *Tranf-planting* and *Communicating* of the feveral *Natural Commodities* of all *Nations,* to other *Airs,* and other *Soils,* and other ways of *Cultivation.* That this is not yet finifh'd is evident, in that there is no *Land* fo well furnifh'd as to produce all the various forts of Things, which its Ground and Temperature is capable to receive ; and alfo becaufe many of the moft fertile *Countries* contain large Spaces that are utterly barren.

§. XXVIII. *Mechanics improveable by Tranf-plantations.*

This *Work* then may be farther advanc'd, by three kinds of Endeavours.

The firft by *Tranfplanting* out of one Land into another, of the fame Scituation in refpect of the *Heavens.* This may be try'd by conveying the Eaftern *Spices,* and other ufeful *Vegetables,* into our Weftern *Plantations.* Nor can it be imagin'd, why they fhould thrive in one *Indies,* and not in the other ; why the *Soil* fhould not be as good where the *Sun Sets,* as where it *Rifes.* Seeing there are parts of both, which lie under the fame Influence of that, and the other *Celeftial Bodies,* to whofe kindly Heat and Neighbourhood, the *Oriental Nations* are fuppos'd to owe their Advantages. This alfo may be attempted in our *Northern Climates:* As for Inftance, the *Flax,* of which we ftand fo much in need, may profper in *Ireland,* in many vaft Tracts of Ground, now only poffefied by wild *Beafts,* or *Tories* almoft as wild.

C c c

The

The second *Advancement* of this *Work* may be accomplish'd by carrying and transplanting *living Creatures* and *Vegetables* from one Climate to another. This will be very beneficial, though it will be perform'd with a various Succefs. Sometimes the *Soil* and the *Air* being chang'd, will give a new Force to the new *Guefts*; as the *Arabian Horfe*, by mingling with our *Breed*, produces a more ferviceable *Race* than either of them fingle. And fometimes the Alteration will be for the worfe; as the *Vine* of *France* brought into *England*, and the *Horfes* and *Dogs* of *England* into *France*; both which are found to degenerate exceedingly : Their *Soil* and their *Sun*, it feems, being fitter to produce Things of *Pleafure* and *Delight*; and our *Air* and our *Earth* being more proper to beget *Valour* and *Strength*.

The third way of *Communication* to be try'd, is by removing the *Plants* and the Productions of the fame Country from one part of it into another ; and by practifing every where all the forts of *Husbandry*, which are us'd in fome Places with Succefs. That this is not enough perfected even in *England*, is manifeft to every one that beholds the *Kentifh* Orchards, and the *Herefordfhire* Hedges; which feem to upbraid the lazinefs of other Countries, whofe High-ways are only fenc'd with Thorns and Briars, or at the beft with Hazel ; while theirs are beautify'd with Apples, Pears, and Cherries.

Now then, in every one of thefe *Tranfplantations*, the chief Progrefs that has hitherto been made, has been rather for the *Collection* of *Curiofities* to adorn *Cabinets* and *Gardens*, than for the Solidity of *Philofophical Difcoveries* : Yet there may be a prodigious Advantage made in them all, both for the one end and
the

the other. And in this it will be found, as in many other Things, that if Men only intend a little *Curiofity* and *Delight*, they will reap not much more by their Pains : But if they regard real Ufe, not only the *Profit*, but a greater *Delight* will alfo follow thereon.

And for our *Encouragement*, whatever Attempts of this Nature have fucceeded, they have redounded to the great Advantage of the *Undertakers*. The *Orange* of *China* being of late brought into *Portugal*, has drawn a great *Revenue* every Year from *London* alone. The Vine of the *Rhine* taking Root in the *Cana-ries*, has produc'd a far more delicious Juice, and has made the Rocks and the Sun-burnt Afhes of thofe Ifland, one of the richeft Spots of Ground in the *World*. And I will alfo inftance in that which is now in a good Forwardnefs : *Virginia* has already given *Silk* for the Cloathing of our *King* ; and it may hap-pen hereafter to give Cloaths to a great part of *Eu-rope*, and a vaft Treafure to our *Kings* ; if the *Silk-worms* fhall thrive there (of which there feems to be no doubt) the Profit will be inexpreffible. We may guefs at it, by confidering what Numbers of *Caravans*, and how many great Cities in *Perfia*, are maintain'd by that *Manufacture* alone, and what mighty Cuftoms it yearly brings into the *Sophi's Revenue*.

But if both thefe Helps fhould chance to fail ; if nothing *new* fhould ever come into our Hands ; and if there could be no farther Alteration made by *Tranf-planting* ; yet we may ftill take Comfort, and rely on the *old Matter* itfelf, on which all our prefent *Arts* have been devis'd. This certainly will take away all diftruft in this Bufinefs : For it may be obferv'd, that the greateft part of all our *New Inventions* have not

§. XXIX. *Mechanics improveable by the old Matter of Arts.*

C c c 2 been

been rais'd from Subjects before untouch'd (though they alfo have given us very many) but from the moft ftudied and moft familiar Things, that have been always in Mens Hands and Eyes. For this I fhall only inftance in *Printing*, in the *Circulation of the Blood*, in Mr. *Boyle's* Engine for the fucking out of *Air*, in the making of *Guns*, in the *Microfcopical Glaffes*, and in the *Pendulum Clocks* of *Hugenius*. What might we have believ'd to be perfect, if not the *Art* of Mens *Communicating* their Thoughts one to another? What was nearer to them than their *Blood*, by which their Life fubfifts? And what more ready to be found out than its *Motion*? In what Subject had the Wit of *Artificers* been more fhewn, than in the variety of *Clocks* and *Watches*? What Thing was more in Mens View than *Glafs*, through which, in thefe Countries, the very Light itfelf is admitted, whereby we difcern all Things elfe? What more natural to us than the *Air* we breath? With which we form every word to exprefs other Things? What was more ftudied than the *Art of Fighting*? What little *Stratagem*, or *Fortification*, or *Weapon*, could one have thought to have been conceal'd from the *Greeks* and *Romans*, who were fo curious in the *Difcipline* of *War*? And yet in all thefe the moft obvious Things, the greateft Changes have been made by late *Difcoveries*; which cannot but convince us, that many more are ftill to come from Things that are as common, if we fhall not be wanting to our felves.

§. XXX.
Mechanics improveable by the fpreading of Civility.

AND this we have good reafon to truft will be effected, if this *Mechanic Genius*, which now prevails in thefe Parts of *Chriftendom*, fhall happen to fpread wider amongft our felves, and other *Civil Nations*;

or

or if by some good Fate it shall pass farther on to other Countries that were yet never fully civiliz'd. We now behold much of the Northern Coasts of *Europe* and *Asia*, and almost all *Afric*, to continue in the rude State of *Nature :* I wish I had not an Instance nearer Home, and that I did not find some parts of our own *Monarchy* in as bad a Condition. But why may we not suppose, that all these may in course of Time be brought to lay aside the untam'd Wildness of their present Manners? Why should we use them so cruelly as to believe, that the Goodness of their *Creator* has not also appointed them their Season of polite and happy Life, as well as us? Is this more unlikely to happen, that the Change that has been made in the *World* these last seventeen hundred Years? This has been so remarkable, that if *Aristotle* and *Plato*, and *Demosthenes*, should now arise in *Greece* again, they would stand amaz'd at the horrible Devastation of that which was the *Mother of Arts*. And if *Cæsar* and *Tacitus* should return to Life, they would scarce believe this *Britain*, and *Gaul*, and *Germany*, to be the same which they describ'd : They would now behold them cover'd over with *Cities* and *Palaces*, which were then over-run with *Forests* and *Thickets* : They would see all manner of *Arts* flourishing in these Countries, where the chief *Art* that was practis'd in their time, was that barbarous one of *painting their Bodies*, to make them look more terrible in *Battel*.

This then being imagin'd, that there may some lucky Tide of *Civility* flow into those *Lands*, which are yet savage, there will a double Improvement thence arise, both in respect of ourselves and them : For even the present *skilful* Parts of Mankind, will be thereby made more *skilful* ; and the other will not
only

only increase those *Arts* which we shall bestow upon them, but will also venture on new Searches themselves.

If any shall doubt of the first of these *Advantages*, let them consider that the spreading of *Knowledge* wider, does beget a higher and a clearer *Genius* in those that enjoy'd it before.

But the chief Benefit will arise from the *New Converts*; for they will not only receive from us our *Old Arts*, but in their first Vigour will proceed to *new ones* that were not thought of before. This is reasonable enough to be granted : For seeing they come fresh and unwearied, and the thoughts of Men being most violent in the first opening of their *Fancies*; it is probable they will soon pass over those Difficulties about which these People that have been long *Civil*, are already tir'd. To this Purpose I might give as many *Examples* as there have been different *Periods* of *civilizing*; that those *Nations* which have been taught, have prov'd wiser and more dextrous than their *Teachers*. The *Greeks* took their first hints from the *East*; but out-did them in *Music*, in *Statuary*, in *Graving*, in *Limning*, in *Navigation*, in *Horsemanship*, in *Husbandry*, as much as the *Ægyptians* or *Assyrians* exceed their unskilful *Ancestors* in *Architecture*, *Astronomy*, or *Geometry*. The *Germans*, the *French*, the *Britains*, the *Spaniards*, the modern *Italians*, had their Light from the *Romans*; but surpass'd them in most of their own *Arts*, and well-nigh doubled the ancient Stock of *Trades* deliver'd to their keeping.

§. XXXI.
Mechanics
are improve-
able by o-
thers besides
Tradesmen.

So then, the whole *Prize* is not yet taken out of our Hands : The *Mechanic Invention* is not quite worn away ; nor will be, as long as new Subjects may
be

be difcovered, as long as our old Materials may be alter'd or improv'd, and as long as there remains any corner of the *World* without *Civility.* Let us next obferve, whether Men of different ways of Life are capable of performing any Thing towards it, befides the *Artificers* themfelves. This will quickly appear undeniable, if we will be convinc'd by *Inftances*; for it is evident, that divers forts of *Manufactures* have been given us by Men who were not bred up in *Trades* that refembled thofe which they difcover'd. I fhall mention Three; that of *Printing, Powder,* and the *Bow-Dye.* The *admirable Art* of *Compofing Letters,* was fo far from being ftarted by a Man of *Learning,* that it was the Device of a *Soldier:* And *Powder* (to make Recompence) was invented by a *Monk,* whofe courfe of Life was moft averfe from handling the *Materials* of *War.* The ancient *Tyrian Purple* was brought to light by a *Fifher*; and if ever it fhall be recover'd, it is likely to be done by fome fuch Accident. The *Scarlet* of the *Moderns* is a very beautiful Colour; and it was the Production of a *Chymift,* and not of a *Dyer.*

And indeed the *Inftances* of this kind are fo numerous, that I dare in general affirm, That thofe Men who are not peculiarly converfant about any one fort *Arts,* may often find out their *Rarities* and *Curiofities* fooner, than thofe who have their Minds confin'd wholly to them. If we weigh the *Reafons* why this is probable, it will not be found fo much a *Paradox,* as perhaps it feem at the firft Reading. The *Tradefmen* themfelves, having had their Hands directed from their Youth in the fame *Methods of Working,* cannot when they pleafe fo eafily alter their Cuftom, and turn themfelves into new Roads of Practice. Befides this, they

they chiefly labour for prefent Livelihood, and therefore cannot defer their *Expectations* fo long, as is commonly requifite for the ripening of any *new Contrivance.* But efpecially having long handled their *Inftruments* in the fame Fafhion, and regarded their *Materials* with the fame Thoughts, they are not apt to be furpriz'd much with them, nor to have any extraordinary *Fancies*, or *Raptures* about them.

Thefe are the ufual Defects of the *Artificers* themfelves : Whereas the Men of freer Lives, have all the contrary Advantages. They do not approach thofe *Trades*, as their dull and unavoidable, and perpetual *Employments*, but as their *Diverfions*. They come to try thofe *Operations*, in which they are not very exact, and fo will be more frequently fubject to commit Errors in their Proceeding : Which very Faults and Wandrings, will often guide them into new *Light*, and new *Conceptions*. And laftly, there is alfo fome Privilege to be allow'd to the *Generofity* of their *Spirits*, which have not been fubdu'd, and clogg'd by any conftant *Toil* as the others. *Invention* is an *Heroic* Thing, and plac'd above the reach of a low and vulgar *Genius*. It requires an active, a bold, a nimble, a reftlefs *Mind :* A thoufand Difficulties muft be contemn'd, with which a mean Heart would be broken ; many *Attempts* muft be made to no Purpofe ; much *Treafure* muft fometimes be fcatter'd without any Return ; much Violence and Vigour of Thoughts muft attend it: fome Irregularities and Exceffes muft be granted it, that would hardly be pardon'd by the fevere *Rules of Prudence.* All which may perfuade us, that a large and an unbounded Mind is likely to be the *Author* of greater *Productions*, than the calm, obfcure, and fetter'd Endeavours of the *Mechanics* themfelves : And
that

that as in the *Generation of Children*, thofe are ufually obferv'd to be moft fprightly, that are the ftolen Fruits of an unlawful *Bed*; fo in the Generations of the *Brains*, thofe are often the moft vigorous and witty, which Men beget on other *Arts*, and not on their own.

THIS came feafonably in, to ftop the undeferv'd Clamours, which perhaps in this humorous *Age*, fome *Tradefmen* may raife againft the *Royal Society*, for entring within the compafs of their Territories. Wherefore I proceed to my third *Particular*, which I have aim'd at in the two former, *that the fureft Increafe remaining to be made in Manual Arts, is to be perform'd by the conduct of Experimental Philofophy.* This will appear undeniable when we fhall have found, that all other Caufes of fuch *Inventions* are *defective*; and that for this very Reafon, becaufe the *Trials of Art*, have been fo little united with the plain Labours of Mens Hands.

§.XXXII. *Mechanics beft improvable by Experiments.*

I have already given this Account of the former *Arts* that we ufe, that the greateft Part of them has been produc'd, either by *Luxury*, or *Chance*, or *Neceffity*; all which muft be confefs'd to be mean and ignoble Caufes of the *Rational Mechanics*.

The firft of thefe has been, that Vanity and Intemperance of Life, which the delights of *Peace*, and greatnefs of *Empire* have always introduc'd. This has been the Original of very many extravagant *Inventions* of *Pleafure*; to whofe *Promotion*, it is not requifite that we fhould give any help, feeing they are already too exceffive. And indeed, if we confider the vaft Number of the *Arts* of *Luxury*, compar'd to the found, and the fubftantial ones of ufe; we fhall find that the Wit of Men has been as much defective in the one, as redundant in the other. It has been the constant Errors of Mens Labours in all *Ages*, that they have still directed them to improve those of *Pleasure*, more than those of *Profit*. How many, and how extravagant, have been the *Ornaments* about *Coaches* ? And how few *Inventions*, about new Frames for *Coaches*, or about *Carts*, and *Ploughs* ? What prodigious Expence has been thrown away, about the Fashions of *Cloaths* ? But how little endeavours have there been to invent new *Materials* for *Cloathing*, or to perfect those we have ? The *Furniture* and *Magnificence* of *Houses*, is risen to a wonderful Beauty within our Memory : But few or none have throughly studied the well-ordering of *Timber*, the hardning of *Stone*, the improvement of *Mortar*, and the making of better *Bricks*. The like may be shewn in all the rest : wherein the solid *Inventions* are wont to be overwhelm'd by *Gawdiness* and *Superfluity* ; which Vanity has been caus'd by this, that the *Artists* have chiefly been guided by the Fancies of the Rich, or the Young, or of vain *Humorists*, and not by the *Rules* and *Judgments* of Men of *Knowledge*.

The second occasion that has given help to the Increase of *Mechanics* has been *Chance* : For in all Ages, by some casual Accidents, those Things have been reveal'd, which either Men did not think of, or else sought for in vain. But of this the *Benevolence* is irregular, and most uncertain : This indeed can scarce be styl'd the *Work* of a Man. The *Hart* deserves as much praise of *Invention*, for lighting on the Herb, that cures it ; as the Man who blindly stumbles on any profitable *Work*, without Foresight or Consideration.

The last that I shall alledge is *Necessity*. This has
given

given rife to many great *Enterprizes* ; and like the cruel Step-Mother of *Hercules,* has driven Men upon *Heroic Actions,* not out of any tender Affection, but hard Ufage. Nor has it only been an excellent Miftrefs to particular Men, but even to whole *States* and *Kingdoms* ; for which reafon fome have preferr'd a *Barren Soil,* for the Seat of an *Imperial City,* before a *Fruitful* ; becaufe thereby the Inhabitants being compell'd to take Pains, and to live induftrioufly, will be fecure from the dangerous Inchantments of *Plenty* and *Eafe* ; which are fatal to the Beginnings of all Commonwealths. Yet the Defects of this fevere *Author* of great *Works,* are very many. It often indeed engages Men in brave Attempts, but feldom carries them on to finifh what they begin : It labours at firft for want of *Bread* ; and that being obtain'd it commonly gives over : It rather fharpens than enlarges Mens *Wits* ; it fooner puts them upon fmall *Shifts,* than great *Defigns* ; it feldom rifes to high or magnanimous Things ; for the fame neceffity which makes Men *inventive,* does commonly deprefs and fetter their *Inventions.*

And now thefe principal Caufes of *Mechanic Difcoveries* being found for the greateft part to be either corrupt or weak : It is but juft, that *Reafon* itfelf fhould interpofe, and have fome Place allow'd it in thofe *Arts,* which ought to be the chief *Works* of *Reafon.* It is a fhame to the Dignity of *human Nature* itfelf, that either Mens Lufts fhould tempt them, or their Neceffities drive them, or blind Fortune fhould lead them in the dark, into thofe Things in which confifts the chief *Prerogative* of their Condition. What greater *Privilege* have Men to boaft of than this ; that they have the Pow'r of ufing, directing, changing, or advancing all the reſt of the Creatures? This is the *Dominion* which *God* has given us over the *Works* of his Hands. And if we will either anſwer the Expectations of *Heaven*, or deſerve ſo high an Honour, we ought rather to manage this *Dominion* by *Diligence* and *Counſel*, than by *Chance*, or *Luxury*, or *Compulſion*.

It is impoſſible for us to adminiſter this *Power* aright, unleſs we prefer the Light of Men of *Knowledge*, to be a conſtant Overſeer and Director of the *Induſtry* and *Works* of thoſe that labour. The Benefits are vaſt, that will appear upon this Conjunction. By this means the *Inventions* of *Chance* will be ſpread into all their various Uſes, and multiply'd into many new Advantages: By this the *Productions* of *Neceſſity* will be amplify'd and compleated: By this thoſe of *Luxury* and *Wantonneſs* may be reduc'd to ſome ſolid Ends: By this may be raiſ'd almoſt as certain a Method to invent new *Mechanics*, as now any particular *Mechanics* can practiſe, to produce their own *Operations*; by this the weak Minds of the *Artiſts* themſelves will be ſtrengthen'd, their low Conceptions advanc'd, and the Obſcurity of their Shops enlighten'd: By this their Thoughts will be directed to better *Inſtruments* and *Materials*; by this their *Poverty* will be aſſiſted, and they will be enabled to attempt more coſtly *Tryals*; by this that will be amended, which has been hitherto the Misfortune of ſuch *Inventions*, that they have commonly fallen into Mens Hands, who underſtand not their *Natures, Uſes* or *Improvements*: By this the Conceptions of Men of *Knowledge*, which are wont to ſoar too high, will be made to deſcend into the *material World*; and the flegmatick Imaginations of Men of *Trade*, which uſe to grovel too much on the Ground, will be exalted.   It

It was faid of *Civil Government* by *Plato*, that then the World will be beft rul'd, when either *Philofophers* fhall be chofen *Kings*, or *Kings* fhall have *Philofophical* Minds. And I will affirm the like of *Philofophy*; it will then attain to Perfection, when either the *Mechanic Labourers* fhall have *Philofophical Heads*, or the *Philofophers* fhall have *Mechanical Hands*; for the proof of this I need only propofe one Inftance, with which I am furnifh'd by *Antiquity*; and it is of *Archimedes*; by this Example alone, we may at once chaftife the floth of all *Ages* fince his time, and confute the prefent Contemners of *Mechanic Knowledge*. This *Great Man* was one of the firft who apply'd his Skill, in the *Mathematics* and *Phyfics*, to the Practices and Motions of *Manual Trades*. And in thefe his Succefs was fo prodigious, that the true Contrivancies of his Hands did exceed all the *fabulous Strength*, which either the *ancient Stories*, or modern *Romances* have beftow'd on their *Heroes*. The *Weights* he mov'd were fo vaft, and the *Engines* he fram'd had fuch dreadful Effects, that his Force could neither be refifted by *Seas*, or *Mountains*, or *Fleets*, or *Armies*, which are the greateft Powers of Nature and Men. He alone fuftain'd the Burden of his falling Country; he alone kept the *Romans* at a Bay, to whom the whole World was to yield. And perhaps he had come off victorious at laft, if he had not contended with the fatal Valour of *Marcellus*: Amongft all whofe Exploits, thefe are recorded as the two greateft, that he firft fhew'd that *Hannibal* might be fubdu'd; and that he vanquifh'd *Syracufe*, though it was defended by *Archimedes*.

Thus

§. XXXIII.   **T**HUS far I hope the way is clear as I go : I have
The Inven- some Confidence that I have sufficiently prov'd, that
tion of new the *Invention* of *Trades* may still proceed farther, and
Mechanics that by the help of Men of free Lives, and by this
will not in-
jure the old. course of *Experiments*. But yet the main *Difficulty* continues unremov'd.   This arises from the suspicions of
the *Tradesmen* themselves : They are generally infected with the narrowness that is natural to *Corporati-*
ons, which are wont to resist all *new Comers*, as profess'd Enemies to their *Privileges :* And by these in-
terested Men it may be objected, That the growth of
new Inventions and *new Artificers*, will infallibly reduce all the old ones to Poverty and Decay.

    But to take off their *Fears* in this Particular, they
are to be inform'd, that there are two sorts of *Experi-*
ments which the *Royal Society* attempts in *Mechanical*
Matters. The first will be employ'd about the revi-
sing, changing, and correcting of the old *Mechanics*
themselves : The second, about inventing of New. In
the first of these they can have no ground of Jealousy ;
seeing they are not intended to bring others over their
Heads, but only to beautify and fasten those which
they already enjoy.   And even this is a Work so necessary to be done, that if there were not a continual
Reparation made in them, they would soon languish,
and insensibly consume away into *Barbarism :* For
the *Arts* of Mens Hands are subject to the same Infirmity with *Empire*, the best *Art* of their Minds, of
which it is truly observ'd, that whenever it comes to
stand still, and ceases to advance, it will soon go back
and decrease.

    Hence it appears, that one part of *Experiments*,
and that a very considerable part, is free from their
Cavils.

Cavils. Let us then go on to the other kinds, which Purpofe the ftriking out of *new Mechanics :* Of thefe I will alfo affert the Innocence, in refpect of their Predeceffors. In few Words, the *Old Arts* are fo far from from being endanger'd by the *New*, that they themfelves will receive a proportionable *Increafe*, as the *New* fhall arife. The Warmth and Vigour which attends new *Difcoveries*, is feldom wont to confine itfelf to its own Sphere, but is commonly extended farther to the Ornament of its Neighbours. This is apparent in the Degree by which all *Nations* ufe to attain to a higher *Civility*. The ordinary Method wherein this happens, is the Introduction of fome one or two *New Arts :* For they appearing with great Activity in the Beginning, do not only eftablifh themfelves; but alfo by ftirring and inflaming Mens Minds, by difgracing the lazinefs of other *Artizans*, and provoking them to an Emulation, they are wont to bring an *univerfal Light* and *Beauty* on thofe *Inventions* into whofe Company they are brought.

It is faid of the *Moral Virtues*, that they have fuch a mutual Dependance, that no Man can attain to *Perfection* in any one of them, without fome Degree of the other. And this alfo is certain in the *Mechanic Arts :* The Connexion between them is fo clofe, that they generally ufe to increafe in the fame Meafure. There is no Time, nor great City, which perfectly excels in any one of them, but it is thereby made more capable of admitting the reft, or of advancing them higher if they were admitted before.

It is true indeed, the Increafe of *Tradefmen* is an injury to others, that are bred up in particular *Trades*, where there is no greater *Employment* than they can mafter : But there can never be an overcharge of
Trades

Trades themfelves. That Country is ftill the richeft
and moft powerful, which entertains moft *Manufactures*. The Hands of Men employ'd are true *Riches*;
the faving of thofe Hands by Inventions of *Art*, and
applying them to other *Works*, will increafe thofe
Riches. Where this is done, there will never a fufficient Matter for Profit be wanting ; for if there be
not vent for their Productions at Home, we fhall have
it Abroad ; but where the Ways of Life are few, the
Fountains of Profit will be poffefs'd by few ; and fo
all the reft muft live in *Idlenefs*, on which inevitably
enfues *Beggery* ; whence it is manifeft, that *Poverty*
is caus'd by the fewnefs of *Trades*, and not by the
multitude.

Nor is it enough to overthrow this, to tell us, that
by this addition of *Labourers* all Things will become
dearer, becaufe more muft be maintain'd : For the
high rate of Things is an Argument of the Flourifhing,
and the cheapnefs of the Scarcity of Money, and ill
peopling of all Countries. The firft is a fign of many Inhabitants, which are true *Greatnefs* : The fecond
is only a fit Subject for *Poets* to defcribe, and to compare to their *Golden Age* ; for where all Things are
without *Price* or *Value*, they will be without *Arts*,
or *Empire*, or *Strength*.

I will explain all this by a familiar and domeftic
Inftance. It is probable that there are in *England* a
hundred times more *Trades* than the *Saxons* or the
Danes found here in their Invafions ; and withal the
particular *Traders* live now more plentifully, and the
whole Nation is wonderfully ftronger than before.
This alfo may be feen in every particular *City* : The
greater it is, the more kinds of *Artificers* it contains ;
whofe Neighbourhood and Number is fo far from being

ing an hindrance to each others Gain, that ftill the *Tradefmen* of moft populous Towns are wealthier than thofe who profefs the fame Crafts in country Mercats.

In *England* it has of late been a univerfal *Murmur*, that *Trade* decays ; but the contrary is evident, from the perpetual Advancement of the *Cuftoms.* Whence then arifes the Complaint ? From hence, that *Traders* have multiplied above the proportionable Increafe of *Trades :* By this Means all the *old* Ways of Gain are over-ftock'd, which would foon be prevented by a conftant Addition of *new.*

The want of a right apprehending this, has always made the *Englifh* averfe from admitting of new *Inventions,* and fhorter Ways of Labour, and from naturallizing new People : both which are the fatal Miftakes that have made the *Hollanders* exceed us in *Riches* and *Trafic :* they receive all *Projects* and all *People,* and have few or no *Poor :* We have kept them out and fupprefs'd them, for the Sake of the *Poor,* whom we thereby do certainly make the poorer.

And here there is fuggefted to me a juft Occafion of lamenting the ill *Treatment* which has been moft commonly given to *Inventors,* not only here in *England,* but in all *Ages* and *Countries.* Nor do they only meet with rough Ufage from thofe that envy their Honour : but even from the *Artificers* themfelves, for whofe Sakes they labour : while thofe that add fome fmall Matters to things begun, are ufually enrich'd thereby ; the *Difcoverers* themfelves have feldom found any other Entertainment than Contempt and Impoverifhment. The Effects of their *Induftry* are wont to be decry'd while they live : the Fruits of their *Studies* are frequently alienated from their Children .

E e e   the

the little *Tradefmen* confpire againſt them, and indeavour to ſtop the Springs from whence they themſelves receive Nouriſhment : The common Titles with which they are wont to be defam'd, are thoſe of *Cheats* and *Projeƈtors.* I cannot deny but many ſuch do often mingle themſelves in the noble Throng of *great Inquirers :* as of old there were ſome that imitated *Philoſophers* only in Beard and Auſterity : So I grant at this time there may falſe *Experimenters* and *Inventors* ariſe, who will ſtrive to make themſelves admir'd by the loud talking of *Mathematical Engines,* and *Glaſſes,* and *Tools* ; and by ſounding in every Place ſuch goodly Words as *Chymiſtry,* and *Agriculture,* and *Mechanics.* But though the Folly of ſuch *Pretenders* cannot be avoided, we muſt not therefore reject the ſober and the judicious *Obſervers.* It is better ſometimes to indure Vanities, than out of too much Niceneſs to loſe any real *Invention.* We ought to do with *Philoſophical Works,* as *Miniſters* of *State* with *Intelligence.* It is the wiſeſt Courſe to give incouragement to all, leaſt by ſhewing ourſelves too ſcrupulous of being impos'd on by *Falſhoods,* we chance to be depriv'd of the *Knowledge* of ſome important *Truths.*

The next *Particular* which I reſolv'd to handle, is the Advantage of *Experiments* in reſpect of *Phyſic.* On this I intended to dilate in many Words, both becauſe of the great weight of the *Subject,* which concerns the very Welfare and Health of our Lives, and alſo becauſe it would afford me abundant matter for Diſcourſe ; for certainly it were eaſy to prove that there may ſtill a vaſt Progreſs be made in the true *Art* of *Medicine,* if either we conſider the imperfection of the *Method* of the ancient *Phyſicians* ; or if we obſerve the Nature of *Diſeaſes,* which alter and
multiply

multiply upon us every *Age*; or if we reflect on the *Cures* themselves, and how little the *Invention* of new ones has hitherto been regarded.

But as I was entring on this *Subject*, I perceiv'd that I might fafely omit it, feeing it is already better perform'd by Mr. *Boyle*, in his Book of the *Ufefulnefs of Experimental Philofophy*. I will therefore withdraw my Pen from this matter, which this noble Gentleman has manag'd in the beft and moft powerful Way, by ufing not only the Force of *Reafon*, but the Conviction of particular *Inftances*.

A N D now with fo good an *Omen* as this Gentlman's *Example*, who has not difdain'd to adorn the Honour of his *Family* with the *Studies* of *Nature*; I will go on to recommend them to the *Gentry* and *Nobility* of our *Nation*. And I am the more encourag'd to make this Addrefs, becaufe I behold that what I would advife is already in good meafure accomplifh'd; fo that I fhall not only have an Occafion to *exhort* them to proceed, but to commend them alfo, for their prefent Zeal towards thefe *Endeavours*.

§. XXXIV *Experiments a proper Study for the Gentlemen of our Nation.*

In this indeed I have much reafon to applaud the *generous Breeding* which has been given to the *Experimental Knowledge* of this *Age* and *Country*, above the bafe and contemptible *Education* of the Opinions of all former *Sects*: for now *Philofophy* being admitted into our *Exchange*, our *Church*, our *Palaces*, and our *Court*, has begun to keep the beft Company, to refine its Fafhion and Appearance, and to become the Employment of the *Rich*, and the *Great*, inftead of being the Subject of their *Scorn*: Whereas it was of old for the moft part only the Study of the *Sullen* and the *Poor*, who thought it the graveft Part of

Science,

Science, to contemn the ufe of Mankind, and to differ
in *Habit* and *Manners* from all others, whom they
flighted as Madmen and Fools. From this arrogant
Sordidnefs of fuch *Principles,* there could not be expected any *Magnificent Works,* but only ill-natur'd
and contentious *Doctrines.* Whatever the *Poets* fay
of the *Moral Wifdom,* that it thrives beft in *Poverty*;
it is certain the *Natural* cannot : for in fuch mean and
narrow Conditions, Men perhaps may learn to *defpife*
the World, but never to *know* it.

Now then, I will proceed not fo much to exhort,
as to confirm the *Gentlemen* of our *Nation,* in the
profecution of this *Art,* to which their *Purfes* and
their *generous Labours* are moft neceffary. And for
their incouragement in this way, I will briefly lay before them the Privileges they have for fuch *Inqui-*
ries, above all the *Gentry* of our Neighbour *Nations,*
and above all the *Nobility* of former *Ages* in this
Kingdom.

One principal Help that they enjoy, for the promoting of thefe *Studies* of Peace, is the prefent *Con-*
ftitution of the *Intereft* of our *Government.* The
cheif Defign of the *Antient Englifh* was the Glory of
fpreading their Victories on the Continent : but this
was a magnanimous Miftake : for by their very *Con-*
quefts, if they had maintain'd them, this *Ifland* had been
ruin'd, and had only become a *Province* to a greater
Empire. But now it is rightly underftood, that the
Englifh Greatnefs will never be fupported or increafed
in this *Age* by any other Wars but thofe at *Sea :* and
for thefe the Service of the Multitude is fitter than of
Gentlemen. This we have beheld practis'd thefe
laft twenty Years, wherein our *Naval Strength* has
more than trebled itfelf : for though fome few *Gen-*
tlemen

tlemen have ftill mingled themfelves in thofe gallant Actions ; yet the Grofs of our *Fleets* have confifted of *common Men*, and of *Mariners* who are bred up in the rude Toils of fuch a Life.

As this *Obfervation* may raife us to the greater admiration of their *Valour*, that fuch *Magnanimity* fhould be found amonft the meaneft of the People ; fo it fhould alfo fuggeft to our *Gentlemen*, who by this means are at liberty from the Employments of greateft Danger, that they ought to undertake thefe, which will give them as great, though a fecurer *Honour*. Nor will it be a Difgrace to them, that the fighting for their *Country* is caft on Men of lower Ranks, if in the mean time they fhall ftrive to enlighten and adorn, while the other defend it : for the fame is ordain'd by *Nature* itfelf in the Order and Offices of her *Works* ; the *Heavenly Bodies* appear to move quietly above, to give Light, and to cherifh the World with a gentle Influence ; while the *Inftruments* of *War* and *Offence* are taken out of the *Bowels* of the *Earth*.

For the Improvement of thefe *Arts* of peaceable *Fame*, they have indeed another Privilege, which can fcarce be equall'd by any Kingdom in *Europe* ; and that is the Convenience and Benefit of being fcatter'd in the *Country*. And in truth, the ufual Courfe of Life of the *Englifh Gentlemen* is fo well plac'd between the troublefome Noife of pompous Magnificence, and the Bafenefs of avaricious Sordidnefs ; that the true Happinefs of living according to the Rules and Pleafures of uncorrupt *Nature*, is more in their power than any others. To them, in this way of Life, there can nothing offer itfelf which may not be turn'd to a *Philofophical Ufe*. Their *Country Seats* being remov'd from the Tumults of *Cities*, give them the beft Opportunity

portunity, and Freedom of *Obfervations*. Their *Hof-pitality*, and familiar Way of converfing with their Neighbourhood will always fupply them with Intelligence. The Leifure which their Retirements afford them, is fo great, that either they muft fpend their Thoughts about fuch Attempts, or in more chargeable and lefs innocent *Divertifements*. If they will confider the *Heavens* and the Motions of the *Stars*, they have there a quieter *Hemifphere*, and a clearer *Air* for that Purpofe. If they will obferve the Generations, Breedings, Difeafes, and Cures of *living Creatures*; their Stables, their Stalls, their Kennels, their Parks, their Ponds, will give them eternal Matter of Inquiry. If they would fatisfy their Minds with the advancing of *Fruits*, the beautifying, the ripening, the bettering of *Plants*; their Paftures, their Orchards, their Groves, their Gardens, their Nurferies, will furnifh them with perpetual *Contemplations*. They may not only make their *Bufinefs*, but their very *Sports* moft ferviceable to *Experimental Knowledge*. For that if it be rightly educated, will ftand in need of fuch Recreations as much as the *Gentlemen* themfelves, from their hunting, hawking, fifhing, and fowling, that is able to receive as much folid Profit as they Delight.

On both thefe Accounts the *Englifh Gentry* has the Advantage of thofe of *France, Spain, Italy*, or *Germany*; who are generally either fhut up in *Towns*, and dream away their Lives in the Diverfions of *Cities*; or elfe are engag'd to follow their *Princes* Wills to foreign Wars.

Nor do they only excell other *Nations* in fuch Opportunities, but our own *Nobility* of all former Times. Firft, they are now far more numerous, and fo more may be fpar'd from the civil Bufinefs of their Coun-

try

try. Befides this, they are now bred up and live in a quite different Fafhion. The Courfe of their *Anceftors Lives* was grave and referv'd : they convers'd with few, but their own Servants ; and feldom travell'd farther than their own Lands : This way ferv'd well enough to keep up their *State* and their *Port* ; but not to help their Underftandings. For the Formalities of *Life* do often counterfeit *Wifdom*, but never beget it. Whereas now they are engag'd in freer Roads of *Education* ; now the vaft Diftance between them and other Orders of Men is no more obferv'd ; now their *Converfation* is large and general ; now the *World* is become more *active* and *induftrious* ; now more of them have feen the Ufe and Manners of Men, and more apply themfelves to *Trafic* and Bufinefs than ever.

This Alteration has been caus'd in our Memory, either by fo many *Families* being advanc'd to the higheft Degrees of *Nobility* for their excelling in the *Arts* of the *Gown* ; or by their frequent Intermarriages with *Citizens* ; or by the Travels of the *King*, and the *Royal Family* ; or elfe by the Civil War itfelf, which is always wont to be the cruelleft *Tyrant*, or the beft *Reformer* ; either utterly to lay waft, or to civilize, and beautify, and ripen the *Arts* of all Countries. And ftill we have reafon to expect, that this Change will proceed farther for the better, if our *Gentlemen* fhall more condefcend to engage in Commerce, and to regard the *Philofophy of Nature*.

The firft of thefe fince the *King*'s return, has been carry'd on with great Vigour by the *Foundation* of the *Royal Company* ; to which as to the Twin-Sifter of the *Royal Society*, we have reafon as we go along to wifh all *Profperity*. In both thefe *Inftitutions* begun
together,

together, our *King* has imitated the two moſt famous *Works* of the wiſeſt of ancient *Kings*; who at the ſame time ſent to *Ophir* for *Gold*, and compos'd a *Natural Hiſtory* from the Cedar to the Shrub.

Nor ought our *Gentry* to be averſe from the promoting of *Trade*, out of any little Jealouſy, that thereby they ſhall debaſe themſelves, and corrupt their Blood: For they are to know, that *Trafic* and *Commerce* have given Mankind a higher Degree than any Title of *Nobility*, even that of *Civility* and *Humanity* itſelf. And at this time eſpecially above all others, they have no reaſon to deſpiſe *Trade* as below them, when it has ſo great an influence on the very *Government* of the World. In former Ages indeed this was not ſo remarkable. The Seats of *Empire* and *Trade* were ſeldom or never the ſame. *Tyre*, and *Sydon*, and *Cades*, and *Marſeilles* had more *Trafic*, but leſs Command than *Rome*, or *Athens*, or *Sparta*, or *Macedon*. But now it is quite otherwiſe. It is now moſt certain that in thoſe Coaſts, whither the greateſt *Trade* ſhall conſtantly flow, the greateſt *Riches* and *Power* will be eſtabliſh'd. The Cauſe of this Difference between the ancient Times and our own, is hard to be diſcover'd: perhaps it is this, that formerly the greateſt Part of the *World* liv'd rudely, on their own *Natural Productions*: but now ſo many *Nations* being civiliz'd, and living ſplendidly, there is a far greater Conſumption of all *foreign Commodities*; and ſo the Gain of *Trade* is become great enough to over-balance all other Strength: Whether this be the *Reaſon* or no, it matters not; but the *Obſervation* is true. And this we ſee is ſufficiently known to all our Neighbours, who are earneſtly bent upon the advancing of *Commerce*, as the beſt Means not only to enrich particular Merchants, but to enlarge the *Empire*.   The

The next Thing to be recommended to the *Gentlemen* of *England* has a near Kindred with the other; and that is the *Philofophy* of *Nature* and *Arts*. For the want of fuch an eafy courfe of Studies, fo many of them have mifcarried in their firft Years, and have ever after abhorr'd all manner of *fober Works*. What elfe do fignify the univerfal Complaints of thofe who direct the *Education* of great Men's Children? Why do they find them fo hard to be fix'd to any manner of *Knowledge?* Their Teachers indeed are wont to impute it to the delicacy of their Breeding, and to their *Mothers fondnefs*. But the chief Caufe of the Mifchief lies deeper. They fill their Heads with difficult and *unintelligible Notions*, which neither afford them Pleafure in Learning, nor Profit in remembring them; they chiefly inftruct them in fuch *Arts*, which are made for the beaten Tracks of Profeffions, and not for *Gentlemen*. Whereas their Minds fhould be charm'd by the allurements of *fweeter* and more *plaufible Studies*; and for this purpofe *Experiments* are the fitteft. Their *Objects* they may feel and behold, their *Productions* are moft popular; their *Method* is intelligible, and equal to their Capacities; fo that in them they may foon become their own *Teachers*.

Nor are they to contemn them for their *Plainnefs*, and the homely *Matters* about which they are often employ'd. If they fhall think fcorn to foul their Fingers about them on this Account, let them caft their Eyes back on the *Orginal Nobility* of all Countries. And if that be true, that every Thing is preferv'd and reftor'd by the fame Means which did beget it at firft: They may then be taught, that their prefent *Honour* cannot be maintain'd by intemperate *Pleafures*, or the gawdy Shews of Pomp, but by true *Labours* and *induſtrious Virtue:* Let them reflect upon thoſe great Men who firſt made the Name of *Nobility* venerable. And they ſhall find that amidſt the *Government* of *Nations*, the Diſpatch of *Armies*, and Noiſe of *Victories*, ſome of them diſdain'd not to *work* with a Spade, to dig the *Earth*, and to cultivate with triumphing Hands the *Vine* and the *Olive*. Theſe indeed were times, of which it were well if we had more Footſtcps, than in ancient *Authors*. Then the Minds of Men were innocent and ſtrong, and bountiful as the *Earth* in which they labour'd. Then the Vices of human *Nature* were not their Pride, but their Scorn. Then *Virtue* was itſelf neither adulterated by the falſe Idols of *Goodneſs*; nor puff'd up by the empty Forms of *Greatneſs:* As ſince it has been in ſome Countries of *Europe*, which are arriv'd at that *corruption* of *Manners*, that perhaps ſome ſevere *Moraliſts* will think it had been more needful for me to perſwade the Men of this Age to continue Men, than to turn *Philoſophers*.

But in this Hiſtory I will forbear all farther *Complaints*, which were acceptable to the humour of this time, even in our *divine* and *moral Works*, in which they are neceſſary. I therefore return to that which I undertook, to the agreeableneſs of this deſign to all *Conditions* and *Degrees* of our *Nobility*. If they require ſuch *Studies* as are proportionable to the greatneſs of their *Titles:* They have here thoſe Things to conſider, from whence even they themſelves fetch the Diſtinctions of their *Gentility*. The Minerals, the Plants, the Stones, the Planets, the Animals, they bear in their *Arms*, are the chief *Inſtruments* of *Heraldry*, by which thoſe *Houſes* are exalted above thoſe of the Vulgar. And it is a ſhame for them to boaſt

of

of the bearing of thofe Creatures they do not underftand. If they value the *Antiquity* of *Families*, and
long Race of *Pedigrees :* What can be more worthy
their Confideration, than all the divers Lineages of
Nature ? Thefe have more proof of their ancient Defcent than any of them can fhew. For they have all
continued down in a right Line, from *Caufe* to *Effect*,
from the *Creation* to this Day. If they fhall confine
themfelves to the *Country*, they have this for their
cheap Diverfion. If they return to the *City*, this will
afford them in every Shop occafions to inform their
Judgments, and not to devour their *Eftates.* If they go
forth to *public Service*, to the leading of *Armies* or
Navies, they have this for their perpetual Counfellor, and very often for their Preferver. There are
fo many *natural* and *mechanical Things*, to be accurately obferv'd by the greateft Captains, as the Advantages of different Arms and Ammunitions, the
Paffages of Rivers, the Streights of Mountains, the
Courfe of Tides, the Signs of Weather, the Air, the
Sun, the Wind, and the like ; that though I will not
determine the *Knowledge of Nature*, to be abfolutely
neceffary to the great Office of a *General*; yet I may
venture to affirm, that it will often prove a wonderful
Affiftance and Ornament, to the courfe of *Glory* which
he purfues.

All *Hiftories* are full of Examples of the great Accidents which have happen'd by the Ignorance of
chief Commanders in *natural Motions* and *Effects* ;
of thefe I will only inftance in three : The firft is of
Cæfar himfelf, who had conquer'd more *Countries*
than moft Travellers have feen, and gain'd more
Battels than others have read of; yet he had like to
have put a Period to all his *Victories*, by the want of

an exact Skill in one of the commoneſt *Works of Na-ture*. This he himſelf relates in his ſecond Paſſage into *Britain*; when his Army was ſo diſmay'd at the ebbing of the *Sea* from their Fleet, believing it to be a Stratagem of their *Enemies*, that ſcarce the Courage and Conduct of *Cæſar*, could hinder them from being terrify'd to their own Overthrow, which had been a fatal Misfortune to the *Britains*, as well as *Romans*; becauſe from his victorious Arms, we firſt receiv'd the dawn of *Civil Arts*. The next Inſtance of this kind, is the Miſchance which befel the *Chriſtian Army* in *Egypt*, in the time of the *Holy Wars*. Their Strength was great and irreſiſtible, if they had only under-ſtood, that which every *Egyptian* could have taught them, the Courſe, and the time of the overflowing of the *Nile*. For the want of that ſlender Knowledge, the braveſt Men of all *Chriſtendom* were led up to the Neck in the River, and were forc'd to yield to their *Enemies* Conditions without ſtriking a Stroke. This was occaſion'd by the Stupidity of the *Cardinal*, who commanded them; if he had been leſs ſkilful in the *Schoolmen*, and more in *Nature*, that dreadful Di-ſaſter had never happen'd. My third *Example* of this kind is to be found in the *Roman Hiſtory* : The *Roman Army* was juſt ready to join Battel, with one of their Enemies; the Sign was given for their Onſet; their Force was equal; a terrible Combat had like to have enſu'd; when on a ſudden the *Sun* was *Eclips'd*; of this the *Romans* were warn'd the Day before. But this ſurpriz'd the other with ſo great Affright, that they were immediately *vanquiſh'd*. So that not the braveſt *Men*, nor the greateſt *Army*, nor the beſt Pro-viſions of *War* got the *Victory*; but that Party which had the beſt *natural Philoſopher* on its ſide.

To

To this Addrefs which I have made to our *Nobility* §.XXXV.
and *Gentry*, I will add as an Appendix another Bene- *Experi-*
fit of *Experiments*, which perhaps it will fcarce be- *ments will*
come me to name amidft fo many Matters of greater *be beneficial*
Weight; and that is, that their Difcoveries will be ve- *to our Wits*
ry ferviceable to the *Wits* and *Writers* of this, and *ters.*
all future *Ages*. But this I am provok'd to mention
by the Confideration of the prefent *Genius* of the *En-*
glifh Nation; wherein the Study of *Wit*, and Humour
of *Writing* prevails fo much, that there are very few
Conditions, or Degrees, or Ages of Men who are free
from its Infection. I will therefore declare to all thofe
whom this Spirit has poffefs'd, that there is in the
Works of Nature an inexhauftible Treafure of *Fancy*
and *Invention*, which will be reveal'd proportionably
to the Increafe of their *Knowledge*.

To this purpofe I muft premife, that it is requir'd in
the beft, and moft delightful *Wit*; that it be founded
on fuch Images which are generally known, and are
able to bring a ftrong and a fenfible Impreffion on the
Mind. The feveral Subjects from which it has been
rais'd in all times, are the *Fables* and *Religions* of the
Antients, the *civil Hiftories* of all *Countries*, the
Cuftoms of *Nations*, the *Bible*, the *Sciences* and *Man-*
ners of *Men*, the feveral *Arts* of their Hands, and
the Works of *Nature*. In all thefe, where there may
be a refemblance of one thing to another, as there may
be in all, there is a fufficient Foundation for *Wit*. This
in all its kinds has its Increafes, Heights, and Decays,
as well as all other human Things. Let us then examine what Parts of it are already exhaufted, and what
remain new and untouch'd, and are ftill likely to be
farther advanc'd.

The

The *Wit* of the *Fables* and *Religions* of the *ancient World* is well-nigh confum'd; they have already ferv'd the *Poets* long enough, and it is now high time to difmifs them, efpecially feeing they have this peculiar *Imperfection*, that they were only *Fictions* at firft: Whereas *Truth* is never fo well exprefs'd or amplify'd, as by thofe Ornaments which are *true* and *real* in themfelves.

The *Wit* which is rais'd from *Civil Hiftories*, and the Cuftoms of *Countries*, is folid and lafting: The *Similitudes* it affords are fubftantial, and equal to the Minds of Men, being drawn from themfelves and their own Actions. Of this the wittieft Nations have always made the greateft ufe; their Writings being adorn'd with a *Wit* that was free of their own *Cities*, confifting of *Examples*. and *Apothegms*, and *Proverbs*, deriv'd from their *Anceftors*. This I alledge, becaufe this kind is fcarce yet begun in the *Englifh Language*; though our own *Civil Hiftory* abounds as much as any other, with great *Examples* and memorable Events, which may ferve for the Ornament of Comparifon.

The Manners, and Tempers, and Extravagances of Men are a ftanding and eternal Foundation of *Wit*: This if it be gather'd from particular *Obfervations* is call'd *Humour*; and the more particular they are, they are ftill the pleafanter. In this kind I may well affirm that our *Nation* excells all others, as our *Dramatic Poetry* may witnefs.

The *Wit* that may be borrow'd from the *Bible* is magnificent, and, as all the other Treafures of *Knowledge* it contains, inexhauftible. This may be us'd and allow'd without any danger of Prophanenefs. The *Ancient Heathens* did the fame; they made their *Divine Ceremonies*

Ceremonies the chief Subjects of their *Fancies* ; by that means their *Religions* had a more awful Impression, became more popular, and lasted longer in force than else they would have done, and why may not *Christianity* admit the same Thing, if it be practis'd with *Sobriety* and *Reverence* ? What Irreligion can there be in applying some *Scripture-Expressions* to *Natural Things* ? Why are not the one rather exalted and purify'd, than the other defil'd by such Applications ? The very *Enthusiasts* themselves, who are wont to start at such *Wit* as *Atheistical*, and more guilty of its Excesses than any other fort of Men : For whatever they alledge out of the *Historical*, *Prophetical*, or *Evangelical Writings*, and apply it to themselves, their Enemies, or their Country, though they call it the Mind of *God*, yet it is nothing else but *Scripture Comparison* and *Similitude.*

The *Sciences* of Mens Brains are none of the best Materials for this kind of *Wit*. Very few have happily succeeded in *Logical*, *Metaphysical*, *Grammatical*, nay even scarce in *Mathematical Comparisons* ; and the reason is, because they are most of them conversant about Things remov'd from the Senses, and so cannot surprize the *fancy* with very obvious, or quick, or sensible Delights.

The *Wit* that is founded on the *Arts* of Mens Hands, is masculine and durable : It consists of *Images* that are generally obferv'd, and such visible Things which are familiar to Mens Minds. This therefore I will reckon as the first sort, which is still improvable by the Advancement of *Experiments.*

And to this I will add the *Works* of *Nature*, which are one of the best and most fruitful Soils for the growth of *Wit*. It is apparent, that the Defect of the *Antients* in *natural Knowledge* did alfo ftrengthen their *Fancies :* Thofe few Things which they knew, they us'd fo mnch, and apply'd fo often, that they even almoft wore them away by their ufing. The Sweet-nefs of Flowers, and Fruits, and Herbs, they had quite devour'd ; they had tir'd out the *Sun* and *Moon*, and *Stars* with their Similitudes, more than they fancy them to be wearied by their daily Journey round the *Heavens*.

It is now therefore feafonable for *natural Know-ledge* to come forth, and to give us the *Underftanding* of new *Virtues* and *Qualities* of Things, which may relieve their Fellow-Creatures, that have long born the Burden alone, and have long been vex'd by the Ima-ginations of *Poets*. This charitable Affiftance *Expe-riments* will foon beftow. The Comparifons which thefe may afford will be intelligible to all, becaufe they proceed from Things that enter into all Mens Senfes. Thefe will make the moft vigorous Impreffions on Mens *Fancies*, becaufe they do even touch their *Eyes*, and are neareft to their *Nature*. Of thefe the Variety will be infinite, for the Particulars are fo from whence they may be deduc'd : Thefe may be always new and unfullied, feeing there is fuch a vaft Number of *Natural* and *Mechanical Things*, not yet fully known or improv'd, and by Confequence not yet fuf-ficiently apply'd.

The ufe of *Experiments* to this Purpofe is evident, by the wonderful Advantage that my Lord *Bacon* receiv'd from them. This excellent Writer was a-bundantly recompenc'd for his noble Labours in that *Philofophy*, by a vaft Treafure of admirable *Imagina-tions* which it afforded him, wherewith to exprefs and adorn his Thoughts about other Matters. But I
will

will not confine this *Obfervation* to one fingle *Author*, though he was one of the firft and moft artificial Managers of this way of *Wit*. I will venture to declare in general of the *Englifh Tongue*, that as it contains a greater Stock of *natural* and *mechanical Difcoveries*, fo it is alfo more enrich'd with beautiful *Conceptions*, and inimitable *Similitudes*, gather'd from the *Arts* of Men's Hands and the *Works of Nature*, than ever any other *Language* could produce.

And now I hope what I have here faid will prevail fomething with the *Wits* and *Railleurs* of this *Age*, to reconcile their Opinions and Difcourfes to thefe *Studies :* for now they may behold that their Intereft is united with that of the *Royal Society* ; and that if they fhall decry the promoting of *Experiments*, they will deprive themfelves of the moft fertil Subject of *Fancy :* and indeed it has been with refpect to thefe terrible Men, that I have made this long Digreffion. I acknowledge that we ought to have a great Dread of their Power : I confefs I believe that *new Philofophy* need not (as *Cæfar*) fear the pale or the melancholy, as much as the humorous and the merry : For they perhaps by making it ridiculous becaufe it is *new*, and becaufe they themfelves are unwilling to take pains about it, may do it more Injury than all the Arguments of our fevere and frowning and dogmatical *Adverfaries.*

But to gain their good Will, I muft acquaint them, that the Family of the *Railleurs* is deriv'd from the fame Original with the *Philofophers*. The Founder of *Philofophy* is confefs'd by all to be *Socrates* ; and he alfo was the famous Author of all *Irony*. They ought therefore to be tender in this matter, wherein the Honour of their *common Parent* is concern'd : it be-

comes

comes them to remember that it is the Fault, and not the Excellence of *Wit* to defile its own Neft, and not to fpare its own Freinds and Relations, for the Sake of a Jeft.

The truth is, the Extremes of *Raillery* are more offenfive than thofe of *Stupidity :* It is a Work of fuch a tender and fubtil Spirit, that it cannot be decently perform'd by all Pretenders to it ; nor does it always agree well with the Temper of our *Nation* ; which as it has a greater Courage than to fuffer *Derifion,* fo it has a firmer Virtue than to be wholly taken up about deriding of others. Such Men are therefore to know, that all things are capable of abufe from the fame *Topicks* by which they may be commended ; they are to confider, that Laughter is the eafieft and the flendereft Fruit of *Wit* ; they are to underftand, that it proceeds from the Obfervation of the *Deformity* of things ; but that there is a nobler and more mafculine Pleafure, which is rais'd from beholding their *Order* and *Beauty :* From thence they may conclude, how great the Difference is between them and the real *Philofophers* ; for while *Nature* has only form'd them to be pleas'd with its Irregularities and Monfters, it has given the other the Delight of knowing and ftudying its moft *beautiful Works.*

In plain Terms, a univerfal Abufe of every thing, though it may tickle the Fancy never fo much, is *inhuman Madnefs*; as one of the *Antients* well expreffes it, who calls fuch Mirth *humanis Bacchari rebus.* If all things were made the Subjects of fuch Humour, all worthy defigns would foon be laugh'd out of the World ; and for out prefent Sport, our *Pofterity* would become barbarous. All good Enterprifes ought to find Affiftance when they are begun, Applaufe when
                                                    they

they fucceed, and even Pity and Praife if they fail. The true *Raillery* fhould be a Defence for *good* and *vertuous Works,* and fhould only intend the Derifion of extravagant, and the Difgrace of vile and difhonourable Things. This kind of *Wit* ought to have the Nature of *Salt,* to which it is ufually compar'd ; which preferves and keeps fweet the good and the found Parts of all Bodies, and only frets, dries up, and deftroys thofe Humours which putrify and corrupt.

This pleafant but unprofitable fort of Men being thus difmifs'd with this fair *Admonition* ; it now follows in the laft Place, that I examine the univerfal Intereft of the *Englifh Nation,* and confider what Effect the *Works* of the *Royal Society* are like to have upon it, by what means their *Labours* may ferve to encreafe our Advantages and correct our Imperfections. In the Entrance of this Subject there are fo many things prefented to my Thoughts, which are worthy to be declar'd to my *Countrymen,* that I rather think it ought to be largely manag'd by itfelf, than to be huddled up in the end of this *Treatife:* and certainly there is fcarce any matter that more deferves to be handled by the beft of our *Englifh Wits,* than the *Intereft* of their *Country.* I do therefore take the Freedom to recommend it to their Hands ; and to befeech them to raife their Thoughts from flighter Bufineffes, from unmanly Flatteries, or Vanities of *Love,* or ufelefs *Burlefque,* to this grave and this noble *Argument* ; and to remember that if *Themiftocles* was in the right, when he preferr'd the making of a fmall *City* great before the playing on a Fiddle, then certainly it is the braveft Employment for a worthy Mind, to endeavour to make a great *Kingdom* greater.

§. XXXVIII.
Experiments advantagious to the Intereft of our Nation.

There

The H I S T O R Y *of the*

There are very many Things in the *natural Genius*
of the *Englifh*, which qualify them above any other
for a *governing Nation*. The Scituation of our *Country* is moft advantageous for *Command* : Its native
Productions are moft ferviceable for *Strength* and *Empire*: The Difpofition of the People is bold in Dangers,
fevere in Difcipline, valiant in Arms, virtuous in Life,
relenting to the Afflicted, and merciful in Conqueft.
The unfortunate Divifions by which our *Force* has been
of late diftracted, are but of one or two *Ages* growth ;
the Vices to which we are fubject are not natural to
our *Soil*, but imported hither from foreign *Countries :*
The *Englifh* Generofity, Fidelity, Magnanimity, Modefty, Integrity, they owe to themfelves ; their Luxury, their Debauchery, their Divifions, their fpiritual
Schifms, they have receiv'd from abroad.

And now what can be a greater Work than the Management of all thefe matters? Here the *Writer* might
have Occafion of doing right to the Honour of his
Country, and yet reproving its Faults with a juft Cenfure : he might explain the Weakneffes and Advantages of our *Kingdom* : he might remove the one, and
confirm the other: he might compare the Actions
of our *Anceftors* with the Manners of this *Time*, and
fhew by what degrees this Diffolution of *Goodnefs*
crept in : he might with a generous and tender Hand,
apply himfelf to the Cure of our *Religious Diftempers* : he might with irrefiftable *Arguments* attempt
to amend what is amifs, reftore the *good*, and by
the Power of domeftick Examples reduce us back to
the ancient fincerity of *dealing*, and *innocence* of *Life*,
and union of *Interefts*.

The Defire of feeing this Work perform'd fits fo much
on my Mind, that I cannot but once more reprefent it

to

to the Confideration of the many Eloquent and Judicious *Authors*, with whom our *Nation* is now more abundantly furnifh'd than ever. But if neither the Neceffity nor Ufefulnefs of the Subject, nor the Benefit of their native Land will prevail with them to fet upon it ; it is my purpofe to excite them by another way, which will indeed be hazardous to my own *Reputation*, yet perhaps may take effect. I will try the fame Stratagem which I have often feen unskilful Singersufe, to make thofe who have excellent Voices fhew their *Art* : for as they by ill *Singing* fome excellent Tune are wont to provoke the othersto *fing*, when no Perfuafions could move them; fo do I intend at my firft Leifure, by ill handling of this *noble Subject*, to ftir up Men of greater Abilities to employ their Skill and their Judgment about it.

Having thus taken this Task on myfelf, it will not be needful here to infift long upon it before hand : I will only in few Words declare, that it is the true Concernment of *England* to fecure itfelf from the *Dominion* of *Strangers*, both *Ecclefiaftical* and *Temporal*; to advance its Induftry in peaceful *Arts* ; to increafe its *People* ; to improve its own *Manufactures* ; to introduce the foreign, of which our Soil is capable ; to make ufe of the two *Kingdoms* that are joyn'd with it under the fame *Monarch*, for thofe Productions which grow not at Home ; to obtain a Union of Mind, both in *Civil* and *Spiritual Matters* ; and to preferve the ancient Form of *Government*.

Of all thefe I will only touch upon thofe Parts of our *Intereft* which have reference to the Defign of the *Royal Society*

The firft thing that ought to be improv'd in the *Englifh Nation*, is their *Induftry*. This, it is true, has

of

of late Years been marvelloufly advanc'd ; as may be fhewn by the enlarging of *Trafic*, the fpreading of many *Fruits*, the Plantations of *Trees*, and the great Improvement of *Manual Arts*. But it is evident, that it may ftill admit of farther Warmth and Activity ; as we may conclude, by the Want of Employment for younger Brothers, and many other Conditions of Men ; and by the number of our Poor, whom *Idlenefs* and not *Infirmities* do impoverifh. The way to compafs this, is not alone by *Acts of Parliament*, and good *Laws* ; whofs Force will foon be evaded by prefent Craft and Interpretation, or elfe will be *antiquated* by Time. This perhaps our *Country* has found above all others : if our *Labourers* had been as diligent as our *Lawgivers*, we had prov'd the moft laborious Nation under *Heaven*. But the true Method of increafing *Induftry*, is by that Courfe which the *Royal Society* has begun in *Philofophy*, by *Works* and *Endeavours*, and not by the Prefcriptions of *Wards*, or *Paper Commands*.

There is nothing whofe promoting is fo eafy as *Diligence*, when it is once fet on foot. This does not only propagate *Works* but *Workers* ; though at firft it may begin on *Neceffity*, yet it will afterwards proceed upon *Pleafure :* So that the farther it goes, the fwifter it advances, becaufe *willing Works* are fooner perform'd than thofe to which we are compell'd. This I will demonftrate by an *Inftance* which I have already alledg'd, and it is of the *Hollanders :* for we may fetch *Examples* of *Virtue* from our own Countrymen, but of *Induftry* from them. At firft they were as lazy as the worft of ours : their Hands were unus'd to labour ; their manner of Life was much like that of the *antient Britains* ; their Coafts lay defolate to the Sea, without

out Banks or Towns, or Ships, or Harbours : and when the *Roman Emperor* gather'd Cockles there, perhaps there was little elſe worth gathering. But when by the number of their People they were forc'd to look abroad, to trade, to fiſh, to *labour* in *Mechanics* ; they ſoon found the Sweetneſs as well as the Toil of their *Diligence :* their Succeſſes and Riches ſtill added new Heat to their Minds ; and thus they have continued *improving,* till they have not only diſgrac'd but terrify'd their *Neighbours* by their *Induſtry.* Nor will it ſuffice to tell us, that they owe this Activity to the Form of their *Government.* That Suppoſition may preſently be confuted by the Example of *France,* the moſt abſolute *Monarchy* of *Chriſtendom :* There it is apparent by the prodigious Toils of their People, both upon the Earth, and in their Shops, that *Diligence* may thrive in a *Kingdom* as well as a *Commonwealth.*

And if ever the *Engliſh* will attain to the *Maſtery* of *Commerce,* not only in *Diſcourſe,* but *Reality,* they muſt begin it by their *Labours,* as well as by their *Swords :* they muſt do it by awakening their Minds, by rouzing themſelves from this Lithargy, by *Action,* by *Trials,* by *Working :* Unleſs this be done, they will in vain be *Victorious :* at the end of their *Wars* they will cool again, and loſe all the Fruits of their *Valour.* The *Arts* of Peace, and their Improvements, muſt proceed in equal Steps with the Succeſs of their *Arms :* The *Works* of our Citizens, our Plough-men, our Gardeners, our Wood-men, our Fiſhers, our Diggers in Mines, muſt be equally advanc'd with the *Triumphs* of our *Fleets* ; or elſe their Blood will be ſhed in vain : they will ſoon return to the ſame Poverty, and want of *Trade,* which they ſtrove to avoid. For as *Tully* profeſſes, *neminem video eloquentem factum eſſe victoriâ :*

riâ : So I will affirm, *that we ſhall never be made Induſtrious by Victory alone.*

The ſecond Thing to be corrected in the *Engliſh Humour,* is an Inclination to every *Novelty* and Vanity of foreign *Countries,* and a Contempt of the good things of our own. This Fondneſs is the uſual Fault of young *Travellers,* but it has alſo ill Effects on Men of full *Age:* For this they are wont to alledge the Excuſe of good *Breeding.* But if we could not ſtudy or underſtand our own Country, without the Imputation of ill Manners, good *Breeding* were the moſt pernicious thing in the World. For there was never yet any *Nation* great, which only admir'd the Cuſtoms of other People, and wholly made them the Pattern of their Imitation. This wandring and affected Humour *Experiments* will leſſen above all other *Studies :* they will employ our Thoughts about our native Conveniences : they will make us intend our Minds on what is contain'd with in our own Seas : and by conſidering and handling them more, will alſo make them more worthy of our Conſideration.

The third *Imperfection* is on the other Extreme, and that is a *norrowneſs of Mind,* and a *puſillanimous confining* our Thoughts to ourſelves, without regarding any-thing that is foreign, or believing that any of their *Arts* or *Cuſtoms* may be preferr'd before our own. This indeed is a Perverſneſs, of which the *Engliſh* are not wholly to be acquitted : it being proper to *Iſlands,* and to ſuch *Countries* that are divided from the reſt of the *World.* This will be cur'd by the effectual *Demonſtrations* that the *Society* will give of the Benefit of a univerſal *Correſpondence* and *Communication.* And this, according to their Method, will be done without falling into the other Vice of affe-

3   ecting

cting foreign *Habits,* and *Manners,* and *Geſtures.* In theſe the *Engliſh* need not be beholden to others ; but in their Fruits, in their Manufactures, in their Engines, in their Works in Gold, and Silver, and Braſs, and Iron, we may follow their Practice, and emulate their Curioſities without Affectation.

There is one Inſtance which will ſhew how our Reſpect to outlandiſh Things is to be regulated. To depend on the *French* for every little Faſhion of Cloaths, and to equal their *Nobility* in their way of Life, is neither for our Honour nor Profit. For the difference between their *Gentry* and ours, and their *Commonalty* and ours, is ſo great, that the ſame Manners will not be decent in us, which become them well enough. But to learn from them their *Skill* in *Horſemanſhip* and *Arms,* their *Building,* their *Cultivation of Fruits,* the *Parſimony* and *Induſtry* of their *Tradeſmen,* is commendable ; for in theſe Things we are defective, and they excell. It is therefore the Admiration of foreign *Extravagances,* and not the Imitation of their *Excellencies* that is to be condemn'd. If we will rather obſtinately be content with our own Store, than borrow what is good from Abroad ; we flatter ourſelves with the ſame fooliſh Imaginations, that all *Countries* had, while they were barbarous. To them their *Acorns* and their *Cottages* were at firſt the utmoſt ends of their Ambition. They knew no more, nor aſpir'd to any farther Addition ; but as ſoon as a new Light ſprung forth amongſt them, they deſpis'd themſelves and their former Condition ; and then they firſt began to underſtand their *Wants,* when they perceiv'd how they might be ſupply'd. As long as we find that all parts of our *Country* are not Ingenious, Inventive, and Induſtrious alike, we cannot preſume, that we

H h h have

have already got beyond all possibility of *Amendment* by others Patterns. As long as we behold any *City* or *Province*, or *Family*, or *Street* of our Neighbours exceed the worst of ours, I will not say the best in Easiness of *Life*, or Pleasantness and Smoothness of *Manners*, we have no reason to arrogate too much to our selves ; but we rather should conceive it to be a less disgrace to tread in their *Footsteps*, than to want their Perfections. As long as there remains any room for our most civil *People* to grow more *Civil*, the Introduction of foreign *Inventions* is not only *pardonable*, but *necessary* ; for such is the Nature of *Civility*, that as it increases, it still requires more *Arts*, though it contents itself with less Forms of living.

The fourth Mischief by which the Greatness of the *English* is suppress'd, is a want of Union of *Interests* and *Affections*. This is originally caus'd by a natural Reservedness, to which our Temper is inclin'd ; but it has been heighten'd by our *Civil Differences*, and *Religious Distractions*. For the sweetning of such Dissentions, it is not best at first to meet and converse about Affairs of State, or spiritual Controversies. For those did first occasion our *Animosities*, and the more they are rubb'd, the rawer they will prove. But the most effectual Remedy to be us'd, is, first to assemble about some *calm* and *indifferent* Things, especially *Experiments*. In them there can be no cause of mutual *Exasperations* : In them they may agree, or dissent without Faction or Fierceness ; and so from enduring each others *Company*, they may rise to a bearing of each others *Opinions* ; from thence to an exchange of good *Offices* ; from thence to real *Friendship* : Till at last by such a gentle and easy *Method*, our several *Interests*, *terefs* and *Sects* may come to suffer one another, with the same Peaceablenefs as Men of different *Trades* live one by another in the same *Street.*

Nor is it the leaft Commendation the *Royal Society* deferves, that defigning a Union of Mens *Hands* and *Reafons,* it has proceeded fo far in uniting the *Affections*; for there we behold an unufual Sight to the *English Nation,* that Men of difagreeing Parties, and ways of Life, have forgotten to hate, and have met in the unanimous Advancement of the fame *Works.* There the *Soldier,* the *Tradefman,* the *Merchant,* the *Scholar,* the *Gentleman,* the *Courtier,* the *Divine,* the *Presbyterian,* the *Papift,* the *Independant,* and thofe of *Orthodox Judgment,* have laid afide their Names of Diftinction, and calmly confpir'd in a mutual Agreement of *Labours* and *Defires :* A Blefling which feems even to have exceeded that Evangelical Promife, *That the Lion and the Lamb fhall lie down together* ; for here they do not only endure each others Prefence without Violence or Fear, but they *work* and *think* in Company, and confer their help to each others *Inventions.*

THE laft part of the *general Intereft* of our *Nation,* in which I will furvey the influence of *Experiments,* is *Obedience to the Civil Government* ; and we ought to be very watchful that they prove not offenfive to the *Supreme Power*; for feeing the *King* has honour'd them with his *Royal Patronage,* it is but juft that the *Prerogatives* of his *Crown* fhould be no lofers by their Increafe. It is indeed a common Accufation, which is wont to be made againft all manner of *Knowledge,* by thofe who have it not, that it renders Men mutinous, arrogant, and incapable of *Superiors* ; but if this be

§. XXXIX.
Experimental Knowledge will not hinder Obedience.

admitted

admitted, we shall asperse *human Nature* and *Govern-ment* with the greatest Calumny. This were to affirm, that Men cannot exercise their *Reason* without being *Factious* and *Unruly*; and that *Civil Government* will be insupportable to all but ignorant Men and Fools; which is so far from being true, that it were easy to prove that those *Nations* which are void of all *Arts* and *Knowledge*, cannot be properly said to pay a right *Obedience* to their *Sovereigns*; but that the Subjection under which they live, rather deserves to be styl'd the Stupidity and Slavery of Beasts, than a just and a manly Submission.

But to limit this Question to the particular kind of *Knowledge*, which is now under debate, it is certain that the Skill of *Nature* ought so little to be suspected for making Men perverse and ungovernable, that it is the best Preservative against *Disobedience*. One of the principal Causes of this is a misguided *Conscience*, and opposing the pretended Dictates of *God* against the Commands of the *Sovereign*. This I have already shewn, that these *Labours* will moderate and reform by abolishing or restraining the Fury of *Enthusiasm*. Another is idle Poverty, which drives Men into Sullenness, Melancholy, Discontent, and at last into resistance of *lawful Authority*. To this *Experiments* will afford a certain Cure; they will take away all pretence of Idleness, by a constant course of pleasant Endeavours; they will employ Men about profitable *Works*, as well as *delightful*; by the Pleasure of their *Discoveries* they will wear off the Roughness, and sweeten the humorous Peevishness of Mind, whereby many are sowr'd into *Rebellion*.

But the most fruitful Parent of *Sedition* is *Pride*, and a lofty conceit of Mens own *Wisdom*; whereby they

they prefently imagine themfelves fufficient to direct and cenfure all the *Actions* of their *Governors*. And here that is true in *Civil Affairs*, which I have already quoted out of my Lord *Bacon* concerning *Divine* : A little *Knowledge* is fubject to make Men headftrong, infolent, and untractable ; but a great deal has a quite contrary Effect, inclining them to be fubmiffive to their *Betters*, and obedient to the *Sovereign Power*.

The *Science* that is acquir'd by *Difputation*, teaches Men to cavil well, and to find fault with accurate Subtilty ; it gives them a fearlefs Confidence of their own Judgments ; it leads them from contending in Sport, to Oppofitions in earneft ; it makes them be-lieve that every thing is to be handled for and againft, in the *State*, as well as in the *Schools*. But the un-feign'd and laborious *Philofophy* gives no Countenance to the vain Dotages of private *Politicians* ; that bends its *Difciples* to regard the Benefit of Mankind, and not the Difquiet ; that by the Moderation it prefcribes to our Thoughts about *Natural Things*, will alfo take away all fharpnefs and violence about *Civil* ; the *Work* of that is fo vaft, that it cannot be perform'd without the Affiftance of the *Prince* ; it will not there-fore undermine his *Authority* whofe Aid it implores ; that prefcribes a better way to beftow our time, than in contending about little Differences, in which both the Conquerors and the Conquer'd have always rea-fon to repent of their Succefs ; that fhews us the diffi-culty of ordering the very Motions of fenfelefs and irrational Things ; and therefore how much harder it is to rule the reftlefs Minds of Men ; that teaches Men *Humility*, and acquaints them with their own *Errors* ; and fo removes all overweening Haughtinefs of Mind, and fwelling Imaginations, that they are better able

to

to manage Kingdoms than thofe who poffefs them. This, without queftion, is the chief Root of all the uneafinefs of *Subjects* to their *Princes.* The World would be better govern'd, if fo many did not prefume that they are fit to fuftain the Cares of *Government.* Tranfgreffion of the *Law* is *Idolatry :* The *Reafon* of Mens contemning all *Jurifdiction* and *Power,* proceeds from their idolizing their own *Wit* ; they make their own Prudence omnipotent ; they fuppofe themfelves *infallible* ; they fet up their own *Opinions,* and worfhip them. But this vain *Idolatry* will inevitably fall before *Experimental Knowledge :* which as it is an *Enemy* to all manner of falfe *Superftitions,* fo efpecially to that of Mens *adoring themfelves,* and *their own Fancies.*

Sect. XL.
The Conclufion, being a general Recommendation of this Defign.

I Have now at laft brought my Reader by a tedious Compafs, to the end of our Journey : And here I defire him to look back, and to make a Reflection on the Matters of which I have treated. In the firft part of my Difcourfe I have alledg'd the Caufes by which thefe *Studies* were fupprefs'd in all former *Ages* ; which have been Interefts of *Sects,* the Violence of *Difputations,* the plaufible Arts of *Speech,* the *Religious Controverfies,* the *Dogmatical Opinions,* the *Poverty* of the *Undertakers,* and the want of a continual Race of *Experimenters.* In the fecond I have fhew'd by what Steps the *Royal Society* arofe, what it has propos'd to attempt, what Courfe it has taken to make its *Obfervations* univerfal and perpetual ; what Affiftance has been afforded it to that Purpofe, and about what Particulars it has been converfant. In the third I have try'd to free it from the falfe Scandals of *Ignorance,* and the Prejudices of feveral ways of Life, and

4   to

to prove that its Effects will more immediately refer to our own Country.

My Reader now beholds an Affembly fettled of many eminent Men of all Qualities, who have engag'd to beftow their Labours on a defign fo publick, and fo free from all Sufpicion of mean or private Intereft. What Foundation they have within themfelves, for defraying the Expence of their *Trials* and *Intelligence,* may be guefs'd by their *Number,* which at this prefent amounts very near to *two Hundred*; as appears by this following *Catalogue,* which I have rang'd *Alphabetically.*

The *King's* Majefty, *Founder* and *Patron.*
His Royal Highnefs the *Duke* of *York.*
His Highnefs Prince *Rupert.*
His Highnefs *Ferdinand Albert, Duke* of *Brunfwick* and *Lunenburgh.*

The *Duke* of *Albemarle,* the *Earl* of *Alesbury,* the *Earl* of *Argile,* the *Lord Afhley,* the *Lord Annefly,* Mr. *Afhmole,* Sir *Robert Atkins,* Mr. *Auftin,* Monf. *Auzout,* Mr. *Awbrey.*

The *Duke* of *Buckingham,* the Lord *George Berkeley,* the Lord *Brereton,* Mr. *Bagnal,* Mr. *Bains,* Mr. *William Balle,* Mr. *Ifaac Barrow,* Dr. *George Bate,* Dr. *Bathurft,* Dr. *Beal,* Monf. *Beaufort de Frafars,* Sir *John Birkenhead* Mr. *Blunt,* Mr. *Boyl,* Mr. *Brook,* Dr. *Bruce,* Monf. *Bullialdus,* Mr. *Burnet,* Sir *Edward Byfhe.*

The Lord *Archbifhop* of *Canterbury*; the Earl of *Clarendon,* Lord *Chancellor* of *England*; the Earl of *Carlile,* the Earl of *Craford* and *Lindfay,* the Lord *Cavendifh,* the Lord *Clifford,* Mr. *Carkefs,* Mr. *Carteret.*

Dr.

Dr. *Charleton*, Sir *Winſtone Churchill*, Sir *John Clayton*, Sir *Clifford Clifton*, Mr. *George Cock*, Sir *Richard Corbet*, Dr. *Cotton*, Dr. *Cox*, Mr. *Thomas Cox*, Mr. *Daniel Cox*, Mr. *Creed*, Mr. *Criſpe*, Sir *John Cluter*.

The Marqueſs of *Dorcheſter*, the Earl of *Devonſhire*, the Earl of *Dorſet*, Monſ. *Vital de Damas*, Sir *George Ent*, Mr. *Elliſe*, Mr. *John Evelyn*, Sir *Francis Fane*, Monſ. *le Febvre*, Sir *John Finch*, Mr. *Henry Ford*, Sir *Bernhard Gaſcoigne*, Mr. *Joſeph Glanvile*, Dr. *Gliſſon*, Mr. *William Godolphin*, Mr. *Graunt*.

The Lord *Hatton*, Mr. *Haak*, Mr. *William Hammond*, Mr. *William Harrington*, Sir *Edward Harley*, Sir *Robert Harley*, Mr. *Harley*, Dr. *Henſhaw*, Monſ. *Hevelius*, Mr. *Abraham Hill*, Mr. *Hoar*, Dr. *Holder*, Mr. *Hook*, Mr. *Charles Howard*, Monſ. *Huygens*.

Mr. *Richard Jones*, the Earl of *Kincardin*, Sir *Andrew King*, Mr. *Edmund King*, the Earl of *Lindſey*, the Lord Biſhop of *London*, Mr. *Lake*, Sir *Ellis Leighton*, Mr. *James Long*, Sir *John Lowther*, Mr. *Lowther*, Monſ. *Hugnes de Lyonne*.

The Earl of *Mancheſter*, Monſ. *Nicholas Mercator*, Dr. *More*, Dr. *Jaſper Needham*, Dr. *Needham*, Mr. *Thomas Neile*, Mr. *William Neile*, Mr. *Nelthorp*, Mr. *Newburgh*, Sir *Thomas Nott*, the Earl of *Peterburgh*, Mr. *Packer*, Mr. *Samuel Parker*, Sir *Robert Paſton*, Dr. *John Pearſon*, Dr. *Pell*, Sir *William Perſall*, Sir *Peter Pett*, Mr. *Peter Pett*, Monſ. *Petit*, Sir *William Portman*, Mr. *Francis Potter*, Mr. *Povey*, Dr. *Power*, Sir *Richard Powle*, Mr. *Pepys*.

The Lord *Roberts* Lord *Privy Seal*, the Lord Biſhop of *Rocheſter*, Mr. *Rolt*, Mr. *Rycaut*, the Earl of *Sandwich*, the Lord Viſcount *Stafford*, the Lord *Stermont*, Mr. *Schroter*, Sir *James Shaen*, Mr. *Skippon*, Sir *Nicholas Slaney*, Mr. *Henry Slingsby*, Mr. *Smethwick*, Mr. *Edward*

ROYAL SOCIETY. 33

Edward Smith, Dr. *George Smith*, Monf. *Sorbiere*, Sir
Robert Southwell, Mr. *Alexander Stanhope*, Mr. *Thomas Stanley*.

The Earl of *Tweedale*, Sir *Gilbert Talbot*, Sir *John
Talbot*, Dr. *Terne*, Mr. *Thomas Thyn*, Dr. *Thruston*, Sir
Samuel Tuke, Sir *Theodore de Vaux*, Mr. *Vermuyden*,
Monf. *Isaac Voffius*.

The Lord *Bifhop* of *Winchefter*, Mr. *Waller*, Dr.
Wallis, Mr. *Waterhoufe*, Dr. *Whiftler*, Mr. *Jofeph
Williamfon*, Dr. *Willis*, Mr. *Francis Willoughby*, Mr.
Wind, Mr. *Winthorp*, Mr. *Woodford*, Mr. *Matthew
Wren*, Dr. *Thomas Wren*, Sir *Cyril Wyche*, Sir *Peter
Wyche*, Mr. *Wylde*, the Lord *Arch-Bifhop* of *York*,
the Lord *Yefter*.

The prefent *Council* are thefe that follow :

William Lord Vifcount *Brouncker*, Prefident ; which
Office has been annually renew'd to him by Election,
out of the true Judgment which the *Society* has made
of his great *Abilities* in all *Natural,* and efpecially
Mathematical Knowledge.

Mr. *William Aerskin*, Dr. *Peter Ball*, Dr. *Timothy
Clerk*, Mr. *Daniel Colwall*, Dr. *Croon*, the Lord *Bifhop*
of *Exeter*, Dr. *Jonathan Goddard*, Mr. *Henry Howard* of *Norfolk*, Mr. *Henfhaw*, Mr. *Hoskins*, Sir *Robert Moray*, Sir *Anthony Morgan*, Dr. *Merret*, the
Earl of *Northampton*, Sir *Paul Neile*, Mr. *Oldenburgh*, Sir *William Petty*, Dr. *Pope*, Dr. *Wilkins*,
Dr. *Chriftopher Wren*.

In this number perhaps there may fome be found,
whofe *Employments* will not give them leave to promote thefe *Studies* with their own *Hands*. But it
being their Part to *contribute* joyntly towards the
Charge, and to pafs *Judgment* on what others fhall
try ; they will appear to be well-nigh as ufeful, as

I i i   thofe

those that *labour*, to the main End of this *Enterprize*.

Whatever *Revenue* they shall raise by this or any other means, they intend thereby to make an Establishment for their *Curators*. To this Office they have already admitted some of their *Fellows*, whom they will employ according to their *Studies* and *Sufficience*: Some shall be sent to travel abroad to search for *Discoveries*; some shall constantly remain in *London*, and represent their *Observations* to the weekly *Assemblies*.

The Places of their *Residence* they have appointed to be two: one a *College*, which they design to build in *London*, to serve for their *Meetings*, their *Laboratories*, their *Repository*, their *Library*, and the Lodgings for their *Curators*: The other the *College* at *Chelsey*, which the *King* has bestow'd on them; where they have a large Inclosure to serve for all *Experiments* of *Gardening* and *Agriculture*; and by the neighbourhood of the *River* they have excellent Opportunity of making all *Trials* that belong to the Water.

And now as I have spoken of a *Society* that prefers *Works* before *Words*, so it becomes their *History* to endeavour after real *Fruits* and *Effects*. I will thereforeconclude, by recommending again this *Undertaking* to the *English Nation*; to the *bravest People*; the most *generous Design*; to the most zealous Lovers of *Liberty*, the surest Way to ransom the Minds of all Mankind from *Slavery*.

The Priviledges that our *King's* Dominions enjoy for this End, appear to be equal'd by no other *Country*. The Men that we have now living to employ, are excellently furnish'd with all manner of Abilities: Their Method is already settled, and plac'd out of the reach of Calumny or Contradiction

The

The Work it felf indeed is vaft, and almoft incomprehenfible, when it is confider'd in Grofs : But they have made it feafible and eafie, by diftributing the Burden. They have fhewn to the World this great Secret, That *Philofophy* ought not only to be attended by a felect Company of *refin'd Spirits*. As they defire that its Productions fhould be *vulgar*, fo they alfo declare, that they may be promoted by *vulgar Hands*. They exact no extraordinary Preparations of *Learning*; to have found *Senfes* and *Truth*, is with them a fufficient Qualification. Here is enough Bufinefs for *Minds* of all Sizes : And fo boundlefs is the Variety of thefe *Studies*, that here is alfo enough Delight to recompence the Labours of them all, from the moft ordinary Capacities, to the higheft and moft fearching *Wits*.

Here firft they may take a plain View of all particular Things, their Kinds, their Order, their Figure, their Place, their Motion : and even this naked Profpect cannot but fill their Thoughts with much Satisfaction, feeing it was the firft Pleafure which the *Scripture* relates *God* himfelf to have taken at the *Creation*; and that not only once, but at the end of every Days Work, when he faw all that he had made, and approv'd it to be good. From this they may proceed to furvey the Difference of their Compofition, their Effects, the Inftruments of their Beings and Lives, the Subtilty and Structure, the Decay and Supply of their Parts; wherein how large is the fpace of their Delight, feeing the very Shape of a *Mite*, and the Sting of a *Bee* appears fo prodigious. From hence they may go to apply Things together, to make them work one upon another, to imitate their Productions, to help their Defects, and with the nobleft Duty to affift *Na-*

ture,

ture, our common Mother, in her *Operations* ; from
hence to all the works of Mens hands, the divers *Artifices* of feveral *Ages,* the various Materials, the improvement of *Trades,* the advancement of *Manufactures* ; in which laft alone there is to be found fo
great Content, that many mighty Princes of the former
and prefent Times, amidft the pleafures of *Government,*
which are no doubt the higheft in the World, have
ftriven to excel in fome *Manual Arts.*

In this fpacious Field their *Obfervations* may wander, and in this whatever they fhall meet with, they
may call their own. Here they will not only enjoy
the cold contentment of *Learning,* but that which is
far greater, of *Difcovering.* Many Things that have
been hitherto hidden, will arife and expofe themfelves
to their view ; many Methods of advancing what
we have already, will come in their way ; nay, even
many of the loft *Rarities* of *Antiquity* will be hereby
reftor'd. Of thefe a great quantity has been overwhelm'd in the ruins of *Time* ; and they will fooner
be retriev'd by our labouring anew in the material
Subjects whence they firft arofe, than by our plod-
ding everlaftingly on the antient *Writings.* Their
Inventions may be fooneft regain'd the fame way by
which their *Medals* and *Coins* have been found ; of
which the greateft part has been recover'd, not by
thofe who fought for them on purpofe in old Rubbifh,
but by digging up Foundations to raife new Buildings,
and by plowing the Ground to fow new Seed.

This is the *Work* we propofe to be encourag'd,
which at once regards the difcovering of new *Secrets,*
and the purifying and repairing all the profitable
Things of *Antiquity.* The Supply that is needful to
finifh it, will neither impoverifh Families, nor ex-

2   hauft

hauſt a mighty Income. So near is Mankind to its Happineſs, that ſo great an *Attempt* may be plentifully endow'd by a ſmall part of what is ſpent on any one ſingle Luſt, or extravagant Vanity of the Time. So moderate is the *Society* in their deſires of Aſſiſtance, that as much Charity as is beſtow'd in *England* in one Year, for the relief of particular Poverty and Diſeaſes, were enough for ever to ſuſtain a *Deſign*, which endeavours to give Aid againſt all the Infirmities and Wants of *human Nature*.

If now this *Enterprize* ſhall chance to fail for want of *Patronage* and *Revenue*, the World will not only be fruſtrated of their preſent Expectations, but will have juſt ground to deſpair of any future *Labours*, towards the increaſe of the *Practical Philoſophy*. If our *Poſterity* ſhall find, that an *Inſtitution* ſo vigorouſly begun, and ſo ſtrengthen'd by many ſignal Advantages, could not ſupport itſelf; they will have reaſon in all times to conclude, That the long barrenneſs of *Knowledge* was not caus'd by the corrupt Method which was taken, but by the Nature of the *Thing* itſelf. This will be the laſt great Endeavour that will be made in this way, if this ſhall prove ineffectual; and ſo we ſhall not only be guilty of our own *Ignorance*, but of the *Errors* of all thoſe that come after us.

But if (as I rather believe and preſage) our *Nation* ſhall lay hold of this Opportunity, to deſerve the applauſe of Mankind, the force of this *Example* will be irreſiſtibly prevalent in all *Countries* round about us; the State of *Chriſtendom* will ſoon obtain a new Face: while this *Halcyon Knowledge* is breeding, all *Tempeſts* will ceaſe; the Oppoſitions and Contentious Wranglings of *Science*, falſly ſo call'd, will ſoon
vaniſh

vanish away ; the peaceable calmness of Mens *Judgments* will have admirable influence on their *Manners* ; the sincerity of their *Understandings* will appear in their *Actions* ; their *Opinions* will be less violent and dogmatical, but more certain ; they will only be *Gods* one to another, and not *Wolves* ; the value of their *Arts* will be esteem'd by the *great Things* they perform, and not by those they speak : While the old *Philosophy* could only at the best pretend to the Portion of *Nepthali, to give goodly words,* the New will have the Blessings of *Joseph* the younger and the belov'd Son ; *It shall be like a fruitful Bough, even a fruitful Bough by a Well whose Branches run over the Wall : It shall have the Blessings of Heaven above, the Blessings of the Deep that lies under, the Blessings of the Breasts and of the Womb :* While the Old could only bestow on us some barren Terms and Notions, the New shall impart to us the Uses of all the *Creatures,* and shall enrich us with all the Benefits of *Fruitfulness* and *Plenty.*

F I N I S.

751704

Printed in Great Britain by
Amazon.co.uk, Ltd.,
Marston Gate.